ECONOMISTS WITH GUNS

BRADLEY R. SIMPSON

Economists with Guns

*Authoritarian Development
and U.S.-Indonesian Relations,
1960–1968*

STANFORD UNIVERSITY PRESS

STANFORD, CALIFORNIA

Stanford University Press
Stanford, California

© 2008 by the Board of Trustees of the
Leland Stanford Junior University.
All rights reserved.

Printed in the United States of America
on acid-free, archival-quality paper.

Library of Congress Cataloging-in-Publication Data

Simpson, Bradley R. (Bradley Robert)
  Economists with guns : authoritarian development and U.S.-Indonesian
relations, 1960–1968 / Bradley R. Simpson.
      p. cm.
  Includes bibliographical references and index.
  ISBN 978-0-8047-7182-5 (pbk : alk. paper)
  1. United States—Foreign relations—Indonesia. 2. Indonesia—Foreign
relations—United States. 3. Indonesia—Politics and government—
1950–1966. 4. Indonesia—Politics and government—1966–1998.
5. United States—Foreign relations—1945–1989. 6. Authoritarianism—
Indonesia—History—20th century. I. Title.

E183.8.I5S56 2008
327.73059809'046—dc22

                                                              2007045246

Typeset by Classic Typography in 10/14 Janson

Contents

Acknowledgments

The writing of one's first book, while agonizingly lonely, is the product of countless acts of kindness large and small. I have been helped along the way by innumerable archivists and staff, teachers, mentors, friends, and family, many of them immersed not in the world of academia but in movements for human rights and social justice in the United States, Indonesia, and East Timor.

This project grew out of my naïve shock as a college student upon discovering that the United States had supported the 1975 Indonesian invasion of East Timor, a tiny island nation that most Americans and I had never heard of. This discovery outraged me as a citizen and intrigued me as a historian, sending me on a search for origins, in this case of the U.S. alliance with the authoritarian regime of Suharto. My research and writing have been guided by the belief that historians are not mere scribes but active participants in shaping collective memory, including of events that most would wish to sweep under the carpet, incompatible as they are with the narrative of American exceptionalism in foreign policy.

I have piled up many debts along the way, especially to the archival staffs of the Lyndon B. Johnson Presidential Library, the John F. Kennedy Presidential Library, the National Archives and Records Administration, the Library of Congress Manuscript Division, the Ford Foundation Archives, the Rockefeller Archives Foundation, the AFL-CIO Archives, the Hoover Institution Archives, and the National Archives of the United Kingdom. I am grateful to the Rockefeller Archives Foundation, the John F. Kennedy Presidential Library, Northwestern University, Idaho State University, and the University of Maryland, Baltimore County, for providing funding to facilitate my research and writing.

I owe a special debt to those who read or commented on all or part of this manuscript and on the conference papers from which they were derived and who helped to get the book to press: John Roosa, David Schmitz, Mark Bradley, David Painter, Anne Foster, Nick Cullather, Robert McMahon, Matthew Jones, Michael Latham, Joe Nevins, Gwyn Sundell, Bob Buzzanco, Christopher Jesperson, Randall Woods, and Baskara T. Wardaya, S.J. My mentors at Northwestern University—Bruce Cumings, Laura Hein, Michael Sherry, and Jeffrey Winters—provided models of engaged scholarship and support along the way. Muriel Bell at Stanford University Press took a chance on this manuscript at an early stage, for which I am forever grateful, and Joa Soarez and Kirsten Oster helped shepherd the manuscript to publication.

Friends and family, of course, bear the brunt of the journey from graduate school to dissertation to first book. My family has offered untiring encouragement—doubtless tempered by relief—while friends have kept me grounded and ever conscious of the need to connect scholarly inquiry to the ongoing efforts of those engaged in grassroots movements. My greatest debt is to Kristin—wife, best friend, and confidant—whose support has eased the way and whose commitment to peace and social justice is a daily inspiration. All errors of fact or interpretation are my own.

Introduction

On the morning of October 1, 1965, Lyndon Johnson's White House received a terse situation report from the Central Intelligence Agency (CIA): "A power move which may have far reaching implications is underway in Jakarta."[1] The night before, six generals from the Indonesian army high command, including army commander Lt. General Achmad Yani, were kidnapped from their homes in Jakarta, killed, and dumped in a well on the outskirts of Halim Air Force Base by self-described participants of the September 30th Movement, who claimed they were acting to forestall a coup by a right-wing "Council of Generals." The Indonesian armed forces quickly labeled the movement a coup attempt against the state and blamed the Indonesian Communist Party (*Partai Komunis Indonesia* or PKI) for the deaths, providing the pretext for one of the great massacres of twentieth-century history—an army-led and U.S.-backed campaign of extermination directed at alleged PKI members and affiliated organizations in which perhaps half a million people were killed in a matter of months. The September 30th Movement

1

and its bloody aftermath is one of the decisive events of postwar Asian history; the events permanently altered the political landscape of Indonesia and led to more than thirty years of corrupt authoritarian rule by General Suharto. Moreover, the annihilation of the largest nonbloc Communist party in the world vividly undermined the rationale for the escalating U.S. war in Vietnam, as former defense secretary Robert McNamara has noted, eliminating at a stroke the chief threat to the Westward orientation of the most strategically and economically important country in Southeast Asia and facilitating its firm reintegration into the regional and world economy after a decade-long pursuit of autonomous development.[2]

Forty years later, millions of Indonesians still carry the scars of the night that changed their country's historical trajectory. But they are mostly suppressed scars, prevented from healing by a regime that between 1966 and 1998 used the September 30th Movement and anti-Communism as a master narrative to justify the dominant role of the Indonesian armed forces (TNI) in the nation's life, the circumscription of political parties, Islam, and civil society, and the ruthless suppression of dissent.[3] Fearful that memories of the fateful night were fading, in 1981 the New Order regime and its most prominent court historian, Nugroho Notosusanto, produced the film *Pengkhianatan Gerakan 30 September* (Treachery of the 30 September Movement), which was broadcast every October 1 and reminded Indonesians in graphic (although fictional) detail of the murders of the generals and the role of the PKI as *dalang*, or puppet master.[4] After Suharto was swept from power in 1998 by the forces of economic collapse and popular mobilization, beginning a slow and unsteady process of democratization that continues today, Indonesians of all political stripes began to reckon with the legacy of his rule. A profound reimagining of the nation's recent past is now under way in the cultural, political, and religious realms, even in school history textbooks, the lessons of which are being bitterly contested.[5] The hegemonic, state-mandated history of the Suharto period is fracturing, buckling under the weight of its own contradictions, but with no clear alternative narrative to replace it. On a 2004 trip to Yogyakarta, for example, banners sponsored by the Front Anti Komunis Indonesia (FAKI) fluttered above the entrance to the famous tourist avenue Jalan Malioboro, reminding me and a thousand backpack-toting tourists to "beware of latent Communism"—three months before the second major terrorist bombing on the island of Bali carried out by homegrown Islamic militants.[6]

Since Suharto's downfall in 1998, Indonesia has experienced myriad problems, including economic instability, environmental degradation, state violence, corruption, religious conflict, and a recrudescent Islamic radicalism, which is locally rooted but has strong transnational links. Although not spawned by the New Order, each of these dynamics was exacerbated, in some cases exponentially, by the political and economic edifice that the Suharto regime created to sustain and legitimize its grip on power. The persistence of these problems in Indonesia's wobbly democratic transition has forced a long overdue reassessment of virtually all aspects of the New Order period by both Indonesians and foreign observers. "The unified coherence of Suharto's New Order," one scholar recently observed, has been "thoroughly discredited, as economic stagnation and growing discord undermined its core themes of stability and state-managed development."[7] Such a reassessment has been a long time coming. Between 1966 and 1998, as the Indonesian government pursued a deeply flawed authoritarian development model, the United States and other powerful governments, social scientists, and international institutions cheered Indonesia's purported success while muting criticism of the Suharto regime's appalling corruption and abysmal human rights record as the regrettable price of stability and growth. As in Brazil, South Korea, Iran, and many other countries during the Cold War, Indonesia during the Suharto period pursued a strategy of what might be termed military modernization, in which the armed forces asserted for themselves a dominant political role legitimized by their commitment to economic and political development.

Such commitments did not spring out of the political ether, nor were they the product of purely local or national historical conflicts. Rather, a complex constellation of national and international political and economic forces lay the foundations for and encouraged the emergence in the mid-1960s of a military-led regime in Indonesia committed to modernization. These forces included the U.S. and other Western governments, which provided military and economic assistance; philanthropic foundations, which trained economists and military officers in management and administration; international financial institutions such as the International Monetary Fund (IMF) and the World Bank, which promoted early variants of what would later be called structural adjustment; and social scientists, who deployed theory to account for and legitimize the growing political and economic role of the military in the development process, not just in Indonesia but throughout the so-called third world.

The discourse and practice of military modernization, however, was not forced on unwitting Indonesians by imperial bureaucrats, philanthropists, and academics. Rather, such ideas dovetailed with the political and institutional priorities of significant elements of the Indonesian armed forces and Western-oriented technocrats whose commitment to military rule stretches back to the country's parliamentary period from 1949 to 1959. In this book, then, I attempt to contribute to a reimagining of Indonesia's recent past by exploring the construction and dispersal of American and Indonesian thinking about Indonesian development and the profound effect these had on the emergence of an authoritarian regime in the world's largest Muslim country in the 1960s. In doing so, I explore one of the central dynamics of international politics during the Cold War: the emergence in the so-called third world of authoritarian regimes pledged to and deriving their legitimacy from their commitment to programs of military-led modernization. I argue that, far from paving the way for the post–Cold War flowering of democratic governments and institutions, U.S. encouragement and embrace of such regimes set back the quest for both democracy and independent development and contributed significantly to some of the chief problems—corruption, weak civil societies, military cultures of violence and impunity, and a militant political Islam—that plague many underdeveloped nations in the aftermath of the Cold War.

Former assistant secretary of state William Bundy once described U.S. policy toward Indonesia during the crucial decade of the 1960s as "no more than a sum of decisions to act or not in the face of unpredictable developments." Bundy's formulation is apt, reflecting not only the blinkered vision with which U.S. officials viewed events outside mainland Southeast Asia but also the judgment of many historians. In contrast to their vast outpourings on the Vietnam War, in which that conflict was explored from nearly every conceivable perspective, scholars of U.S. foreign relations have accorded scant attention to Indonesia, despite the tremendous importance American policymakers accorded the archipelago in their postwar strategic and economic considerations.[8] One would never know from reading the voluminous recent literature on the Kennedy and Johnson administrations and Southeast Asia, for example, that until the mid-1960s most officials still considered Indonesia of far greater importance than Vietnam and Laos.[9]

Historians who have explored U.S. relations with Indonesia during this period have portrayed U.S. policy as basically reactive, focused on short-term strategic and political concerns and rooted in bureaucratic conflict. H. W. Brands writes that "the importance of Indonesia to the U.S." in the 1960s "did not require explanation" owing to its self-evident strategic and economic significance, as if everyone agreed on what that meant and in what context it mattered.[10] American policy throughout is attributed primarily to strategic concerns that the world's fifth most populous nation would fall to Communism, either boring from within (the PKI) or subverting from without (the Soviet Union from 1960 to 1963, China from 1964 to 1965), contentions that are backed up by boxes of National Security Council (NSC) and Joint Chiefs of Staff (JCS) documents attesting to Washington's determination to prevent Indonesia's "loss to communism" and encourage its "free world orientation."[11]

Unfortunately, we have yet to answer some of the most basic questions confronting Americans and Indonesians during the 1960s. What was the relationship between Washington's short-term policy goals for Indonesia and its long-term vision for Indonesian political and economic development? How were U.S. priorities for Indonesia related to the policies it pursued in other parts of the world? How did Indonesians envision their country's economic and political development, and how did they navigate the difficult shoals of great power conflict and the structural limits of their role in the world economy? How did the destruction of the Indonesian Communist Party and the ascendance of the New Order regime of General Suharto affect these goals? Perhaps most important for our purposes, how did Washington and Jakarta's commitment to a program of military-led modernization emerge, and what were its long-range implications? Existing accounts of U.S.-Indonesian relations obscure or ignore the long-range developmental vision inextricably linked to the geopolitical and anti-Communist concerns articulated by U.S. officials, social scientists, and businessmen and many Indonesians throughout the 1960s. That vision held out for Indonesia a military-dominated, development-oriented regime integrated into the regional economy and bound to multilateral institutions. It was a vision firmly embedded in a discourse of modernization, shaping both the ways in which U.S. officials and their Western and Indonesian counterparts thought about Indonesia and the policies they advocated to contain the PKI and lay the foundation for Indonesian political and economic development.

In his magisterial *Global Cold War*, Odd Arne Westad argues for a basic reconceptualization of the dynamics of superpower rivalry in which "the most important aspects of the Cold War were neither military nor strategic, nor Europe-centered but connected to political and social development in the Third World" and the destructive consequences of U.S. and Soviet intervention there.[12] Competing U.S. and Soviet visions of development and the programs of military, economic, and technical assistance that purported to realize them often constituted the most important forms of intervention. In recent years historians have produced a rich literature exploring the role that social scientific theories of development and modernization played in shaping both U.S. and Soviet foreign policy and the developmental visions of people throughout the so-called third world. Modernization theory as a social science paradigm emerged out of postwar concerns with the problems of development and their significance for the United States and as part of a "determined, deliberate drive toward a comprehensive theory of society" that would make it possible to better understand and manage social change in developing countries.[13] Its proponents generally held to a few core assumptions: the distinction between traditional and modern societies; the integrated and interdependent nature of economic, political, and social change; the universality of linear development toward a common modernity; and the conviction that contact with the West could accelerate the progress of developing countries.[14]

By the early 1960s modernization theory dominated social science thinking about political and economic development in both the academic and policy realms. Modernization theorists drew in expected ways on deeply embedded discourses that emphasized both the uniqueness and appropriateness of America's developmental model for the rest of the world and the cultural superiority of the West in general and the Anglo-Saxon tradition in particular. In the case of the United States such ideas also "resonated with previous combinations of missionary vision and imperial control," asserting America's right and ability to transform the underdeveloped world in its image even as officials questioned the capacity of non-Western peoples to overcome "Oriental fatalism" and other "ancient cultural obstacles" to modernity.[15] World War II, however, marked a decisive break with these earlier visions, focusing the attention of policymakers and social scientists on the development of postcolonial nation-states within an integrated world system.[16]

But modernization theory was more than a social science paradigm driving research agendas and facilitating cozy relationships between scholars and the national security state.[17] Michael Latham suggests that modernization was "an ideology, a political instrument, an analytical model, a rhetorical tool, a cognitive framework, and a system of beliefs"; in short, "an element of American culture." It was also a discourse in the Foucaultian sense, a language of development "bound up with actions, practices, and institutional networks . . . of power and authority."[18] This discourse identified and named "backward" countries according to "universal" and "neutral" criteria set out by social scientists, government agencies, and international institutions such as the IMF, catalogued their shortcomings, and prescribed policies and packages of military, economic, and technical assistance to hasten their inevitable march toward development and modernity. Policymakers held up the U.S. and British experience as universally valid models, ignoring their unique historical circumstances and advantages.[19] By arguing that all countries followed similar paths to development and that the speed with which this was accomplished was largely a matter of timing, contact with the West, national volition, and cultural differences, the discourse of modernization also naturalized and dehistoricized economic and political inequality on a global scale, wiping out the vastly different colonial experiences, for example, of Korea under the Japanese (where colonialism helped to lay the groundwork for late economic development) and Indonesia under the Dutch (where it did nothing of the sort).[20] The ideology of modernization thus conflated the historically contingent roles that states played in regional economies and the world system with their stage of development, thereby rationalizing the role that U.S. officials thought countries should play in the international division of labor with their supposed level of cultural and material advancement.[21]

The architects of U.S. policy toward Indonesia heartily embraced this discourse from the moment of their arrival in Washington.[22] The Kennedy administration's Basic National Security Policy for 1962, for example, analyzed U.S. policy toward "underdeveloped areas" wholly within the framework of modernization. It urged the creation of comprehensive country plans for developing nations with "a clear understanding of the desired pace and direction of modernization, based on our objectives and on the limits and possibilities set by the particular country's stage of political, social and economic development." By scrutinizing comprehensive national development plans, MIT social scientist Paul Rosenstein-Rodan suggested that Washington could determine which nations were primed for "take-off" and which were still developing the "pre-conditions" for sustained growth, adjusting the type and amount of aid accordingly.[23]

Although modernization theory as a social science paradigm may have originated in the United States in the postwar period, it was part of a larger, widely dispersed fabric of thinking about the process of becoming modern, the origins of which stretch back to the Enlightenment.[24] The ideological lure of using state power as an agent for social transformation, however, particularly animated early twentieth century development schemes, taking root not just in New Deal America in the form of the Tennessee Valley Authority, but also in the Soviet Union in the form of collectivized agriculture and the Virgin Lands scheme, in rural redevelopment plans in francophone West Africa, and elsewhere.[25] Such schemes resonated in postindependence Indonesia as well.

Concerns about modernization and development, terms used interchangeably by U.S. officials, shaped the policies of both the Kennedy and Johnson administrations toward the developing world.[26] In January 1961 Soviet premier Nikita Khrushchev famously (if briefly) suggested that Moscow would support "wars of national liberation," and Soviet officials pointed to their country's rapid industrialization as a model for postcolonial states. Moreover, Soviet bloc foreign aid and technical assistance expanded dramatically in the late 1950s and early 1960s, targeting countries such as Cuba, Indonesia, India, Egypt, and Ghana. Deputy national security adviser Walt Rostow, the MIT economist and author of *Stages of Growth: A Non-Communist Manifesto*, warned that unless the United States could respond in kind, the Soviets and Chinese would succeed "in projecting an image of communism as the most efficient method for modernizing the underdeveloped regions." The Cuban revolution added greater urgency to this challenge.[27]

The Kennedy administration responded to these challenges by declaring a "Decade of Development," creating the Agency for International Development (AID) and initiating programs such as the Alliance for Progress and the Peace Corps. Perhaps more important, President Kennedy oversaw a worldwide expansion of economic and military assistance and inaugurated a global turn toward counterinsurgency, paving the way for the emergence or consolidation of military modernizing regimes in Asia, Central and Latin America, and the Middle East. The Johnson administration shared its predecessor's commitment to these policies, persisting in the belief that U.S. military and economic assistance, advice, scientific expertise, technology, and culture could decisively shape the economic, political, and social trajectory of developing nations and speed them along the road to a modernity that policymakers defined almost wholly in terms of their own experience.

U.S. officials during the 1960s viewed these challenges in strongly gendered terms, as had their predecessors.[28] John F. Kennedy arrived in office amid a perceived crisis of American masculinity linked to allegations of declining U.S. power. William Lederer and Eugene Burdick's best-selling 1958 novel *The Ugly American* charged that flabby, effeminate bureaucrats holed up in U.S. embassies were losing the Cold War in Southeast Asia to their Communist adversaries, who were "out in the villages . . . winning converts to their cause" through hard work, sacrifice, and grassroots economic development programs. *The Ugly American's* portrayal of the Eisenhower administration's foreign policy, Robert Dean argues, "reflected and embodied ideas about foreign aid and counterinsurgency current with Kennedy and many of his advisers," including skepticism of large-scale aid programs involving "military highways, dams, and industrial infrastructure." Washington's support for counterinsurgency, civic action, and Peace Corps activities in countries such as Indonesia during this period can thus be viewed in part as an attempt to promote modernization using more vigorous, individualistic, and masculine aid techniques (the Peace Corps contingent in Indonesia consisted entirely of physical education instructors, Sargent Shriver explained to President Kennedy, in part because "athletics is a matter of national pride and importance" to Sukarno).[29]

Indonesia loomed especially large in Washington's eyes as one of the few countries in the world where U.S. and Soviet officials competed directly for influence with military, economic, and technical assistance. U.S. aid policy toward Indonesia thus offers a particularly valuable window into the developmental model America was offering as an alternative to Communism,

Socialism, and state-led industrialization. U.S. officials believed that integrated programs of technical, military, and economic assistance and multilateral efforts to stabilize the Indonesian economy, while plugging holes in the containment dike being poked by PKI activists and Soviet aid technicians, could set it on the path to economic rationality, political stability, and Western-oriented development. This is the vision that lurked in the background of the military and economic aid package that the Kennedy administration proposed for Indonesia in late 1962 following the brokered settlement of the West New Guinea dispute with the Netherlands. But it was a contested strategy, vulnerable domestically to congressional and hard-line opponents, dependent on the domestic strength of Western-oriented technocrats in Indonesia and on Sukarno's willingness to adopt policies urged upon it by the United States and the IMF, and contingent on Washington's allies playing roles that complemented its regional policies. Chief among these unforeseen contingencies was Britain's formation of Malaysia out of the remnants of its Southeast Asian empire in the early 1960s—London's own attempt to contain and channel Southeast Asian nationalism and development along acceptable lines. Indonesia's opposition to Malaysia's creation in the fall of 1963 would lead over the next two years to a major military and political confrontation with Malaysia, Britain, and, indirectly, the United States, torpedoing the Kennedy administration's plans and accelerating Jakarta's domestic political polarization and economic collapse in late 1965. In the wake of the September 30th Movement, which brought General Suharto to power in 1965, however, this modernizing vision reemerged in slightly altered form to guide policy toward Jakarta as Washington embraced the New Order and sought to restore political and economic stability in Indonesia.

Kennedy's much-maligned undersecretary of state Chester Bowles deftly articulated the broader impulses animating U.S. policy, explaining to Indonesian president Sukarno in November 1961 that Washington's goal was to develop a "stable group [of] independent Asian nations as [an] offset and counter to Chinese Communist power" by creating "an arc of stable and free Asian states based on Japan, Indonesia, India and Pakistan" with the United States as a "helpful bystander"—in other words, former secretary of state Dean Acheson's "great crescent." Bowles drew comparison to the nineteenth-century British empire, whose naval fleet shielded American development, prompting one of Sukarno's ministers to urge similar protection for Jakarta, noting that the "British fleet was just like your seventh fleet today."[30] A few months later Bowles wrote a "Draft Memorandum on East and Southeast Asia," offering an unusually explicit definition of long-term U.S. goals for the region. Casting Washington's short-term goals in largely strategic terms, Bowles argued that over the long term the United States should foster "increased cooperation among nations of the region" along lines that "must follow the natural flow of economic utility":

> In this context, the U.S. role must remain subtle, sophisticated, and unostentatious. If the fragmentation of free Asia is to be bridged, persistent U.S. leverage is essential: leverage toward increased intra-regional trade, increased productivity, multinational economic development, regional communications arrangements, commodity stabilization plans, and cultural and information exchange.
>
> Our *ultimate* aim, however difficult to achieve, must be the gradual economic integration of the free Asian rim land, from Japan and Korea to India and Pakistan. In the long run, such integration is the only viable basis for increasing political cooperation and for coordinated security planning by the free states of the region.

These ambitious goals necessitated a long-term U.S. presence in the region as a "military shield for the developing nations of South and Southeast Asia" and "as the major outside contributor to technical training, economic planning and economic development."[31] Here geopolitical and strategic means served world economy ends, a formulation precisely the opposite of most accounts of U.S.-Indonesian relations.[32] This was a mature hegemonic vision for the region, gracefully articulating the relationship between power and plenty and the role of the United States in exercising that power—the gloved hand rather than the mailed fist.

The assumptions underpinning U.S. thinking about Indonesia changed remarkably little in the postwar period, tracing ever back to the early postwar period and visions of Indonesia's role in an integrated regional economy centered on Japan. Upon coming to office, Kennedy administration policymakers began pushing Japan to develop closer ties to Indonesia and urged Tokyo to help underwrite development assistance to Jakarta. As the curtain rang down on the Sukarno era in 1966, the State Department continued pressing Japan to take the lead in organizing multilateral assistance to Jakarta, arguing that "the economies of Japan and Indonesia are complementary" even as it concluded that Japanese capital intended to push American oil companies out of Indonesia—all while American exporters howled about losing markets to Tokyo.[33]

Several themes emerge from the account that follows, themes that characterized U.S. relations with Jakarta through the 1960s and its policy in much of the so-called third world during the Cold War.[34] The first is Washington's near obsessive fear of Communism in Indonesia, a concern that persisted throughout the period, led U.S. policymakers to substantially exaggerate the likelihood of the Indonesian Communist Party (PKI) coming to power, misjudge the balance of Indonesian social forces, and support the mass killings of alleged PKI supporters in the months following the September 30th Movement. The second theme is the Kennedy and Johnson administrations' commitment to military-led economic and political development, a project that many Indonesian officials also embraced and considered synonymous with modernization. This commitment emerged in heightened fashion following the destruction of the PKI and General Suharto's rise to power in 1966, but, as we will see, it produced its own contradictions for Suharto's New Order regime. The third theme, which flowed directly from Washington's developmental concerns, is Washington's consistent support for authoritarianism in Indonesia and its reliance on the armed forces as the guarantor of economic and political stability, a policy that would guide its relations with Jakarta for the next thirty years and substantively affect the course of Indonesian history.

Four decades after Suharto came to power, the United States continues to intervene politically and militarily in the Islamic world, now under the guise of the so-called war on terror and with the goal of "nation building" in Afghanistan and Iraq and "democracy promotion" elsewhere in the world. And despite endless high-flown rhetoric emanating from the White House about its commitment to freedom and democracy, the United States continues to align itself with authoritarian regimes and armed forces from the Middle East to Southeast Asia, incubating the same forces of political instability, corruption, and political Islam that the modernizing New Order regime helped to unleash in Indonesia. It is to that story, which also began with hopes in Washington and Jakarta for the prospects of democratic development, that I now turn.

CHAPTER I

Imagining Indonesian Development

The only prophet without a significant Indonesian following is probably Adam Smith.

—Max Millikan

The collapse of Japanese and European colonialism and the rise of revolutionary nationalist movements in East and Southeast Asia in the 1940s was a signal event of twentieth-century international history.[1] The post–World War II attempt by a generation of U.S. and European policymakers to direct the inevitable process of decolonization along lines compatible with Western interests and the efforts of indigenous forces to assert their own visions of self-determination helps to explain much of the Cold War in Asia, which produced two devastating wars in Korea and Indochina and myriad instances of covert intervention. The historical trajectory of Indonesia, then the world's fifth most populous nation and its largest Muslim state, would be decisively shaped by these efforts. Since the surrender of Japanese forces in August 1945, which ended World War II, U.S. policy toward the former Netherlands East Indies has lagged consistently behind the aspirations of its nationalist leaders to sever the economic, political, and cultural sinews of European colonialism. Concerned more with the implications of rapid decolonization of

Asian empires for Europe and Japan than with the demands for independence of anticolonial leaders, the Truman administration initially acquiesced to Dutch efforts to reestablish control over their former colonial empire, expressing the same ambivalence about the fitness of Indonesians for self-government that it did for Vietnam. For three years the United States publicly professed neutrality in Indonesia's independence struggle while The Hague used lend-lease equipment and funds freed up by U.S. Marshall Plan aid to repress Indonesia's republican forces. Not until the fall of 1948 did Washington decisively back Indonesian independence by threatening to withhold military and economic aid after the Netherlands unilaterally violated a U.S.-brokered settlement. Not only did Dutch military actions threaten the Truman administration's European priorities, but U.S. officials also feared that the anticolonial struggle might unleash more radical and less easily controlled forces, such as the "emergence of a Pan-Asian bloc, which . . . may follow an independent path."[2] Equally important, the young republican government demonstrated its anti-Communist bona fides to the Truman administration by bloodily crushing a PKI uprising in September 1948 in the East Java city of Madiun.[3] While White House officials congratulated themselves for their newfound devotion to Indonesian independence, many Indonesian nationalist leaders remained profoundly suspicious of both U.S. and Soviet intentions. Washington's near simultaneous decision to back the French effort at colonial reconquest in Indochina and continued British control over Malaya—both also challenged by radical independence movements—underscored the fragile nature of Washington's support for Asian self-government, as Indonesia's new leaders readily recognized.[4]

In the wake of Indonesia's independence in 1949, U.S. officials and social scientists identified the Southeast Asian nation as a linchpin in Washington's strategy of regional economic integration and as a line of containment against the expansion of Soviet and later Chinese power. Washington hoped that its support for Indonesian independence and the provision of a modest program of economic and technical assistance beginning in 1950 would help foster the emergence of a representative, capitalist, and pro-Western government.[5] The vast majority of Indonesians, however, associated Western-style democracy and capitalism with colonialism and sought a collectivist, social democratic (or even socialist), and indigenously rooted path to political and economic development. Sukarno's articulation of the famous five principles known as the *Pancasila*—national unity, social justice, belief in God, humanitarianism, and democracy—was an imprecise attempt at formulating a distinctly Indonesian vision of democracy through consensus, as opposed to the "free fight" democracy of a competitive parliamentary system.[6] Mohammed Hatta, Indonesia's first vice president and its foremost advocate of a decentralized Indonesian state and a democratic, participatory government, likewise firmly rejected Western-style democracy (even as he battled against Sukarno to rescue the parliamentary system), arguing in 1956 that "political democracy alone cannot bring about equality and fraternity. Political democracy must go hand in hand with economic democracy," a "social democracy covering all phases of life."[7] Throughout the mid-1950s both visions reflected a fragile optimism both within and outside Indonesia over the prospects for democratic development, even if they profoundly differed over the meaning of democracy.[8]

The rising strength of the Indonesian Communist Party (PKI) in the years after independence, however, tempered such hopes, as did Indonesia's firm commitment to neutralism and national development along lines that clashed repeatedly with U.S. goals in the region. Growing U.S. frustration with Indonesia mirrored its concerns during the decade over the rise of indigenous radicalism, neutralism, and nationalism throughout the so-called third world.[9] By the mid-1950s U.S. support for and optimism about the prospects for democracy in Indonesia proved to be highly contingent. As in countless other nations, Washington began encouraging, alongside technical and agricultural assistance, military aid programs that prioritized stability over democracy and envisioned U.S.-trained military establishments as vanguards of modernization. Indonesia's abandonment of parliamentary democracy and the outbreak of a U.S.-backed civil war during the late 1950s marked a turning point toward the Indonesian and American embrace of an authoritarian regime as the appropriate vehicle for modernizing the world's fifth largest nation. When the Kennedy administration arrived in Washington in 1961, visions of military modernization framed the boundaries of American and Indonesian thinking about possible paths to the country's future.

Imagining Indonesian Development

Indonesia's postindependence hopes for political and economic development flowed directly from its experience under Dutch colonial rule and the near insuperable challenge of creating an integrated nation out of a far-flung, multiethnic archipelago poorly prepared by its former colonial power for independence. The bewildering complexity of Indonesian politics in the decade after independence, with nationalist, Socialist, Catholic, Communist, and Islamic parties and organizations offering fundamentally different proposals for the nation's basic political and economic structure, testified to the difficulty of constructing a unified nation and political system. The persistence of local and regional identities in places such as Aceh as well as Dutch attempts to weaken the new republic through federalist schemes exacerbated these challenges, leading Sukarno in August 1950 to abandon the federal arrangement agreed to in the 1949 Roundtable Conference and guaranteeing conflict between the island of Java, with two-thirds of the nation's population, and the rest of the archipelago. Indonesian views on economic development were likewise conditioned by the exploitative nature of Dutch colonialism—which concentrated much of the economy in foreign hands and oriented it toward production of commodities, such as rubber, tin, palm oil, and petroleum, for the world market. Consequently, Indonesian nationalists, beginning with the country's first president, Sukarno, hoped to take back control of the economy from foreigners and establish a basis for national unity, development, and self-sufficiency.[10]

U.S. officials, on the other hand, framed Indonesia's strategic, economic, and political importance squarely in regional terms that flowed from their commitment between 1947 and 1950 to seek the reconstruction of Japan, regional economic integration, and the containment of Communism throughout Asia. Dean Acheson's State Department laid out the goals in a series of planning documents, in particular PPS (Policy Planning Staff) Paper 51 and NSC 48/2, which called for both the economic integration of Southeast Asia through the linkage of its raw materials with Japanese industrial capacity and Western access to the region.[11] These core commitments, for which containment and anti-Communism were the means, not the ends, remained the unspoken assumptions guiding U.S. policy toward Indonesia through the end of the Sukarno era and indeed throughout the Cold War.[12]

Indonesia's commitment to a nonaligned foreign policy, its pursuit of state-led development, and its tolerance of a strong and growing Communist party, however, posed profound challenges to U.S. goals that mirrored those it faced elsewhere in the developing world. Indonesia's postindependence leaders, committed to a nonaligned foreign policy, "proved resistant, from the first, to American direction and obdurately refused to join the American alliance system or even to accept any American aid that might come with strings attached."[13] Republicans in Washington, who viewed foreign aid as "a global extension of the New Deal Programs they loathed," sought to link such assistance to pro-U.S. military and economic policies, with predictably counterproductive results.[14] In 1952 popular outrage at U.S. demands that Indonesia sign a mutual security agreement as a condition of receiving U.S. military aid brought down the Sukiman cabinet. First the Truman and then the Eisenhower administration tried to cement Jakarta's ties to the West and to the regional economy through programs of military, technical, and economic assistance, only to express exasperation as civilian and military leaders of all stripes proved willing to accept aid but unwilling to take sides in the Cold War.

Sukarno's hosting of the Bandung conference of nonaligned nations in 1955 symbolized Indonesia and other postcolonial nations' determination to chart an independent course in foreign affairs and the broader challenge that nonalignment posed to both the United States and the Soviet Union. The Eisenhower administration initially opposed the convening of the Bandung conference (called "a vast illuminated soapbox where the malcontents of the world—the black, the yellow, the brown, and even some whites—could have their say" by *Newsweek*) and at turns sought to accommodate itself to or undermine the efforts of Yugoslavia, India, Egypt, Indonesia, and other nations to pursue a neutralist path in the Cold War.[15] The Soviet Union, likewise initially hostile to nonalignment, under Khrushchev revised Communist development doctrine to account for and appeal to its proponents, developing the notion of the "national democratic state" as a way station on the road to Socialism.[16] China's Communist leadership, even as they participated in the Bandung meeting, were also unsure of how to relate to neutralist and anti-imperialist leaders such as Nehru, Nasser, and Sukarno, who were often lukewarm or hostile to domestic Communist parties. Although Mao publicly praised Sukarno for his anticolonialism, Deng Xiaoping confessed to Soviet ambassador to China Stephan Chervonenko that "the struggle with bourgeois figures of this sort is one of the most important problems facing the international communist movement."[17]

The threat that the U.S. and other Western governments identified at Bandung, however, extended beyond the obvious political challenge that nonalignment posed to the imperative of Cold War alliance building. In his opening speech to the conference, Sukarno implored, "I beg of you, do not think of colonialism only in the classic form which we of Indonesia, and our brothers in different parts of Asia and Africa, knew. Colonialism has also its modern dress, in the form of economic control, intellectual control, actual physical control by a small but alien community within a nation."[18]

As Sukarno suggested, the creation of the nonaligned movement raised the specter of more than just an unprecedented alliance of what American conference attendee Adam Clayton Powell called "the two billion colored people of the earth."[19] U.S. officials also feared that political nonalignment might extend to the economic sphere as well, presaging collective attempts at independent state-led development, regional trading blocs, or declarations of support for Soviet or Chinese models of industrialization. Many neutralist leaders embraced socialist ideals, at least rhetorically, and viewed Western-style capitalism as an exploitative extension of formal colonialism. Eisenhower administration officials could only express relief when the nations attending the Bandung meeting seemed to acknowledge their continued dependence on foreign investment and technical assistance from the West and refrained from explicit calls for autonomist programs of development.[20]

Training for Development

It was to this challenge of explaining and attempting to direct the scope of change in the so-called third world that the U.S. government and a host of nonstate and international organizations turned their attention as the Cold War solidified. The establishment of area studies programs in the late 1940s and early 1950s by a constellation of academic institutions, philanthropic foundations, and the U.S. intelligence community was a crucial development in the history of American hegemony. Both as intellectual adjuncts to the creation of a national security state and as sites for the figurative naming and categorization of the world, area studies programs at Harvard, the University of Chicago, the University of California at Berkeley, MIT, Johns Hopkins University, Cornell University, and elsewhere played a crucial role in the construction and dispersal of social scientific thinking about political and economic development in the developing world and in the production of relevant policy knowledge.[21] This was nowhere more true than in Indonesia, where programs funded by the Ford and Rockefeller Foundations, among others, shaped both American and Indonesian understandings of the possibilities and limits of Indonesia's development.

The historian Henry Benda in 1964 wrote without exaggeration that "no country in Southeast Asia has in postwar years received greater attention, institutional support, and dedicated individual scholarship than Indonesia."[22] Much of that attention resulted from a massive outpouring of foundation funding for the study of Indonesian politics, economics, and society in the years between 1950 and 1964. During this period the Ford and Rockefeller Foundations alone disbursed nearly $20 million for education, agriculture, medical, and technical assistance in both the United States and Indonesia.[23] These philanthropic institutions not only facilitated a dramatic expansion of social scientific research on Indonesia but also funded participant and educational exchange programs for Indonesian technicians, economists, teachers, agrarian specialists, military personnel, and engineers—what U.S. ambassador to Indonesia from 1958 to 1965 Howard Jones termed a long-term "struggle for the Indonesian mind."[24] Ford and Rockefeller Foundation funds underwrote the creation of area studies programs in the United States, including the Social Science Research Council's Committee on Comparative Politics, which also funded studies of Indonesian politics and economics. These efforts intersected with and helped to shape wide-ranging debates taking place within Indonesian society during the 1950s over the nature and direction of economic and political development, debates that would have far-reaching implications.

The Ford Foundation arguably played the most significant (and doubtless most well-publicized) role. Ford-funded education training for Indonesian social scientists directly shaped Indonesian development thinking.[25] Between 1956 and 1962 Ford Foundation fellowships, in addition to AID participant training programs, provided training for an entire generation of Indonesian economists through the creation of a partnership between the University of Indonesia and the University of California at Berkeley and the funding of graduate economics study at MIT, Cornell University, and other institutions.[26] The young republic's need for trained economists was acute; in 1956 only fifteen Indonesians had pursued advanced study. Two years later Ford Foundation officials reported that its economics training program had "become increasingly associated with the internal development of Indonesia."[27]

The experience of the economist Subroto was illustrative. After Subroto had completed a master's degree in economics at McGill University in 1956, Sumitro Djojohadikusomo, dean of the Faculty of Economics at the University of Indonesia (FEUI), arranged for Subroto to continue graduate work at MIT, where he worked with Ben Higgins, Charles Kindleberger, and Paul Samuelson studying Indonesia's terms of trade in primary commodities. A year later Subroto returned to teach at FEUI, leaving again in 1960 and 1961 to study management at Stanford University and business at Harvard, both on Ford Foundation fellowships.[28]

Sumitro told officers of the Rockefeller Foundation that his hope was to reorganize the Economics Department at the University of Indonesia "along American lines" in terms of both research and organization. Sumitro, a former minister of trade and minister of finance, was Indonesia's most prominent economist, a member of the Indonesian Socialist Party and a leading supporter of the PRRI (Revolutionary Government of the Republic of Indonesia) rebellions in 1958. Forced into exile in 1957, he maintained close ties to the State Department and CIA throughout the Guided Democracy period until invited back to Indonesia by Suharto in 1966 following Sukarno's ouster.[29] The group of economics professors from the University of Indonesia who surrounded Sumitro, the most significant of whom include Widjojo Nitisastro, Mohammed Sadli, Subroto, Ali Wardhana, and Emil Salim, would after the fall of Sukarno in 1966 play a crucial role in setting Indonesian economic policy and dismantling the edifice of Sukarno's Guided Economy, prompting radical scholars to dub them the "Berkeley Mafia."[30] U.S. officials assiduously cultivated these Western-oriented technocrats, who in the spring of 1963 were the chief supporters of an ill-fated attempt by First Minister Djuanda to commit Indonesia to an IMF-sponsored program of structural adjustment. The State Department's Policy Planning Council later cited the political destruction of these "modernizers" as a major factor in Indonesia's subsequent economic disintegration between 1963 and 1966.[31]

The support of the Ford and Rockefeller Foundations for U.S. and Canadian social scientific research on Indonesia during this period had an equally significant impact on American and Indonesian development thinking. Between 1952 and 1956 alone the foundations helped fund the establishment of the Southeast Asian Studies Center and the Contemporary Indonesia Project at Cornell University, Harvard University's Development Advisory Service, the Southeast Asian Studies Program at the University of California at Berkeley, and the Center for International Studies at MIT.[32] The bulk of U.S.-based social scientific research on Indonesia during the 1950s and early 1960s took place either directly under the auspices of these grants or through foundation-funded centers for international and area studies.[33]

Cornell University's Modern Indonesia Project and MIT's Center for International Studies (CENIS) illustrate the central role that such funding played in the creation and dissemination of research on Indonesian politics and society. As early as 1951, Ford Foundation director Paul Hoffman, the former CEO of Studebaker and Marshall Plan administrator, began discussing with Economic Cooperation Administration officials the need for greater policy-relevant research concerning Indonesia.[34] A year later the Ford Foundation provided funding for the establishment of programs at MIT and Cornell, the latter headed by George McT. Kahin, a founder of Southeast Asian studies and author of the seminal 1952 book *Nationalism and Revolution in Indonesia*.[35] In 1953 Kahin requested funding for a comprehensive and interdisciplinary study of contemporary Indonesian political life, including its central and local governments, parliament, labor, youth, modernist Muslim organizations, non-Islamic parties, and Indonesian Chinese community. An overarching goal of these studies was to achieve a "greater understanding of [the] problem of Communism in Indonesia." The Modern Indonesia Project also emphasized the creation of an indigenous social scientific community, noting that in its first year it had more than doubled the number of Indonesians conducting social science research.[36]

MIT's CENIS, created in 1953 under the leadership of former CIA official Max Millikan, aimed more broadly to serve as an interdisciplinary space for the construction of a comprehensive theory of development.[37] In 1953 CENIS director Millikan proposed a three-pronged study of nations at various stages of the development process, focusing on Italy, India, and Indonesia (the last two an early focus of the Soviet Union's tentative embrace of nonaligned states).[38] The MIT Indonesia project sought, in the words of one scholar, "to develop a comprehensive theory of Javanese culture and society," in part to explain the failure of Indonesia to produce a vibrant entrepreneurial class.[39] But the project's goals were as much prescriptive as descriptive. The CENIS grant proposal for its Indonesia project identified its chief goal as determining the country's "possible alternative courses of future development" and how these could "be affected by the policy and action of the governments concerned, the U.S. government and international agencies."[40]

Beginning in 1953, CENIS supported a team of anthropologists, sociologists, economists, communication specialists, and political scientists to conduct research along four major themes in Indonesia: "1) the process of capital formation; 2) social aspects of agricultural development; 3) the emergent alignment of political forces with special reference to their effect on economic development; [and] 4) sources of political and social disaffection."[41] The Indonesia project identified its goals in consultation with the head of the National Development Planning Agency (BAPPENAS) of the Indonesian government and the director of the Social Science Department of the University of Indonesia. As the Center's 1954 annual report noted, the major premise underlying its research was that "the major obstacles to Indonesian economic development have to do with the *organization* of the country's human and natural resources" and not with its historic (and historically constrained) role in the world economy. Explicitly rejecting the development framework offered by Indonesian nationalists—*pembangunan* as nation building and the creation of a noncolonial national economy—CENIS scholars described the country in classically Ricardian terms of comparative advantage and asked, "What, in terms of its position in regional and world markets, should Indonesia's pattern of industrialization be?"[42]

Over the next ten years the MIT Indonesia project provided some of the answers, producing some of the most significant social science research on Indonesia in the fields of economics, anthropology, political science, and communication studies.[43] The research of anthropologist Clifford Geertz, doubtless the most famous of the MIT-affiliated scholars, illustrates the ways in which the project shaped both popular and official understanding of Indonesian culture and the framework within which Americans and Indonesians thought about the country's development. CENIS director Max Millikan recruited Geertz, a student of Talcott Parsons, to travel to Indonesia in 1954. Upon returning to Cambridge, Geertz urged the young anthropologist to write a study that would "explain why Java had failed to achieve an agricultural evolution that would set the stage for industrialization."[44] The resulting works, most famously *Agricultural Involution*, located Indonesia's economic backwardness in the response of colonial-era peasants to exploitative Dutch agricultural practices.[45] Rather than provoking a flight of peasants to urban areas where they might become fodder for industrialization, Geertz argued, agricultural poverty in Indonesia resulted in more intensive cultivation of ever-shrinking plots of land and a downward spiral—his "involution"—of overpopulation, technological stagnation, and disempowerment.[46]

Although the involution thesis has since come under heavy criticism, it carried important implications for U.S. policy in Indonesia and for Indonesian development.[47] In addition to confirming the arguments of modernization theorists that the barriers to Indonesian development were partly cultural in nature, Geertz's work buttressed the claims of U.S. policymakers that the solution to Indonesia's agricultural problems lay in educating farmers in American farming methods, greater technical expertise, and agricultural mechanization, all of which would gradually push peasants from rural areas and toward urban centers where they might provide an industrial workforce. The most important example of such thinking was the International Cooperation Administration– (and later AID-) sponsored agricultural extension program linking the University of Kentucky to the Agricultural University at Bogor. Between 1957 and 1966 this program brought more than 200 Indonesian agricultural experts for study to the United States and an equal number of Americans to Indonesia. The goals of U.S. officials, who pushed technical training, extension programs, and the capitalization of peasant agriculture, clashed directly with those of many Indonesian development planners, who prioritized agricultural self-sufficiency and rural employment over technological modernization. Although both Indonesian and Americans "shared the important belief that the goal of development was transformation to a Western ideal of economic growth and productivity," they differed profoundly in their views on the means to these ends.[48] Moreover, by the late 1950s and early 1960s Indonesian officials, frustrated with American priorities, could—and did—increasingly turn to the USSR for similar forms of assistance.

The Soviet and Chinese Challenge

The concerns among U.S. officials about Indonesia's possible drift to the left in the 1950s reflected broader anxieties about the Soviet Union's growing focus on the developing world. Following the death of Joseph Stalin, Soviet premier Nikita Khrushchev inaugurated a fundamental turn in Soviet foreign policy, including the pursuit of peaceful coexistence with the West, an accommodation to nonalignment, and initiation of expansive programs of economic and technical assistance to countries such as Indonesia, India, Egypt, and Afghanistan. In addition to denouncing the former dictator's domestic crimes, Khrushchev criticized Stalin for his shortsightedness in seeking rigid control over local Communist parties and in failing to actively pursue closer relations with newly independent countries where conditions were not immediately ripe for revolution.[49] As John Foster Dulles told the National Security Council in November 1955, this shift marked the beginning of a Soviet economic and political offensive with grave implications for U.S. interests in the third world. Not only did Soviet overtures undermine U.S. attempts to forge closer political ties with neutralist states, Dulles argued, but such efforts also could fray the trade and military ties that effectively bound developing countries to the West.[50]

Between May and October of 1956 Sukarno undertook a series of visits— to the United States, much of Western Europe, the Soviet Union, Mongolia, Yugoslavia, China, and Czechoslovakia—that highlighted these contrasting models of economic development.[51] On his May trip to the United States, during which the Eisenhower administration pledged $25 million in aid, Sukarno offered lavish public praise for American technological and economic might, quoting Thomas Jefferson in an address to Congress that received a standing ovation and making a favorable impression on the American press. Privately, however, the Indonesian president commented that the United States had little to offer as a model for a country as poor as Indonesia. In Moscow, Sukarno secured a Soviet pledge of $100 million in economic assistance and invited Soviet president Kliment Voroshilov to come to Jakarta. (The visit inspired the CIA's famously bungled attempt to create a pornographic film showing Sukarno in a compromising position with a Russian stewardess. The shapely blond had been seen with Sukarno on his visit to Moscow and accompanied Voroshilov to Jakarta.)[52] In a 1957 meeting of the CPSU Central Committee, Plenum Deputy Premier Anastas Mikoyan argued that although Sukarno and other non-Communist leaders were "bourgeois nationalists," closer political and economic ties to nonaligned states such as Indonesia created opportunities for "undermin[ing] the influence of the imperialist powers on the countries of Asia."[53]

U.S. officials and social scientists largely agreed with Mikoyan's assessment, if not his choice of words. The Soviet—and later Chinese—challenge was always as much economic as it was political and military. Indeed, in the late 1950s "the Soviet Union seemed to possess a number of distinct advantages over the West," which had little to do with its military capabilities, "in any competition for the loyalties of the emerging postcolonial societies of Asia and Africa."[54] One was political, stemming from the Soviet Union's opposition to colonialism (outside Eastern Europe) and in favor of civil rights for nonwhite peoples, a stance that appealed to anticolonial nationalists and radicals throughout the developing world. The U.S. practice of racial apartheid at home, the AFL-CIO's representative in Indonesia wrote to George Meany, was "withering the reputation of the USA citizens and government here in Southeast Asia." Moreover, from Southeast Asia to southern Africa, Washington's political and military alliances with both current and former European colonial powers made the task of winning the support of postcolonial states immeasurably more difficult.[55]

No issue highlighted this dilemma more than West New Guinea. The Dutch had administered West New Guinea as part of the Netherlands East Indies, but in the 1949 Round Table Agreement that gave Indonesia its independence, The Hague insisted on retaining control. Indonesian officials thought Netherlands officials would complete the transfer of West New Guinea to the Republic of Indonesia once the political situation was more amenable.[56] The Dutch had other ideas. After repeated talks and appeals to the United Nations failed, Indonesia in 1957 seized Dutch economic assets, expelled Dutch citizens, and three years later severed relations. The takeover of Dutch assets carried tremendous implications for Indonesia's internal balance of power, its development prospects, and its foreign relations. The Indonesian armed forces quickly assumed supervision of formerly Dutch-controlled extractive and manufacturing enterprises, securing an independent revenue base, increasing their political power, and bringing them into direct conflict with organized plantation and oil field workers.[57] The United States, which pledged neutrality and abstained on U.N. resolutions concerning West New Guinea, incurred the wrath of Indonesian nationalists. Not so the Soviets, who, like the PKI, emerged after 1957 as a loud and persistent defender of Indonesia's position.[58]

Perhaps more important than their anticolonial rhetoric, Soviet officials pointed to their country's experience with rapid industrialization as a model for developing nations to follow. This appeal only grew as the leaders of almost all newly independent nations faced enormous pressure to rapidly increase the standard of living of their populations and enormous obstacles in achieving these goals, because their position in the world economy, rapid demographic changes, and colonial developmental schemes oriented them toward export-oriented growth on the basis of raw materials production for the West rather than industrialization. U.S. officials and modernization theorists performed impressive acts of intellectual gymnastics trying to criticize the legacy of European colonialism while advocating development plans that continued colonial trade structures. Max Millikan wrote to the Ford Foundation that "in view of the great importance to the United States and the Western World of adequate supplies of relatively inexpensive raw materials, ways must be found to make continued high-level raw material output consistent with the economic development of the producing countries."[59] By the early 1950s, however, the rising expectations for economic growth in the developing world were being dashed by the failure of foreign investment to materialize and by declining terms of trade in these same raw materials, increasing the appeal of statist solutions.[60]

Indonesia's experience highlights the challenge that many other nations faced in squaring this circle. Before World War II Dutch colonial policy accelerated Indonesia's integration with world markets but retarded the creation of an integrated national economy and failed to lay the foundation for industrialization. At independence Indonesia depended for foreign exchange on exports of oil, rubber, palm oil, tin, copra, and other commodities largely produced on Dutch-, British-, and American-owned estates, which had "few linkages with the surrounding economies." For government revenue Indonesia relied not on a base of taxpayers but on royalties and import duties. The new nation chafed under the burden of a heavy debt and suffered from severe shortages of capital, technology, managers, economists, skilled labor, and industrial production for local use. Beginning in the 1950s Indonesia also faced declining prices for tin (in part the result of U.S. strategic stockpiling policies) and rubber (because of the increasing market share of synthetics and poor replanting practices), leading to chronic foreign exchange shortfalls and balance of payments deficits, which exacerbated the difficulties of capital accumulation and increased tensions with the Eisenhower administration.[61]

Many Indonesians viewed this colonial legacy as an indictment of Western-style capitalism and as an argument for relying on the state, rather than private capital, as the engine of economic development. Indonesia's first prime minister, Sutan Sjahrir, expressed beliefs held throughout much of the developing world when he wrote in 1956 that "nationalism in Indonesia is anti-capitalist—largely because capitalism here is Western, and, specifically, Dutch."[62] Although in agreement on basic principles, Indonesian elites shared no consensus on whether to pursue an independent developmental path or seek integration with the world economy, "whether or to what extent . . . to rely on foreign experts, foreign aid, and foreign investment," and how to square demands for social justice and national development with the economic realities of its peripheral status in the world system.[63]

Little wonder, then, that like many developing nations Indonesia looked with interest to the Soviet Union as a possible model for economic development.[64] Even Western observers admired the Soviet Union's economic achievements, rationalizing the unimaginable human cost of its rapid development model with the same tropes of Russian backwardness and passivity that marked postwar discussion of the obstacles to modernization in Asia.[65] The Soviet Union's achievement of rapid industrialization in a single generation, its emphasis on heavy industrialization, the prominence of state planning—all carried great appeal to nationalist leaders who sought to rapidly cast off the burdens of colonialism and modernize economy and society. Soviet technological advances in the 1950s—in particular the explosion of a hydrogen bomb in August 1953 and the launching of Sputnik in 1957—suggested that the socialist state was rapidly catching up to the capitalist West. Upon his return from a March 1960 visit to India, Burma, Indonesia, and Afghanistan, Nikita S. Khrushchev remarked approvingly to a crowd in Moscow:

> The American Senators say with alarm that the strengthening of the Soviet Union's economic strength will permit it to expand aid on easy terms to the underdeveloped countries. Noting that the Soviet Union is an example of rapid industrialization for these underdeveloped countries, the Senators write that the exchange of technical specialists, economic aid, trade opportunities, the growing prestige and strength of the Soviet Union, the Sputnik and Lunik—all these factors strengthen the impression that the Soviets represent the future. Again, not badly put.[66]

Besides the USSR's actual achievements, Soviet officials' confidence raised concerns among U.S. policymakers about the vitality and relevance of the U.S. model of development for the third world and for Indonesia in particular. As

Max Millikan ruefully noted, "The only prophet without a significant Indonesian following is probably Adam Smith."[67]

China's adoption of a rapid industrialization model potentially posed even greater challenges, given the similarities it shared with other newly independent Asian nations seeking accelerated economic growth.[68] Western officials and scholars in the 1950s paid insufficient attention to Indonesian perceptions of China as a possible development model, although many Indonesians viewed China's experience with foreign domination and revolution and its rapid industrialization as an inspiration—even if many rejected its Communist form.[69] Following his 1956 trips to Moscow and Beijing, Sukarno expressed "ready acceptance" of the "apparent achievements, especially material, under Communist rule," as did a wide range of Indonesian observers. Vice President Hatta remarked after a three-week visit to China in 1957, "What we have seen in the past ten days is very amazing and exciting. Amazing, because everywhere we saw people were energetically working for development. New factories, which had not existed before and had not even been thought about by the old government, were emerging all over the place."[70] In February 1959 the PKI held a major economic seminar which concluded that "the state sector should be given the prime role in transforming the country from a backward, agricultural, export-oriented economy into an advanced, industrialized, balanced economy." Like nationalists in India, many Indonesians viewed the lessons that the United States, the USSR, or China might offer in economic terms—shearing modernization of its political content in ways that baffled officials in Washington.[71] Western-trained Indonesian technocrats and economists readily accepted Soviet technical assistance, adopted a Soviet-style five-year development plan in 1957, written with the help of Canadian development economist Ben Higgens—who from 1955 to 1957 headed CENIS's Indonesia Project—and incorporated large-scale industrial projects into national development schemes.[72]

Mirroring their U.S. counterparts, Soviet social scientists paved the way in advocating comprehensive development and technical assistance programs to the third world, believing that ascendant elite groups, such as students, technocrats, and the armed forces, would be open to Communist ideas.[73] As Michael Adas has demonstrated, both the United States and the USSR, despite their many differences, "tended to favor development assistance that promoted industrialization and large scale infrastructural projects, including hydroelectric dams and transportation systems."[74] Between 1956 and 1964 Soviet and Eastern European development assistance to Indonesia averaged more than $120 million per year; heavy industrialization and infrastructure development were emphasized: chemical, cement, and textile plants; iron, steel, and nonferrous metal factories such as the Cilegon steelwork; road building, mechanized agriculture, and atomic power; and massive irrigation projects such as the Asahan Hydroelectric project. During the same period thousands of Indonesians received technical training in the USSR and Eastern Europe, and more than 2,000 Soviet and East European technical and agricultural advisers served in Indonesia.[75] Yet even as Indonesian technicians and economists welcomed Soviet bloc assistance, they rejected Soviet advice that conflicted with the government's need to mobilize mass political support for development goals.[76] Sukarno viewed China's achievements primarily in ideological terms, concluding that Mao's success stemmed not so much from long-range industrial planning as from mass mobilization and a relentless emphasis on national unity, and he specifically rejected Chinese political doctrine as inappropriate to Indonesia's situation. Economist Sarbini Sumawinata, although a proponent of what would later be called the developmental state model of Asian industrialization, likewise criticized development plans from the Soviet Union that called for austerity in basic consumption at the expense of mass support (just as many Indonesians would in 1963 reject similar calls for austerity by the IMF). He argued that "the implementation of the socialist system such as being held in the Soviet Union and China does not present an improvement to the capitalist system."[77]

The Eisenhower administration attempted to counter the Soviet Union's appeal in Indonesia not just through technical and economic assistance but also through a massive cultural diplomacy initiative by the U.S. Information Agency (USIA) and, covertly, through the CIA-funded Congress for Cultural Freedom. Utilizing the Voice of America, pamphlets, books, newspapers, movies and magazines, the USIA campaign stressed the superiority of American-style liberal capitalism and democracy and U.S. goals for the region of liberal modernization and anti-Communism. In 1953 alone, U.S. embassy officials estimated that 10 million Indonesians saw American films screened from the back of USIA trucks traveling around the country. The Congress for Cultural Freedom published and distributed Indonesian translations of

George Orwell's *Animal Farm*, Miliovan Djilas's *New Class*, and the famous collection of anti-Communist essays *The God That Failed*. The Congress even helped fund the publication of Indonesian writer Mochtar Lubis's novel *Senja di Jakarta* (Twilight in Jakarta), which it viewed as antitotalitarian in tone.[78] The USIA and the Ford and Rockefeller Foundations provided tens of thousands of fiction and nonfiction books, especially foundational texts in social science and comparative politics, to reading rooms, libraries, and universities around the country. Between 1951 and 1955 nearly 900 Indonesians in all fields of study traveled to the United States on publicly and privately funded grant initiatives for technical training.[79] In addition, the U.S. government, the Ford Foundation, and the AFL-CIO devoted substantial resources to funding and training rivals to Communist-affiliated labor federations, promoting depoliticized bread-and-butter trade unionism and seeking to split the labor movement off from Sukarno.[80]

Indonesians viewed the U.S. culture to which they were exposed with a mixture of wonder at the country's seemingly inexhaustible material wealth and resentment of its power and seeming spiritual shallowness. British and Dutch officials criticized the U.S. campaign as insulting and counterproductive, and Indonesian officials feared that U.S. propaganda would create unreasonable expectations for the possibilities of mass consumption in one of Asia's poorest nations. Fascinated Indonesians, meanwhile, paid up to $20 on the black market—an extraordinary sum in 1955—for Sears catalogs with their cornucopia of consumer goods on display. Yet among Indonesian nationalists in 1955 the U.S. image in Indonesia was "hardly a positive one: an economic and military superpower eager to lure Indonesia into the camp of the 'free world,' . . . a culture symbolized by big black cars, Western movies, and greediness, and a society characterized by segregation and racism."[81] Moreover, President Eisenhower himself recognized the inapplicability of the U.S. development model to Indonesia, telling the NSC that he was unperturbed by the thought of Indonesia taking a socialist road, declaring that "there was obviously no basis in Indonesia . . . for a free enterprise economy such as that of the United States."[82]

Toward the PRRI Revolts

Indonesia's long authoritarian period—which began in the late 1950s with the inauguration of Sukarno's Guided Democracy and lasted through Suharto's New Order regime until his ouster in 1998—has tended to obscure in both national memory and historiography a simple fact. From 1949 until 1957 Indonesia was a thriving parliamentary democracy, the collapse of which was hardly an inevitable tale of declension, as later observers seem to suggest.[83] Through the mid-1950s the public and official discourse in the United States on Indonesian development reflected this fact and operated within an ideological framework that stressed optimism about the prospects for modernization along parliamentary, democratic, and technocratic lines, as did analyses of development in postcolonial states more generally. Many scholars have argued that modernization theorists "always subordinated" democracy to concerns about stability, even during the 1950s.[84] Yet the U.S. and Indonesian commitment to military modernization did not emerge until late in the decade, and the evidence is persuasive that belief in the possibilities for democratic development was genuine. In its 1953 grant proposal to the Ford Foundation for an Indonesia field project, CENIS officials identified as their chief objective determining which "programs and policies in the United States . . . will do most to encourage economic growth on the basis of expanding, rather than contracting, democratic foundations."[85] Benedict Anderson argues that in the years following Indonesia's independence, Western scholars—most funded by the Ford Foundation—generally hewed to a perspective popularized by George McT. Kahin that suggested that "Indonesian nationalism was a historically determined and progressive force moving Indonesia away from colonial authoritarianism and exploitation and toward a liberal constitutional order."[86] As late as August 1956 the Eisenhower administration's National Intelligence Estimate for Indonesia concluded that "the prospects appear moderately favorable that Indonesia will continue to advance slowly in the direction of a modern democratic state over the next few years."[87]

U.S. optimism, however, was tenuous. The rising power of the PKI convinced many officials that democracy was incompatible with Indonesian political realities, a conclusion that many Indonesians—led by Sukarno and the armed forces—were coming to at the same time, although often for different reasons. Indonesia's landmark 1955 parliamentary elections, in which the PKI emerged as the nation's fourth largest party with 16.4 percent of the vote, raised red flags in Washington, which had attempted to ensure the victory of the moderate Masjumi Party with an infusion of up to $1 million. When the PKI improved its position further in local elections in 1957—taking nearly 30 percent of the vote in Java and displacing the Indonesian Nationalist Party (PNI) as the largest party in Yogyakarta—Secretary of State John Foster Dulles, CIA Director Allen Dulles, and U.S. Ambassador Hugh Cumming began waving those red flags.[88] Between 1954 and 1959 party membership grew from less than 200,000 to more than 1.5 million, with attendant gains in youth, women's, labor, and other affiliated organizations. Vice President Richard Nixon echoed the sentiment of many Eisenhower administration officials in late 1956 when he opined that "Sukarno was probably right in believing that a democratic government was not the best kind for Indonesia" because "the Communists could probably not be beaten in election campaigns because they were so well organized."[89] The United States would support democracy in Indonesia only if it resulted in the election of non- or anti-Communist forces.

As fears about the rising threat of the PKI increased, U.S. officials naturally looked to the armed forces as a counterweight. The Pentagon established links with the Indonesian military as early as 1948 and in August 1950 began training and assistance to Indonesia's fledgling police force. Training for Indonesian army officers, especially at U.S. service schools, assumed even greater importance as a means of transmitting ideas and influence. By January 1956 Hugh Cumming reported without exaggeration that "all lines of command in the Army now flowed through officers who had been trained in the United States."[90] A decade later approximately 2,800 members of Indonesia's officer corps had received training at U.S. service schools, many at the General Command and Staff College (GCSC), which imparted both modern operational doctrines and loyalty to the United States. General Yani, who attended the GCSC from 1955 to 1956, consciously patterned the Indonesian military academy at Magelang after the U.S. military academy at West Point. Army Chief of Staff General Nasution, who formulated Indonesia's doctrine of territorial management and warfare, told the U.S. embassy of his plans to use U.S. Army and West Point training manuals at the national military academy.[91] Former U.S. military attaché Willis Ethel recalled that the "Staff college in Bandung used our manuals. We sent people here to service schools . . . they'd go back loaded with all sorts of material and tried to run the staff college pretty much as they'd run Leavenworth."[92] U.S. military training and assistance also reinforced the proclivity of Indonesian armed forces officers to envision themselves as guardians of political order, an institutional identity dating back to Indonesia's independence struggle and growing in rough proportion to their perceived declining power under parliamentary rule.

By the end of 1956 Secretary of State Dulles and his brother, CIA Director Allen Dulles, were convinced that Indonesia's government and military were falling under the influence of the PKI. In the fall of 1957 rebel officers, backed by regional political parties and religious groups such as the Masjumi, began to set up local revolutionary councils. Administration officials—fueled by generally inaccurate intelligence reports from the CIA—decided to aid regional military officers alienated by the centralization of wealth and power in Java and the republic's excessive bureaucracy, corruption, and economic neglect of the outer islands. In February 1958 these dissident officers formed the Revolutionary Government of the Republic of Indonesia (*Pemerintah Revolusioner Republik Indonesia*, or PRRI), igniting a brief but fierce civil war. In response, Sukarno proclaimed martial law with broad support from Javanese military officers and brought an end to Indonesia's system of parliamentary democracy, centralizing power more firmly in Java and replacing it with a system he called Guided Democracy.[93] Indonesian troops, under the command of General Nasution and loyal to Sukarno, crushed the rebellion by June, although isolated rebel units continued to resist the central government in Jakarta for nearly two more years.

In the fall of 1957 the Eisenhower administration launched one of the largest and most disastrous covert operations of the Cold War, providing millions of dollars in covert funds and modern weapons to the dissident colonels leading the regional rebellions. In an operation hidden from the State Department's own ambassador to Jakarta, the CIA sought to reverse Indonesia's supposed leftward drift by either weakening or overthrowing Sukarno, checking the power of Java-based units of the military and the PKI, or even forcibly breaking up Indonesia to preserve Western access to resource-rich western Sumatra. In January 1958 the Eisenhower administration intervened directly by providing air cover to rebel military units and positioning U.S. naval vessels for possible intervention in Sumatra. In addition, U.S. forces and PRRI rebels operated freely from the British base complex in Singapore and trained at U.S. facilities throughout the region, including Taiwan, Guam, and the Philippines.[94]

Administration officials publicly insisted that the PRRI rebels were operating on their own, a convenient fiction in Washington that no one in Indonesia took seriously. U.S. support could no longer be denied, however, after CIA pilot Allen Pope was shot down and captured in April 1958. It soon became clear that Washington's allies were heading toward disaster and that the United States had made a terrible miscalculation. The Soviet Union, which backed Sukarno and the central government throughout the civil war, launched a major program of military and economic assistance in its wake, totaling nearly $750 million. Between 1956 and 1962, when deliveries peaked, Moscow provided Indonesia with hundreds of tanks, armored personnel carriers, artillery pieces and guided missiles, 170 jets and fighter-bombers, and most of the ships in the Indonesian navy. Soviet military aid significantly strengthened Moscow's position among the navy, air force, and Java-based army officers such as General Nasution, who long after remained suspicious of the United States for backing the PRRI.[95] Eisenhower administration officials were forced to admit what newly installed ambassador Howard Jones had been arguing all along, that the United States was fueling a civil war between two anti-Communist factions of the same military. In May 1958 the White House abruptly resumed military aid to the government it had been seeking to overthrow, as Secretary of State John Foster Dulles and others expressed dismay at the role Soviet weapons had played in the rebels' ignominious defeat.

Washington's involvement in Indonesia's civil war left deep scars on its relationship with Jakarta. But U.S. officials just a few years later could not imagine why Indonesians—after thousands of their countrymen had died in a U.S.-backed civil war—might still harbor anger or mistrust their intentions, a startling myopia. The U.S. embassy in Jakarta reported in late 1960 that Sukarno "is still suffering from the misapprehension [that the] U.S. is gunning for him." Paranoia, apparently, was the only possible explanation, a view shared by Lucian Pye, who viewed anti-Americanism in postcolonial states as a form of psychological pathology.[96] The episode, and Washington's unwillingness to acknowledge its lingering effects, offered stark confirmation of Marilyn Young's observation that U.S. officials during the Cold War were often "able to operate without awareness of the way in which even minor exercises of U.S. power affect[ed] the lives of others; sometimes without even remembering that anything happened at all."[97]

Unsurprisingly, the PKI emerged from the rebellions with its strength and nationalist credentials enhanced. The British Commissioner General's Office in Singapore observed in April 1958 that "if an election were held now the PKI would be returned as the largest single party."[98] Beginning in 1960 and periodically thereafter, Sukarno would call for a NASAKOM cabinet representing the central tendencies of Indonesian political culture—nationalism, religion, and Communism (*Nasionalis*, *Agama*, and *Komunis*). Anti-Communist parties, such as the Muslim Masjumi and the PNI, which supported the rebels, on the other hand, lost much of their power. The political fallout from the civil war left the country bereft of organizations that might stand as a counterweight to either the PKI or the military, laying the foundation for the terrible bloodletting of late 1965. The army also strengthened its political clout, using its powers under martial law to entrench itself in important ministries and to take over management of formerly Dutch-owned enterprises, a move with decisive implications for Indonesia's development strategy.[99]

The year 1959 saw military takeovers in a number of nonaligned countries, including Indonesia's neighbors Thailand and Burma as well as Iraq, Pakistan, and Sudan. The trend toward political authoritarianism and economic statism suggested to U.S. officials that the postcolonial world was abandoning democracy—and if Indonesia was any guide, this might not be unwelcome. In response the State Department prepared a major study which observed that "political and economic authoritarianism prevails throughout the underdeveloped world" and argued that this offered "certain short-run advantages to the United States." The recent history of Latin America, the study claimed, "indicates that authoritarianism is required to lead backward societies through their socio-economic revolutions. . . . The trend toward military authoritarianism will accelerate as developmental problems become more acute and the facades of democracy left by the colonial powers prove inadequate to the immediate tasks."[100] On June 18 the National Security Council met to discuss the report, which President Eisenhower declared as "the finest . . . he had ever heard given before the National Security Council." Secretary of Defense Neil McElroy concurred, offering that "in these backward societies, it was desirable to encourage the military to stabilize a conservative system" and pointing to General Nasution in Indonesia as an example of the sort of anti-Communist military leaders the United States ought to be backing.[101]

Defense Secretary McElroy's support for military rule in Indonesia, coming just months after Washington's disastrous intervention in the country's civil war, was symptomatic of a broader shift by the Eisenhower administration in favor of military dictatorships in the third world. The decline of parliamentary democracy in Indonesia now made nationalism and democracy seem antagonistic. U.S. officials and social scientists writing about Indonesia correspondingly focused increased attention on the Indonesian military as a modernizing force and less attention on prospects for a return to democracy.[102] Washington now began to view the armed forces as they viewed themselves: as a bulwark against the PKI's rise to power that could play a leading role in laying the groundwork for economic and political modernization.

CHAPTER 2

The Kennedy Administration Confronts Indonesia

While the incoming Kennedy administration scoured Harvard Yard in December 1960 for what David Halberstam later termed the "best and the brightest," the National Security Council surveyed Indonesia in a major analysis, NSC 6023, that would guide Washington's thinking for the next five years. In the wake of the PRRI rebellions, the Soviet Union had emerged as Indonesia's single largest aid donor and military supplier. The Indonesian economy was in a shambles, U.S. prestige in the country was at a nadir, and pro-U.S. political and military forces were banned, in exile, or on the defensive.[1] Howard Jones warned that the United States faced a far narrower range of choices than just two years earlier: "to match or surpass Soviet offers; to decide Indo is not worth saving for the free world, abandoning Indo to the Communist bloc; or to continue a moderate program of economic and military assistance sufficient to bolster our friends." To Jones, only the last alternative offered any hope of preserving U.S. interests in Indonesia and in the region.[2]

The NSC warned of the dangers the United States faced from increased Sino-Soviet economic and military assistance to Indonesia and especially from the PKI, which was "unique among Indonesian political parties in its discipline, unity of purpose, and command of the techniques of political action." Ironically, the PKI was also perhaps the most modern of Indonesia's modernizing forces; its members were "the only men here who frankly admire American efficiency and have attempted to inculcate it into their cadres," journalist Neil Sheehan observed. The NSC lamented that "open measures of repression against the PKI . . . are difficult to justify on internal political grounds," given its relatively moderate political program. The party, now firmly ensconced as defenders of Guided Democracy and national unity, stood in marked contrast to the "internecine quarrels, venality and incompetence" of the non-Communist organizations.[3]

More than its predecessors, NSC 6023 emphasized the link between economic crisis and political instability, noting that anti-Communism alone served as an insufficient guide to policy. "Ultimately," the NSC argued, "actions to defeat communism in Indonesia must be supplementary to long-range effective programs to improve the living standards of the masses" and must solve Indonesia's "serious economic and social problems." In the short term, however, containing or rolling back the PKI remained a major priority. The NSC thus recommended employing "all feasible means, including . . . the use of U.S. armed force if necessary and appropriate," to prevent Indonesia from falling under Communist control. Priority was to be given to "programs and projects which offer opportunities to isolate the PKI, drive it into positions of open opposition to the Indonesian government, thereby creating grounds for repressive measures politically justifiable in terms of Indonesian national self-interest."[4] Ambassador Howard Palfrey Jones similarly urged "preparation for [a] possible major psychological war campaign coordinating covert and overt resources when [the] proper climate can be developed," a portentous mouthful considering Washington's recent covert operations.[5] The implications here were straightforward. Just two years after its disastrous covert intervention in Indonesia, the United States committed itself to provoking a clash between the army and the PKI, on the presumption that the army would emerge victorious over its well-organized but unarmed and basically defenseless opponent. Once the PKI was eliminated as a threat, a military-led regime could hopefully lay the groundwork for economic development that U.S. officials believed was Indonesia's best hope for long-term economic and political stability.

Howard Jones believed that John F. Kennedy's arrival provided an opening for the improvement of U.S.-Indonesian relations and the realization of these goals. Unlike Kennedy's predecessor, Jones thought, the new president was less reflexively anti-Communist, seemed better to understand the force of third world nationalism, and was more likely to deal constructively with nonaligned nations.[6] The "time has come," he wrote the State Department, "when U.S. interests demand a reassessment of the situation in Indonesia" and consequently of U.S. policy. The current diplomatic and economic offensive by the Soviet Union and China required the United States to seize the initiative and undertake a "positive program" if it was to prevent Indonesia from falling under Communist control.[7] Like embassies in many countries, the U.S. mission in Jakarta bemoaned Washington's unwillingness to engage in the sort of comprehensive, multiyear planning and diplomacy that marked Soviet aid policy in the developing world. A year earlier Max Millikan and Donald Blackmer of CENIS published a report at the request of the Senate Foreign Relations Committee that reached similar conclusions and called for long-term integrated planning for the underdeveloped world.[8] Ambassador Jones now called for the same, believing that Kennedy stood a good chance of reversing the decline in U.S.-Indonesian relations. Sukarno, like many Indonesians, viewed the young president as an opponent of colonialism, having read the then-senator's June 1956 denunciation of French colonial rule in Algeria.[9] In January 1961 Jones urged the president to invite Sukarno to Washington for an official visit, hoping that the trip would build a personal rapport between the two leaders. The new secretary of state, Dean Rusk, agreed, observing that, however loathsome, the Indonesian president was "in nearly absolute control of Indonesia's destiny for the time being."[10]

Sukarno promptly accepted the White House's invitation and announced he would come to Washington in early April—just ten weeks away. The scramble to prepare for the Indonesian president's visit highlighted deep divides within the Kennedy administration over its strategy for Indonesia.[11] Scholars have characterized the divides over Indonesia policy during the early 1960s as between those who were "accommodationist" and favored working with Sukarno and those who were "hard-line" and favored isolating Sukarno or even seeking his overthrow and replacement by a military regime. But bureaucratic and factional debates over Indonesia tapped into broader policy currents—identified by Bruce Cumings as nationalist and internationalist—that defined basic cleavages in U.S. foreign policy in the postwar period. The internationalist current characterized those who stood for a regulated, open world economy and a wide-ranging U.S. hegemony seeking to ensure global order through collective security and multilateralism.[12] Its staunchest supporters included members of Thomas Ferguson's "hegemonic bloc" of high-tech, competitive, multinational industries, banks, and law firms; in the early 1960s these organizations advocated expansive foreign aid programs to build the human capacity and social infrastructure for development and foreign investment in the third world.[13] Nationalists, in contrast, tended to support mercantilist forms of political economy, opposed collective security arrangements and multilateralism in favor of the unilateral projection of American economic and military power, and advocated the rollback rather than the containment of Communism. This current found some of its strongest support among declining industries and local or national firms that feared foreign competition and multinational rivals; its advocates emerged as some of the fiercest critics of the New Frontier approach to foreign aid and liberal developmental vision.[14] Policy differences over narrow questions of military or economic aid to Indonesia thus cut across geographic and ideological lines, reflecting differing conceptions of the country's strategic and economic importance vis-à-vis Europe, Japan, and the Soviet bloc, as well as conflicting visions of Indonesian modernization.

As a form of shorthand, the debate between accommodationists and hard-liners over Indonesia can serve as a useful jumping-off point for illuminating larger patterns. The hard-liners were based primarily in the State Department's European division, the Pentagon, and the CIA's Deputy Directorate for Plans for the Far East. The Europeanists concerned themselves primarily with West New Guinea and the threat that Indonesian ambitions to recover the territory posed to the Netherlands and NATO. Inveterate cold warrior and rollback advocate Richard Bissell, a veteran of covert operations against Guatemala, Cuba, and Indonesia, rode horse for the hard-line faction in the CIA. In the 1950s, as Franz Schurmann notes, "American anti-communism and Asian rollback began to interact with each other in such a way" that rollback was "the *de facto* stance of the CIA" in East Asia, taking the form of covert war and military intervention.[15]

Washington's support for the PRRI rebellions in 1957–1958 was a paradigmatic attempt at covert rollback in Asia, replete with soldiers of fortune such as Allen Pope, who was still in prison in Indonesia in 1961. But rollback failed utterly in Indonesia, and its advocates in 1961 were in decline, engaged in a holding operation and finding unlikely allies in Europe-oriented internationalists such as U.S. ambassador to the U.N. Adlai Stevenson and containment bureaucrats such as Dean Rusk. Each group, however, cast its gaze in a different direction, one faction toward Europe and the other toward mainland East and Southeast Asia. If Rusk represented the former, then the latter was typified by Commander in Chief of the Pacific Fleet (CINCPAC) Admiral Harry Felt. Felt was a traditional navy conservative and rollback advocate who opposed the introduction of U.S. ground forces in Vietnam but backed air- and carrier-based containment. He also hated Sukarno, who threatened to block Western access to Southeast Asia's strategic waterways.[16]

The hard-liners also attracted nationalists such as Howard L. Hunt, the reclusive Texas oil billionaire and bankroller of the far right. Hunt wrote Kennedy in April 1961 to oppose Sukarno's visit, arguing that he was "second only to Khrushchev in the conspiracy to destroy freedom." Hunt's primary concern with Indonesia was the inability of independent oil companies such as his own to gain access to a market still controlled by multinational oil giants Caltex, Stanvac, and Shell. He warned Kennedy not to trust the major oil companies because they would "not give a true account of the situation in Indonesia" and lumped them in for good measure with the State Department, the United Nations, and Dwight Eisenhower, under whose watch "we had lost hundreds of millions of people to communism."[17] Of course none of this made any sense—Eisenhower losing China, a line of straight march drawn from John Foster Dulles (who represented Wall Street and Big Oil) to Dean Rusk (who represented the Rockefellers and Europhile intellectuals)—without an understanding of where a nationalist like Hunt fit into the American political economy and the world oil market. In his classic account of the "Seven Sisters," Anthony Sampson observed that "the independents liked to depict the majors, who were importing oil from Arabia, as potential traitors," quoting Russell B. Brown, general counsel for the independent's trade association; Brown had complained in 1955 that "their motivations have taken on a new and foreign accent as they have become companies of the world rather than of this nation." H. L. Hunt could not have agreed more, and he will return to the story in 1968, with Suharto firmly entrenched in power, angling for oil concessions off the coast of West Irian and complaining again about how the big oil companies and the U.S. embassy were conspiring to exclude independents.[18] For now Hunt helps to illustrate a simple but crucial point: that policy factions and strands of modernization thinking were linked to identifiable social constituencies with concrete interests in the outcome of seemingly byzantine disputes about policy toward a state on the periphery of American hegemony.

The accommodationists gathered around Ambassador Howard Jones in Jakarta, in the State Department's Bureau of Far Eastern Affairs, in the Agency for International Development, and at the NSC, where Jones had the support of National Security Adviser Walt Rostow and his deputies. Averell Harriman's appointment to assistant secretary of state for Far Eastern affairs in November 1961 and his replacement in early 1963 by Roger Hilsman solidified their position. Containment internationalists all, this core policy group, which would direct Indonesia policy roughly until the spring of 1965, was the most consistent advocate of a long-term developmental approach to Jakarta. They also attracted support from oil giants such as Stanvac and Caltex; plantation companies such as Goodyear and U.S. Rubber; construction firms such as Morrison Knudson and Brown and Root; and banking and manufacturing companies such as Singer Sewing Machine, Westinghouse Electrical, Morgan Guarantee Trust, General Motors, and Union Carbide. All were world-competitive multinational firms that had invested in Indonesia in the preindependence period, and all were anxious to preserve their position—and that of Western capital more generally—as the Sukarno regime moved to the left and expressed greater hostility to foreign investment.[19]

The questions of West New Guinea and U.S. military and economic assistance dominated interagency discussion in the weeks leading up to Sukarno's visit. Deputy Director of Central Intelligence (DCI) Robert Amory suggested before a meeting of Kennedy's "Tuesday Lunch Group" in late March that U.S. neutrality on West New Guinea was "no longer tenable" and should be abandoned in favor of Indonesia, eliminating an issue "which unites the Army, Sukarno and [the] Communists."[20] Richard Bissell attacked this logic, arguing that such a policy would only "cement relations between Indonesia and the USSR" and "help to consolidate a regime which is innately antagonistic toward the U.S." In a cryptic passage he mused that "the influence that the United States can exert, at least in the short run, is extremely limited, if (as must be assumed) crude and violent intervention is excluded. Only [Sukarno's] removal from power," he inveighed, "would offer some hope that trends that now seem inexorable can still be reversed."[21]

Robert Komer was unconvinced. In an angry response to McGeorge Bundy, he dismissed the reasoning behind the hard-liner's case:

> I disagree with so many of the half judgments in [excised] Indonesia paper that I don't know where to begin. The thesis is that Sukarno, the devil incarnate, will take Indonesia so far down the road as to make it a pushover for PKI in predictable future. However, the paper admits there are no countervailing forces left. Hence, all it comes up with is sterile oppositionism, i.e. we tell Sukarno sternly he can go to hell without our help. . . . What we need is holding operation which will preserve our ties with Army and other elements until such time as Sukarno comes a cropper with other side or disappears from scene. . . . Bissell paper opposes both but has no better answer.

In a handwritten note to Walt Rostow at the bottom of his letter, Komer scribbled "Walt—despite Pye, Pauker, Bissell I'll stick with Amory and *Jones*. None of these others," all hard-liners, "have any answers at all."[22]

The exchange between Bissell and Komer demarcated the boundaries of the bitter debate over Indonesia policy at the outset of the Kennedy administration. At a cursory level we see factional disputes among bureaucratic actors defending regional turf, the legacy of past policies, and personal animosity. At a deeper level the debate reflects competing conceptions of the strategic and economic importance of the Netherlands and Indonesia to U.S. global priorities, both in the near term, where anti-Communist and geopolitical concerns were often paramount, and over the elusive long-term, where developmental and security concerns merged. It also reflects divergent views on the vision for modernization held out for Indonesia by U.S. policymakers and social scientists, with Bissell, Lucian Pye, and Guy Pauker advocating what historian Ron Robin has termed "coercive" counterinsurgency programs as the desired path to this goal, in contrast to the "constructive" program held out by Jones and others.[23]

"That Bit of Colonial Debris Called West New Guinea."[24]

The Kennedy administration's policy toward West New Guinea framed the discussion leading up to Sukarno's visit. In fact, West New Guinea emerged as the single most important issue in U.S.-Indonesian relations after the collapse of the PRRI revolts and remained so until the United States brokered an agreement on the future of the territory in August 1962 under the threat of a looming Indonesian invasion. Indonesia posed problems unique for the United States in Southeast Asia in the 1960s, because its two major foreign policy fixations, first West Irian and later Malaysia, intimately involved Washington's European allies, raised questions about U.S. treaty obligations in the region, and drew into sharp focus the conflicts between other nations' regional concerns and the hegemonic responsibilities of the United States.

The Dutch and Indonesian positions by 1960 were well defined and endlessly reiterated. The Netherlands argued that West New Guinea was geographically distinct and that Indonesia could make no claim to it based on common history, culture, language, or religion. The rightward shift in the Dutch Parliament in the early to mid-1950s entrenched political forces opposed to negotiations with Indonesia, bitter at the anti-Dutch policies of the Indonesian government, and committed to self-determination for the Papuans—so long as the end result was not integration with Indonesia.[25] Indonesian leaders countered that their entire country was a creation of Dutch colonialism and that their revolution would remain incomplete until all the territories of the former Dutch East Indies reverted to Indonesian rule. Moreover, so long as the Dutch maintained a foothold in the archipelago, they could continue potentially to threaten Indonesian security by supporting separatist movements or by engaging in economic sabotage. The U.S. government, Ambassador Jones wrote, was "fully informed of fact that all Indo foreign policy, [and] much of Indo internal political life, revolves around this cardinal issue."[26]

For those Americans who could find it on a map, West New Guinea was a blank slate upon which they could write their fantasies about primitive peoples and the benefits of encounter with the West.[27] Its inhabitants were "contemporary ancestors" of a more modern way of life, people with no past, no history, and no agency except as a function of their interaction with the

West and Indonesia: a "flat, unchanging, primitive landscape," as Frederick Cooper has described the parallel French and British imperial discourse on African development in the postwar period.[28] One member of the West New Guinea council bemoaned "the inclination of the world to search for nothing but the most primitive" in the territory, whose dark-skinned inhabitants prompted comparisons with African primitivism.[29] Whereas modernization theory served in the wake of decolonization movements to recast older notions of racial hierarchy onto the plane of culture and development, West New Guinea was a throwback to the earlier ideas of missionary vision and imperial control from which it derived. Appropriately, American visitors at the time consisted almost entirely of evangelical missionaries, anthropologists, art collectors, and mineral prospectors.[30]

Until 1960 the United States proclaimed "passive neutrality" on the future of West New Guinea, a position that translated into de facto support for continued Dutch rule. When President Kennedy arrived in Washington, the debate over U.S. policy intensified, in part because Dean Rusk professed support for Papuan self-determination and backed the Dutch position, whereas outgoing secretary of state Christian Herter had recently shifted in favor of U.N. trusteeship leading to eventual independence.[31] But for all the ink spilled about West New Guinea, neither supporters nor opponents of the Dutch or Indonesian position cared about the territory's inhabitants. Rather, the debate concerned what West New Guinea stood for. For the Dutch, as well as for many recalcitrant members of Congress, West New Guinea symbolized Indonesia's treachery and Sukarno's irredentism. For the State Department and the NSC, on the other hand, support for self-determination in West New Guinea was an expedient, a function of containment logic applied to Indonesia that could be discarded if needed.[32] "As we get closer and closer to a dangerous impasse over that bit of colonial debris," Robert Komer reminded Carl Kaysen in January 1962, "we have simply got to keep our eye on the object of the exercise—which is Indonesia, not West New Guinea."[33] When Dutch ambassador J. H. Van Roijen demanded assurance from Dean Rusk that self-determination was not merely a "façade to turn over the area either directly or indirectly to Indonesia," Robert Johnson, the NSC staffer responsible for the Far East, responded that this was *precisely* the intent of the State Department's position. "If we talk to [Dutch officials] in a way that suggests . . . that we really believe self determination is a significant principle in this backward area," he warned Walt Rostow, "we will gain no capital with the Indonesians and we shall only be deluding ourselves."[34]

At a time when U.S. officials were already hampered by looming crises in Berlin, Laos, and Vietnam, the White House's overriding concern was to avoid an armed regional conflict—over a territory with no intrinsic economic or strategic importance—that could threaten the entire U.S. position in Southeast Asia and push Indonesia closer to Moscow. Moreover, with Soviet political backing and a massive military aid package on the way, U.S. officials recognized that Sukarno was in a position to make good on his threat to take West New Guinea by force.[35] On a private visit to The Hague, former secretary of state Dean Acheson bluntly told Dutch foreign minister Joseph M. A. H. Luns that "the real interest of the West, including the Dutch, was not in ascertaining the doubtfully existent wishes of naked and illiterate Papuans about a sovereignty which they did not understand, but to prevent, for the sake of Australia, New Zealand and the Philippines, a Communist takeover of West New Guinea through the collapse or other stratagem of Sukarno."[36] Kennedy and Rusk made the same point in more muted fashion when Luns visited Washington shortly before Sukarno, emphasizing the "total global struggle" the West faced "in Berlin, the Congo, Laos, the Taiwan Straits, and elsewhere" and cautioning that the United States "did not intend to bluff or be caught bluffing" if the Dutch tried to invoke NATO commitments to come to their aid in the event of an Indonesian attack. In short, no defense guarantees.[37]

Military and Economic Aid on the Eve of Sukarno's Visit

Equally intractable conflicts surrounded the question of U.S. military and economic assistance to Indonesia. Since the failure of the PRRI rebellions, the United States had sought to repair its battered relations with the Indonesian armed forces by restarting a program of military aid and training.[38] Indonesia's need for aid was acute, and despite Washington's recent history, the odds were tilting in its favor. Both General Nasution and Sukarno were anxious to begin modernizing the Indonesian military, a job for which both Washington and Moscow played ardent suitor but for which most Indonesian officers favored U.S. equipment. Nasution and Sukarno hoped to assuage the services' demands for the replacement of outdated equipment, cement their loyalty to the state, and enhance Indonesia's regional military position, thereby decreasing its vulnerability to outside intervention, including from the United States. Military modernization would also provide the leverage Indonesia needed to press for the return of West Irian.

The massive Soviet military aid push magnified the urgency of these demands and prompted a major U.S. response. As George and Audrey Kahin have demonstrated, the resumption of "token aid" during the months after the collapse of the PRRI rebellion masked the true size of Washington's effort to regain its lost political capital with the Indonesian army. In absolute terms U.S. military assistance to Indonesia tripled between 1958 and 1959, from $5.4 million to $16.9 million, but this figure hardly tells the whole story.[39] The Pentagon utilized all the accounting tricks at its disposal to cook the real figures, accepting token payment in Indonesian rupiah, selling weapons and transportation at giveaway prices with virtually no repayment obligation, and providing advanced equipment designated as "excess stocks" at a bare fraction of their market value. As a result, military assistance to Indonesia valued on the books at $42.8 million nearly matched the more than $300 million in assistance from the Soviet Union over the same period.[40]

The increased flow of military aid continued until December 1960, when Sukarno broke relations with the Netherlands and declared that Indonesia would recover West Irian before the next year was out. A few weeks later General Nasution announced that Indonesia would continue to seek arms from the Soviet Union. The moves prompted an outcry from Congress, which chafed at providing aid to a country whose leader condemned Western "imperialism," bought arms from the Soviet Union, threatened NATO allies, and gave comfort to domestic Communists.[41] In response, the Pentagon quietly slowed the pace of military equipment deliveries.[42]

Although aware of the growing criticism of Indonesia in Washington, Jones was convinced that a transformation of U.S. military assistance was needed. As Richard Bissell and his supporters at the CIA attacked the logic of accommodation, the ambassador made his case to Rusk for a reevaluation of the U.S. military assistance program for Indonesia. He argued that U.S. military aid up to this point had rested on a limited strategy of inducements, offering "token aid" for token changes: "a little more anti-communism, a little more aid, etc." Now Jones called for the inauguration of a comprehensive aid program, as called for by the administration's new Basic National Security Policy, to facilitate long-range country planning and escape the "straitjacket" of political restrictions and year-to-year appropriations battles. To compete with the Soviet Union's long-term military aid programs, the United States needed to gain the confidence of Indonesia's military leadership and provide "modern, complex" equipment that would lock Indonesia into long-term training and maintenance relationships. The "fundamental purpose in providing aid is political," Jones argued, namely, "strengthening the anti-Communist military leadership."[43]

Along a parallel track, the Pentagon began pushing for a civic action program for Indonesia, part of a worldwide expansion of such programs begun in 1961 with the creation of the Office of Public Safety and the Special Group for Counterinsurgency.[44] In his first foreign aid message to Congress on March 22, Kennedy declared that "military assistance will in the future more heavily emphasize the internal security, civil works and economic growth of the nations thus aided."[45] Indonesia was a prime candidate for this new emphasis. On the eve of Sukarno's visit, counterinsurgency guru General Edward Lansdale proposed a civic action program (CAP) for Indonesia, arguing that it would strengthen the Indonesian army, bring it "closer to the Indonesian people" through involvement in rural reconstruction and development projects, and "take some of the emotional heat off the West Irian issue." Lansdale and other U.S. officials viewed civic action not only as an adjunct to counterinsurgency but also as a modernizing program that would encourage the military in its dual role as both guardian and shepherd of the development process.[46]

Indonesia's critics, however, rejected the logic behind Jones's and Lansdale's calls for increased military aid.[47] First, they insisted, Sukarno was so far along the pro-Soviet path that he could not be decisively influenced by changes in U.S. policy. Second, any increase in U.S. military aid would reward Indonesia for its efforts to seize West New Guinea by force. Finally, the only justifiable rationale for an increase in military aid would be to stiffen the resolve of the army vis-à-vis the PKI, a dubious prospect in the estimation of scholars such as Guy Pauker of the RAND Corporation, who doubted whether the army under General Nasution (who still mistrusted the

United States for its support of the PRRI rebellion) was politically unified and ruthless enough to do the job.[48]

Similar considerations underlay the debate over economic assistance. Between 1949 and 1960 Washington extended more than $470 million in aid to Indonesia, concentrated in technical assistance, participant training, Export-Import Bank loans for infrastructure projects, and PL 480 (Food for Peace) commodity assistance. But the Eisenhower administration's emphasis on covert war, hostility toward Sukarno, and lack of bureaucratic coordination precluded long-term development planning aid for Indonesia. As a result, U.S. assistance assumed an ad hoc and token character that was hamstrung by congressional appropriations schedules, and it paled in comparison to Soviet outlays. In Afghanistan, Vietnam, and many other countries it was the United States that promoted massive infrastructure projects, but in Indonesia the Soviets held the initiative.[49] Ambassador Jones complained in early 1961 that "at the moment there are no Indonesian applications for substantial U.S. loans at [a] time when books are being filled with [Soviet] bloc projects ranging from multi-purpose hydro projects to steel mills, chemicals, textiles, etc."[50] Typical was a massive Soviet-funded steel mill at Cilegon on the western tip of Java, which Soviet officials promoted as a harbinger of rapid industrialization when construction began in the early 1960s.[51]

Food for Peace aid exemplified the logic of U.S. assistance. Between 1956 and 1961 sales of rice, cotton, tobacco, and wheat to Indonesia under PL 480 totaled $288 million. During this same period poor planning and Indonesia's deteriorating economic situation turned the country from a net rice exporter into one of the world's leading importers. Foreign rice undercut domestic producers, and rapid inflation made imports of U.S. fertilizer and equipment, the proclaimed engines of agricultural modernization, prohibitively expensive. Food for Peace, however, served powerful domestic constituencies in southern states—especially those with a large stake in maintaining exports at a time of declining commodity prices. It also generated counterpart funds at the local level and lowered dollar outlays while serving the long-range purpose of developing new markets and lowering the U.S. balance of payments deficit, a persistent concern of the Kennedy administration. But PL 480 aid did nothing to enhance Indonesia's long-term capacity for producing rice, a problem the program reproduced in other countries.[52]

The U.S. aid program contrasted sharply with Sukarno's Eight-Year Plan for Indonesia's economic development, inaugurated in August 1960. The Eight-Year Plan was the most concrete expression of Sukarno's concept of Guided Economy, a rough blueprint for state-led development that advocated intervention in basic industries to promote long-term development needs, the "subordination of foreign capital to national social and economic goals," and a transition from an import and export dependent economy to self-sufficiency, especially in basic commodities and foodstuffs. In broad outline the plan reflected the affinity many postcolonial governments had for Soviet-style five-year plans, but Jones described it as "thoroughly Indonesian, derived spontaneously from their own compulsion."[53] The ambassador's pitch for expanded aid to Indonesia was thus a partial answer to one of the key questions facing U.S. policymakers: How should Washington relate to (and hopefully redirect) Indonesia's ramshackle attempt at state-led development?

U.S. officials and Indonesia scholars—and later Suharto—routinely cast the country's economic woes as emblems of Sukarno's personality, cultural defects, irrationality, a vague anti-Western bias, or simple incompetence but rarely as the result of an intentional plan for national development, however poorly executed or funded.[54] Despite widespread criticism of Sukarno's economic plan, however, Kennedy's advisers had no alternative to offer at the time, and Sukarno's detractors rarely acknowledged the simple fact that after 1957 it was the armed forces in control of much of the economy and Washington that emphasized the modernizing potential of the military and encouraged this increased role.[55] By 1960 Indonesia was devoting approximately half its national budget to defense expenditures, far more if one counts funds from military-controlled enterprises, corruption, and smuggling. This extraordinary diversion of resources precluded any serious attempt at economic development while deepening the military's stakes in deflecting challenges to its budgetary prerogatives and economic position. The CIA observed that "a growing budgetary load will have to be borne in order to fund Indonesia's preparations for a showdown over West Irian," a problem that only deepened during Indonesia's *Konfrontasi* with Malaysia. Both campaigns reinforced the growing power of the military in Indonesian political life and contributed to the "continuing and accelerated decline" in Indonesian economic performance.[56]

Opponents of the New Frontier approach to foreign aid were aghast at the prospect of any assistance to Jakarta. The *Wall Street Journal* warned that

"American aid is helping to build a socialist economy here in Indonesia" by directing Export-Import Bank funds to the Indonesian government for economic development projects rather than to the indigenous private sector, which apart from the Chinese (who dominated small-scale production), was wholly incapable of effectively using foreign capital on a large scale. "Rather than lower the bars to private foreign investment and encourage the growth of profit generating free economies," the *Journal*'s editors complained, "the Socialist visionaries of the new lands of Asia and Africa expect to have their profits beforehand, as gifts from the West, and to invest these unearned 'profits' in rigidly centralized economic systems that may require perpetual subsidy." William Henderson, executive director of the Council on Foreign Relations, wrote to Kennedy that "one wonders whether any American representative has even taken the opportunity to speak frankly and fully about the realities of international life as we see them."[57] Ambassador Jones countered that the United States needed to "suppress our inclination to assess projects mainly on our own preconceptions of economic soundness" rather than according to the priorities of Indonesians. To compete with the Soviets, Washington would have to loosen up the criteria for aid and play for the long haul. "In political warfare," Jones argued, "we must accept [the] reality that circuses may be more vital than bread."[58]

Sukarno's visit took place against the backdrop of the disastrous attempted invasion of Cuba at the Bay of Pigs. The parallels to U.S. support of the PRRI rebellions could not be clearer, yet Sukarno refrained from mentioning either event. President Kennedy heeded the State Department's advice to cater to Sukarno's ego and marked his trip with the pomp and circumstance befitting a head of state, while the Secret Service attempted to cater to what White House officials charged was Sukarno's "insatiable demand for call girls." But on the issues of substance that so divided the NSC and Foggy Bottom, Arthur Schlesinger concluded, "The meetings with Sukarno were no great success."[59] The Indonesian president's hopes that Kennedy would support Indonesia's claims to West New Guinea went unrealized. The president continued to stress U.S. loyalty to a NATO ally and Indonesia's international obligations, and Sukarno located Indonesia's demands in the broader stream of Asian anticolonialism. "Why does America never say that we have a just claim to West Irian?" he asked, adding, "You must see this problem through the glass of nationalism." Foreign Minister Subandrio, however, suggested that Indonesia was prepared to find "ways and means for the Dutch to save face" and would consider a trusteeship "to make the transition to Indonesia's possession easier."[60] The CIA later reported that Sukarno had been favorably impressed by his visit with President Kennedy, despite the lack of concrete progress on West New Guinea. Kennedy himself was a little more sanguine. "An inscrutable Asian" was how he summed up his opinion of the Indonesian president. Nevertheless, he mused that the trip might have done some good to convince Sukarno that his White House "was taking a different view of Indonesia."[61]

Resolving the West New Guinea Crisis

If the administration was taking a different view of Indonesia than its predecessor, it was difficult to discern in early 1961. The United States had yet to formulate a policy and aid framework for dealing with Indonesia's deep-seated economic and political challenges. Moreover, the brewing crisis with the Netherlands over West New Guinea had produced a stalemate in Washington and threatened to overwhelm U.S.-Indonesian relations.[62] The crisis forced policymakers to choose squarely between perceived Cold War imperatives, NATO obligations, and their professed support for liberal ideals of self-determination. "We have tried bilateral negotiations," the Indonesian president pleaded with Ambassador Jones. "We've tried that seriously and for years. We have tried using the machinery of the United Nations, and the strength of world opinion expressed there . . . hope evaporates; patience dries, even tolerance reaches an end. West Irian is a colonial sword poised over Indonesia. It points at our heart, but it also threatens world peace." Most U.S. officials had no reason to doubt the Indonesian president's warning.[63]

Sukarno's outspoken opponents in Congress, the CIA, the State Department, and at think tanks like the RAND Corporation considered West New Guinea a greased skid to power for the PKI and to increased Soviet influence. But supporters of the Dutch position failed to recognize West New Guinea's importance to Indonesian nationalists, as both a geographic and an imaginative space where the "rival centralities" of state-led nationalism, Communism, and militarism converged, each seeking to fulfill its own ideological and institutional needs. At stake was Indonesia's claim to postcolonial modernity, the completion of its revolution, and the legitimacy of state power, which lent fervor to Sukarno's campaign that few in the United States could comprehend. Indonesia was unlikely to back down, even at the risk of war, in its quest to return the territory to the national fold.[64]

Advocates of a shift in favor of Indonesia agreed. As Walt Rostow recalled, "It was clear that if Indonesian political life was ever to turn to the laborious tasks of modernization and of finding regional harmony in Southeast Asia, the issue of West Irian would have to be removed from its agenda." Indonesian officials nurtured this hope by suggesting that once they had "recovered" West New Guinea, they would begin resolving the country's long-term economic problems.[65] In the wake of Sukarno's visit, Walt Rostow wrote Deputy Under Secretary of State U. Alexis Johnson that the United States faced "a unique but transient opportunity" to resolve West New Guinea.[66] Sukarno thought President Kennedy sympathetic, and Dutch public opinion was showing signs of flexibility, especially among businesses anxious to return to Indonesia. But Washington still lacked a coherent policy, and continuing U.S. neutrality was becoming unsustainable.[67] Given the enormous attention historians have devoted to Vietnam and Laos, it is easy to forget that in early 1961 the NSC listed Indonesia and West New Guinea among its most "urgent planning priorities." It was West New Guinea, after all, that threatened war with a key European ally and it was Indonesia where the United States and the Soviet Union competed most directly for influence.[68]

Secretary of State Rusk, preoccupied with more pressing concerns in Europe and elsewhere in Southeast Asia, suggested dumping the issue in the lap of the U.N. and urged the embassy in Jakarta to explore the possibility of U.N. trusteeship, a position that pleased no one. Dutch, British, and Australian officials feared that Afro-Asian countries would back Jakarta in the U.N. General Assembly, whereas Indonesia viewed U.N. trusteeship as "a delaying action" that might encourage centrifugal forces elsewhere in the archipelago.[69] Why, then, press forward with a policy that everyone opposed? Foggy Bottom, generally sympathetic to the Dutch, reasoned that trusteeship offered the possibility of a face-saving Dutch withdrawal from West New Guinea that "sidesteps the self-determination issue"—enabling the United States to maintain its position of neutrality. But in separate meetings with Adlai Stevenson in New York on September 16, Sukarno and Foreign Minister Luns insisted they would consider U.N. involvement only "as a 'conduit'" for handing the territory over to Indonesia (Sukarno) or as a means of guaranteeing self-determination for Papua and keeping it out of Indonesian hands (Luns).[70]

NSC officials expressed bewilderment with Rusk's solicitude of Dutch officials and questioned his understanding of Indonesia's long-range importance, especially after Sukarno told Chester Bowles that Jakarta would turn toward Washington "overnight" if the United States backed Indonesia on West New Guinea.[71] Walt Rostow grew so frustrated that he finally just went around Rusk and urged the president to impress upon the secretary of state the need for the State Department to take a position "that looks to Indonesian control" rather than backing a "meaningless" Dutch proposal on self-determination at the U.N.[72] The brewing conflict over trusteeship came to a head at the U.N. General Assembly session in November, when the United States abstained on an Indian-sponsored resolution, supported by Jakarta, that called for bilateral negotiations between Indonesia and the Netherlands.[73] Indonesian officials were "furious." To make matters worse, as the CIA observed, the U.S. stance undermined Indonesian moderates such as General Nasution, who was having a hard time defending a negotiated solution in the face of calls by the PKI, Subandrio, and others for an outright invasion of the territory.[74]

U.S. policy toward Indonesia and West New Guinea at this time resembled nothing so much as a rugby scrum, moving imperceptibly downfield with little to show but lots of kicking, biting, and scratching. The scrum loosened a bit with the arrival of Averell Harriman as assistant secretary of state for the Far East in November 1961, shifting the balance of power in the State Department on Indonesia in favor of the accommodationists.[75] The Far East division had borne the brunt of the McCarthy era purges, which destroyed the careers of most of the department's best Asia analysts and left the remainder peering over their right shoulders at the rollback constituency, with their rigid anti-Communism, penchant for ill-conceived covert operations, and intolerance for neutralists such as Sukarno.[76] Into this trench warfare waded Harriman, who declared the Far East Bureau "a disaster area filled with human wreckage" and set about recruiting young staffers, such as Roger Hilsman and Michael Forrestal, who would chart a more independent course on Asia policy, especially with regard to Vietnam. Harriman had developed his own animus toward Rusk after the secretary of state refused him permission to meet with Chinese foreign minister Chen Yi during negotiations over the neutralization of Laos; as assistant secretary of state he also went behind Rusk's back and dealt directly with Kennedy, encouraging his staff to do likewise.[77] The former governor of New York was a diplomat and banker by training, a genuine internationalist by temperament, and a fierce, although pragmatic, anti-Communist. As the scion of one of America's great railroad fortunes, Harriman also possessed a worldview that merged economic, political, and security concerns with a deep sense of the United States's global interests, a concern for the whole that his titular boss, Dean Rusk, lacked. And although Harriman cut his diplomatic teeth working in Europe, he wasn't one to automatically subordinate Asian to European concerns.[78]

As Harriman took up his new post, the State Department was completing a long-awaited policy review on Indonesia, initiated in response to the Joint Chiefs of Staff's call for a "detailed and dynamic national plan to take the political, economic and psychological offensive" on Indonesia from the Soviet Union. The review concluded that U.S.-Indonesian relations would continue to flounder until Washington removed the West New Guinea dispute "from Communist exploitation" and divested itself of its image as a "protector of colonial interests."[79] From Jakarta, Howard Jones pointed out that Indonesia's military mobilization was also wreaking havoc on its already unstable economy, leading to acute foreign exchange shortages, skyrocketing inflation, and balance of payments deficits.[80] A long-term decline in the production of foreign exchange–earning agricultural commodities was making a mockery of Indonesia's eight-year development plan, and recent political attacks on Chinese businessmen, the takeover of Dutch enterprises, and looming signs of a government offensive against foreign oil interests were prompting a growing capital flight.[81] Although Foreign Minister Subandrio told the U.S. embassy that "the economic situation is so desperate that a military attack on West New Guinea is impossible," the British Foreign Office observed that the Indonesian armed forces were "making serious preparations for an invasion" and looked to the recent Indian takeover of Goa as a precedent.[82]

The pressure on Rusk to accommodate a shift in favor of Indonesia came from all directions. McGeorge Bundy bluntly told the president that area specialists thought that Rusk's position "can only help the Communists" and urged him to consider the problem in terms of Indonesia's "longer run economic development."[83] At Kennedy's urging, the secretary of state finally signed off on a letter to Sukarno offering to facilitate negotiations between Indonesia and the Netherlands. But Rusk, Adlai Stevenson, and the State Department's European desk still would not publicly break with The Hague, and in meetings with Dutch ambassador Van Roijen indicated that the United States might support military action under U.N. auspices if Indonesia attacked.[84] An exasperated Robert Johnson told Bundy that although the United States needed to facilitate a face-saving solution, it also needed to "shock the Dutch into a realization that the U.S. is *not* in their corner" and that the United States would *not* back them militarily in the event of an Indonesian attack. President Kennedy agreed.[85]

Just as it appeared that Dutch-Indonesian negotiations might be in the offing, Sukarno gave his famous *Trikora* (*Tri Komando Rakyat* or Triple Command of the People) speech of December 19, 1961, in which he demanded the dismantling of the Dutch "puppet state" of West Irian, called for the mobilization of the "entire Indonesian people" to regain the territory, and pledged to plant the Indonesian flag there by the end of 1962. The speech came just days after PKI chair D. N. Aidit secured the official imprimatur of Communist parties at the twenty-second Communist Party of the Soviet Union (CPSU) congress in Moscow for Indonesia's demand for a return of the territory.[86] Sukarno also created the *Mandala* command for the liberation of West New Guinea, headed by the young General Suharto. Suharto's ostensible aim was to infiltrate troops into West New Guinea, incite Papuan dissidence, and establish a foothold, but the military campaign was organized "on a piffling scale and . . . with well-nigh total ineptitude"—perhaps by design. General Nasution and other army leaders were extremely wary of provoking war with the Dutch, which would damage relations with Western governments, further weaken a tottering economy, increase Indonesian dependence on Soviet military hardware, and bolster the fortunes of the PKI.[87]

Britain and Australia also looked upon the brewing crisis in West New Guinea with great anxiety, but for different reasons. The Foreign Office's primary concern, shared by Malayan prime minister Tunku Abdul Rahman, was that West New Guinea would destabilize regional security and disrupt British plans for merging Malaya, Singapore, Borneo, and Brunei into a Malaysian federation.[88] London had given assurances to the Netherlands in 1959 that it would come to their aid in the event of an Indonesian attack and were hoping that The Hague would not invoke such commitments. Moreover, both the Foreign Office and the Commonwealth Relations Offices, looking to their imperial holdings elsewhere, were leery of implying even indirectly that colonial fragments deserved self-determination. As the British ambassador to the U.N. bluntly put it, "I see no reason for endangering British and thus free world interests through adherence to the Dutch point of view."[89]

Australia also adopted a complicated and contradictory stance that reflected its subordinate position within the British Commonwealth, dependence on British and U.S. defense guarantees, and economic and geographic proximity to Indonesia. Before 1959 Australia openly favored the Dutch position both in and out of the U.N., preferring "a friendly Netherlands to an uncertain Indonesia in possession of West New Guinea." Two years later Australia tilted uneasily in favor of self-determination for West New Guinea, although officials in Canberra told Washington they were opposed to any solution that involved "turning over West Irian to the Indonesians."[90] Uppermost in the mind of Australian prime minister Sir Robert Gordon Menzies was the possibility that after absorbing West New Guinea, Indonesia would turn its sights eastward to Papua New Guinea. Like The Hague, Australian Foreign Ministry officials also sought guarantees from Washington that an attack on Australia or Papua New Guinea would bring the ANZUS Treaty into effect.[91] Dean Rusk was solicitous of such concerns, but for reasons having more to do with Vietnam than West Irian. The United States "could not possibly hope for Australian support" in shoring up Ngo Dinh Diem's tottering regime in South Vietnam, the director of the State Department's Vietnam Task Force wrote Averell Harriman, unless Washington pledged to defend it in the event of an Indonesian attack stemming from the West New Guinea dispute.[92]

Far more likely was the possibility of hostilities erupting out of miscalculation, as happened in January 1962, when Dutch and Indonesian naval forces inadvertently clashed off the coast of West New Guinea. In the wake of the clash U.N. Secretary General U Thant brought heavy pressure on both countries to resume dialogue. But talks went nowhere.[93] Washington had unwittingly emerged as the indispensable third party in the conflict, George Ball observed, and "both sides know that we hold the key to a solution."[94] In mid-February Attorney General Robert F. Kennedy visited Jakarta to meet with Sukarno, one of dozens of such efforts in early 1962, and after much wrangling, he extracted a promise of unconditional negotiations—on the condition that the transfer of West New Guinea to Indonesia be included on the agenda.[95] Shortly after, Foreign Minister Luns visited Washington, where President Kennedy bluntly told him that "West New Guinea as such is of little consequence" to the overall Western position in Asia. The United States, he suggested, was looking after the whole, the Dutch after a barren fragment of a moribund empire.[96] Within days of the Luns visit, the Netherlands and Indonesia agreed to secret preliminary talks with no preconditions under the auspices of the U.N. and with U.S. mediation. Ambassador Ellsworth Bunker, former ambassador to India, future ambassador to Vietnam, and—like Acheson—a former rowing protégé of Harriman at Yale, got the nod as mediator. The hegemonic hand of the United States loomed large in these meetings between Dutch, Indonesian, and U.S. officials. Even in a part of Asia where both Britain and the Dutch had more direct interests and where the United States had no military bases and at a time when the United States was preoccupied with two major crises in mainland Southeast Asia, it was Washington's word that counted.[97]

Talks over the future of West New Guinea began on March 21 at a secluded estate in Middleburg, Virginia, with just Adam Malik, Dutch ambassador Van Roijen, Bunker, and several staff present.[98] In an effort to break the negotiating deadlock, the State Department floated a new proposal developed by Ambassador Bunker, under which the Dutch would transfer administrative authority over West New Guinea to a transitional U.N. administration, resulting one to two years later in transfer of the territory to Indonesia and at some future date in an act of self-determination. The Kennedy administration considered the so-called Bunker Formula a sufficiently face-saving device to meet Dutch concerns. No provision was made for ascertaining the opinions of the Papuans themselves, whose views most U.S. officials plainly considered irrelevant.[99] Sukarno immediately accepted the proposal, but Dutch officials expressed outrage at what they considered to be a "sudden, complete and unexpected reversal of the attitude of the U.S." and broke off talks for more than three months.[100] The collapse of negotiations came just as Averell Harriman and AID assistant administrator for the Far East Seymour Janow testified before House and Senate subcommittee hearings on the Foreign Assistance Act of 1962, where Democratic senator Thomas Dodd of Connecticut charged that of the territorial claims made by newly independent states, Indonesia's claim to "Netherlands New Guinea is the most arrant, the most baseless, the most flagrantly imperialistic, the most threatening to the free world, and the most offensive to the spirit of the United Nations Charter."[101] The RAND Corporation's Guy Pauker went further, making the preposterous claim in *Foreign Affairs* that the Soviets were exploiting West New Guinea to further their "master plan" for destroying the Indonesian economy by drowning it in military debt and sowing chaos and despair that would help the PKI come to power.[102] Such criticism served as a warning of the political price the Kennedy administration might pay for backing Indonesia's claims.

As talks stalled, the danger of war between Indonesia and the Netherlands increased markedly, as did the frustration of U.S. officials. A spring National Intelligence Estimate concluded that "as Indonesian military capabilities improve, Sukarno will become increasingly prone to employ military measures short of an all-out invasion to weaken the Dutch bargaining position." Intelligence reports confirmed both Indonesia's increased military activity in West New Guinea and a doubling of the Dutch troop presence, which included sending U.S.-provided destroyers and submarines (intended for NATO use) to the area.[103] More ominously, Sukarno sent Foreign Minister Subandrio to Moscow to request accelerated delivery of more than $70 million in military assistance. Pentagon officials, concerned that the army's influence was waning in favor of navy and air force officers more sympathetic to Moscow, pushed for the full resumption of Military Assistance Program (MAP) deliveries, ostensibly suspended in February.[104] Prime Minister Luns, meanwhile, refused to inform the Dutch parliament of the Bunker plan and insisted on guarantees for Papuan self-determination before talks would restart. "The Dutch are playing us for suckers," Ellsworth Bunker told participants of a meeting at the State Department, to general agreement. The White House finally played the only card it had left, authorizing U.N. ambassador Adlai Stevenson to leak the Bunker Formula in an effort to force The Hague to resume negotiations.[105]

By this point Sukarno was ill-disposed to compromise.[106] In July the Indonesian president kicked General Nasution upstairs as defense minister, replacing him as armed forces chief of staff with his U.S.-trained rival General Achmad Yani, an advocate of increasing military pressure against the Dutch. Politically outflanked by Sukarno and the PKI, which publicly called for an invasion of West New Guinea, the military "abandoned their earlier pattern of restraint" and dropped hundreds of troops into the territory using U.S.-supplied Hercules troop transports, where they engaged in numerous but ineffective clashes with Dutch forces.[107] The Netherlands repeatedly complained to the U.N. Security Council but to no avail, as Washington was at that moment extending new military aid to the army. Over the strong objections of Secretary of State Rusk and Dutch officials, President Kennedy reversed the partial freeze on military aid to Jakarta and authorized $4.3 million in new MAP assistance.[108]

Under heavy U.S. and U.N. pressure, Indonesia and the Netherlands finally agreed in mid-July to resume talks on the basis of the Bunker proposal. Despite rising international criticism, Sukarno refused to even accept a cease-fire, recognizing the tilt toward Indonesia and concluding that it was the threat of full-scale Indonesian military action in West New Guinea that had brought the Dutch this far.[109] On July 30 Indonesia and the Netherlands finally reached agreement to transfer West New Guinea administration to a United Nations Temporary Executive Authority (UNTEA) and to Indonesia as early as May 1, 1963. A limited number of U.N. personnel would ostensibly remain in place to advise Indonesia in preparation for the act of self-determination it was responsible for holding no later than 1969.[110] Formal negotiations finally began on August 14 at the United Nations in New York and concluded two days later when Indonesia and the Netherlands signed a final agreement. U.S. officials greeted the signing with relief.[111]

Not everyone cheered. In fact, public reaction to the agreement and to Washington's role in facilitating it was overwhelmingly negative. Dutch Prime Minister Luns complained bitterly that the Netherlands had been abandoned by its allies and compelled by Indonesian military threats to agree to the Bunker plan. *New York Times* columnist Arthur Krock denounced U.S. acquiescence in "the latest of the triumphs of the threat of armed force as a means of territorial aggression," a view seconded by the British Foreign Office.[112] More important, Kennedy's congressional critics were outraged. Senator Mike Broomfield termed the agreement an "Asian Anschluss," and Republicans soon began calling for congressional hearings over the administration's West New Guinea policy.[113] The critics were right. Indonesia quickly set about ensuring that West New Guinea would be firmly and irrevocably integrated into the Indonesian republic and that West Irian's "act of free choice" in 1969 would leave Papuans with no choice at all.[114]

As Indonesian and Dutch officials inked the U.N. agreement, the army finally defeated the long-running Darul Islam guerrilla movement in West Java and a kindred Islamic revolt in northern Sumatra, extending Jakarta's administrative control over the entire archipelago for the first time since independence. Indonesia's diplomatic-cum-military triumph in West Irian thus brought a close to a long chapter in Indonesian nationalism that from its inception had been defined by its striving for national self-realization through territorial consolidation. But victory also deepened the split between the Kennedy administration and Congress over Indonesia policy; highlighted the tensions between policymakers' often conflicting definitions of U.S. strategic, economic, and political interests; and exposed the shallowness of U.S. support for the principle of self-determination.

Resolution of the West New Guinea problem would only confront the United States with new challenges. The Kennedy administration's diplomatic success ironically alienated a Congress already deeply skeptical about foreign aid, especially to Indonesia. Most members of Congress rejected the administration's case that the United States had little choice but to accommodate Sukarno, whom they considered a Communist sympathizer and all-around tyrant. Indonesia's campaign, financed in part by massive Soviet aid and an increased diversion of already scarce resources to the Indonesian military, accelerated its deepening economic crisis, which Washington now expected Jakarta to resolve. Indonesia's campaign to retake West New Guinea strengthened the political power of both the armed forces *and* the PKI, further polarizing Indonesian society. Moreover, Washington's accommodation of Indonesia likely encouraged Sukarno's belief that Indonesia's neighbors would back down in the face of confrontational diplomacy. This belief would prove disastrously mistaken when Jakarta launched its policy of confrontation (*Konfrontasi*) with the British over the formation of Malaysia, threatening to scuttle Washington's ambitious post–West Irian plans for Indonesia's modernization.

CHAPTER 3

Developing a Counterinsurgency State

As Indonesia intensified its efforts to recover West New Guinea from the Netherlands in 1962, Deputy Undersecretary of State for Political Affairs U. Alexis Johnson wrote an article for the State Department's in-house journal titled "Internal Defense and the Foreign Service." In it he spelled out the challenge Washington faced as backward peasants in developing countries awoke from centuries of apathy and became "exposed to the material goods and way of life which we in the U.S. take for granted." The United States must meet this legitimate "revolution of rising expectations" among the modernizing masses, Johnson argued, or risk losing them to Communism. How was the United States to meet this challenge? Through integrated military and economic programs directed at both "the roots of subversion" and their "overt manifestation"—that is, through a strategy of counter*subversion* aimed at developing "effective police and military capabilities" to maintain "internal security" coupled with economic and technical assistance to create the human and material infrastructure for development. Once the United

States helped new nations achieve internal stability, he suggested, policy-makers could turn to the long-term goal of encouraging political and economic modernization.[1]

Johnson's short piece neatly summed up American thinking about much of the non-Western world in the early 1960s. It offered the reader a pithy account of the decolonizing world's transition to modernity, the nature of the threat posed by Communist and other "subversive" forces, and the relationship between military and economic aid in U.S. policy, all filtered through the lens of modernization theory. Johnson's schema also reflected acceptance at the highest levels of the Kennedy administration of what was becoming known as "military modernization" theory, a conceptual and policy turn toward the explicit embrace of military-led regimes as vanguards of political and economic development.[2] In the wake of the U.N.-brokered settlement of the West Irian crisis in the fall of 1962, this vision of military modernization emerged as a guide to U.S. policy toward Jakarta as Kennedy administration officials laid out a blueprint they argued would lead to the short-term stabilization and long-range modernization of Indonesia. Through technical assistance, counterinsurgency, and civic action programs and through a multilateral effort to stabilize the Indonesian economy and set it on the path to economic rationality, U.S. officials thought they had a formula for overcoming the country's seemingly insurmountable economic and political problems. Western-oriented Indonesian officials expressed Walt Rostow–like confidence that "within two years we can build a solid foundation in Indonesia to enter a stage of self-sustaining growth," whereas the Indonesian armed forces embraced the notion of military modernization, which legitimized their own emergent doctrine of civil-military relations and territorial warfare.[3]

Policy planning during this period offered a glimpse of the elusive long-term goals that U.S. officials held out for Indonesia, goals largely submerged since the Indonesian revolution by short-range strategic and political concerns about Sukarno and the threatening rise of the PKI. A year later, however, hopes for a dramatic aid expansion and embrace of the Indonesian armed forces was eclipsed by the logic of containment, as Sukarno initiated *Konfrontasi* with Malaysia and aborted Indonesia's short-lived attempt at moving toward a market-led, Western-oriented program of economic development. The Kennedy administration's post–West Irian strategy for Indonesia was firmly embedded in a discourse of military-led modernization, providing both a cultural and ideological frame of reference for policymakers and a set of prescriptions in the economic and security realms. But it was a contested strategy, vulnerable to congressional and hard-line opposition at home, dependent on Indonesia's willingness to accede to the formation of Malaysia and to adopt policies urged upon it by the United States and the IMF, and contingent on U.S. allies playing roles that complemented America's larger policies in the region.

The Humphrey Mission and Modernization

The Kennedy administration began laying the groundwork for its post–West Irian strategy well before Indonesia settled with the Dutch; in fact, the first brick was laid shortly after President Sukarno visited Washington in April 1961. Administration officials at the time began developing plans for a civic action program for Indonesia, one of many being inaugurated as part of a new global focus on counterinsurgency. Kennedy also sent an economic mission, headed by Donald Humphrey of Tufts University and Walter Salant of the Brookings Institution, to study conditions in Indonesia and to make recommendations for U.S. aid.[4] The Humphrey mission's recommendations became the basis for the Kennedy administration's aid proposals for Indonesia, demonstrating the ways in which the discourse of modernization theory influenced U.S. thinking about Indonesia and concrete policy initiatives.

The Humphrey mission report illustrates how Kennedy administration officials transformed modernization ideology into political practice in a national context, concluding:

> We found Indonesia in the early stages of economic development but moving in the right direction. . . . The native ability of her people and her rich natural resources make the outlook . . . promising once the pre-conditions of self-sustaining growth are developed. . . . Indonesia is not yet ready for the take-off into sustained growth; the plane has only been brought out of the hanger. But . . . we predict that when the Indonesian economy does take off it will fly high and fast.[5]

Seeking applicable lessons from the United States's colonial past, the study team compared Indonesia and its "separatist" tendencies with the United States and its federal structure after independence from Britain, arguing that

U.S. success proved that the country's problems were rooted in internal dysfunction and mismanagement.

The Humphrey mission analyzed Indonesia as a classic peripheral economy, exporting raw materials to the United States, Europe, and Japan in exchange for consumer and manufactured goods, capital, and spare parts. The report characterized Indonesia as socially and economically backward at independence; its problems seemed to multiply as it sought economic and political autonomy. The ouster of Dutch nationals in 1957 and the takeover of Dutch firms left Indonesia with a dearth of trained technical and managerial personnel at all levels of the economy, resulting in poor administration and maintenance of the country's capital stock and incompetent long-term planning.[6] These problems were complicated by a foreign exchange crunch, which rippled through the economy in 1961–1962, exacerbating shortages of raw materials and spare parts needed to feed factories that were operating at from one-fourth to one-half capacity. Of its chief commodity exports (rubber, oil, coal, bauxite, and tin), only production in the foreign-dominated oil sector continued to rise, whereas poorly maintained rubber plantations deteriorated from lack of upkeep and replanting, in sharp contrast with prosperous Malaya. Indonesia's roads, railroads, and shipping infrastructure were all in various states of decay, providing little incentive for foreign direct investment in the extractive sector. Moreover, the "casual attitude toward government finance and the problem of inflation" exhibited by officials in Jakarta exacerbated these problems, diverting revenues from capital imports and production for exports to production for domestic consumption while the government enacted what the U.S. investigators saw as "irrational" state-directed price controls on commodities and consumer goods.[7]

Humphrey mission members did see a few bright spots amid the grim signs of economic mismanagement and irrationality: The "centers of government activity staffed with well-trained personnel," who recognized Indonesia's economic problems, sought "pragmatic, rather than ideological solutions" and displayed "a desire for resolute action"—in other words, Indonesian versions of the action-oriented, hypermasculine intellectuals of the Kennedy administration.[8] The Humphrey mission report placed great faith in the ability of these (overwhelmingly) Western-trained Indonesians to overcome the country's many economic problems and pursue a "rational" program of development, with U.S. experts supplying "the kind of ideas that . . . are appropriate for their development." "Inappropriate" in this analysis were import-substitution and other state-led development schemes that Washington not only tolerated but encouraged in such strategically vital countries as Japan, Taiwan, and South Korea, which occupied semiperipheral or core positions in the world economy.[9]

The Humphrey mission called for the United States to commit $325–$390 million in aid for Indonesia beginning in FY 1963, with nearly half of that to be financed multilaterally through Europe and Japan. The purpose of the expanded aid was to increase educational assistance and technical training, improve Indonesia's transportation infrastructure, bring on line excess industrial capacity, expand resource extraction and agricultural production, and provide assistance to private capital for the development of light industry. Aid in succeeding years would "strengthen elements of the government and the society that will exhibit greater economic rationality," putting off heavy industry and other major capital investments until some point far off in the future, if ever.[10] For now, technical assistance would allow Indonesia to "imitate and absorb other countries' methods of production," especially in declining light industries, with the goodwill generated by contact with Westerners "worth many a highway or dam."[11]

U.S. officials and social scientists were convinced that foreign (preferably U.S.) capital, advice, and contact would act as a catalyst for developing nations. Economist Theodore Morgan, who served on President Johnson's Council of Economic Advisers, told a conference on economic planning in Southeast Asia attended by University of Indonesia economist Emil Salim that "low income countries that seek economic growth can stand on the shoulders of the high-income countries in important respects. They can draw on the techniques and the capital of these countries; and more important in the long run, their people know that major economic advance can be achieved, whereas the people of Western Europe in, say, the 14th century did not."[12] Policy debates centered primarily on the question of whether private or public assistance should take the lead, with Congress and conservative nationalists tending toward private assistance and modernization theorists and internationalists tending toward public aid. In short, differences were rooted in both ideology and political economy, in the role policymakers thought Indonesia ought to play in the world economy and the role they thought state power ought to play in development planning and funding.[13]

The views of Humphrey mission member Walter S. Salant are illustrative. A member of the Council of Economic Advisers under Truman, Salant was a prominent proponent of U.S. public foreign investment in the developing world, arguing that technical assistance and private foreign investment were "necessary but limited solution[s]" to the third world's developmental needs. An international Keynesian, Salant linked U.S. public assistance directly to the modernization process and insisted that external financing of development could help to create markets for U.S. and European goods by building up indigenous infrastructure and increasing the purchasing power of third world nations, especially in Asia.[14] It is in this context that we can understand the charges lobbed by American nationalists that the Kennedy administration's foreign aid program represented an internationalization of the New Deal and an attempt to subsidize socialist development abroad.[15] As they developed these ambitious plans, proponents of increased aid to Indonesia, such as Ambassador Howard Jones and Roger Hilsman, also prepared a "minimum" fallback program of more limited quantities of Food for Peace (PL 480) aid, AID technical assistance, and Military Assistance Program (MAP) funding in the likely event that Congress stymied the Kennedy administration's efforts.[16] As *Konfrontasi* heated up and prospects for an expanded program of aid evaporated amid fierce congressional opposition, this minimum program (modernization lite) ironically became the basis for continued U.S. assistance to Indonesia.

The Military Moment

The economic aid program envisioned in the Humphrey mission report was only one component of an integrated political and aid strategy for Indonesia. The flip side to economic aid was MAP, which provided military and police training, weapons, and civic action equipment for the Indonesian armed forces. The increased U.S. commitment to military assistance, aimed at encouraging a greater role for the Indonesian armed forces in economic development and internal security, marked a conceptual and doctrinal turn for the Kennedy administration that went far beyond the mere preference voiced by Kennedy's predecessors for military regimes as bastions of anti-Communism and stability. For U.S. officials and social scientists thinking about development, the early

1960s represented a military moment when they began linking military aid more tightly to comprehensive programs of economic and technical assistance—a shift with profound significance for both U.S. foreign policy and the internal politics of many developing countries. In much of the under-developed world such doctrines resonated with the increasing role in state and society that many armed forces establishments envisioned for themselves, as the daunting challenges of pursuing economic growth and political stability strained the capacities of civilian governments.

The U.S. government's embrace of military modernization in the early 1960s arose in tandem with, and in many cases drew on, a growing body of American social science research that until the late 1950s had displayed what one scholar characterized as "a liberal opposition to military regimes."[17] This broad shift was in part a response to the growing Soviet provision of military and economic assistance in the developing world, anxiety over the impact of the Cuban Revolution, a wave of military coups in Asia and Africa, and the growing political and economic role that armed forces establishments were carving out for themselves throughout the third world. Before 1959 much of the political science literature on the armed forces in the developing world focused broadly on civil-military relations and the phenomenon of the military coup d'etat, often portraying the armed forces as bulwarks of stagnation and reaction. Such criticisms were consistent with the optimism that modernization theorists displayed toward the prospects of democratic development, although they were at odds with the Eisenhower administration's often warm relations with military dictators.[18] By the end of the decade, however, both scholars and U.S. officials began constructing the policy and intellectual apparatus for a turn toward military modernization, offering more positive assessments of the military's possible role as a governing force and as a spur to economic and political development.

The March 1959 release of the Draper Committee report on military assistance marked an important step on the road toward military modernization. The committee, chaired by former under secretary of the army William H. Draper Jr. and a roster of foreign policy luminaries, including John McCloy and Joseph Dodge, was formed in the fall of 1958 and tasked with offering a broad assessment of the U.S. MAP.[19] The committee recommended a reorganization of the U.S. aid program to enable long-range planning and short-circuit annual congressional budget battles, a major concern of scholars at the Center for International Studies who bemoaned the State Department's inability to engage in the sort of long-range planning practiced by Soviet officials. More significantly, the Draper Committee's second interim report, "Military Contributions to Economic and Social Projects," recommended a reorganization of U.S. military assistance programs to "encourage the use of the armed forces of underdeveloped countries as a major transmission belt of socioeconomic reform and development." It was one of the first official endorsements of military-led development and an early call for the dramatic expansion of what became known as civic action programs.[20] Discussing the results of the State Department's recent study on the political implications of military takeovers in the third world, Admiral Arleigh Burke and CIA director Allen Dulles argued at a June 18 NSC meeting that the United States ought to expand military training programs in Asia to include a wide range of civilian responsibilities and to encourage Military Assistance Advisory Groups (MAAGs) to "develop useful and appropriate relationships with the rising military leaders and factions in the underdeveloped countries to which they were assigned."[21] A few months later the semigovernmental RAND Corporation held a conference at which Lucian Pye, Guy Pauker, Edward Shils, and other scholars expanded on these ideas, exploring the role of the military as a potential modernizing force in the underdeveloped world through a series of historical case studies.[22] In the spring of 1960 CENIS published a report commissioned by the Senate Foreign Relations Committee that echoed the conclusions of the scholars at the RAND meeting, proposing that the United States consider military dictatorships as a vehicle for advancing modernization.[23]

On the eve of the Kennedy administration's dramatic turn toward internal security, counterinsurgency, and civic action in the developing world, these scholars and officials lay the intellectual and policy groundwork for an embrace of military dictatorships. Over the next few years a proliferation of empirical and theoretical studies positively assessed the military's role as a possible modernizing force in every part of the world.[24] These works made a number of broad claims. The first was that armies could help to break down local, tribal, religious, and class identities and train soldiers to identify with the nation as a whole, replacing particularistic affiliations with universal ones and providing both solidarity and a degree of class and social mobility. The second claim was that in most developing countries the armed forces were among the most modern organizations, embracing innovation, technology, and administrative rationalization and serving as catalysts for the rest of society.[25] Moreover, by their very nature, as Marion Levy put it, armies "are the most efficient type of organization for combining maximum rates of modernization with maximum levels of stability and control."[26] In theory, the armed forces' technocratic identity also gave them an "anti-political orientation" and a "sense of realism and detachment" with which to contemplate the national interest. In practice, however, what U.S. officials and social scientists most admired about armies in the developing world was *precisely* their political orientation, in particular, their willingness to repress radical political and social forces in the name of maintaining political stability and order.[27]

Although supporters of U.S. military assistance both inside and outside the academy had long promoted armies as conservators of political stability, proponents of military modernization also accepted and promoted a far greater role for the armed forces in directly managing the economies of developing countries. This conceptual turn carried two important policy implications that rippled through both the foreign aid establishment and the intersecting worlds of academia and private foundations in the early 1960s. Beginning in 1961, the State Department recommended supplementing traditional military training for Indonesian officers with "specialized instruction designed [to] improve their ability [to] discharge civil administrative responsibilities," including training in "legal [affairs], public safety, public health, welfare, finance, and education, economics, property control, supply, management, [and] public communications."[28] Training programs would thus penetrate both horizontally, across wide sectors of the economy and civilian bureaucracy, and vertically, with civic action and police assistance enabling closer surveillance and control over rural populations. Encouraging armies to play a greater role in economic development and civilian administration, however, meant accepting a greater degree of statism in economic policy than would previously have been conceivable, especially in countries like Indonesia where the armed forces assumed control of significant sectors of the economy after the takeover of Dutch enterprises in 1957. Rather than facilitate a turning away from autonomy, U.S. support for military modernization in the developing world might instead pit armies committed to state-led development and collective enterprise against Western-oriented technocrats willing to rely on foreign capital, raw materials production, and open markets as engines of growth.

The RAND Corporation's Guy Pauker acted as chief pitchman in promoting the Indonesian armed forces as a modernizing force. The Harvard-educated and Rumanian-born Pauker exemplified the crucial nexus between the intelligence community and academia in the 1950s and 1960s. A founder of the Committee on Comparative Politics at the University of Chicago, Pauker first traveled to Indonesia under the auspices of the Center for International Studies Indonesia project in 1954 to explore the political barriers to Indonesian development.[29] During this and subsequent visits with the RAND Corporation, which he joined in 1958, Pauker cultivated close ties with many of the Indonesian army's highest ranking officers, as well as with high-level NSC, Pentagon, and CIA officials. He rather immodestly claimed that he was "the first who got interested in the role of the military in economic development"; in nearly a score of scholarly articles and RAND Corporation reports he relentlessly argued the hard-liners' case for relying on the Indonesian army to promote U.S. interests and Indonesian development, even as he doubted whether it was ruthless enough under Nasution's leadership to do the job.[30] One scholar has suggested that Pauker, like other military modernization theorists, "did not insist that rule by military men was the best of both worlds but only that regimes controlled by military men still left open the possibility of development in a democratic direction."[31]

Collectively, however, Pauker's works, prefiguring Samuel Huntington's conservative critique of modernization theory in the late 1960s, strongly suggested that democracy ought not be the goal of modernization and that Washington should side with military-led regimes as a matter of both expediency and principle as developing nations passed through the turbulent middle phases of economic and political development. Political scientist Amos Perlmutter even suggested that "praetorianism" might itself be a phase of development, a natural and inevitable feature of the modernization process and therefore morally neutral with regard to its implications for U.S. policy.[32] Surveying the field in 1971, as challengers to modernization theory were picking it apart from all sides, Henry Bienen observed that between 1959 and 1965 "military rule was seen as a practicable and stable alternative when parliamentary, democratic regimes faltered; as the only noncommunist rule possible in power vacuums, and as the most efficient organizations for modernity and stability." During this period "academic opponents of the conception of militaries as modernizing institutions largely left the field" as the institutional, professional, and financial encouragement for such research evaporated and as Washington's support for military assistance to developing world armies grew.[33]

By 1963 military modernization theory had become widely accepted in policy-making circles. Under Walt Rostow's guidance in January of that year the State Department Policy Planning Staff (PPS) prepared a lengthy study, "Role of the Military in the Underdeveloped Areas." In the past, the study argued, American policy had emphasized civilian supremacy over the armed forces in postcolonial states, in line with its general optimism about the prospects for democratic, parliamentary development. The United States, however, had failed to take into account the potential of the military as "a powerful potential group of 'modernizers' and a conduit [for] contemporary Western thought and values." The PPS suggested that "contemporary analyses of modernization, which dramatize the evolutionary character of movement from a traditional to a modern democratic society, which account for the inevitability of the military role and, which in a sense legitimize that role to a degree, provide a basis for a more coherent U.S. doctrine." This meant encouraging patterns of economic development "in which the military see themselves as deeply involved in the process of modernization but in a role as cooperative partnership with civil authorities" and instilling a new concept of "total security" in which soldiers view themselves as insurance against both external invasion and internal subversion. In short, the PPS paper proposed a political doctrine that wedded modernization theory to U.S. support for national security states everywhere that alleged insurgency and subversion reared their ugly heads.[34] It also represented a clear synthesis of an emergent scholarly consensus in favor of military-led development. (Not everyone joined in the chorus, however. George Kennan offered a trenchant critique of the intellectual underpinnings of the Basic National Security Policy [BSNP] and modernization theory more generally in a long memo to Walt Rostow, writing, "I suspect rapid social change itself to be the deepest cause of political instability and violence. For this reason, I expect no good to come of the sort of precipitate development which you so warmly embrace." Kennan also recognized the extent to which his thinking "has departed from that which is not only reflected in your paper but is already accepted by a large portion of our intellectual community.")[35]

The Kennedy administration's military assistance proposals for Indonesia can be understood only in the context of this broader shift in favor of military modernization and the administration's doctrinal commitment to civic action and counterinsurgency throughout the developing world.[36] Kennedy administration officials arrived in Washington convinced that the Soviet Union had shifted its tactics to exploit the turmoil accompanying the process of modernization, especially in Latin America and Asia. Just a year earlier the Cuban Revolution had awakened many policymakers to the possibility of revolutionary change sweeping the Western hemisphere. The formation of the National Liberation Front in Vietnam and the intensification of a Communist-based insurgency in Laos augured similar challenges in Southeast Asia. As a result, Kennedy concluded that both the U.S. foreign aid program and the U.S. way of war fighting itself had to change.[37] In many ways Washington's effort to delineate and police the boundaries of acceptable political and economic development was predictable, even in the absence of Soviet or Chinese opportunism, and transcended Cold War concerns.[38] But Nikita Khrushchev's January 6, 1961, speech offering rhetorical support for "wars of national liberation" appeared to confirm the Soviet Union's new strategy, prompting U.S. embassies everywhere to look for signs of incipient subversion behind every protest by restive workers or repressed peasants.

The newly elected president responded to this challenge by promoting a bureaucratic and doctrinal shift away from conventional military tactics and toward "unconventional warfare and paramilitary operations" directed at internal unrest.[39] The State Department's Western Hemispheric Division developed a comprehensive plan in late 1960 to redirect Latin American militaries away from their previous focus on hemispheric defense toward internal security and military modernization, a shift ratified by Kennedy in September 1961 when he issued National Security Action Memorandum (NSAM) 88. Now MAP resources, training, and equipment would "encourage military involvement in both internal security and economic development" throughout the hemisphere and, eventually, throughout the developing world.[40] Similar efforts to institutionalize a new focus on counterinsurgency sprouted like spring bulbs in the national security bureaucracy as administration officials began to review U.S. counterinsurgency policy and evaluate the organizational and material requirements for an intensified focus on unconventional warfare.[41] In January 1962 Kennedy signed NSAM 124, creating the special group for counterinsurgency, which was responsible for developing and reviewing counterinsurgency programs.[42] Attorney General Robert Kennedy, who shared his brother's fascination with counterinsurgency, joined the special group shortly after its formation and gave the group both the president's imprimatur and a direct line to the White House.

The operational results of this commitment to counterinsurgency varied according to the perceived threat of guerrilla or other insurgent movements in particular nations. In large swaths of Central and Latin America this reorientation led predictably to the formation of U.S.-backed national security states and nascent death squad regimes, with Guatemala—a showcase for the new focus on counterinsurgency—leading the way.[43] Counterinsurgency doctrines "linked development to internal defense," argued Michael McClintock, "making it dependent upon enhanced security" and "placing development at a disadvantage from the start" virtually everywhere the doctrine took root.[44] This was also the case in Indonesia, where the army simultaneously pursued a counterinsurgency strategy against internal opponents while greatly expanding its political and economic power following the 1957 declaration of martial law and the takeover of Dutch enterprises, in part by creating clientelistic businesses and functional organizations serving the armed forces' institutional and economic interests.

Civic action programs dovetailed perfectly with modernization theorists' emphasis on the constructive role of the military in safeguarding stability and shepherding the development process.[45] As noted earlier, Lucian Pye of MIT, among others, argued that military elites in developing countries, because of their devotion to "professionalism, order, efficiency, industrial development and technological progress," could serve as modernizing agents while maintaining internal security "in the face of efforts of communist forces to exploit the existing conditions of wide-spread poverty."[46] In countries that sought to establish the preconditions for self-sustaining growth but that had large armies, poor infrastructure, and shortages of skilled personnel, civic action programs could thus meet multiple needs at once. The armed forces could adapt their mission by helping to build civilian infrastructure, establishing closer links between the military and rural populations, and serving as transmission belts for Western ideas, all while expanding military control in areas threatened by real or imagined insurgency.[47]

By the fall of 1961, as NSC staff assistant Harold Saunders pointed out, two distinct lines of thought on civic action had developed, reflecting both jurisdictional disputes and differing perspectives on the goals of civic action as a military-political doctrine. Pentagon officials saw civic action playing a limited role in such countries as Vietnam, with short-term military goals predominating and "economic development an incidental by-product." They were joined by Guy Pauker of the RAND Corporation, who brandished studies based on rational choice theory, which "questioned the efficacy of psychological, social and civic action as effective weapons for winning the insurgent brushfires of the Cold War." Nonmilitary planners, mostly within AID and the State Department, stressed the "nation-building" potential of civic action programs, viewing them as "a tool in long-term economic and social development." Klaus Knorr of Princeton's Center for International Studies argued that "civic action is not just a useful way to hedge one's bets in an internal war situation . . . but the key to the whole situation." As MAP plans for FY 1963 worked their way through the bureaucracy, Saunders warned Walt Rostow that a "basic choice of emphasis" about civic action was required.[48] At Rostow's prompting, in December 1961 Saunders drafted NSAM 119, which split the difference between the competing visions of civic action by insisting it could serve differing roles in countries "fighting active campaigns against internal subversion," those threatened by external aggression, and those "where subversion or attack is less imminent." Indonesia fell into the last category. Where possible, such activities were to be coordinated with other programs directed at the same goals, including military assistance, paramilitary assistance, police training, the Peace Corps, and covert operations.[49]

From the start U.S. officials held up Indonesia as a crucial testing ground for this vision of civic action: as a nation building exercise, as a counterinsurgency strategy, and, not incidentally, as a front for covert operations aimed at undermining the PKI. In December 1961 the special group for counterinsurgency authorized the use of funds for the "covert training of selected personnel and civilians, who will be placed in key positions in the (*deleted*) civic action program" and engage in various anti-Communist activities.[50] With the approval of pro civic action forces in the Department of Defense, the NSC, and Jakarta, the Pentagon included $4 million in FY 1963–1964 funding, out of a proposed two-year total of $53.3 million in military aid for Indonesia, for a modest civic action program.[51] But the conflict over West Irian and opposition from supporters of the Netherlands, including Dean Rusk, derailed civic action plans for much of 1962. The State Department predicted it might be a year before civil action programs were implemented in Jakarta. Robert Komer complained to McGeorge Bundy that "we're a long way from self-sustaining growth" because civic action and police training "are regarded as marginal to the main tasks of the agencies concerned."[52] The Pentagon and Congress never really bought the developmental logic behind such programs, viewing short-term security interests as paramount and dismissing programs that distracted from that focus. In many ways Indonesia typified the problems that civic action advocates had in pressing their case for aid to nations not threatened by active insurgency. "It is simply much easier to get people moving on active problems like Laos, Vietnam or Thailand," Komer explained, "than to get them to focus on the preventative medicine needed to forestall such problems arising elsewhere."[53] As Indonesia and the Netherlands lurched toward a settlement on West Irian, however, mid-level NSC and State Department officials began pushing harder for such medicine. Ambassador Jones led the charge from Jakarta, pointing to Indonesia as a "major test case for civic action in a relatively peaceful environment" and as a challenge to proponents of the military as a modernizing force in developing nations.[54]

The development of military modernization theory in the United States paralleled the emergence between 1958 and 1962 of the Indonesian army's own doctrine of territorial warfare and management. Following the outbreak of the PRRI revolts, in 1958 the army began reviewing its own requirements for counterinsurgency warfare and concluded that the armed forces needed to develop greater grassroots support and involvement throughout the country in order to effectively defend the nation from external attack or internal subversion. The declaration of martial law, takeover of Dutch estates, and army leaders' deeply held belief that leadership in the independence struggle conferred the right and duty to involve themselves in all areas of national life reinforced this conviction. Moreover, Sukarno's declaration of Guided Democracy, which the army supported, appeared to vindicate the mistrust that many military leaders held for the political parties, especially the PKI, whom they judged responsible for the nation's political and economic problems and the regional crisis.[55]

More than any Indonesian military figure, General Abdul Harris Nasution deserves credit for formulating the doctrine of territorial warfare and management. A brilliant soldier and military strategist, Nasution, after graduating from the Bandung Military Academy in 1942, led civil defense forces in Bandung during the Japanese occupation. After the Japanese surrender he commanded the crack Siliwangi Division of the Indonesian army, fighting against the Dutch, before being named armed forces chief of staff in 1949 and again in 1955. In 1953 Nasution wrote a lengthy analysis of guerrilla warfare based in part on his understanding of Indonesia's success against militarily superior Dutch military forces during the Indonesian independence struggle. In his writings on conducting both guerrilla and counterguerrilla operations, Nasution emphasized the need to address the socioeconomic causes of revolt and to build local support for the government, arguing that such goals necessitated the creation of counterinsurgency units oriented toward internal defense and operationally distinct from the regular army.[56]

Under the doctrine Indonesia was divided into regions that would be independently organized to defend against external attack, a notion that also provided the basis for the army's doctrine of civic mission. As explained to Guy Pauker, the army's intention was "not to establish a military regime but to pursue Nasution's 'third way'" between civilian supremacy and outright military rule, declaring itself a "functional group" under Guided Democracy that merited inclusion in the Parliament, cabinet, and state bureaucracies. Far more than a mere war-fighting plan, however, the doctrine of territorial warfare and management was a statement of the military's view on civil-military relations, a permanent justification for maintaining its prominent role in politics, the state, and the economy and laying the foundation for possible military rule. The August 1959 creation of the National Development Planning Agency (BAPPENAS) and its subsequent formulation of the Eight-Year Overall Development Plan in 1960 spurred the armed forces leader to name a committee headed by air force commodore Siswadi and army colonel Suwarto, working in consultation with U.S.-trained economists such as Mohammed Sadli, Widjojo Nitisastro, and Subroto of the University of Indonesia's School of Economics, to outline their own plans for the military's role in the nation's economic development.[57]

Armed forces leaders' efforts derived added urgency from three related developments: their campaign to defeat the Darul Islam insurgency in West Java and Aceh, the PKI's increasing emphasis on the organization of rural areas, and the prospective end in 1963 of the state of emergency declared during the PRRI revolts. The insurgency in Aceh reflected long-running local grievances and a fierce independence on the part of its largely conservative Muslim inhabitants, many of whom resisted both Dutch (who never fully pacified the region) and Indonesian control and sought to create an Islamic state or an autonomous region in control of its own resources.[58] Hoping finally to bring the insurgencies in Aceh and West Java under control, Brigadier General Adjie of the army's Siliwangi Division inaugurated a homegrown version of the civic action programs then gaining currency among State Department and Pentagon planners in Washington. Adjie targeted those areas most heavily damaged in the fighting with the Darul Islam for rural development and reconstruction projects by local army units, who repaired rice fields and roads and built public buildings in a bid to gain popular support.[59]

The Indonesian armed forces' doctrinal shift also stemmed from the PKI's turn toward the countryside and the prospective end of martial law. Beginning in 1959, party leaders proposed a "concerted effort to organize the peasantry" and began encouraging an elite cadre to move to and work in rural areas, forming farmer and peasant organizations and propagandizing in favor of implementing long-stalled land reform legislation.[60] Sukarno's proclamation of Guided Democracy, the subsequent constriction of the PKI's political options, and the party's steady gravitation toward China in the Sino-Soviet split provided additional impetus for a turn toward the countryside. Although the PKI's rural campaigns would achieve mixed success and provoked considerable and often violent opposition, especially among Muslim organizations in East and Central Java, military leaders expressed great anxiety at the party's growing radicalism and viewed rural development and civic mission projects as a means of diluting the PKI's appeal among Indonesian peasants.

By 1962 the army's civic mission was absorbing some 40 percent of its manpower in rural development projects and had become "a major preoccupation of the Ministry of Defense and of the Army General Staff." Military leaders used the dramatic expansion of the army's noncombat role to rebut critics, including the PKI, who charged that chronic budget deficits and the looming end of the country's state of emergency in 1963 warranted a reduction in the size of the 350,000-strong armed forces.[61] Indonesia's Western supporters viewed civic action in similar terms. At a time when ongoing Dutch-Indonesian negotiations limited Washington's ability to supply heavy arms, civic action also provided a "cheap and non-controversial" way of backing the Indonesian military.[62] What Indonesia's doctrine of civic mission and territorial warfare also demonstrates is how theories of military modernization promoted in the United States found willing audiences in many countries where armed forces establishments were already seeking to justify a greater role in the economy, state, and society.

What civic action supporters needed was White House approval to reverse the freeze on MAP funds for Indonesia imposed in January because of its military campaign in West New Guinea. The Dutch were firmly opposed to any resumption of military aid to Indonesia so long as Sukarno threatened West New Guinea, a position backed by Secretary of State Rusk and the European desk of the State Department. In an effort to break the logjam, William Bundy recommended that Kennedy restore the MAP for Jakarta but reassure the Dutch that U.S. aid would not enhance Indonesia's military capabilities against West New Guinea.[63] The president supported Bundy's position and, over Rusk's opposition, authorized $4.3 million in MAP funds in June 1962, including the initial installment on an archipelago-wide fixed communication system for the army. Kennedy's actions also signaled to CAP supporters that they could accelerate plans to send a civic action team to Indonesia and lay the groundwork for a full-fledged program.[64]

Police training also played a crucial and underappreciated role in the United States's counterinsurgency approach to Indonesia. Indonesia in the early 1960s posed distinct counterinsurgency challenges for U.S. officials compared to South Vietnam, Laos, or Guatemala—countries that faced active guerrilla or insurgent movements, benefited from massive U.S. military assistance and training, and received little or no Soviet aid. Indonesia in the summer of 1962 was the largest non-Communist bloc recipient of Soviet military and economic aid—directed primarily at the navy and air force—and was home to the world's largest nonbloc Communist party; it faced no significant internal threats and received comparatively little U.S. military assistance. Moreover, Indonesia's economy was deteriorating almost as rapidly as the fortunes of the PKI were rising. The United States thus faced the challenge of devising tools commensurate with the nature of the threat posed by Communism in Indonesia and with the relatively limited reach of its own influence.

Police training fit the bill. Kennedy's support for police training in Indonesia reflected both long-standing U.S. practice and a renewed interest in police assistance programs as an "essential element in our counterinsurgency effort."[65] Director of the Office of Southwest Pacific Affairs Francis Underhill explained that "the rationale for help to the police was that internal order and stability was essential for economic development just as development was the essential underpinning of stability."[66] Without strong and modern police services, the International Cooperation Administration (ICA) warned that "much of the development effort may be dissipated in disorder, confusion and frustration."[67] U.S. police assistance could help rationalize police forces using the latest technology and training and, in doing so, help rationalize the development process itself.

In addition, by their nature and function police forces were ideally suited to detecting and neutralizing domestic subversion in its early stages.[68] U.S. police assistance to Indonesia fudged the line between counterinsurgency and civic action, providing training—as did assistance to the army—for participation in rural reconstruction and road-building projects in addition to its more traditional functions. AID administrator David Bell explained to Congress in 1965 that "the police are a most sensitive point of contact between government and people, close to the focal points of unrest, and . . . better trained and equipped than the military to deal with minor forms of violence, conspiracy and subversion." Effective police assistance, as Robert Kennedy put it to Dean Rusk and Robert McNamara, would enable friendly governments to maintain order "without the necessity of firing upon civilian demonstrators who are often composed of students."[69] The United States had offered limited assistance to Indonesia's Mobile Police Brigade as early as 1949 and began formal police training in Indonesia in 1955 under the auspices of the ICA's Public Safety Program. In 1960 the police were formally incorporated into the armed forces and brought under military command, institutionalizing their increasing focus on internal security. Both the Defense Department and the CIA also retained their own role in supporting paramilitary police forces in Indonesia. According to a secret 1962 report on police training, the CIA "financed and directed police assistance programs in Turkey, Thailand and Indonesia which had overt as well as covert aspects" and which aimed at "neutralizing . . . subversive individuals and organizations."[70] Robert Amory, the deputy director of intelligence for the CIA in the Kennedy administration, recalls that the CIA worked "very closely with AID" on the task of developing internal police forces, which was "dangerous ground because you can get to Gestapo-type tactics."[71] Congressional critics of U.S. assistance to Indonesia's police drew just this connection.[72]

The ICA's Public Safety Program helped to shape both the organization and the practices of the Indonesian police. U.S. funds helped to develop an integrated police educational system in Indonesia based on U.S. pedagogy, and American advisers gave lectures and wrote lesson plans and texts for Indonesia's police academies, with more than 300 police officers training in the United States or other allied countries. AID funds also helped to construct a police communications center in Jakarta and established the "first link in an archipelago-wide radio-teletype system," and PL 480 counterpart funds were used to construct a "secure message center and code room" at the National Police Headquarters, at the time the only secure communications network in Indonesia.[73] As it expanded its counterinsurgency commitment to Indonesia, the Kennedy administration naturally looked to the Mobile Police Brigade, a 23,000-strong paramilitary police force focused on counterinsurgency and the prevention of "disturbances, demonstrations, riots," and other offenses "of a political, economic and criminal nature."[74] Both the chief of the Indonesian State Police, General Sukarno Djojonegoro, and the chief of the Mobile Police Brigade, First Colonel Soetjipto Joedodihardjo, had been to the United States for training or to visit with their American counterparts.[75] Both Indonesian and U.S. officials recognized the symbiotic relationship between the civic action program and aid to the Mobile Police Brigade. They argued that, to prevent the PKI from ascending to power, the army must "shift from primary reliance on its military security mission to a greater contribution to economic development"; this shift would increase the Mobile Police Brigade's importance in the overall U.S. counterinsurgency program.[76]

U.S. officials naturally sought to apply successful civic action and counterinsurgency lessons from Indonesia to Vietnam. General Maxwell Taylor's November 1961 report to President Kennedy recommended a dramatic hike in U.S. military assistance and training to South Vietnam; the aid included expanded civic action and police training. A concurrent study by the State

Department's Bureau of Intelligence and Research (INR) on the implications of the turn to guerrilla warfare in southern Vietnam recommended the Indonesian police force, and U.S. training for it, as a particularly effective example of the possibilities of police involvement in civic action, intelligence gathering, and counterguerrilla activity.[77] The significance of American police assistance to Indonesia can only truly be appreciated by comparison with other leading aid recipients. Indonesia trailed only South Vietnam in public safety assistance in 1963 and received 50 percent more aid than Thailand. Had the United States not curtailed assistance because of *Konfrontasi*, the projected U.S. Public Safety Program for Indonesia in 1964 would have been the world's largest, more than twice the size of Vietnam's and twice the size of the programs for Pakistan and Thailand (the next two leading recipients) combined. For the period 1956–1973 only Vietnam and Thailand received more overall police aid than Indonesia.[78] Although unrecognized by historians, police assistance was an anchor of the Kennedy administration's development and counterinsurgency strategy for Indonesia.[79]

The West Irian settlement was a boon to advocates of police assistance and civic action in both governments. In Washington the settlement removed the primary barrier to a closer relationship with the Indonesian armed forces even as it raised congressional ire over the Kennedy administration's perceived support for Sukarno. In Indonesia it temporarily strengthened the hand of General Nasution, who had long advocated a partial demobilization of the military as a way to streamline and professionalize the services and reduce their burden on the fragile economy.[80] Demobilizing thousands of soldiers in the midst of rapid economic decline, however, invited political instability, and the army "feared the social consequences of unemployment and the potential gain for the PKI." U.S. officials hoped that a big civic action program would help cushion this "inevitable army letdown" and stave off pressure for a reduction in the army's size or influence.[81] Along with police assistance programs, civic action offered a solution to the country's security and development needs that matched the ideological and organizational requirements of the Indonesian army in a "post–West New Guinea climate" with the ideological focus of U.S. officials on the military as a modernizing force.[82]

As Indonesia and the Netherlands initialed the New York Agreement, which formally ended Jakarta's long struggle to "regain" West New Guinea,

Kennedy administration officials looked to capitalize on the U.S. role in bringing about a settlement to expand economic and military assistance to Indonesia. "Capital of the sort we've gained is a transitory asset to be used while it's still good," Robert Komer wrote President Kennedy, adding that "we cannot afford not to compete [with the Soviets] for such a prize."[83] Kennedy agreed and signed off on NSAM 179, which called for an interagency review to explore "expanded civic action, military aid, and economic stabilization and development programs" for Indonesia, with the goal of coordinating the emerging strands of U.S. strategy into a coherent plan of action.[84]

The Humphrey mission estimated in early 1962 that Indonesia needed $250–$330 million to stabilize its economy and lay the foundation for long-range development.[85] In return for mobilizing the international community and a skeptical Congress to support a long-range development program, U.S. officials expected the Indonesian government to commit to a far-reaching IMF-led regime of economic stabilization. Submitting to IMF strictures would effectively reverse Indonesia's nascent attempt to pursue a program of state-led development, and the Kennedy administration viewed Indonesian compliance as a "necessary *quid pro quo* to our effort to provide resources for a pragmatic, rationally managed development program."[86]

Officials at Foggy Bottom, the Pentagon, and AID quickly agreed to fund what the Humphrey mission had called its "minimum" program of aid—AID technical assistance, Food for Peace surplus agricultural sales, and a MAP involving expanded civic action and police training. But while accepting the logic of modernization, many officials questioned whether the United States could effectively intervene on the scale needed to stabilize Indonesia's economy and steer it along this path. For starters, U.S. officials disagreed about how serious Indonesia's economic and political situation really was and what this implied for U.S. action.[87] Even assuming that Indonesia faced an immediate crisis, as Ambassador Jones and AID officials argued, critics of the maximum program of aid were skeptical about Sukarno's commitment to a serious stabilization effort.[88] Many Indonesian economists remained unconvinced that inflation was an impediment to economic development and viewed U.S. and IMF calls for fiscal austerity and monetary reform with derision.[89] Skeptics also worried that the Indonesian economy was "not currently organized to digest a crash program of aid efficiently," that it lacked the absorptive capacity for a large aid program at its current state of development.[90] The problem, Harold Saunders explained to Kennedy, was that despite Indonesia's grave economic situation, the United States did "not have a great deal of leverage to bring them around to a more realistic economic policy."[91] Washington, however, would inevitably be linked to the results, and if stabilization failed, Michael Forrestal observed, the United States could not "hide behind the skirts of the IMF." To avoid blame for the "necessarily harsh and negative" consequences of an IMF stabilization program, George Ball argued, Washington needed to combine stabilization with a "positive developmental approach."[92]

Ambassador Jones and his supporters argued persistently that Indonesia was worth the risk "of at least partial failure" accompanying a larger aid commitment because the worst scenario—the PKI's ascension to power— was almost too grim to contemplate. Michael Forrestal, Harold Saunders, and others were not so sure, predicting that "it would take something of a political revolution to get a meaningful program through Congress" and that the political outcry from "even indirectly paying off [Indonesian] debt incurred for military equipment in the Soviet Union would be deafening" on Capitol Hill.[93] Interagency discussion of the administration's plans for Indonesia, however, ratified two crucial shifts in U.S. policy. First, even if officials disagreed on the timing, U.S. policy would now aim to "solve Indonesia's stabilization and recovery problems and eventually launch a national development plan."[94] Second, the United States now gave the nod to multilateralism and emphasized the need to work with other Western countries through the Development Assistance Committee (DAC), the IMF, and the World Bank, an emphasis that would guide U.S. policy through the rest of the 1960s.

The Kennedy administration particularly sought a greater Japanese role in aiding Jakarta, wanting Tokyo to develop greater trade and aid ties to Southeast Asia both to underwrite economic development and to forward regional economic integration. Writing to Dean Rusk, Roger Hilsman "envisioned Japan playing a special role of 'consultation and collaboration' in the 'development of free Asian societies.'"[95] U.S. officials, for example, encouraged Japan to tie reparations payments to Indonesia (amounting to more than $200 million) to the purchase of Japanese goods and services and used PL 480 credits to Jakarta to channel cotton through Japan for processing. Japanese reparations funded construction of irrigation and flood control projects, nearly half of Indonesia's textile and paper mills, and a dam on the

Brantas River in East Java. More spectacular were the fourteen-story Hotel Indonesia in Jakarta (built in 1962) and the National Monument (*Monas*) in Merdeka Square. In the period 1950–1963 Japan provided $623 million in economic assistance to Jakarta, second only to the United States at $711 million and eclipsing it by 1965, when Indonesia "came to be seen as the centerpiece of Japanese policy in the region."[96] It is no coincidence that the Kennedy administration's interest in Japanese assistance to Jakarta heightened just as it was developing its post–West Irian strategy.

The plan of action developed in the wake of NSAM 179 envisioned a three-pronged approach: committing Sukarno to economic stabilization, collaborating with "those Indonesian civilian leaders who are most interested in the modernization and development of Indonesia," and strengthening the army's role in "economic and social development activities."[97] U.S. and international assistance, in turn, would be made contingent on Indonesia's adoption of a "far-reaching" stabilization program along the lines recommended by the IMF in July, allowing Jakarta to draw up to $82.5 million in additional loans from the IMF.[98] If stabilization succeeded, Indonesia's balance of payments recovered, and Sukarno stayed on the road to economic reform, the United States could look toward the long-term development assistance outlined in the Humphrey mission report and aimed at building up Indonesia's industrial, agricultural, and transportation infrastructure. Benjamin Higgins, whom Ben Anderson has called the "doyen of the Indonesianist economists," asserted that in Indonesia "a 'big push' is needed, not only from the economic point of view but from the sociological and political viewpoint," arguing that the country was at an "optimal moment for launching development, a short period of time when sociological, political and economic factors coalesce to provide a climate unusually favorable for takeoff into economic growth."[99]

Many U.S. officials agreed. George Ball sent President Kennedy the interagency plan of action on October 10, the day before he met with Ambassador Jones, who was in Washington for consultations related to the NSAM 179 process. Jones argued that "time was of the essence" if the United States was to "effectively exploit the favorable position we had in Indonesia."[100] Michael Forrestal, however, warned Kennedy against indicating "at this stage even by implication that we stand ready to finance stabilization," at least until Sukarno had proved his commitment to enacting basic reforms.[101] At least on paper, Forrestal, Saunders, and other advocates of the slow and steady road won out. On October 22, while the world's attention was fixed ninety miles off the coast of Florida, President Kennedy took time out to sign NSAM 195. The president approved the so-called minimum program of aid and ostensibly deferred the thorny question of Washington's role in Indonesia's long-term development for future consideration.[102]

The debate over the Kennedy administration's post–West Irian strategy for Indonesia was framed by the logic and language of military modernization. In the goals they set out, the means they devised, and even their criticism of different policy options, administration officials demonstrated their faith that the right mix of economic and military aid, properly timed and guided by Western expertise, could propel Indonesia along the developmental path trod by the United States. The key questions, at least within the White House, were ones of timing. Most administration officials probably agreed with Roger Hilsman when he explained to a skeptical congressman that the United States was now "in a position to press discreetly for a re-direction of Indonesia's economy toward a more rational pattern which cannot help but affect the country's political orientation." The next step was convincing Indonesia to adopt an IMF-led program of stabilization, the indispensable first step in the Kennedy administration's post–West Irian strategy.[103] However, U.S. officials had yet to acknowledge the contradictions between their far-reaching ambitions for Indonesia, the limited means and determination at their disposal, congressional opposition to their plans, and Indonesia's determination to chart an autonomous trajectory of political and economic development.

CHAPTER 4

The Road from Stabilization to *Konfrontasi*

With the resolution of the West New Guinea crisis Indonesia had achieved the territorial unity that it had been seeking since independence, although at enormous cost to its economy. Now the nation's neighbors and Western observers wondered what Sukarno would do to refocus the political passions he had harnessed to the *Trikora* mobilization. The British Foreign Office concluded that "excessive optimism is unjustified" and that the "essentially military nature" of Indonesia's victory would likely encourage it to make territorial claims elsewhere in the region, especially given Washington's reluctance to threaten military force.[1] Few, however, thought that Sukarno might attempt to block British plans to create Malaysia out of the remains of its former Southeast Asian empire, launching in the fall of 1963 a policy of confrontation that would accelerate Indonesia's economic decline, internal political crisis, and alienation from the West.

President Sukarno suggested that Indonesia might now redirect political attention to the mammoth task of economic development, and U.S. officials hoped to direct those energies to an integrated program of economic and military assistance. The day after the signing of the U.N. agreement on West New Guinea, Robert Komer prompted President Kennedy to issue National Security Action Memorandum (NSAM) 179. The memorandum called for an interagency review of Indonesia policy to explore the possibility of expanded military and economic assistance and support for economic stabilization and development along lines desired by the IMF and Western foreign aid donors. "Having invested so much in maneuvering a West New Guinea settlement for the express purpose of giving us leverage" in Washington's competition with the Soviet Union, he wrote the president, "we'd be foolish not to follow through."[2]

Although the State Department and IMF officials spoke of "economic stabilization" in morally and politically neutral terms as a return to economic rationality, the potential implications of economic stabilization for Indonesia were dramatic. They involved the liberalization of the Indonesian economy, acceptance of the strictures of foreign creditors, the elimination of subsidies for basic consumption, encouragement of foreign investment in the extractive sector, and a diminished role for the state—in short, the dismantling of Indonesia's plans for Guided Economy and integration into the regional and world economy on Western terms. Critics of IMF policies toward the developing world now have the language to describe what was being proposed—a structural adjustment policy, or SAP. The Kennedy administration was reluctant to involve itself in the politics of "sapping" Indonesia because support in both Jakarta and Washington was slim, the prospects for success dubious, and the consequences of failure potentially catastrophic. But stabilization was the sine qua non of the administration's post–West Irian strategy. Moreover, U.S. officials recognized that Indonesia's willingness and ability to embark on this uncertain course was directly tied to the degree of backing Indonesia could expect from the United States.

Their task was threefold: to convince Sukarno to embrace the need for liberal economic reforms and reject conflict with Malaysia, to mobilize U.S. allies and the IMF in support of Jakarta, and to ram the U.S. aid package for Indonesia through a hostile Congress. As with civic action and police assistance, the United States began working on this track with the IMF and its allies long before Kennedy signed his Plan of Action for Indonesia.[3] In May 1962 an IMF study team traveled to Indonesia and called for what would later be seen as a classic structural adjustment package: fiscal austerity, increased production of raw materials for export, an end to state subsidies for domestic consumption, devaluation of the rupiah, termination of multiple exchange rates, and tight credit policies to reign in runaway inflation.[4] U.S. officials concurred with the IMF's recommendations, although they were convinced that only an end to the West Irian crisis would create the conditions for tackling Indonesia's economic problems. Even so, Ambassador Jones suggested, "It is . . . not premature to attempt to lay [the] groundwork for [a] later stabilization effort" and "to bring facts of life to [the] attention of the government."[5] Sukarno saw things a bit differently. After being given a watered-down version of the Humphrey report that downplayed U.S. concerns, he illustrated his expectations of U.S. aid to Assistant Secretary of Commerce Hickman Price by "making sweeping motions of hands as if raking in [a] bountiful harvest of dollars."[6]

U.S. officials and their allies in other capitals and multilateral institutions had little confidence that Sukarno would take the lead in this process. Instead, the U.S. embassy in Jakarta planned to work with the "small but important group of non-leftist officials" close to First Minister Djuanda who were "seriously interested in economic development" and modernization. Many of these officials had trained in the United States on Ford Foundation fellowships or under participant exchange programs at the University of California in Berkeley, Stanford, Harvard, MIT, and other elite universities.[7] Supporters of stabilization, especially Ambassador Jones, assiduously cultivated this group of Indonesian officials. Keenly aware of the narrow basis of support for such policies within the Indonesian state, U.S. officials sought to encourage their Indonesian counterparts, raise their political profile with Sukarno, and provide protection from the social forces that could be counted on to attack them.

First Minister Djuanda and Indonesian representative to the IMF Sutikno Slamet led the push for stabilization, working with economist Khouw Bian Tie, Indonesian ambassador to the United States Zain, Governor Soemarno of the Bank of Indonesia, and Minister of Mines Chaerul Saleh. These officials were leading advocates of a measured retreat "from nationalism and indigenism," rejecting heavy state control of the economy and attacks on private investors and looking toward Chinese and foreign capital as engines of capital accumulation and development.[8] Slamet received help from U.S.

advisers such as the economist Bernard Bell, previously brought in by Ambassador Jones to advise BAPPENAS on Indonesia's Eight-Year Plan and to consult with the Humphrey mission. Slamet argues that Bell was a "decisive factor" in getting stabilization off the ground, having persuaded Djuanda to go with the "all at once" approach urged by the IMF.[9] In late September Governor Soemarno of the Bank of Indonesia (Bank Negara Indonesia) and Slamet invited the IMF to investigate economic conditions and help Indonesian officials draft stabilization measures that would be needed to secure a standby loan and to improve the country's standing with foreign creditors.[10] Working with BAPPENAS and First Minister Djuanda, Bernard Bell outlined a "Program of Economic Action for Indonesia" that was "adopted . . . virtually verbatim as the RI position paper" for negotiations with the IMF and later as the May 26 Regulations. It called for a slashing of budget deficits, ceilings on bank credit, simplification of exchange rates for imports, redirection of state capital toward basic production, elimination of direct controls on prices and production, and efforts to secure foreign aid to finance general imports of food, raw materials, and spare parts.[11] The challenge was to convince Sukarno, the armed forces, and political parties to support stabilization measures that were guaranteed to provoke a harsh public response (as they would thirty-five years later in the spring of 1998, when the public backlash from IMF-imposed stabilization measures helped to bring down Suharto). Sukarno himself remained unconvinced of the need to undertake monetarist measures to reduce inflation, arguing that the solution was to mobilize the Indonesian masses to increase production and self-sufficiency—as he saw Mao doing in China—rather than imposing austerity on them.[12]

Despite its misgivings, the White House began working to support Jakarta's efforts, forming an interagency advisory group on stabilization and encouraging Indonesian officials to meet with U.S. corporate leaders, banks, and business associations to promote private investment and explain Indonesia's proposed scheme of production-sharing contracts for resource extraction.[13] The Kennedy administration placed a special emphasis on working through multilateral institutions to accomplish its goals. Beginning in the 1960s Washington began relying on multilateral banks as "key instruments" for integrating nations—especially those attempting to pursue statist or mercantilist development paths—into a U.S.-led and U.S.-guided world economy, preferring "the virtues of a multilateral economism to the vices of direct coercion or intervention." Through its leverage in these banks the United States "linked the economic and financial reforms they demanded to U.S. political goals . . . especially during debt renegotiations when borrowing nations were most vulnerable."[14] Washington also relied on the Development Assistance Committee (DAC) of the Organization for Economic Cooperation and Development (OECD) and, at a meeting in Paris in December 1962, convinced DAC members Japan, Britain, France, and West Germany (all heavily invested in Indonesia) to finance stabilization measures "on the condition that Indonesia put its own financial house in order" and secure similar terms from the Soviet Union.[15] Days later President Kennedy authorized a $17 million loan to provide spare parts and raw materials for Indonesian industry, something Indonesia hardly qualified for on economic grounds but that Averell Harriman characterized as a signal to other nations that the United States was serious about underwriting Indonesian economic development.[16]

Indonesia's negotiations with the IMF and Washington would scarcely merit a footnote in the history of the era if not for the fierce struggle it detonated within Indonesia over the direction of economic policy. Following the West Irian settlement, Sukarno declared that Indonesia would turn its attention to the great unfinished task of increasing production and providing food and clothing for the Indonesian masses, the first step on the road to national industrialization and economic development. To accomplish this task, Indonesia needed massive foreign aid (its Eight-Year Plan was premised on such assistance), but many Indonesians chafed at the political costs of accepting the harsh conditions sought by U.S. and IMF officials, which promised to adversely affect the relationship between the Indonesian state and foreign capital and between the government and managers of state-owned capital, especially the military.[17] Ironically, the long-run impact of acceding to the IMF's demands would be to undermine the role of the military in Indonesia's economy precisely at the moment when the U.S. government and private foundations were engaging in a substantive effort to encourage an even greater role.

PKI chairman Aidit denounced proposals for acceding to U.S. or IMF demands, declaring that "the real way out of Indonesia's economic difficulties is not by begging for loans from abroad or making the Indonesian people the servants of foreign capital in Indonesia." The PKI urged instead that Indonesia continue working to increase production and build a self-sufficient national economy independent of foreign aid.[18] Indonesia, however, lacked both the raw materials and the spare parts to increase production and the foreign exchange with which to buy them.[19] Roger Hilsman and Michael Forrestal, on a visit to Jakarta, told a group of high-ranking civilian and military officials that Indonesia had to "face up to [the] politically difficult but economically essential decisions" the IMF was demanding before the United States could consider more substantial aid.[20] Forrestal's trip came on the eve of a crucial meeting of the Supreme Operational Command (KOTI), where Djuanda made his case for a far-reaching program of economic reform, arguing that the only way for Indonesia to increase production for export was to keep inflation (which destroyed export incentives and soaked up foreign reserves) in check, in effect splitting the difference with those who opposed monetarist measures to contain prices. In response, Sukarno formed a cabinet-level committee to flesh out Djuanda's proposals, but he included stabilization opponents such as PKI deputy chair Njoto, who emphasized self-reliance (*Berdikari*) and downplayed foreign aid.[21]

With Sukarno's tentative approval of stabilization in hand, Sutikno Slamet returned to Washington to begin negotiating an IMF agreement. Slamet recognized the thin reed of political support that the IMF-proposed measures had at home and was determined to drive the hardest bargain possible to ease the almost certain domestic outcry.[22] A secret brief by Bernard Bell, prepared as a position paper for the IMF meetings, spelled out many of the positions eventually adopted by Indonesia: a balanced budget in two to three years, the lifting of price controls on basic goods such as rice, and a system of tiered increased exchange rates for imports.[23] In return for these concessions the Indonesian delegation hoped to secure an $82.5 million stabilization loan from the IMF. Sukarno gave Slamet's efforts an important boost when he announced on February 28 that the 1963 budget would "reflect efforts toward stabilizing the nation's economy and finance." IMF officials expressed cautious approval and returned to Indonesia to oversee the formulation of the new economic regulations.[24]

Two weeks later Sukarno issued his Economic Declaration (DEKON), later referred to by the People's Consultative Assembly (Majelis Permusyawaratan Rakyat Sementara, or MPRS) as Sukarno's "Political Manifesto of the Economy." The DEKON declared that Indonesia was in the first phase of its revolution, which entailed wiping out the vestiges of imperialism and feudalism and attempting to "create an economic structure that is national and democratic in character." The declaration was in essence a call for state-led development with partial assistance from domestic and international capital—scarcely a ringing endorsement of IMF policies. But it was vague enough that both opponents and supporters of stabilization could (and did) use it to justify their positions.[25] The Kennedy administration expressed cautious optimism that "if Indonesia can survive [the] short run we should be able to assure ourselves of a neutral, independent, and non-Communist nation."[26]

U.S. optimism was tempered, however, by continued Soviet and Chinese aid overtures.[27] At the end of March Soviet defense minister Marshal Malinovsky arrived in Jakarta for a highly publicized ten-day visit, where he offered Sukarno an additional injection of military aid. Close on his heels came Chinese chairman Liu Shao-Chi and Foreign Minister Chen Yi, the first visit by a Chinese head of state to a non-Communist country and at a time when China "was making a big effort to woo the third world in an effort to offset the damaging impact of the Sino-Indian border war and to strengthen her position internationally against the Soviet Union."[28] Both U.S. and British officials closely monitored these high-profile trips, which highlighted the growing competition between Moscow and Beijing for Indonesia's favor as the Sino-Soviet split widened.[29]

Malinovsky and Liu both publicly endorsed Indonesia's stance against Malaysia, but as Soviet officials hinted that they were not going to back Indonesia as enthusiastically as they had on the West Irian issue, Sukarno began drawing closer to Beijing.[30] Liu's visit foreshadowed a growing political convergence of China's interests with Indonesia that would continue through 1965 despite their strategic rivalry and the reservations that Chinese officials had about the political "revisionism" of Sukarno and PKI chairman Aidit. Subandrio told Ambassador Jones that Indonesian policy "would continue to be directed at maintaining correct, friendly relations with China since Indonesia could not afford to antagonize this great power."[31] But Sino-Indonesian cooperation also generated growing concerns among groups wary of Chinese economic and military influence, as anti-Chinese riots in West Java in early May—which enjoyed indirect army support—suggested.[32] Moreover, Indonesia's economic crisis demanded the sort of assistance that neither China nor the Soviet Union could provide. As Chairman Liu departed from Jakarta, Sukarno authorized Djuanda to begin drafting with AID assistance the stabilization measures called for by the IMF and Washington. Despite Indonesia's growing affinity with China, Robert Komer observed hopefully, Sukarno "now sees no real alternative to reliance on U.S. and Western aid and has become reconciled to doing what is necessary to get it."[33]

The Congressional Battle over Aid to Indonesia

Congressional opponents of aid to Indonesia, on the other hand, did see clear alternatives to Indonesia's reliance on U.S. assistance, and in 1963 it was they, not the PKI, who posed the greatest challenge to the White House's modernizing vision. Their salvos on Indonesia spotlighted the broader attack on New Frontier foreign aid waged by many of the same conservative nationalist voices who opposed the Trade Expansion Act of 1962 and later the Great Society, many of them Republicans from states with declining manufacturing sectors and low-wage industries under threat from increased foreign trade. H. R. Gross (R-Iowa), a staunch opponent of aid to Jakarta, entered a statement into the *Congressional Record* from the National Economic Council—representing middle-size firms producing for the national market—that argued that "if Western civilization is to go on" the United States must reestablish a "self-renewing economy," end large-scale government spending, and end "this New Deal–Fair Deal–New Frontier madness" of foreign aid, a madness "that dwarfs every madness reported in history."[34] Congressional opposition to the Kennedy administration's foreign aid proposals highlighted a fact that scholars of modernization theory as ideology have for the most part ignored: that the prescriptions of modernization theorists were tied to particular social constituencies and were rooted in a particular conception of the American political economy at home and abroad.[35] James Burnham, former spokesman for the rollback current and founder of the *National Review*, drew similar connections. He condemned both the economic "irrationalism" of the Sukarno regime and Washington's support of him and asked, "Isn't it self evident that what the masses want is more food, clothing, houses, cars, Medicare? Isn't it a fact that Castro, Nasser, Kenyatta, Ben Bella reduce the economies of their countries to shambles? So doesn't it follow . . . or is it just possible that—in relation to the masses of men as they really are—it is the Welfare State, the Great Society that is irrational?"[36]

Senator William Morse (R-Ore.), a traditional conservative whose state was home to timber and mining companies chomping at the bit to get into Indonesia, articulated the strategic thinking that underlay the nationalist criticism of foreign aid. Morse dismissed the domino theory as a liberal attempt to export the New Deal to Asia, asking, "Does any Senator think that Indonesia protects us in Southeast Asia? America is defended in that part of the world by the seventh fleet, American airpower, American troops in the Pacific." Morse spelled out a unilateralist vision of U.S. security in the Pacific centered on the projection of air and sea power and aimed at protecting the Western Hemisphere, and he argued, "It is time that we stopped pouring the American taxpayers' money into one rat hole after another in that area of the world."[37]

Sukarno was a poster child for these conservative and nationalist opponents of the New Frontier approach to foreign aid who rejected both the short-term logic and the long-term strategy of the administration's modernizing vision for Indonesia. He was a self-proclaimed socialist and nationalist who thumbed his nose at the West, disparaged private property and attacked foreign capital, favored state-led development, accepted aid from the USSR and China, and sought to dominate the region, colonize his neighbors, and drive out Western influence—seemingly with the administration's help.[38] The *Congressional Quarterly* observed that Indonesia was "the aid recipient which appears to be coming under the sharpest attack" by congressional aid opponents. Representative William Broomfield of Michigan was blunter still: "You will have one hell of a fight," he told Roger Hilsman, "when this foreign aid bill hits the floor."[39]

Administration officials were not helped any when the Kennedy-appointed Committee to Strengthen the Security of the Free World issued its recommendations in late March.[40] The committee, headed by General Lucius Clay, was stacked with international lawyers and bankers who served on the boards of corporations invested (or interested) in Indonesia, including Robert Lovett of Freeport Sulphur and former treasury secretary Robert B. Anderson of Goodyear Tire and Rubber.[41] Kennedy assembled the "Clay Committee" in an effort to bolster the case for the administration's worldwide expansion of economic and military aid to developing nations. Instead, the committee issued a sharp rebuke to his aid priorities and called for a half-billion-dollar reduction in foreign assistance. "Too much money, too little thought" was how the *Wall Street Journal* summarized its conclusions. The report criticized the administration for dispensing foreign aid on political grounds, neglecting internal security, and supporting state-controlled firms rather than private enterprise; instead, it called for more rigorous aid standards, a focus on "self-help and self-discipline," aid tied to market reforms, the vigorous promotion of private enterprise, and an emphasis on multilateralism—the strategy the Johnson administration would follow after Sukarno's ouster in 1966.[42] Portrayed at the time as closet allies of nationalist aid opponents, the committee's work makes more sense when viewed as "a manifesto of free enterprise sentiment regarding overseas assistance," opposing the administration's modest drift toward public investment and public-private aid partnerships such as the Alliance for Progress.[43] The report also underlined concerns by George Ball and Dean Acheson that current levels of military and economic aid were exacerbating the U.S. balance of payments deficit and undermining international confidence in the dollar, a worry that would grow rapidly as the United States escalated its war in Vietnam.[44]

The Clay Committee singled out Indonesia for particularly harsh criticism:

> We cannot leave this area of the world without special reference also to Indonesia. Because of its population, resources, and geographical position, it is of special concern to the free world. However, we do not see how external assistance can be granted to this nation by free world countries until it puts its internal house in order, provides fair treatment to foreign creditors and enterprises, and refrains from international adventures.[45]

The media gave the Clay report widespread and sympathetic coverage, amplifying congressional calls for slashing foreign assistance in general and aid to Indonesia in particular.[46]

During three months of House Foreign Affairs Committee hearings, lasting from April to June, the administration's critics gleefully attacked aid to Indonesia. Congressman J. L. Pilcher (R-Ga.) told Robert McNamara on the first day of hearings, "I just don't see how you can justify American taxpayers' money going to a Communist country." Having begun the year with ambitious plans, Kennedy officials now hoped to simply weather the storm and repel efforts to eliminate aid to Jakarta entirely. *Business Week* predicted after two weeks of hearings that "Indonesia may well become a focal point in the Congressional battle over the reshaping of American foreign aid policies."[47] A parade of congressmen denounced Sukarno as a "dictator," "black-mailer," "lower case bum," and "junior grade Hitler" and Indonesia's government as "Communist," "pro-Communist," or "Communist-leaning socialist." Congressman William Broomfield (R-Mich.), a former supporter of aid to Jakarta, brought the hearings to a close by railing against the Indonesian president for nearly an hour. Coddled by U.S. assistance, he charged, Sukarno had squandered Indonesia's resources, destroyed its economy, and neglected economic development in favor of a Soviet-funded arms buildup and threats against Malaysia. Shortly after, he offered an amendment to the Foreign Assistance Act that would ban all military and additional economic aid to Indonesia entirely without a presidential determination stating that it was in the national interest.[48]

Administration officials worked diligently to kill the Broomfield amendment while conceding privately that a presidential determination could probably be circumvented. Military aid was another matter. "Our military assistance program," a State Department position paper for the hearings stated, "is a major weapon not only in the fight for continued Indonesian independence but also in the fight to increase Indonesian receptivity to Western political and economic institutions and practices." U.S. officials viewed police training and civic action programs as an indispensable way to "maintain a foothold" with the Indonesian military and to help the army "develop grass roots political power." General Clay and Admiral Felt, alarmed by the undifferentiated opposition to aiding Indonesia, made a point of emphasizing their confidence in the Indonesian military's anti-Communist credentials and their support for continuing with civic action and other programs of military assistance and training, even as they called for a reduction in economic aid.[49]

The bottom line, argued aid supporters such as Roger Hilsman, appointed in April 1963 as assistant secretary of state for the Far East, was that Washington could not give up the game to the Soviets or the Chinese no matter how anyone felt about Sukarno. They urged Congress to consider the importance of Indonesia in the larger framework of American regional policy—in short to accept the assumptions and analysis underlying their strategy for modernizing Indonesia and to reject the assumptions underlying the "hard-line" stance of Guy Pauker, the CIA, the British, and congressional critics. "Look at a big map of Asia," Roger Hilsman told the House Foreign Affairs Committee. "Visualize it. You can look at it over there—Korea, Japan, and in the north, the great arc down in the corner, Southeast Asia is a salient projecting through all this, and over the salient are the islands of Indonesia which are at the crossroads of the Pacific." "If Indonesia should fall into Communist hands," commander in chief of the Pacific Fleet Admiral Felt warned, it would be "a catastrophe to the free world."[50] Many congressmen were unconvinced. Representative Wayne Hays (R-Ohio) told AID director Frank Coffin, "I think anything you give to this dictator out there, Sukarno, is just down the drain."[51]

British officials agreed and told the White House with increasing frequency that U.K. and U.S. interests regarding Indonesia were beginning fundamentally to diverge. As *Konfrontasi* heated up, the Foreign Office concluded that, although Western aid was vital to preventing Indonesia's economic collapse, such assistance "would likely be employed in shoring up the Indonesian economy so that the Indonesians could devote themselves" to attacking Malaysia.[52] Indonesia's threats had already forced the Macmillan government to increase defense aid to Malaysia, strengthening the hand of officials who opposed looming (and still secret) plans for a possible retrenchment of British military forces from east of the Suez. Whitehall had not yet attempted to block U.S. efforts, but an explosive, unpublished White Paper on Indonesian covert operations in Malaya and Borneo—which would surely inflame Congress—suggested that it was in their power to do so.[53]

Just a few months after the U.S.-brokered settlement of the West New Guinea crisis, the Kennedy administration's ambitious plans for Indonesia appeared dead in the water.[54] At the height of the congressional debate in Washington, however, Jakarta took a series of steps that raised the hopes of U.S. officials that Indonesia might seek political stability through accommodation with Malaysia and economic stability through Western-led and market-oriented development. In late May 1963 President Sukarno expressed his support for new economic regulations drafted by First Minister Djuanda, after which he oversaw crucial negotiations with American and British oil companies over their future concession rights in Indonesia. Simultaneously, the Indonesian president signaled his willingness to seek a rapprochement with Tunku Abdul Rahman over the formation of Malaysia, leading to a summit two weeks later in Manila where the prime ministers of Indonesia, Malaysia, and the Philippines announced their intention to form an indigenous "Maphilindo" alliance and to seek the help of the United Nations in resolving *Konfrontasi*.

Finally, Indonesia reached an agreement with the Soviet Union to reschedule payments on its outstanding debt of $800 million, helping to clear the way for the possible expansion of Western economic assistance. The rapid succession of events at the end of May illustrates the extraordinarily complicated and interwoven nature of Indonesia's political and economic problems as well as the challenges the United States faced as it urged Sukarno to move forward on all four fronts *and* attempted to mobilize Congress, the IMF, and its DAC allies to support its efforts.

U.S. officials were deeply concerned that the emerging conflict with Malaysia would derail Indonesia's timid steps toward Western-oriented reform. But it was the question of oil that posed the greatest challenge to U.S. hopes for Indonesian development and placed Washington's priorities in sharpest relief. In the spring of 1963 U.S.-Indonesian relations threatened to implode as long-running negotiations over the future of U.S. and British oil concessions ground to a halt, threatening to force the oil companies out of Indonesia and with them Jakarta's hopes for Western economic and political support. Short of an outright PKI takeover or war with Malaysia, no Indonesian action in the 1960s posed a graver threat to basic U.S. interests than the possible expulsion or takeover of Western capital, of which American oil companies were by far the most important representative. The collapse of oil negotiations threatened to unravel the Kennedy administration's careful efforts to lock in Indonesia's integration with the regional and world economy through training, multilateral aid, and IMF-led stabilization. U.S. intervention in the negotiations between the oil companies and the Indonesian government in 1963 was a sharp reminder of the leverage that Washington could bring to bear when Indonesian actions bumped up against the limits established by U.S. hegemony.

American oil companies first became interested in Indonesia in the mid-1880s when the Netherlands East Indies became a major consumer of Pennsylvania kerosene, importing more than half a million barrels per year. A decade later Standard Oil Company began seeking concession areas, but Dutch, British, and French oil companies successfully kept Standard out until 1912, when a Dutch-headquartered subsidiary of Standard Oil of New Jersey finally gained footholds in Aceh, Sumatra, and Java. During the 1920s the Netherlands bowed to pressure from the State Department and effectively split future oil concessions between U.S. companies and the Anglo-Dutch-owned Royal

Dutch Shell, leading to the entry of Standard of California (SOCAL) and Texaco, which formed a joint venture (Caltex) to exploit its Asian concessions.[55] Japan also eagerly sought entry into the Netherlands East Indies oil market as a way of reducing its dependence on imports from the United States and Europe, and the cutoff of U.S. oil exports following Tokyo's invasion of Indochina in 1939 was a major factor in Japan's decision to later attack Pearl Harbor and take over the Netherlands East Indies during World War II.[56]

The Japanese wartime occupation of Indonesia helped to lay the foundation for the postwar transformation of the Indonesian oil industry. While stealing millions of barrels of oil, the Japanese trained many Indonesians in petroleum engineering and management, establishing the Permina oil academy and the Oil and Gas Institute at Bandung to develop skilled workers for the oil industry. Japanese military officials also organized the Oil Workers Militia Association (Himpunan Laskar Minyak), which after the war reformed itself as the Indonesian Oil Workers Union (Persatuan Pegawi Minyak). The return of Western workers to the oil fields at the end of the war, along with the racial segregation and wage hierarchies that marked life in the oil camps, increased the desire of many Indonesian revolutionaries to establish national control over and create state-owned corporations in the extractive sector. After independence, however, each of the oil companies enjoyed "let alone" agreements that preserved the favorable contractual rights they had enjoyed under the Netherlands East Indies government. In 1951 the Indonesian parliament created a commission to look into its extractive industries and determine appropriate pricing and tax structures, suspending the granting of new concession areas in the oil industry until new regulations could be written. The concession freeze lasted ten years.

The three major foreign oil companies in Indonesia—the Dutch- and British-owned Shell and the American-owned Stanvac and Caltex—were each affected differently by the freeze. Shell and Stanvac, which were long on refining and storage capacity and short on new reserves, suffered the most as existing concessions began to dry up. Caltex, on the other hand, operated the Minas oil field, the largest in Southeast Asia, and until 1960 was exempted from participating in the unprofitable domestic petroleum market. The American consul in Medan reported that Caltex, "with a record production of 8,000,000 barrels of oil from its Sumatran fields in August 1960," was "one of the most significant factors in Sumatran and indeed, in Indonesian life," a position that made it "practically impossible" to avoid involvement in the country's political affairs. With their small armies of foreign technical staff, air-conditioned buildings, schools, and hospitals, the oil company operations were also viewed as an "outpost of modernity" in "a backward country," as *Fortune* described it.[57]

Jakarta's turbulent relations with foreign oil companies in the 1960s flowed directly from these efforts to extirpate the legacy of Dutch colonialism by rewriting the laws governing exploitation of the country's resources. The conflict in Indonesia was a local manifestation of a broader shift in the world oil industry, in which producer states sought to increase their revenues and leverage through more favorable splits on royalties, the increased training of indigenous personnel, concession agreements with independent companies, and other mechanisms aimed at weakening the power of the multinational oil companies and securing a measure of racial and economic justice in the foreign-controlled oil camps. Washington worried that as Indonesia considered a new oil law, it would adopt statist policies precluding further profitable investment by U.S. companies. These concerns were magnified when Soviet president Nikita Khrushchev visited Jakarta in February 1960; Khrushchev pledged $250 million in economic and technical aid and stationed eight Romanian oil advisers in Indonesia. Embassy officials speculated that this might be a first Soviet step toward "reorient[ing] oil exports from Indonesia and . . . making [it] dependent upon the Soviet bloc."[58] Caltex president Henry F. Prioleau suggested as much to George Ball, pointing to the recent visit to Moscow by Foreign Minster Subandrio and Defense Minister Nasution to hint that oil company problems were linked to Moscow's recent overtures.[59]

Indonesia unveiled its long-awaited Regulation 44 in September 1960. The regulation voided colonial-era concessions and stipulating that foreign oil companies would essentially become contract workers, each operating with one of Indonesia's state-owned oil companies: Permina, controlled by Ibnu Sutowo and linked to the army; Pertamin, linked with the PKI-affiliated oil workers union; or Permigan, which had been formed by Minister of Mines Chaerul Saleh to dilute Sutowo's power and bolster his own.[60] The *Wall Street Journal* blared in response to the regulations that Indonesia "had taken on the trappings of a totalitarian Communist state," but oil analysts rightly observed that Jakarta lacked the technical expertise and the marketing outlets to nationalize its oil industry and that the new legislation was likely just the opening gambit by First Minister Djuanda and Chaerul Saleh in what would be a lengthy and bitter negotiating process.[61] Previously the companies and the Indonesian government worked with a straightforward 50–50 revenue split, but now their take threatened to decline significantly as the Ministry of Mines demanded a 60–40 split on future oil revenues. Indonesia's Eight-Year Plan projected a heavy reliance on increased royalties from natural resource extraction, and without a favorable agreement Sukarno's economic ambitions were dead in the water.[62]

After passage of the new oil law, Indonesian officials began soliciting bids from independent European, Japanese, and U.S. oil companies. The major oil companies feared that independent oil companies, as they were attempting to do elsewhere, would undercut them and enter the Indonesian market with lower profit margins and on less favorable terms than the majors were willing to accept. Shell, Caltex, and Stanvac executives also feared the political implications of accepting a 60–40 split, especially in the Middle East where their concessions dwarfed those in Indonesia.[63] The entry of independent oil companies globally (Anthony Sampson's classic account of the Seven Sisters called the chapter on this period "The Intruders") led to a "flood of oil coming online in places like Libya," sharply reducing prices and prompting producing nations to create OPEC in August 1960.[64] Import-dependent nations such as Japan (which imported more than 95 percent of its oil), meanwhile, were forming state-owned companies to secure their own sources of crude, as Tokyo did in 1957 when it negotiated a concession agreement with Saudi Arabia offering the kingdom a 57 percent share of profits. Three years later Japan reentered the Indonesian oil market when Permina signed a co-production agreement with a Japanese consortium, the North Sumatra Oil Development Company, for concession areas in East Aceh.[65]

The start of negotiations in 1962 illustrated just how difficult it was to separate the fortunes of U.S. oil companies from Washington's relations with Jakarta and from the conflicts that the renegotiation of concession agreements had triggered among Indonesian social and political forces. In May the Ministry of Basic Industry and Mining began negotiations with Pan American Oil, an independent subsidiary of Standard Oil of Indiana, for possible concessions in Sumatra, but after talks with Djuanda "hit a snag," Chaerul Saleh told a Pan Am representative that the first minister "had been 'captured' by Stanvac . . . and was opposed [to the] Pan Am proposal."[66] Saleh in turn told Jack Anderson of Caltex that Sukarno was "anxious [to] make [an] arrangement with Pan Am soonest because Pan Am had supported a Pro-Indonesian West Irian policy at [the] White House." On June 16, however, Pan Am officials traveled to Jakarta to initial an agreement, altering the status of Caltex, Stanvac, and Shell negotiations and forcing them to tailor their proposals for new exploration areas to the conditions met by Pan Am—most importantly, a 60–40 profit split.[67] The entry of Pan American into the Indonesian market was a textbook example of the disruptive impact that "outsiders" could have on the environment in which the major oil companies operated, scrambling their political calculations as well as those of their Indonesian partners.

The West Irian settlement also shifted the political terrain of the Indonesian government's oil negotiations, increasing Western pressure on Sukarno to move forward with economic reforms. An IMF staff report in August concluded that the government "has done little to date to stabilize the economy" and was "financially irresponsible" at a time when it lacked foreign exchange and promoted policies hostile to foreign investment. IMF and U.S. officials suggested that successful conclusion of negotiations with the oil companies, the most visible example of the American presence in Indonesia, would help restore the confidence of foreign creditors and investors and demonstrate Jakarta's good faith with the IMF and a hostile Congress, which in the spring would consider a major aid package.[68] But two could play this game of linkage. Chaerul Saleh warned that he would not sign an agreement with the oil companies until he had successfully obtained further aid from the United States, remarking to one oil company official, "I am frank, am I not?"[69]

Through early 1963 the Indonesian government's talks with Stanvac, Caltex, and Shell dragged on without resolution. The companies agreed in principle to a 60–40 profit split on new concessions, to the transfer of refining equipment, and to the sale of marketing and distribution facilities to Indonesia's state-owned oil companies, but they continued to dispute the valuation of facilities the companies were preparing to sell and how to finance them, as well as the issue of so-called "blocked Rupiah" accounts, whereby the oil companies were forced to spend domestically acquired and inflation-ravaged rupiah in Indonesia.[70] Averell Harriman assured Stanvac and Caltex representatives that the State Department wanted "to be as helpful as we can," asking if "there is anything specific the oil companies want the U.S. to do."[71] By March the companies were complaining that they had reached an impasse with Indonesian officials, as Caltex balked at demands that it provide all crude for Indonesian domestic consumption, which would "be virtually impossible for any American company to comply with." Howard Jones agreed, telling the State Department after a meeting with Julius Tahija, the top Indonesian official at Caltex, that a "real crisis is approaching."[72]

As they had earlier, oil company representatives raised the specter of Chinese oilmen "waiting in the wings" to take over for Caltex and Stanvac should negotiations fail. U.S. and British analysts, however, doubted that China could absorb or refine the quantity of oil Indonesia currently exported, however much Beijing desired to reduce its dependence on Soviet imports. But Averell Harriman was incensed, warning Chaerul Saleh that Indonesia should give "very careful consideration to economic consequences for their whole stabilization program if they pursue unreasonable demands which would force oil companies out of business." The meaning of the threat was perfectly clear: no oil contracts, no stabilization.[73] Although neither Caltex nor Stanvac had yet asked the U.S. government to intervene directly, the negotiations had become inseparable from broader U.S. policy concerns regarding stabilization, development, and the long-term position of foreign investment in Indonesia.[74] British officials voiced similar concerns, worrying about the implications of negotiations for the conflict with Jakarta over the formation of Malaysia.[75]

Before the breakdown in negotiations in the spring of 1963, the State Department and U.S. oil corporations pursued a corporatist arrangement in Indonesia that left Caltex and Stanvac to pursue their own foreign policies, despite the obvious geopolitical implications of their position in the country.[76] As Indonesia's position hardened, however, Stanvac and Caltex officials began signaling their desire for the Kennedy administration to intervene. In early March CIA director John McCone phoned Averell Harriman after speaking with Standard of California director Gwen Follis, who told him that negotiations in Indonesia were going down the tubes. "What exactly *was* going on?" he asked Harriman. The governor snapped back that the oil companies should have called him instead of McCone, a former board member of Standard Oil and founder of Bechtel-McCone Corporation, complaining that he had "repeatedly asked them what they want the government to do and each time they had asked that we keep hands off." Later that day Harriman called Follis himself, telling him, "This is a pretty deep-seated battle that is going on there. . . . We could not be helpful unless you put up a fight. If you would, we would do all we can to back you."[77]

Kennedy administration officials were perplexed. Why risk alienating the oil companies or even forcing them out of Indonesia when Jakarta was cooperating with the IMF on stabilization? The vice president of Union Oil Company suggested part of the answer when he observed that "one cost of doing business in Indonesia is that of being caught in [the] cross fire of domestic politics."[78] The recent entry of independent oil companies such as Pan American had emboldened Indonesian officials to take a tougher line in talks. But the negotiations had also sparked a political battle between First Minister Djuanda, Chaerul Saleh, and Ibnu Sutowo, each of whom favored the foreign company tied to the state-owned company with which he worked. What perplexed U.S. officials was for Indonesians a high-stakes battle over royalties, possibilities for patronage and political power, and control over the bulk of the country's foreign exchange earnings. The State Department was growing worried. "The failure [of] negotiations," George Ball cautioned, "could result [in a] dangerous strategic setback for [the] U.S. as well as [a] disastrous blow to possible Indonesian economic recovery." If the Indonesian government imposed a settlement on the oil companies, they would most likely be driven out, ending any possibility of U.S. support for a structural adjustment program and for foreign assistance to Jakarta more generally.[79]

As rumors swirled in Jakarta that the government had drafted an oil decree stopping "just short of nationalization," U.S officials made more explicit links between oil negotiations, the IMF stabilization program, and the foreign aid bill that Congress had just begun to consider. State Department officials warned First Minister Djuanda that the "unreasonable and unremitting GOI [Government of Indonesia] attitude with respect to [the] oil companies might interfere with U.S. support" for stabilization.[80] Pressure from Washington, however, threatened to stoke the fires of Indonesian nationalism, making it more difficult for Djuanda to implement the deeply unpopular IMF-backed measures. Chaerul Saleh told embassy officials that the companies and the Kennedy administration "had to consider [the] situation from [a] political as well as economic standpoint" and take into account both Indonesia's desire to control its own resources and the potent domestic opposition to Western demands.[81] On April 26 Saleh pushed through a decree [Regulation 18] giving the three oil companies just seven weeks to sign a contract according to the terms of Indonesia's new oil law. Failure to reach agreement would nullify the companies' concessions and allow the government to unilaterally impose new terms.[82] At a State Department meeting the next day, Caltex CEO Harold Arnold said now was the time to put the heat on Sukarno, remarking that "the three oil companies have reached a complete impasse with the government." We can "scarcely exaggerate harmful effect in U.S. which will be produced when Indonesian intention to administer Regulation [18] becomes known," Roger Hilsman fretted to Ambassador Jones. At stake was Indonesia's economic stability, the prospects for foreign assistance, international support for stabilization, and the confidence of foreign investors, already fragile and dissipating rapidly.[83]

With the administration already facing harsh criticism on Capitol Hill, a breakdown in oil talks could not have come at a worse time. Michael Forrestal relayed the news to President Kennedy, noting "there is already sentiment [in Congress] for barring all aid to Indonesia and news of this might pull down the house of cards." Christian Herter Jr. of Stanvac had already raised this possibility with Senate minority leader Everett Dirkson, who canvassed congressional opinion and concluded that the oil companies should "be very quiet." Averell Harriman told Fred Dutton, the State Department's assistant secretary for congressional relations, that he "could not emphasize too strongly how damaging it would be to let anybody talk about this on the Hill."[84] Howard Jones remained cautious about approaching Sukarno, insisting that such an appeal "can effectively really only be made once and should be made when real threat to American interests is clearly evident." Chaerul Saleh and Sukarno, he noted, "have had the Hickenlooper Amendment"—which in 1962 barred foreign aid to any country that expropriated U.S. property—"dinned into their ears for months."[85]

Historians have wholly overlooked the importance of the oil dispute, which threatened the position not just of U.S. capital but also of foreign investors more generally and potentially Indonesia's alignment in the Cold War. Averell Harriman argued that "U.S.-Indonesian relations have reached [their] most serious turn since Indonesian independence"—an amazing claim given Washington's massive recent covert operations in the country.[86] The time to act, the Kennedy administration concluded, was now. After conferring in London, U.S. and British officials proposed an official approach to Sukarno. The administration selected international oil consultant Walter Levy, State Department lawyer Abraham Chayes, and Wilson Wyatt—the lieutenant governor of Kentucky, Kennedy fund-raiser, and Democratic Party stalwart—to serve as the president's special emissaries to meet with Sukarno and persuade him of the need to accept a 60–40 settlement and resolve the other outstanding issues. Harriman warned Walter Levy that they had "about four weeks in which to negotiate or else the whole thing collapses and Indonesia falls into the hands of the Chinese and Russians."[87]

During this period Harriman, James Bell, and Roger Hilsman attended more than a dozen meetings with representatives of the oil companies and British officials to hammer out a strategy for the upcoming talks. From the mass of technical details a few themes emerged. First, the breakdown of negotiations had exposed the divergent interests of Washington and London. Shell's fortunes were tied to British policy on Malaysia, and the administration was not about to let U.S. oil companies suffer for it.[88] Kennedy administration officials had also concluded that Washington's interests did not necessarily coincide with Caltex and Stanvac's. Although they viewed the oil crisis in terms of the prospects for Indonesian economic stabilization and U.S. strategic interests in the region, the oil companies were primarily concerned about the repercussions of the negotiations for world oil markets and the Middle East, concerns that "reflected [a] thorough understanding of relationship of their Indonesian interests and properties everywhere else." Ambassador Jones's démarche to Sukarno emphasized that Caltex and Stanvac's Middle East interests were "obviously far more important than Indonesia"—a local market in a global constellation of interests.[89]

Finally, despite protestations to the contrary, members of the Wyatt mission had little doubt about the larger political implications of their task. Walter Levy told the oil companies that "economic and policy arguments [are] much more important" than contractual ones, a recognition that Jakarta's challenge to foreign investors in Indonesia was as much political as economic.[90] The *New York Times* warned that Sukarno's treatment of the companies was "a major test of his intentions" toward economic stabilization, Malaysia, and Western influence generally.[91] Ambassador Jones warned, however, against presenting Sukarno with such an apocalyptic picture, which would "indicate a power of life and death over Indonesia that would . . . confirm his suspicion that we are both imperialistic and out to topple him. I do not see how any self respecting head [of] State could bow to such pressure let alone one of Sukarno's ego."[92]

The Wyatt mission met with President Sukarno in Tokyo on May 29. Wyatt emphasized to Sukarno the importance of U.S. public opinion and Congress in the making of foreign policy, the need to conclude the negotiations as soon as possible, and the likely impact in Congress on aid for Indonesia if the negotiations failed.[93] Next, Walter Levy gave an overview of the Indonesian oil industry and its position in the world oil economy. He cautioned that despite its enormous potential, Indonesia needed technical expertise and equity that could be supplied only by private capital, without which Indonesia's petroleum future was bleak. Levy might have been speaking to officials from any of a dozen oil-producing countries where the paternalistic practices of the major oil companies had retarded the emergence of a large number of trained high-level officials and skilled workers and where they still controlled the refining, distribution, and marketing networks that made going it alone nearly impossible. The thrust of Levy's presentation was clear: Jakarta had no choice but to reach an accommodation with the oil companies, without which its oil industry and economy would quickly collapse.[94]

Over the next three days the Wyatt mission and Indonesian officials engaged in intensive discussions over the remaining issues: the terms for the transfer of local assets from the oil companies to the Indonesian government and Chaerul Saleh's demand that Caltex and Stanvac help finance the transfer of these distribution and refining facilities and the companies' blocked rupiah accounts. On June 1 they emerged with a preliminary "Heads of Agreement," including a straight 60–40 split on realized profits, an agreement for the remission of foreign currency after profits had been deducted, a depreciation schedule for the sale of the companies' marketing and refining assets, commitment by the companies to provide crude oil for Indonesian domestic consumption, and unrestricted use of the rupiah generated by the oil companies' Indonesian operations. Shell Oil, satisfied with the outcome of the talks, signed an identical agreement with the Indonesian government that same day.[95]

U.S. officials and the media greeted the agreement with elation, relieved that another attempt by a commodity-producing third world nation to exert greater control over its resources had been resolved on terms ultimately acceptable to U.S. multinational corporations. *Business Week* observed frankly that "in the case of economically underdeveloped nations that are the recipients of much-needed U.S. aid and are also hosts to important U.S. investments, recent efforts to link foreign aid policy with the protection of private investment give very real advantages to U.S. negotiators." *Fortune* welcomed the end to an impasse that "might have turned out to be more serious than a crisis in Berlin."[96] A representative of Socony Mobil who wrote to thank Harriman called the agreement "an especially significant example of effective coordination between government and business in the national interest." Ambassador Jones mused that "with the oil issue settled and tempers subsiding on Malaysia, a meaningful stabilization program, based on Western cooperation, now seems really possible."[97]

The May 26 Regulations

As oil negotiations began in Tokyo, First Minister Djuanda announced a series of measures aimed at demonstrating Indonesia's commitment to economic restructuring along the lines laid down by IMF and Western creditors. The regulations attempted to accomplish a number of related tasks: the dismantling of price controls and subsidies; elimination of export duties; an upward revision and simplification of exchange rates; devotion of scarce foreign exchange to a crash program of imports for industry; fiscal austerity, including major budget cuts; severe credit tightening to restrict the money supply; and pension and salary increases to compensate for price hikes. With these measures, an infusion of $300–$350 million in loans and international aid, and the rescheduling of the country's external debt, Indonesia could conceivably achieve fiscal and monetary stability within a year. Although some observers carped that the May 26 Regulations did not meet all the IMF's demands, it is hard to see what more Djuanda could have done; he had given in on almost every point of substance to a stabilization program that had almost no public support and that was guaranteed to inflame nationalist resentment at Western meddling in Indonesian affairs. Moreover, the ailing Djuanda's hopes for building political support for the regulations were complicated by the fierce power struggle taking place for his position, as Foreign Minister Subandrio, Chaerul Saleh, Information Minister Ruslan Abdulgani, and others circled "like jackals" for a shot at his position and the ear of Sukarno, who appeared content to watch from Tokyo and wait opportunistically for the dust to settle.[98]

The impact of the regulations was swift, severe, and widespread, seemingly confirming the judgment of one historian that "Sukarno's highly authoritarian and broadly based government was unable to apply policies which hurt supporters—unless suddenly and indiscriminately."[99] Prices on basic commodities, transportation, and utilities rose by 200–500 percent virtually overnight, easily outpacing cost-of-living adjustments for civil servants and taking a heavy toll on urban workers and those with fixed incomes.[100] The tight credit policies—designed to mop up the excess money supply and shift funds from state trading corporations importing luxury goods to sectors producing for export—instead caused a liquidity crisis.[101] Previously hoarded basic commodities reappeared in the market as prices rose, but now far fewer people could afford them. Export incentives also prompted a surge in exports from Sumatra to Singapore, much of it copra and rubber previously smuggled by military commanders as a way to line their pockets and finance their units.[102]

The May 26 Regulations generated strong opposition from across the Indonesian political spectrum. The PKI denounced the measures as an attack on the poor, a sign of Indonesia's dependence for aid on the United States and the IMF, and a betrayal of the revolutionary rhetoric of the DEKON.[103] The National Front, Nahdatul Ulama, the Catholic Party, the Indonesian Nationalist Party, and numerous student groups soon joined the chorus.[104] The army, in contrast, maintained a studied public silence. Sutikno Slamet recalls that the technocrats "did not see the army as either an ally or an enemy of the stabilization plan," but Nasution privately told Sukarno of army leaders' widely shared perception that "reliance on Western aid would mean a diminution of independence."[105] On the one hand, the regulations would deal a blow to the long-range interests of the PKI by enmeshing Indonesia in a web of IMF rules and Western aid arrangements. But the armed forces, particularly the navy and the air force, stood to lose from balanced budget plans that promised to slice Indonesia's bloated defense by at least one-third.[106] Army leaders had already anticipated the possibility of reduced defense spending in the wake of the West Irian settlement, shifting resources to their civic mission capacity and more economically productive activities, taking over state trading corporations, and creating army-run foundations to provide off-budget financing for local units.

The wild card was, of course, Sukarno, who approved the May 26 Regulations, inexplicably did nothing to mobilize mass opinion in their favor, and then virtually guaranteed their failure when he escalated Indonesia's *Konfrontasi* against Malaysia a few months later, foreclosing the possibility of international financial assistance upon which the regulations were predicated. Historians can only guess at his motives. The Indonesian president certainly didn't relish the prospect of attempting to mobilize support for an unpopular, foreign-backed economic program that would diminish his nationalist credentials and shift the terrain of national struggle from the plane of revolutionary discourse to the desks of technocrats charged with implementing the demands of Western creditors. But Sukarno's willingness to allow Djuanda to introduce the May 26 Regulations suggests that he recognized the gravity of the country's economic challenges, which technocrats and Ambassador Jones had been warning him about for months. It also suggested that he expected the Kennedy administration and its allies to tolerate his conflict with the British over Malaysia's formation for the sake of ensuring the regulations' implementation.[107] Julius Tahija of Caltex told Howard Jones that Sukarno planned to take "prompt and vigorous action" against those opposing stabilization, raising the possibility of "real confrontation between [the] government and [the] PKI."[108] The Indonesian president, however, did nothing and never spoke or acted forcefully on behalf of stabilization efforts. Instead he adopted an opportunistic position until *Konfrontasi* foreclosed on his choices, literally watching from afar on a lengthy foreign trip while domestic social forces slugged it out.

In addition to reaching a settlement with Western oil companies and floating his long-awaited economic stabilization plan, Sukarno in July also reached agreement with Khrushchev to reschedule Indonesia's massive debt to the Soviet Union. The administration's aid proposals for Indonesia were "all premised upon [a] Soviet debt moratorium," both as a political requirement for further economic assistance and as a signal of Sukarno's intentions vis-à-vis Western influence. Without it, neither the United States nor its allies could risk extending new loans to Jakarta for fear it "would use them to pay off debts to the Bloc," causing a predictable explosion in Congress.[109] Indonesia's debt to the USSR alone, much of it undertaken in the aftermath of the PRRI rebellions, represented one-fourth of its balance of payments deficit and 40 percent of its debt-servicing load.[110] Indonesian officials first broached the debt issue during the visit of Soviet Defense Minister Malinovsky in late March. A few weeks later, shortly before Soviet technicians arrived to begin negotiations, Indonesia announced it was unilaterally cutting payments on Eastern European debt by 50 percent over the next two years (from $83 million to $41 million) and deferring payment on the rest. *Antara* reported that Indonesian and Soviet officials had agreed to reschedule Jakarta's debt payments, apparently codifying Indonesia's unilateral decision.[111]

Dean Rusk called Jakarta's actions over the past few months the "most significant move towards [a] West orientation of [the] Indonesian economy since independence."[112] The agreement with the Soviets opened the door for IMF action on a stabilization loan and for a DAC agreement on increased aid to Indonesia. "The Indo[nesians] have complied sufficiently with our pressure for stabilization and Bloc debt rollover," Robert Komer told Kennedy, "that we ought to go ahead on getting Europeans to chip in" at the DAC meeting about to begin in Paris.[113] Indonesia was perilously close to exhausting its foreign exchange reserves, a scenario with potentially devastating consequences. But despite continued protest against the May 26 Regulations, the Indonesian economy was showing signs of improvement, with commodity prices leveling off, exports rising, and import receipts surging.[114] U.S. officials looked back on the events of the past two months with cautious optimism, aware of the precariousness of their position yet hopeful that Sukarno was inaugurating a meaningful shift toward the West.[115]

CHAPTER 5

From High Hopes to Low Profile

As the Kennedy administration sought in the spring and summer of 1963 to mobilize support for its Indonesian aid strategy, it anxiously scanned the Southeast Asian horizon for potential trouble. U.S., European, Australian, and Japanese observers worried that Sukarno and the military had aims of regional dominance and that the campaign of brinkmanship to recover West Irian had only whetted their appetite.[1] Critics now portrayed Sukarno as harboring expansionist ambitions—casting his gaze toward Papua New Guinea, North Borneo, or Portuguese Timor, which U.S. officials thought "ripe for the plucking at any time."[2] Moreover, support in Washington for the White House's vision of Indonesian military modernization rested on a thin reed. Just how thin would be demonstrated a few months later when Sukarno, with tentative support from the military and the enthusiastic backing of the PKI, launched Indonesia on a campaign of confrontation (*Konfrontasi*) with Britain and Malaya over the formation of Malaysia.

Konfrontasi would dramatically transform Indonesia's foreign relations and the regional strategies of the United States and the United Kingdom, each inseparable from the widening war in Vietnam. The South Vietnamese government's repression of Buddhist demonstrators in May 1963 provoked a major political crisis that eventually led to the overthrow of the government of President Ngo Dinh Diem. The deepening spiral in Vietnam heightened the stakes of halting Indonesia's perceived leftward drift at the same time that it constrained the options available to American and Commonwealth policymakers. *Konfrontasi* would also accelerate Indonesia's economic decline, exacerbate the conflict between the armed forces, anti-Communist political and religious groups, and the PKI, and substantially raise the risks of a domestic conflagration. Over the course of the next year, as *Konfrontasi* expanded in tandem with the U.S. war in Vietnam, the Johnson administration would gradually jettison its "accommodationist" strategy of working with Sukarno to promote military-led modernization in Indonesia; in its place the U.S. adopted a covert strategy aimed at ousting Sukarno and thus sparking a violent conflict between the armed forces and the PKI.

Britain and Southeast Asian Decolonization

Britain's formation of Malaysia marked the end of its imperial role in Southeast Asia. Beginning in 1957, when the British granted Malaya independence while retaining formal or informal control over the territories of Sabah, Sarawak, Singapore, and the tiny oil-rich sultanate of Brunei, London sought a decolonization process that would both meet legitimate nationalist demands in the region and maintain British dominance over its Far Eastern territories by enmeshing them in a network of economic, political, and security relations.[3] That challenge was especially acute in Singapore, which was granted self-government in 1959; there, anti-Communist prime minister Lee Kuan Yew faced demands from the left-wing Barisan Socialist Party for immediate independence, a socialist constitution, and the removal of the British base complex. Sukarno disliked Lee because Singapore cooperated with the CIA during the PRRI rebellions and tolerated anti-Sukarno dissidents and smugglers who wandered freely back and forth across the straits.[4]

Although Singapore handled fully half of Indonesia's export trade, it also turned a blind eye to the massive export of rubber, copra, and tin by local military units in Sumatra, including future army leaders such as Ibnu Sutowo and Suharto.[5]

British officials had long urged a federation among their former colonial possessions in the region, but until mid-1961 Malaya's prime minister Tunku Abdul Rahman (known as the Tunku) and other conservatives opposed a merger with Chinese-dominated Singapore, prompting the Foreign Office to suggest adding the territories of Sabah, Sarawak, and Brunei to ensure a Chinese minority in Malaysia.[6] A commission of inquiry in Sabah and Sarawak concluded in June that, despite evidence of widespread local opposition, the population favored federation with Malaysia, leading to an agreement in November 1961 that paved the way for a Malaysian federation.[7] Through the end of 1962 Indonesian officials voiced little opposition to the proposed merger, although the CIA reported that Indonesian intelligence, local army units, and left-wing parties were assisting opponents of Malaysia in Kalimantan and Brunei. Preoccupied with the mobilization to recover West Irian, however, Sukarno paid little public attention to the matter. Foreign Minister Subandrio assured British prime minister Harold Macmillan during a visit to London that Indonesia supported Malaysia; he repeated his assurances in an address to the United Nations General Assembly.[8] But the Indonesian president's ideological commitment to the doctrine of the new emerging forces and to a permanent struggle against colonialism convinced the British that Sukarno would be drawn to oppose Malaysia after he had settled accounts with the Dutch. The White House offered muted support for Malaysia, considering it "a neat and positive arrangement whereby British influence and military presence could still be sustained in the region." Malaya had the most prosperous economy in Southeast Asia in 1962, producing nearly one-third of the world's rubber and tin and providing its citizens with a per capita income more than double that of Indonesia. But U.S. officials also recognized that Indonesia viewed Malaysia as a threat, and they were leery of taking on added defense burdens. Already tied down in Laos and Vietnam, officials such as Averell Harriman were determined that the United States not become involved.[9] As Washington intervened more deeply in Southeast Asia, the strategic implications of Britain's military presence weighed heavy in its considerations.

The Brunei Uprising

British plans for Malaysia rested on a surprisingly shaky foundation. On December 8, 1962, two thousand poorly trained and ill-equipped members of the little known North Borneo National Army (Tentara Nasional Kalimantan Utara, or TNKU) launched an ill-fated revolt against the Sultan of Brunei and proclaimed the Unitary State of Kalimantan. Within hours local police and British troops flown in from Singapore crushed the clumsy operation. Lee Kuan Yew immediately used the revolt as a pretext for arresting scores of political opponents, much to the delight of the Tunku, who had demanded repression of Singapore's restive left wing as the price of admission to Malaysia.[10] The Tunku quickly charged Indonesia with supporting the Brunei rebels, but contemporary evidence suggests that, although supportive, Jakarta was surprised by the revolt. The Kennedy administration wasn't taking any chances, however, and on a visit to Jakarta NSC staffer Michael Forrestal bluntly warned Sukarno against trying to block Malaysia's formation, which he said the United States "intend[s] to support vigorously."[11] A few days later Subandrio accused Malaysia's leaders of being "accomplices of the neocolonialists and neo-imperialists pursuing a hostile policy towards Indonesia" and announced that Jakarta "cannot but adopt a policy of confrontation," the contours of which he left deliberately vague. British officials immediately pressed Washington to publicly back Malaysia while they sped up the timetable leading to its formation.[12]

The Kennedy administration's response highlighted its commitment to maintaining good relations with Jakarta. The CIA had known that the TNKU was training in Indonesian Borneo and was well aware of the level of anti-Malaysia sentiment inside Brunei. But Washington's priority was reinforcing Indonesian support for stabilization, and it considered the likelihood that Indonesia would risk war with Britain to be quite low.[13] As the State Department signed $40 million in new aid deals with Jakarta, Averell Harriman told British ambassador Sir David Ormsby Gore that the United States would not subordinate its regional priorities to Britain's parochial interests. Although the United States supported Malaysia's formation and needed British support on Vietnam and Laos, it would do everything possible to avoid publicly siding with Britain at a moment when it was asking Indonesia to enact painful economic reforms and turn to the West.[14]

U.S. officials were at a loss to explain what Jakarta hoped to accomplish in a seemingly irrational conflict with no clear goals, no chance of success, and potentially disastrous consequences. Most historians have concluded that Sukarno's support for *Konfrontasi* stemmed from a complicated combination of ideology, domestic politics, and strategic calculations. His radical nationalism, visceral hatred of colonialism, enormous ego, and belief that Indonesia had a legitimate right to shape events in Southeast Asia inclined him to oppose the manner in which Malaysia was being created—as a colonial project rather than as an outcome of struggle.[15] Indonesia's critics charged that Sukarno embraced *Konfrontasi* primarily as a means of distracting Indonesians from the country's economic crisis.[16] Most Indonesian elites viewed the proposed Malaysian federation as a neocolonial project, a view reinforced by London's crushing of the Brunei revolt, the Tunku's insistence on moving ahead quickly with federation, and Britain's confrontational diplomacy in the summer of 1963. But the army and the PKI had their own institutional and ideological reasons for supporting *Konfrontasi*. The army feared British might and sought to recoup the power lost at the end of the West Irian campaign; it used the dispute to delay the end of martial law, put off national elections scheduled for 1964, and resist budget cuts demanded by the IMF. The PKI sought to bolster its position vis-à-vis the army and Sukarno, enhance its nationalist credentials, derail Djuanda's economic efforts, and steer Indonesia's foreign policy away from the West.[17] There were few countervailing forces.

Indonesian concerns about Chinese influence in Southeast Asia also shaped the politics of *Konfrontasi* but in ways that defied straightforward calculation. "The problem of the Chinese," Robert Barnett wrote Averell Harriman, "is infinitely complex." The Sino-Indian border war and Mao's battle with Khrushchev for international leadership suggested to many Kennedy administration officials that Communist China was becoming expansionist and posed the chief threat to U.S. interests in the region.[18] Sukarno, Nasution, and almost all Indonesian elites thought China was "naturally expansionist," not because it was Communist but because it was China, a country of 700 million whose overseas population—2.5 million of them living in Indonesia—dominated the trading economies of many Southeast Asian countries. Chinese Indonesians were often the targets of nationalist wrath, discriminatory regulations, and occasional physical attacks by Indonesians who resented their relatively privileged economic position, measures sometimes tacitly or directly backed by Sukarno and the PKI even as they forged closer ties with Beijing.[19] It was such logic that spurred Sukarno to offer rhetorical support for Philippine president Diosdado Macapagal's proposal for a loose federation of Malaysia, Indonesia, and the Philippines, telling him that "the time now had come when petty quarrels should be set aside in order to join forces in the face of a common Chinese enemy."[20]

On February 13, as his economic advisers went to Washington to negotiate with IMF officials, Sukarno spoke before a mass rally in Jakarta where he charged that the formation of Malaysia was "the product of the brain, the thinking, the goals, the effort, the initiative of neo-colonialism."[21] Indonesia's rhetorical escalation of what was now being called *Konfrontasi* convinced the British government of the need to push Malaysian federation as quickly as possible. Prime Minister Macmillan called for a quadripartite meeting in Washington, but he was bitterly disappointed when Australian and New Zealand officials balked at backing Britain without firm U.S. security guarantees; in addition, Averell Harriman said that American influence with Sukarno "would be used solely to keep Indonesia out of the Communist bloc and not as a means of forcing him to support Malaysia" so long as Indonesian behavior stayed within tolerable bounds.[22] An attack by Indonesian troops in the border region of Sarawak, held on the eve of tripartite talks between Philippine, Indonesian, and Malaysian officials, suggested that Washington could be quite tolerant.[23]

Over the next few months, however, Indonesia took significant steps to de-escalate *Konfrontasi*. In early June Malayan foreign minister Tun Razak, Subandrio, and Philippine foreign minister Emmanuel Pelaez negotiated what became known as the Manila Accord. The accord affirmed shared responsibility for guaranteeing the stability and security of the region and endorsed Philippine president Macapagal's proposal for a grouping of the Malay nations, called Maphilindo. The Philippines and Indonesia also announced that they would "welcome" Malaysia, provided that the U.N. could ascertain that the populations of Sabah and Sarawak were supportive.[24] The Macmillan government was unimpressed, dismissing Maphilindo as "a complete sham" and pointing to continued Indonesian cross-border incursions as a better signal of Jakarta's intentions.[25] But at an ANZUS council meeting in Canberra, Indonesian stabilization and oil negotiations—not Malaysia—topped the State Department's agenda. "The loss of Indonesia to the Bloc," the State Department argued, "would be an infinitely more grave threat to our mutual security than any development we now anticipate as likely to arise from Indonesia's position in the Malaysia dispute."[26]

A month after the Manila Accord, Indonesia's progress on stabilization, oil negotiations, and Malaysia seemed to signal a shift toward the West, fulfilling the Clay Committee's benchmarks for continuing U.S. assistance.[27] Defeating congressional attempts to limit U.S. aid now became a priority for the White House, which lobbied Representative William Broomfield, fed articles to sympathetic congressmen to enter into the *Congressional Record*, and enlisted lobbying help from Caltex and Stanvac executives.[28] In Jakarta the embassy pointed to continued congressional hostility to pressure Indonesia. Howard Jones recalled that "hovering wraith-like in the background" of his meetings with Indonesian officials "was [the] obvious specter of [the] Broomfield amendment and [the] serious market reaction here which could occur if speculators began to discount [the] likelihood [of] continuance [of] U.S. assistance."[29]

The "Manila spirit" on which U.S. officials pinned so many of their hopes lasted all of a month. On July 9, 1963, British officials signed an agreement with the Tunku, Lee Kuan Yew, and the leaders of the North Borneo territories to establish Malaysia on August 31, signaling that they intended to go ahead regardless of the outcome of any U.N. ascertainment. Sukarno was furious, and on July 11 he angrily announced the resumption of *Konfrontasi*.[30] The Indonesian military was more cautious, in part because of the explicit warnings given by U.S. officials that "overt military activity against Malaysia would entirely foreclose all prospects of U.S. aid."[31] But Congress was ill-inclined to search for shades of gray in Jakarta's actions. On July 25 the House Foreign Affairs Committee let the air out of the administration's tires and approved the Broomfield amendment, which banned further aid to Indonesia.[32] The administration now faced the difficult prospect of convincing its allies to provide aid for Indonesia that Congress had just rejected, and opponents of stabilization in Indonesia pointed to the Broomfield amendment as a prime example of why Indonesia could not trust the West and should not bow to pressure over Malaysia.[33]

Hoping to prevent a widening of the conflict, Sukarno and Philippine president Macapagal met with the Tunku to discuss the timetable for Malaysia's formation. At this meeting Sukarno traded his demand for a plebiscite in the

North Borneo territories in exchange for the Tunku's agreement that Malaysia's formation might be delayed slightly to accommodate a U.N. mission of inquiry in Sabah and Sarawak.[34] The White House realized that the West would now need to provide political cover for a dignified retreat from *Konfrontasi* by showing it was serious about helping Indonesia. "Sukarno's expectation of substantial external assistance from the west and notably the United States *must not be disappointed*," Robert Barnett wrote to Averell Harriman upon returning from a lengthy tour of Southeast Asian capitals.[35] With the early returns on Indonesia's stabilization program trickling in, IMF officials returned to Jakarta to evaluate its eligibility for a $50 million stabilization loan, shortly before the Development Advisory Committee (DAC) was to meet in Paris to consider an additional Indonesian request for $250 million to meet its balance of payments obligations, finance essential imports, and avert an exchange rate meltdown.[36] The United States convinced the IMF to approve Jakarta's request, even though it had met few of its austerity requirements, but DAC members balked.[37] Congressional critics of Indonesia were outraged that the Kennedy administration was even trying to bail out Sukarno. The House took a sharp knife to the administration's proposed foreign aid budget for 1964, slicing 20 percent from the White House's original request for $5 billion.[38]

As Congress was slashing the administration's foreign aid budget, the U.N. mission conducted its survey in Sabah and Sarawak. Into this powder keg strode the short-fused Commonwealth secretary Duncan Sandys, who encouraged the Malayan cabinet to declare that Malaysia would come into being regardless of what the U.N. determined. When U Thant's report, issued on September 14, concluded that "there is no doubt about the wishes of a sizeable majority of the peoples of [Sabah and Sarawak] to join the Federation of Malaysia," both the Indonesian and Philippines cabinets decided to withhold recognition.[39] Two days later the Tunku proclaimed Malaysia Day, sparking massive and violent demonstrations in both countries. When Malaya recalled its ambassador and broke relations with Indonesia, demonstrators, partly organized under the auspices of Sukarno's National Front, sacked and burned the British embassy and destroyed British residences throughout Jakarta.[40] The next day Sukarno announced the administrative takeover of all British companies and the severing of all trade with Malaysia, including Singapore, through which half of Indonesia's imports and exports passed.[41]

Sukarno's decision to cut off trade with Malaysia—an act of "economic idiocy" in the words of one administration official—was a dramatic act with far-reaching consequences, among the least of which was depriving Indonesia of the bulk of the foreign exchange earnings it needed to meet its commitments to the IMF.[42] Severing trade ties also deprived Stanvac and Shell Oil of their Malaysian markets for fuel oil and cut off access to entrepôt and refining facilities in Singapore, which were used for distributing oil throughout Southeast Asia. Exports of smallholder rubber, tin ore, copra, and coffee fell sharply, and the earnings of many small-scale producers and exporters of agricultural goods simply "disappeared."[43] The severing of economic ties with Malaysia "shattered the keystone" of the Kennedy administration's post–West Irian plans for Indonesia. Jones and other accommodationists had long argued that, faced with economic collapse, dependence on the Soviet bloc, or a potential PKI rise to power, Sukarno would respond by bolstering internal security and deepening Indonesia's economic ties to the West. In fact, Sukarno seemed to be doing the opposite. The escalation of *Konfrontasi* also alienated Indonesia from other nonaligned nations, many of which, as Pakistani officials told Lord Home and Dean Rusk, considered the conflict "an entirely different matter from the colonial issue of West Irian since it involved two Afro-Asian states."[44]

On September 23 an interagency working group met at the White House to consider the future of U.S. assistance to Indonesia.[45] Given the fierce reaction to Sukarno's actions, many officials favored a significant aid reduction or even a total cutoff, but Kennedy's "strong, clear stand for restraint" held them in check. "With a strong president whose views were known," Michael Forrestal recalls, "no one person felt strong enough to want to buck him."[46] Congress was another matter, with Representative Broomfield and other opponents calling for an immediate aid suspension. "If history has taught us one lesson," the Michigan congressman said, "it is that you cannot appease a power-mad dictator." The next day the United States announced that it was halting all new economic assistance to Jakarta and temporarily holding up shipments of weapons and ammunition. Shipments of rice, technical assistance, MAP aid, and assistance to the Mobile Police Brigade would continue.[47] Sutikno Slamet ruefully told AID officials that he now saw "virtually no hope for stabilization," as *Konfrontasi* galvanized domestic opponents, who called for wholesale revision or repudiation of the May 26 regulations.

As Washington went, so did the IMF, which suspended $30 million in undisbursed aid from its standby arrangement with Jakarta. The DAC likewise canceled its upcoming meeting on Indonesia.[48]

Once again, Indonesian foreign relations spilled over into oil politics. PKI-affiliated unions attempted to seize Shell Oil facilities and attacked Shell properties.[49] Whitehall feared the worst. "I cannot but feel," Prime Minister Macmillan wrote President Kennedy, "that to allow Sukarno to drive a wedge between us in this matter of the oil companies would give him exactly the sign for which he was looking."[50] Although Kennedy hoped to avoid linking British fortunes in Jakarta to those of the United States, Macmillan was right. Indonesian actions against Shell Oil and other British properties posed a general threat to the position of foreign capital in Indonesia, forcing the hand of U.S. officials. On September 21 Ambassador Jones met with Sukarno and demanded the immediate return of all British properties and prompt compensation for all properties destroyed in the anti-British rioting.[51] A few days later Indonesia signed contracts with Caltex, Stanvac, and Shell, "one of the very few bright signs that have come out of Jakarta" in an otherwise dismal week, NSC staffer C. L. Alexander told McGeorge Bundy.[52] The events of the previous weeks were a blunt reminder of Washington's limited leverage in Indonesia. The United States had to set more modest goals now, the State Department cabled ambassadors in the region: maintaining crucial ties to the army and police, continuing with a scaled-back program of assistance, and facilitating a way for Sukarno to climb down from *Konfrontasi*. As relations with Jakarta deteriorated, the Kennedy administration and later the Johnson administration were forced to grapple with the possibility that Washington's plans for drawing Indonesia toward the West had failed and that a new strategy, commensurate with the gravity of the perceived threat posed by Sukarno's continued march to the left, was needed.[53]

Pulling Sukarno's Chestnuts out of the Fire:
U.S. 'Konfrontasi' Diplomacy

Sukarno's resumption of *Konfrontasi* in the fall of 1963 decisively altered Indonesia's political and economic trajectory and its relationship with the United States. For the Kennedy administration *Konfrontasi* spelled the decline of the accommodationist policy current and the end of its ambitious plans for using economic, military, and multilateral assistance to accelerate Indonesia's modernization. Walt Rostow later expressed his frustration "that Sukarno could not bring himself to settle down to the modernization of Indonesia and let the matter of Malaysia be dealt with peacefully." The escalation of *Konfrontasi* signaled that "a point of no return [had been] passed," wrote J. A. C. Mackie; it marked the end of Indonesia's attempts at economic stabilization, accelerated the unraveling of the economy, and exacerbated the political polarization of Indonesian society.[54]

With the stakes so high, administration officials had no choice but to involve the United States more directly in diplomatic efforts to defuse *Konfrontasi*. The dispute threatened to escalate into a major regional conflict at the very moment when the Vietnam War was emerging as America's single most significant foreign policy challenge and the British were expressing serious doubts about U.S. strategy.[55] Even at the zenith of its power, Washington could ill afford to become directly involved in the Malaysia conflict without adversely affecting its commitments elsewhere in Southeast Asia, and over the next two years it would struggle with this conflict between its ambitious goals toward Indonesia, the limited reach of U.S. aid and influence, and the pressing commitments of its regional allies. The White House's chief goal in the fall of 1963 was to defuse *Konfrontasi* and force Indonesia, Malaysia, and the Philippines back to the bargaining table. Howard Jones warned Rusk that it would be a "serious mistake" to publicly attack or otherwise isolate Sukarno, a move that would only increase his militancy and dependence on the PKI.[56] The Tunku, however, refused to consider a return to talks until Sukarno agreed to a cease-fire and a total withdrawal of Indonesian troops from Sarawak and Sabah.

The British dilemma was especially acute. As the CIA observed, *Konfrontasi* had exposed "a critical gap between its commitments in the Malaysian areas and its capabilities," disrupting its goal of reducing regional military expenditures and partially withdrawing from east of the Suez. British intelligence recognized that a prolonged Indonesian insurgency in Borneo would hemorrhage the nation's resources, but policymakers in London wavered between the need to end *Konfrontasi* as quickly as possible and their desire to punish Indonesia by provoking an army-PKI clash leading to Sukarno's ouster. James Cable, head of the Southeast Asian Department of the Foreign Office, argued that "an army *coup d'état* would become a real possibility if it were evident that Malaysia could not be broken and the Indonesian economy appeared to be on the point of collapse."[57] Although U.S. officials in principle supported Sukarno's ouster, they thought that such talk was irresponsible and premature while there was still a chance that a combination of threats, pressure, and incentives might lead to a negotiated settlement. The contrast with Vietnam—where the administration was working to block negotiations and where support for a coup against Ngo Dinh Diem was growing—was striking.

The divergent aims and priorities of the United States and its closest allies over Indonesia emerged in crystalline form at quadripartite talks held in mid-October 1963. Averell Harriman argued that Sukarno had no "concrete long-range plan for expansion" in the region, was not as vulnerable to outside pressure as the British thought, faced "no significant domestic threat," and would be unlikely to change his policy on *Konfrontasi* in response to an aid cutoff.[58] Australian prime minister Menzies and New Zealand prime minister Keith Holyoake were by now being pulled in opposite directions. Whitehall persistently pressed Australia and New Zealand to commit troops to Borneo, both to reinforce the British presence and to invoke Washington's commitments under the ANZUS Treaty. Washington's goal on the other hand, "was to establish mechanisms by which [it] would maintain a degree of control over Australasian military involvement in confrontation" while ensuring that its allies could not inhibit U.S. action.[59]

In Jakarta Howard Jones doggedly defended U.S. engagement with Sukarno and the Indonesian armed forces. He continued to insist that the army was not the primary threat to British interests in the region. Congressional critics disagreed.[60] At the end of October William Broomfield and Clement Zablocki, chairman of the Far East and Pacific Subcommittee of the House Foreign Affairs Committee, returned from a two-week trip to Southeast Asia condemning Indonesian expansionism. A week later Wisconsin senator William Proxmire introduced an amendment to cut off all remaining aid to Jakarta barring a presidential determination, branding Sukarno "a new oriental Hitler."[61] The amendment passed in a lopsided vote, as did the Gruening amendment, which barred assistance to countries "engaging in or preparing for aggressive military efforts," setting up the confrontation with Congress over aid to Indonesia that Kennedy had wished to avoid.[62]

It was on this dour note that Ambassador Jones returned to Washington in early November to propose, with Assistant Secretary of State Roger Hilsman and Averill Harriman, a last ditch "package deal" to President Kennedy: In exchange for Sukarno's commitment to tripartite negotiations and a withdrawal of Indonesian forces from Kalimantan, the president would resuscitate multilateral aid and visit Indonesia as part of a broader Southeast Asian tour. The president approved, and as a sweetener authorized the sale of 40,000 tons of rice and a visit by General Nasution to the United States.[63] Linking his commitment to military modernization with the administration's goal of regional economic integration, Hilsman also urged President Kennedy to use the Southeast Asian trip to push for a "new pacific partnership" that would join "the developed countries of the pacific" to the "less developed countries in a program of nation building," linking "deterrence of Communist aggression" with "the construction of a viable system of free-world societies through economic and technical assistance."[64]

Kennedy's approval of Jones's gambit is a testimony to the strategic and economic importance he ascribed to Indonesia. Michael Forrestal recalls that Kennedy "used to say quite brutally, 'Indonesia is a nation of 100 million with perhaps more resources than any other nation in Asia. . . . It doesn't make any sense for U.S. to go out of way permanently to alienate this large group of people sitting on these resources, unless there is some very, very persuasive reason for doing it.'"[65] Three days later the president was assassinated in Dallas, magnifying the impact of First Minister Djuanda's death from a heart attack just two weeks earlier. Ambassador Jones characterized Djuanda as "the only member of the cabinet who saw the Indonesian problem 'whole.'" He was also the only person whom Sukarno seemed to trust on economic matters. He was an architect of IMF-led stabilization, a lightning rod for PKI criticism (and therefore acceptable to the army), and the most powerful Sukarno-era proponent of cementing Indonesian ties to the West while giving the state a leading role in economic development.[66]

Lyndon Johnson and Indonesia

In the days following Kennedy's death, Lyndon Johnson spent much of his time on the phone with heads of state, domestic business leaders, and members of Congress to reassure them that he was firmly in control and intended to carry through with Kennedy's policies. Nowhere was such continuity needed more than in Southeast Asia. The assassination of Ngo Dinh Diem in South

Vietnam had opened a chaotic scramble for power that only highlighted that country's dependence on U.S. largesse and firepower for survival. President Johnson harbored real worries about the growing U.S. military presence in Vietnam and even greater worries about the domestic consequences of failing. In a meeting with Henry Cabot Lodge and other advisers he argued "now that it was done, we have to see that our objectives are accomplished." He pledged to Bill Moyers, "I am not going to lose Vietnam. I am not going to be the President who saw Southeast Asia go the same way China went."[67]

Indonesia was on the far periphery of Johnson's concerns when General Nasution arrived in Washington just two days after Kennedy's assassination. The State Department encouraged Johnson to receive the armed forces chief, noting that he was the "chief counterweight" to Sukarno and "by far the most likely successor" should the president die or be overthrown. The CIA was less gracious, describing Nasution as "an apologist" for *Konfrontasi* and soft on the matter of ousting Sukarno. In their meeting Johnson broke new ground, giving the general perfunctory assurances of the continuity of U.S. policy.[68] Two weeks later, on the eve before he returned to Jakarta, Howard Jones also met with President Johnson, stressing the importance of establishing a close relationship with Sukarno and urging him to meet Indonesia's president at the earliest opportunity. Johnson again was unmoved, musing, "I wonder whether the closer we get to Sukarno the more difficult he becomes."[69]

Historians have spilled much ink arguing whether Kennedy's death altered the basic direction of the U.S. war against Vietnam, but the assassination unquestionably changed the direction of U.S. policy toward Indonesia. Forrestal noted that "an Indonesian policy requires a positive effort by the President because there are not that many people in the government who care and there are many who oppose." Kennedy had cared and was willing to expend political capital; Johnson decided early on that "he was not going to bear any political burdens on behalf of Indonesia." The new president described his dislike of Sukarno in visceral, strongly gendered terms. "When you let a bully come in and start raiding you in your front yard, if you run, he'll come in and run you out of your bedroom the next night," he told Robert McNamara. "I don't think we ought to encourage this guy [Sukarno] to do what he is doing there. And I think any assistance just shows weakness on our part."[70] Lyndon Johnson was neither interested in Indonesia nor inclined to spend political capital pushing policies that were unpopular in Congress, where he had much more pressing concerns—such as passing the martyred president's civil rights bill. Unsurprisingly, when aide Kermit Gordon showed up at Johnson's ranch over Christmas bearing the presidential determination Johnson would need to sign to keep aid to Indonesia flowing, Johnson balked. "I talked to Dick Russell about that and he says that I ought to be impeached if I approve it," he half-joked to Robert McNamara. But the decision provoked bitterness among some Kennedy administration officials. "Everyone down the line," Roger Hilsman later wrote, knew that "Kennedy would have signed the determination routinely."[71]

Two weeks later the NSC met to discuss the presidential determination amid a backdrop of repeated Indonesian military incursions into Malaysia.[72] The president's advisers were in a difficult position; they were unified in their increasing opposition to Sukarno and sensitive to the pressure created by passage of the Broomfield and Gruening amendments, but they were wary of cutting aid much further. The State Department had already slashed funding for FY 1964 by 80 percent to just over $15 million, and reducing aid much further would mean severing crucial links to the Indonesian military.[73] "Nobody likes Sukarno, and with good reason," McGeorge Bundy observed, "but . . . we are contending for the long-range future in a country of 100 million with great resources in a strategic location." Rusk agreed. "More is involved in Indonesia," he argued, "than is at stake in Vietnam." Cutting aid further would eliminate one of the few remaining sources of U.S. leverage, have little effect on Sukarno's efforts to undermine Malaysia, and, according to CIA director John McCone, probably lead to the takeover of U.S. investments.[74]

The question, then, was what to do about Congress. Bundy suggested that Johnson send Robert Kennedy to Jakarta to "tell Sukarno the hard and brutal truth," as the embassy seemed unwilling to do. After remaining silent for much of the meeting, Johnson finally spoke. Do we have to make a decision now? he asked Rusk. The administration had just been through a prolonged and bitter fight with Congressman Otto Passman over the foreign aid budget for FY 1964. "I'm really humiliated that I'm President [and] that a goddamn Cajun from the hills of Louisiana has got more power than all of us," he told Speaker of the House John McCormick. Dismissing his aides' advice, Johnson directed Rusk and McNamara to discreetly consult with congressional leaders about the possibility of continuing aid already in the pipeline without a determination, so long as no new aid commitments were made.[75] To convince Congress that he took its concerns seriously, Johnson dispatched Robert Kennedy to Jakarta, a move that both conveyed the proper resolve and got his disliked attorney general out of town for a few weeks. "I am going to send Bobby Kennedy to Indonesia and just let them put it in his lap," he confided to Richard Russell. "Let him go out there and have whatever row there is with Sukarno."[76]

The younger Kennedy did not relish his task. "I did not like him from what I heard of him," he told Arthur Schlesinger after his first visit to Indonesia in 1962. "I did not like him when I was there and I haven't liked him since." The British weren't excited either, viewing any U.S. attempts at mediation as a prelude to demands for concessions from Malaysia.[77] After a week of whirlwind meetings, Kennedy convinced President Sukarno, Philippine president Macapagal, and Tunku Abdul Rahman to meet, and he secured an Indonesian commitment to halt military action in Kalimantan.[78] It looked as though Kennedy might finally have gotten *Konfrontasi* "out of the jungle and onto the conference table," Robert Komer wrote President Johnson.[79] The attorney general's satisfaction at having brokered a cease-fire quickly dissipated when he returned to the White House to brief the president and found an "open klieg lit Cabinet meeting" filled with reporters. He felt sandbagged, convinced that neither Lyndon Johnson nor Dean Rusk gave "a damn about his effort."[80] Appropriately, the cease-fire on which Washington pinned its brief hopes collapsed almost before it began, as the Tunku and Sukarno came to starkly different conclusions over whether the cease-fire required Indonesian forces to withdraw from Malaysian territory. Three months later Ambassador Jones wrote that the meaning of Kennedy's agreement still was "not entirely clear."[81]

The Foreign Office opposed negotiations altogether, arguing that Sukarno's goal was the destruction of Malaysia and the expulsion of Britain from Southeast Asia and that talks would raise only nonnegotiable issues, such as British base facilities in Singapore and the Anglo-Malaysian defense agreement. Officials in Canberra and Wellington largely shared these concerns. British policymakers were similarly dismissive of the State Department and White House's efforts to differentiate between Sukarno's and the armed forces' attitudes toward Malaysia, fearing that close aid and training ties had blinded them to the danger that the Indonesian military posed to Western interests in Southeast Asia.[82] Over the course of the winter they stepped up efforts to block weapons sales and military training for Jakarta not only from the United States but also from Germany, Italy, France, Japan, and Canada, and they delighted in pointing to Indonesia when pressed by U.S. officials on the issue of continued British trade with Cuba, the Soviet Union, and China.[83] At quadripartite talks held in Washington in early February 1964, Edward Peck, head of the Far Eastern Department of the British Foreign Office, argued that by pushing negotiations, the United States was letting Sukarno off the hook, drawing out *Konfrontasi*, and pressuring Malaysia to make unacceptable concessions. It would be far better, argued Australian ambassador to Indonesia Keith Shann, to isolate Indonesia and let things "deteriorate to a point where internal difficulties will either force the overthrow or neutralization of Sukarno."[84] U.S. officials responded that they "just did not want to be dragged into a ten year jungle war to support a country like Malaysia against a country like Indonesia." American intelligence estimates uniformly concluded that the Indonesian president's grip on power was unlikely to be challenged during his lifetime. The United States had no choice but to try to maintain decent relations with Sukarno, Averell Harriman argued, "unless, of course, some of our friends wished to try to overthrow him."[85]

The Hard-Line Resurgence

Although the White House maintained to Congress and its British allies that U.S policy toward Indonesia had not changed, many officials were losing patience with Ambassador Jones's approach to Sukarno and the logic of accommodation, and those who disagreed were losing their jobs. Over the course of 1964 Jones's allies in Washington fought a rearguard battle against a rising tide of hard-line sentiment on Indonesia. The accommodationists were felled as much by the regional and global implications of the escalating U.S. commitment to Vietnam as by the growing frustration with Sukarno and *Konfrontasi*. Within months of Kennedy's death, policymakers critical of the drift of U.S. policy on Vietnam—especially the introduction of massive ground forces—resigned, were removed, or simply lost their influence and were ignored as McGeorge Bundy, Robert McNamara, and Dean Rusk cemented their control over the policy-making process. Among the casualties were Averell Harriman, Roger Hilsman, and Michael Forrestal, the strongest backers of the Kennedy administration's post–West Irian strategy of integrated military and economic assistance aimed at Indonesia's long-range political and economic modernization.[86] Rusk quickly became one of the president's closest and most loyal advisers—bad news for those who had harshly criticized him or gone over his head to President Kennedy just a few months earlier.[87] Harriman's exile was particularly hard. Kennedy's ambassador to Malaysia, Charles Baldwin, credited him with being the architect of the administration's Indonesia-Malaysia policy. AID assistant administrator for the Far East Seymour Janow argued that Harriman "more than any other, knew the pitfalls, the political obloquy to be expected upon" the Kennedy administration for its aggressive commitment to Indonesia.[88]

With Hilsman and Harriman out of the bureaucratic loop, hard-liners in Washington and Kuala Lumpur began pushing for a more aggressive approach toward Sukarno and the Indonesian military, adopting elements of the British government's critique of Washington's embrace of the army. It was "about time we took some action" against Sukarno, McGeorge Bundy told his staff. "The essence of the problem," David Cuthell wrote Howard Jones in a telegram signed off on by Dean Rusk, was that "Sukarno recognizes our refusal to support confrontation . . . and is willing to face [the] possible loss of both current and potential U.S. aid." The Indonesian military for the most part seemed to "lack understanding of where Indo policy is leading," and those officials that did understand were unwilling to act, all of which made it harder to justify continued military training and civic action assistance before a hostile Congress.[89]

The criticism was off the mark. The Malaysia campaign, as U.S. intelligence realized, had opened up fissures within the armed forces. The navy and air force—the branches of the military closest to Sukarno and Moscow—pushed for a more aggressive posture, including attacks on the Malaysian mainland, whereas the army sought to limit military action to Borneo, because it would bear the brunt of any military escalation. Cuthell proposed that the "time has come to draw on relationship we have built with [the] Indo military in [an] effort [to] head off GOI before it's too late," a position Ambassador James Bell was pushing from Kuala Lumpur.[90] The push came as the State Department's Policy Planning Council revived its interagency working group to draft new policy guidelines for Indonesia. Lest anyone wonder about the implications of the debate, the draft policy paper asked, "Are we simply seeking a change in Indonesia's external policies or do we see the withholding of assistance as a means of stimulating change within Indonesia itself?"[91]

Over the next few weeks, Howard Jones and other embassy staff met with key Indonesian military leaders to outline the dire picture before them and the advantages of moving against Sukarno. Looming in the background of these conversations was the specter of further reductions in U.S. economic and military assistance. In a meeting with Ambassador Jones in early March, General Nasution pledged that the armed forces, while committed to *Konfrontasi*, had no intention of going to war with either the British or Malaysia and would try to keep the conflict within acceptable limits.[92] Army leaders were still reluctant to force a showdown with Sukarno, fearing a split in the military or even civil war. Jones continued to press the defense minister, suggesting broadly that Washington would back a coup against the Indonesian president. But General Nasution "avoided like the plague any discussion of possible military takeover, even though this hovered in [the] air . . . throughout [our] talk," he reported back to the State Department "and at no time did he pick up obvious hints of U.S. support in time of crisis."[93]

"To Hell with Your Aid"

Although the continuation of U.S. aid to Indonesia was generating heated internal debate, administration officials doggedly—if unenthusiastically—continued to defend the limited aid program before a hostile Congress. On March 25 Dean Rusk told the Senate Foreign Relations Committee that the United States had "initiated no new aid programs in Indonesia" and would not until *Konfrontasi* had ended; meanwhile, White House and State Department officials privately assured aid opponents that remaining assistance would not enhance Indonesia's ability to threaten Malaysia. But military and counterinsurgency training continued, Michael Forrestal confided to McGeorge Bundy, with "some categories of training now going on, and some starting soon which would make British hair stand on end."[94]

Rusk's testimony was widely covered by Indonesian newspapers. The next day in Jakarta, at a groundbreaking ceremony attended by 2,000 people and numerous diplomats, the Indonesian president pointedly looked at Howard Jones and shouted, "To hell with your aid! We can do without aid. We'll never collapse!" Sukarno's comments sparked predictable outrage. "It's easy for President Sukarno of Indonesia to tell us to 'go to hell' with our foreign aid—now that he has already received $894 million worth," declared an ambitious Texas oilman named George H. W. Bush, whose Zapata Off-Shore was drilling for oil off the coast of Borneo.[95] Jones criticized the "emotional, uninformed U.S. reaction to Sukarno's recent outburst," but the damage had been done. Both houses of Congress introduced bills to completely ban U.S. assistance to Indonesia.[96] McGeorge Bundy was by now hardening his stance—gloomily telling White House staff that "it was inevitable that we would have to cut off aid"—and opposing a presidential determination for Indonesia.[97] Despite their frustration with the Indonesian military's unwillingness to act decisively in the face of Sukarno's leftward drift, however, many administration officials insisted that long-term U.S. interests demanded continued aid and close ties to the army and other anti-Communist groups. These connections would bear fruit in a post-Sukarno era, when the United States expected the military and its allies to run the country. The crucial question remained: What political price was the administration willing to pay to maintain a foothold in Jakarta?

Defending aid to Indonesia would have been easier if U.S. officials could have pointed to progress in defusing *Konfrontasi*. But intelligence reports indicated that Indonesia was once again stepping up its military incursions in Kalimantan and Borneo, prompting the Malaysian government to announce that it was calling up 100,000 conscripts and refusing talks until Indonesian forces withdrew. Not to be outdone, Sukarno announced the formation of a Volunteers' Command (Komando Gerakan Sukarelawan) with 21 million members committed to "crushing" Malaysia.[98] Whitehall was exasperated with the Johnson administration's reliance on the ever-receding possibility of talks, arguing instead that Indonesia should be given a "bloody nose." But as Dean Rusk told the Australian minister for external affairs Sir Garfield Barwick, President Johnson was "not going to put in boys from Nebraska and Kansas just because the Tunku won't go to a meeting."[99]

Indonesia's hopes that domestic pressure might force the Tunku to compromise with Jakarta evaporated when the returns came in from Malaysia's April 25 national elections. The Tunku's Alliance Party soundly defeated Lee

Kuan Yew's People's Action Party and won an overwhelming majority of seats in the Malaysian Parliament, with the government's handling of *Konfrontasi* looming large in the background.[100] Sukarno responded by forming the Dwikora (Dwi Komando Rakyat, or Two Commands of the People) and by creating a military command (the Komando Siaga, or KOGA) headed by air force commander vice air marshal Omar Dhani to oversee *Konfrontasi*.[101] Not even a looming rice shortage, the economy's continued downward spiral, and the outbreak of a "fairly widespread" regional revolt in Sulawesi seemed to moderate Sukarno's position.[102] In this atmosphere of near total mistrust and mutual recrimination, Sukarno, Macapagal, and the Tunku met in Tokyo on June 20, 1964, surprising no one when they departed in failure two days later with neither Indonesia nor Malaysia willing to moderate its demands.[103] Surveying the depressing landscape, President Johnson told McGeorge Bundy that "the only question is how gradually we disengage."[104] A National Intelligence Estimate drafted in July reflected the deepening pessimism, concluding that the "road ahead for Indonesia is a troubled one of domestic deterioration, external aggression, and overall Communist profit."[105]

As the Johnson administration's exasperation with Jakarta grew, hard-liners pressed for a closer embrace of Malaysia. The White House's decision to invite the Tunku to visit Washington in July confirmed the slow but steady ascension of the hard-liner current and ratified an important shift in U.S. policy toward Malaysia.[106] Four months earlier, in February, Prime Minister Douglas Home and President Johnson had struck a tacit bargain that amounted to an imperial division of labor in the region, exchanging Washington's political support on Malaysia for British support on Vietnam.[107] After two days of meetings, the Tunku and President Johnson announced a U.S. offer of military assistance and condemned violations of Malaysia's territorial integrity by its neighbors—a clear reference to Indonesia.[108] The Tunku's trip to Washington doubtless confirmed the Indonesian president's belief that the United States was settling more firmly on Malaysia's side in its dispute with Jakarta. Equally important, the commitment to Kuala Lumpur enabled the White House to press New Zealand and Australia to commit their limited forces to Vietnam rather than to Malaysia.[109]

The Tunku's visit was marred by the outbreak in Singapore of race riots between Chinese and Malay residents; the riots highlighted Malaysia's political fragility and vulnerability.[110] Indonesia accordingly stepped up its attacks and shifted the locus of military activity from Sarawak and Borneo to mainland Malaysia and Singapore, where Indonesian troops began sabotage efforts in late June. On August 17, as Sukarno was proclaiming *Vivere Pericoloso* (the year of living dangerously) in his Independence Day speech, a group of forty well-armed guerrillas landed on the Malaysian coast just north of Singapore, where they were quickly captured after singularly unsuccessful efforts to stir up local Indonesian migrants. It was the first substantial Indonesian attempt at extending *Konfrontasi* to the Malaysian mainland. U.S. officials continued to suggest that negotiations were a live option, although "neither [Malaysia nor Indonesia] appears interested."[111]

The Tower Amendment and 'Vivere Pericoloso'

Throughout the spring and summer of 1964 the Johnson administration doggedly hung on to its limited program of aid to Indonesia in the face of harsh criticism from both allies and Congress, insisting that the United States had to "keep our foot in the door for the long-term stakes."[112] But in the space of a few weeks Indonesia's diplomatic shift to the left, its dramatic escalation of *Konfrontasi*, and a withering congressional attack on the remainder of the U.S. aid program gutted the political rationale behind this policy. On August 10, Indonesia established formal diplomatic relations with North Vietnam, prompting the South Vietnamese government to suspend relations with Jakarta. Sukarno made no secret of his bitter opposition to the U.S. war against Vietnam. "I think your Asian policy is wrong," Sukarno told Howard Jones as he left for consultations in Washington. "It is not popular with Asian people generally. It looks to them as though you are interfering with the internal affairs of Asian Nations. . . . Why should you become involved?"[113] The Indonesian president probably spoke for most Indonesians, who viewed the Vietnamese as first and foremost fighting for national liberation. Indonesia's defiant recognition of Ho Chi Minh came just three days after Congress passed the Gulf of Tonkin resolution, which authorized "retaliatory" strikes against North Vietnam after alleged attacks against two U.S. warships engaged in covert operations off the Vietnamese coast.[114]

Sukarno's actions sparked the usual outrage on Capitol Hill. First Representative Birch Bayh and then Senator John Tower introduced amendments barring further aid to Indonesia and immediately halting U.S. military train-ing.[115] U.S. assistance to Indonesia, Tower argued, highlighted the problems with a foreign aid program that specialized in building "roads that go no-where" and providing "TV sets for bush country natives." Tower's amend-ment passed in the Senate by a nearly two to one margin, despite intense lobbying by administration officials. The next day hundreds of youth from the Sukarnoist National Front entered and occupied the USIS library in Yogyakarta, forcing it to close.[116] This poke in the eye doubtless intensified President Johnson's already intense dislike of Sukarno, but U.S. options were limited. "With Vietnam and Laos already on our Southeast Asian plate," McGeorge Bundy wrote the president, "we can ill afford a major cri-sis with Indonesia right now."[117] Although fed up with Sukarno, White House advisers were just as angry at the Senate's interference with the pres-ident's foreign policy prerogatives. The Tower amendment "not only puts you on [the] spot," Robert Komer wrote the president, "but moves us dan-gerously close to a final break with Indonesia." Johnson agreed. "Give us some discretionary power," he barked at George Ball. Ball went to Senators Everett Dirkson and William Fulbright, who told him they could "bury the amendment" in committee—at the price of deep cuts in remaining aid.[118]

If the administration was looking for wiggle room, it was not going to find it in Jakarta. Sukarno's fiery August 17 Independence Day speech re-peatedly condemned the United States for supporting Malaysia and attack-ing Vietnam, suggested that the days of foreign capital in Indonesia were numbered, and called for a "retooling" of reactionaries in the military and bureaucracy. Sukarno proclaimed that 1965 would be Indonesia's "year of living dangerously," a time for broadening the struggle against Malaysia to include confrontation with imperialism on all fronts. The speech "cannot be shrugged off as more of the same," Francis Galbraith cabled the State De-partment that day. Sukarno was charting a course "fundamentally opposed to our thought, our influence and our leadership," he argued, "for Marxism, against liberal democracy, for Asia and Africa, i.e. the colored races, against Europe and the U.S., for struggle against rather than cooperation with us."[119] Passage of the Tower amendment and the continued erosion of U.S.-Indonesian relations decisively undermined advocates of accommodation and strengthened the hand of administration hard-liners. The State Depart-ment, supported by AID officials and the Bundy brothers, argued that the time had come to "terminate aid to [the] Indonesian military and paramilitary org[anizations]."[120]

Although resigned to a drawing down of the aid program, officials from the Joint Chiefs of Staff, the Department of Defense, and the CIA argued strongly against an end to military assistance. Having spent years cultivating close training, personal, and intelligence ties with the Indonesian army, these advocates of military modernization, led by Robert Komer and James Thomson, were reluctant to sever relations that could be "meaningful in terms of continuing contact and future influence." They drew unexpected support from Francis Galbraith, Howard Jones's in-house critic in Jakarta. Galbraith argued not only for the maintenance of military ties but also for the initiation of new covert operations and contingency planning to stem the tide, calling on the White House to "be alert to development potential for meaningful dissidence, especially in outer islands and West Java, and be prepared to move rapidly in support [of] Army should Sukarno-PKI pressures on Army leaders or other occurrences precipitate army revolt against Sukarno."[121]

Advocates of maintaining ties to the Indonesian armed forces blunted but did not deflect the attack on remaining assistance. William Fulbright helped to beat back the Tower amendment, but the joint Department of State/AID/Department of Defense policy approved by President Johnson at the end of August 1964 would halt completion of a proposed archipelago-wide military communications system and suspend delivery of remaining military equipment for the police and the Mobile Police Brigade. "Nonmilitary" training and equipment deliveries for police and Mobile Police Brigade units would continue, as would a stripped-down civic action program. Meanwhile military attaché George Benson was instructed to seek out Generals Yani and Nasution for a "where the hell do we go from here" discussion on the reduction or elimination of military training for the army. The key was to make the aid cuts with minimal fanfare. "The very fact that we're on a slippery downward slope makes it all the more important not to burn our bridges to Indonesia," McGeorge Bundy wrote Johnson. "We do not want to be the ones who trigger a major attack on U.S. investments there."[122]

The slope got a lot more slippery when at the beginning of September more than 100 Indonesian paratroopers landed in the town of Labis on the Malaysian mainland and at five other points along the Malaysian coast. The attacks marked a significant escalation of *Konfrontasi*, prompting the Tunku to declare a state of emergency and the British to urge Malaysia to take its case to the U.N. Security Council. In Washington Dean Rusk quickly assured British officials of U.S. backing at the U.N.—but then warned them not to overreact in the expectation that U.S. forces were standing by to help.[123] "We cannot give them a blank check and pick up the tab for escalation by the use of U.S. forces," Rusk cabled the U.S. ambassador in London.[124] The British embassy in Washington was unimpressed with the White House's tepid support, complaining with racist disdain that there were "in the State Department, and elsewhere 'nigger lovers' who believe you can make a silk purse out of Sukarno's ear."[125]

Johnson administration officials watched the British response to the attacks with great apprehension. The United Kingdom's Far East Command diverted a full aircraft carrier battle group toward Singapore, and the Chiefs of Staff in London prepared a list of targets for retaliatory air strikes and secretly authorized British troops to begin striking Indonesian forces up to 10,000 yards on the Indonesian side of the Kalimantan border. The British "sound just as hysterical as Sukarno," Robert Komer told McGeorge Bundy. Australian and New Zealand defense officials pledged their support to Malaysia and quickly offered troops, but they worried that Washington was being kept in the dark about British military plans, which included counter-guerrilla operations in North Sumatra aimed at disrupting Indonesian infiltration efforts.[126] On September 17 William Bundy flew to London and met with Permanent Under-Secretary at the Foreign Office Sir Harold Caccia, Deputy Under-Secretary of State Sir Edward Peck, and other Commonwealth officials. He demanded that the White House be kept informed of London's plans, because military action might invoke Washington's obligations under the ANZUS Treaty or provoke attacks against U.S. interests in Indonesia.[127] But the Johnson administration had turned a corner in endorsing Britain's right to take retaliatory action. As William Bundy cabled Howard Jones, "If you think Sukarno believes we can or will restrain British, he should be disabused of any such idea."[128]

Given the uncertainty over British intentions, U.S. officials welcomed the U.N. Security Council debate over the Indonesian attacks, hoping it would restrain Sukarno's defense officials in London and Capitol Hill all at once. After a week of debate the United States voted for a moderate resolution deploring Indonesia's actions, but it fell to a Soviet veto.[129] The Security Council vote pleased no one, and it deepened Sukarno's alienation from the U.N., which he now viewed as a tool of the "old established forces," his designation for the former colonial powers. But it was Britain's military mobilization more than the debate in New York that deflected a further escalation of the conflict. The Indonesian army was anxious to avoid a clash with Britain's vastly superior forces and embarrassed at the failure of raids carried out by Vice Air Marshal Omar Dhani's troops. To regain control over military operations from incompetent air force and navy units, armed forces chief General Yani appointed General Suharto as deputy commander of the renamed Kolaga (Komando Mandala Siaga), centralizing decision making and undermining those who favored aggressive operations against mainland Malaysia. Meanwhile, both the army and Sukarno separately opened backdoor channels with Malaysian officers and civilian leaders to discuss ways of reducing hostilities.[130]

Although Indonesia had pulled its chestnuts out of the fire, intelligence reports predicted that attacks would continue for the foreseeable future and that Sukarno's objectives would remain unchanged. Indonesia seemed to be shifting, a National Intelligence Estimate concluded, "from narrow confrontation of Malaysia to more diffuse confrontation with the entire West."[131] Johnson administration officials concluded grimly that *Konfrontasi* "is essentially without solution" and that "for the present, we see no useful role the United States Government might play." In lieu of renewed diplomatic initiatives, the British military deterrent in the area would have to suffice.[132] The prognosis for Indonesia's internal political situation was much the same. Sukarno had identified himself with the PKI's demands for a retooling of "reactionary" elements in the bureaucracy and "bureaucratic capitalists," shorthand for the army heads of state-owned enterprises. He had also endorsed the party's campaign for forceful implementation of a long-stalled land reform bill bitterly opposed by the military, landlords, and Muslim organizations and had taken small but significant steps to increase PKI representation in the cabinet. Although not a Communist himself, the CIA argued, Sukarno's "emotional bias toward Marxism" and the need to build mass support for his policies had led to a marriage of "mutual exploitation" that showed no signs of weakening. So long as Sukarno remained in power and the army remained on the defensive, the PKI would continue to grow in strength, until Indonesia eventually became a "modified Communist regime."[133]

Rollback Resplendent

The steady deterioration in U.S.-Indonesian relations and widespread frustration at Washington's inability to restrain Sukarno emboldened supporters of direct military rule. The push for such a hard-line approach, involving an intensification of covert operations aimed at provoking a coup against Sukarno or a clash between the army and the PKI leading to the PKI's destruction, came primarily from the Far Eastern Bureau of the State Department, the CIA's Directorate of Operations, and from opponents of Ambassador Jones at the embassy in Jakarta. Local events provided the impetus, but the CIA had spelled out its rationale several months earlier, in an analysis that deserves to be quoted at length:

> The major change of the past few years has been the growing inability of the great powers to control the situation in [Southeast Asia]. Local leaders and local political movements have become increasingly powerful and less disposed to follow the advice or dictates of others.
>
> The Viet Cong of the south, dependent largely upon their own resources but under the direction and control of the North, are pressing their offensive more vigorously than ever.
>
> Larger stakes are involved in the contest between Indonesia and Malaysia. Sukarno and his supporters fear Malaysia and particularly the greater energy and efficiency of the Chinese in Singapore and North Borneo. Above all, they hope to make Indonesia a world power able to negotiate in equality with China, the USSR and the U.S., having brought the Philippines and the mainland states under Indonesian hegemony.
>
> One consequence of this disorder and of the inhibitions upon open involvement is likely to be an increase in clandestine activities designed to influence the course of events in a desired direction or to block similar activities by other powers. In many places the situation may be so soft, the issues so undefined, and the parties so difficult to identify that outside powers will be unable to develop an acceptable rationale for intervention.
>
> Thus many situations will be resolved by local leaders or groups sponsored and supported covertly from the outside. This will be an attractive course of action, not only because of the inhibitions upon open intervention, but because it will often cost so little in money and effort if an investment is made early enough to be effective.[134]

Parts of the CIA's analysis were certainly overblown. For example, there was scant evidence of Indonesia's capability or desire to dominate the Philippines, much less mainland Southeast Asia. But the implications were clear: Independent nationalism, not Communism, posed the greatest threat to both Soviet and U.S. interests in the region, necessitating greater covert efforts to bring it under control. And much of the logic fit Indonesia like a glove.

Within days of the Indonesian paratrooper landing at Labis, the CIA sent the State Department a proposal for "a program of covert action aimed at affecting the current trend of events." Reciting the familiar litany of ominous trends, the CIA noted that the United States still had allies in Indonesia "who are willing to work for the things they believe in." They had shown "a capacity for limited but effective clandestine political action" and had approached the U.S. embassy seeking assistance—almost certainly a veiled reference to former supporters of the PRRI rebellion.[135] Until this point U.S. policy "had been essentially constructive and forward looking, predicated on the concept of contributing to Indonesia's economic development"—that is, the internationalist vision of Indonesian modernization. Likewise, the CIA's covert activities had been limited to contacting and grooming "potential leader types" and engaging in "limited harassment" of the PKI. Now the CIA proposed stronger stuff—intensified covert operations aimed at "building up strength among non-communist and anti-communist groups and organizations" and "encouraging direct action against the PKI as a party." "The purpose of this entire exercise," the memo offered, "is agitation and the instigation of internal strife between communist and non-communist elements."[136] The CIA's proposal—at least those parts that have been declassified—scrupulously avoided using the word *coup*, but there is no doubt, as Frederick Bunnell has observed, that army moves against the PKI "necessarily involv[ed] some form of coup d'état whether with or without Sukarno's acquiescence." Later stages of the action program, the CIA noted, went beyond "the framework of the existing policy"—that is, seeking Sukarno's overthrow rather than maintaining links with the military in the hopes of outlasting him. The risks were substantial, the CIA acknowledged, but "this risk must be taken."[137] Although the CIA has yet to declassify the barest fraction of its operational files for this period, its intent to provoke a bloody clash in Indonesia is now beyond doubt.

The CIA's turn toward rollback in Indonesia was hardly new, coming just five years after the Eisenhower administration's disastrous and massive intervention in Indonesia's civil war. NSC 5901, drafted two years before Kennedy entered office, had prioritized military aid "programs and projects which offer opportunities to isolate the PKI, drive it into positions of open opposition to the Indonesian government, thereby creating grounds for repressive measures politically justifiable in terms of Indonesian national self-interest."[138] Both Indonesian observers and American policymakers agreed, however, that the Indonesian army was unwilling to challenge Sukarno and risk its fragile unity by striking first to crush the PKI, and before the fall of 1964 the risks of moving against them outweighed the likely benefits. Given the size of the PKI and its affiliated organizations, any decisive move against the party would almost certainly involve extraordinary violence. A group of pro-Western Indonesian economists lamented to Howard Jones that the army "would always react, not act" against the PKI and would do so only when "its interests were acutely and obviously threatened." This statement prompted Thomas Hughes of the State Department's Bureau of Intelligence and Research to ask, "Is there anything that would make [such a] clash inevitable?"[139]

U.S. officials had already repeatedly indicated to Indonesian army leaders that a coup against Sukarno, an attack on the PKI, or both would enjoy American support.[140] The differences between Ambassador Jones and Robert Komer and their opponents in the CIA and the State Department's Far East Bureau regarding a coup were tactical, not principled, questions of timing, not propriety. Jones and his supporters believed that active U.S. support for mediation of *Konfrontasi* and engagement with Sukarno would be more effective in the long run than highly risky covert operations that, if disclosed, might lead to the defeat of the army and the PKI's rise to power. As Robert Komer put it to his boss, "We would not take the steps necessary to unseat Sukarno. . . . This is why I have been so strong on preventative diplomacy."[141]

Over the next two months CIA and State Department officials met regularly to discuss the emerging covert action proposal.[142] The program that emerged identified two broad objectives. The first involved using covert propaganda to "create an image of the PKI as an increasingly ambitious, dangerous opponent of Sukarno and legitimate nationalism." In pursuit of this objective the United States would help anti-PKI forces develop "a broad-gauge ideological common denominator, preferably within the framework of

Sukarno's enunciated concepts, to which practically all political groups except the PKI can adhere," accentuating the cleavage between Communists and "legitimate" nationalist forces. Second, the CIA would encourage, coordinate, and, where possible, covertly assist "individuals and organizations prepared to take obstructive action against the PKI." Over the longer term this meant identifying and keeping tabs on "anti-regime elements" and other potential leaders of a post-Sukarno regime. William Bundy approved the proposal at an interagency meeting on November 19, 1964, two weeks after President Johnson's landslide victory over Barry Goldwater.[143]

Bundy's approval of the covert operations proposal inaugurated a shift toward what might be described as a "low-posture" rollback strategy. Johnson administration officials were aware of the limits of U.S. power and conscious of the risks a covert action strategy entailed, but they were also anxious to take some initiative in resisting what they perceived as the PKI's steady progress. The policy shift did not end efforts by Ambassador Jones, Robert Komer, and others to jump-start negotiations between Indonesia and Malaysia or to induce Sukarno into easing *Konfrontasi*. But low-posture advocates now viewed such efforts in light of their possible impact on the covert action policy track. After Jones proposed backdoor talks between Indonesia and Britain in late November, for example, the State Department cabled back that a "major consideration is whether U.S. initiatives to re-open talks would help or harm anti-com[munist] forces."[144] As in Vietnam, the Johnson administration began actively opposing efforts at negotiations that conflicted with its broader foreign policy goals.

The expansion of covert operations in Indonesia came on the heels of a similar CIA operation in Brazil, where on March 31 right-wing military officers launched a coup, with Washington's support, against the progressive, nationalist regime of João Goulart. U.S. officials accused Goulart of collaborating with the local Communist party and other radical forces in an effort to "seize dictatorial power."[145] Like Sukarno, Goulart was an economic nationalist committed to nonalignment, an economic program of state-led development, and the political mobilization of the overwhelmingly poor rural majority.[146] As in Indonesia, the Goulart regime was challenging the prerogatives of foreign investors, especially in the oil sector, where in the spring of 1964 the Brazilian state oil firm Petrobas completed the nationalization of refining capacity. Like Indonesia, Brazil suffered from runaway inflation and increasing economic and social turmoil that fed its political crisis. And as they would in Indonesia, CIA covert operations in Brazil aimed to destabilize the economy, sow confusion, and offer support to a wide range of forces that opposed Goulart while the U.S. embassy maintained close contact with coup plotters in the Brazilian army.[147] The embarrassing speed with which the Johnson administration recognized the military regime in early April spoke volumes about the White House's likely response to similar events in Indonesia.[148]

Washington's acceleration of covert operations was also predicated on similar British efforts. Beginning in 1963 the Foreign Office, Ministry of Defense, and the Cabinet Defense and Overseas Policy Committee (DOPC) began discussing the possibility of offensive covert actions "with the short term objective of dissipating Indonesia's military effort against Malaysia." At the end of the year the DOPC approved a covert operation program involving aid for regional dissidents in Sulawesi, northern Sumatra, and Kalimantan, offensive military action against Indonesian forces in Borneo, and propaganda and psychological warfare activities directed from Singapore and Malaysia. The propaganda campaign of the Foreign Office's Information Research Department aimed, as did the CIA campaign inaugurated several months later, at "stirring up dissension between different factions inside Indonesia" and portraying the PKI and China as grave threats to the country's future.[149]

Foreign Office officials in London continued to chafe at U.S. efforts to prop up anti-Communists in the Indonesian armed forces (and therefore their ability to wage *Konfrontasi*) even as they welcomed signs of a tougher line in Washington. Sukarno's escalation of *Konfrontasi* in September appreciably hardened official attitudes and solidified British determination to defend Malaysia with force, ruling out of public consideration "any concessions that might strengthen moderates . . . such as Adam Malik who were seeking to moderate Confrontation." The election of Harold Wilson as prime minister the next month and the Labor Party's return to power did little to change these attitudes. More worrisome for British policy than a Labor victory was a fall Cabinet review of overseas military commitments and their deleterious impact on the British economy. The Cabinet concluded that the United Kingdom simply could not afford to maintain a sizable long-term military presence in the Far East while waiting for *Konfrontasi* to end;

their commitment was hemorrhaging the budget and contributing heavily to an £800 million balance of payments deficit. The review reinforced the Foreign Office's preference for a more aggressive policy aimed at provoking "a prolonged struggle for power leading to civil war or anarchy" in Indonesia, which it hoped would make it impossible to wage *Konfrontasi* and divert the army's attention from Malaysia. British and U.S. intelligence agreed that the PKI was unlikely to come to power in the immediate future and that the army was reluctant to crush the PKI unless first provoked. For officials in both countries the crucial question was, How do we make such a clash inevitable? Edward Peck, assistant secretary of state in the Foreign Office, suggested that "there might be much to be said for encouraging a premature PKI coup during Sukarno's lifetime."[150] The New Zealand high commissioner in London agreed, arguing that a premature PKI coup "might be the most helpful solution for the West—provided the coup failed."[151]

CHAPTER 6

Indonesia's Year of Living Dangerously

Looking back over the sorry state of his domain in early 1965, Ambassador Howard Jones sketched an "almost unrelieved picture of adverse trends in Indonesia, both domestically and in regards to U.S.-Indonesian relations."[1] On the eve of Kennedy's death fifteen months earlier, Jones and other officials had expressed cautious optimism that they could rein in Sukarno, defuse the conflict with Malaysia, and coax Jakarta back on the road to Western-oriented economic reform and eventually modernization.[2] Just a month earlier, however, Sukarno had announced that Indonesia was quitting the United Nations over the world body's stance on Malaysia, *Konfrontasi* showed no signs of resolution, and Indonesia's economy continued to deteriorate as inflation soared, production plummeted, and foreign investors came under steady harassment—trends that all redounded to the benefit of the PKI. To make matters worse, Indonesian radicals now identified the United States as the chief threat to their interests, targeting the U.S. war in Vietnam and American corporations and cultural and social installations. "The interests of the U.S. and Sukarno now conflict in nearly every quarter," the CIA observed pessimistically. Dean Rusk warned that "before long Indonesia may be for all practical purposes a Communist dictatorship."[3]

The question dogging policymakers in 1965 was, What, if anything, could the United States do to halt or reverse these trends? The massive U.S. escalation of its war against Vietnam in the spring of 1965 to include air strikes against the north and the introduction of tens of thousands of combat troops significantly raised Washington's stakes in Indonesia. Ambassador Jones argued that "for [the] U.S. to watch [Indonesia] fall to early communist domination without making an effort to stop it seems unthinkable."[4] But Indonesia suffered from what Chester Cooper called benign neglect as Vietnam consumed the energies of top administration officials.[5] The Johnson administration recognized its limited leverage in Jakarta—much less in rural Java or Sumatra where the PKI was engaged in determined organizing through affiliated peasant organizations—and often despaired of the army's unwillingness to unseat Sukarno or crush the PKI, despite persistent encouragement. Moreover, army leaders fretted that U.S. support tarnished their nationalist credentials and hampered their political battle against their domestic opponents.

Rightfully noting the Johnson administration's limited ability to control events in Indonesia, scholars have wrongly concluded that the United States was a passive bystander in 1965, battening down the hatches to weather the storm while "waiting for the eventual dawning of a post-Sukarno era." But for Washington to stand by helplessly while the world's fifth largest country "went Communist" would present one of the great anomalies of the Cold War.[6] U.S. policy toward Indonesia, however, was no anomaly, even if it was constrained by American commitments elsewhere in Asia and by political dynamics in Jakarta. Even as officials in Washington and Jakarta reduced the overt U.S. presence, they sought through an expanded program of covert action to exploit the increasing social and political polarization in Indonesia and to provoke a violent clash between the army and the PKI or a military coup against Sukarno. The resulting low-posture policy recognized that open military intervention in Indonesia to forestall a PKI victory could not be seriously considered, especially given the rapidly expanding military commitment to Vietnam. Instead, Johnson administration officials made a prudent, if risky wager: that by minimizing the open U.S. presence in Indonesia while ramping up covert operations, they could still achieve their short-term goal of preventing the country's slide to the left.

The Polarization of Indonesian Politics

Indonesian politics in late 1964 and early 1965 became "more polarized than ever before as President Sukarno aligned himself more openly with the PKI against the army leadership" and continued to sever Jakarta's ties to the West, all while accelerating economic decline exacerbated by the bitter internal struggle at home.[7] The collapse of promising anti-Communist organizing efforts, a renewed PKI political offensive, Indonesia's abrupt withdrawal from the United Nations, a tacit alliance with China, and Sukarno's broadened confrontation with the West posed decisive challenges to U.S. policymakers, who sought to reconcile the limited means at their disposal with the gravity of Indonesia's political and economic crisis.

For anti-Communist forces the crucial question at the end of 1964 was How to blunt the PKI's political offensive? A year earlier the PKI, in a major strategic shift, launched the Unilateral Action (*Aksi Sepihak*) campaign, which involved the mass mobilization of peasants to implement Indonesia's stalled 1960 land reform legislation. PKI chairman Aidit recognized that the campaign would arouse intense opposition from both the armed forces and Muslim organizations, both of whom stood to lose land and rural power if the law was fully implemented. The party's decision nevertheless to move forward with the campaign suggested for many observers that the PKI was "bidding in their own name for the villages."[8] Over the course of 1964 the PKI also urged an intensification of *Konfrontasi*, demanded greater political representation, and began calling for the suppression or "retooling" of the party's adversaries. In late August PKI chairman Aidit suggested in a speech that the ideology of *Pancasila* might no longer be needed once Indonesia had achieved its unity, prompting the party's opponents to charge that the PKI was anti-*Pancasila*. As Sukarno left for a two-month world tour, a coalition of forces led by elements of the Indonesian National Party, the Murba Party, various Muslim groups, and anti-Communist newspapers in Jakarta announced the formation of the Body to Protect Sukarnoism (BPS).[9] Trade minister Adam Malik, a leading spokesman, insisted that the purpose of the BPS was simply to spread Sukarno's teachings. However, the movement "quickly became a rallying point for anti-communist sentiment," and by early October it had enlisted army leaders, members of the army-affiliated SOKSI union, and scores of politicians, including Foreign Minister Subandrio.[10] The PKI rightly considered the BPS a mortal threat and bitterly denounced it as an attempt to "confuse and divide" the Indonesian people; Sukarno remained characteristically aloof as he assessed the balance of forces.[11]

U.S. officials watched hopefully, but the CIA noted presciently that the BPS "could well collapse overnight if its strategy of winning the President's support should fail and Sukarno should move to suppress its growth."[12] And collapse it did. Subandrio, reading Sukarno's continued silence as opposition, withdrew his support from the BPS in early December and accused it of fomenting internal conflict. The Indonesian National Party (PNI) quickly followed suit and called for Sukarno to disband the BPS, which he did on December 17. A few days later the KOTI (Supreme Operational Command) met and warned Indonesia's political parties against mounting similar efforts in the future. For good measure Sukarno banned the Murba Party, rounded up two dozen of its members on trumped-up charges, and closed several anti-PKI newspapers in Jakarta, branding them "henchmen of the BPS." The CIA reported that the banning of the Murba Party nearly sparked a coup attempt against Sukarno. Howard Jones offered a gloomy postmortem: The BPS was "likely [the] last organized attempt by civilian moderates to stem [the] PKI advance," he wrote. "We now believe [the] evidence [is] fairly persuasive that effective internal anti-communist resistance will not develop during Sukarno's lifetime."[13]

Indonesia's sudden withdrawal from the United Nations at the end of December deepened the pessimism of U.S. officials. The proximate cause for Sukarno's decision was Malaysia's long-awaited ascension to a seat on the U.N. Security Council. However, the Security Council vote against Indonesia in September (Soviet veto or not) had already convinced Sukarno that the U.N. could not represent the interests of anticolonial nations and strengthened his desire to create an alternative Conference of the New Emerging Forces (CONEFO). Although few Western officials thought Indonesia had either the political clout or the resources to peel nonaligned nations away from the U.N.,

Sukarno's commitment to the idea of CONEFO suggested an increasing willingness to abandon traditional Western principles of diplomacy.

Jakarta's close ties to Beijing bolstered this perception. The Indonesian tilt away from the Soviet Union and toward China marked a turning point in Indonesia's growing confrontation with the West and in the Sino-Soviet split. When Sukarno visited Beijing in early November—three weeks after China exploded its first nuclear weapon—Mao Tse-tung and Zhou Enlai urged him to intensify Indonesia's *Konfrontasi* with Malaysia, endorsed his plans for CONEFO, and apparently offered to provide limited military assistance.[14] An exchange of visits by Chinese foreign minister Chen Yi in November and Subandrio in January confirmed the rapidly improving relationship. The British embassy in Jakarta noted that more than twenty economic experts and a dozen military advisers accompanied Subandrio to Beijing and that sixty Chinese economic advisers made the reverse trip to Jakarta, an exchange the semi-official *Indonesian Herald* argued was of "special importance in view of the unique experience of people's China in establishing a policy of self-reliance in the field of economic rehabilitation."[15] Chinese leaders also expressed their support for PKI militants, who continued to distance themselves from Moscow despite continued (and far greater) Soviet economic and military aid and began calling for the formation of an armed "fifth force" of workers and peasants and "Nasakomization" at all levels of government. Nasakomization referred to Sukarno's long-standing but unrealized call for a NASAKOM cabinet representing the nationalist, religious, and Communist streams. Hoping to assuage opponents of his tilt toward Beijing, Sukarno told a gathering of right-wing political leaders that Indonesia's "current affinity with Communist China strategy [is] aimed at buying support from U.S. on Malaysia," explaining that he expected the United States and China to be at war within the next five years, at which point Washington would have to petition for Jakarta's support on its own terms.[16]

Chinese policy was driven only in part by a confluence of interests with Sukarno and the PKI, which practiced a brand of "Marxist revisionism" that it condemned elsewhere. (Mao in May 1965 sent a personal message to the PKI Central Committee praising the party for developing an "Indonesian-ized Marxism-Leninism" that "conform[ed] to the basic interest of the Indonesian people.")[17] More important were the geopolitical imperatives of the Sino-Soviet split and the U.S. war in Vietnam, which Chinese leaders were convinced would extend to Beijing as it increased support for North Vietnam. When Subandrio traveled in May to Guangzhou for talks, Zhou Enlai told him that Beijing was preparing for an invasion of Vietnam in the event of a U.S. attack on China.[18] Indonesian army leaders as well as U.S. and Soviet officials watched the signs of a tacit Sino-Indonesian alliance with acute anxiety. Soviet officials responded to the tilt toward Beijing by attempting to patch up relations with the Indonesian army, viewing it as a counterweight to the increasingly pro-China PKI and—reflecting Soviet theorists' embrace of military modernization theory—as a vanguard of development. Accordingly, the Soviet embassy in Jakarta began turning away from the PKI and toward the armed forces, the PNI, and even the Nahdlatul Ulama (NU), approvingly quoting NU officials who argued that the "PKI is working against the Soviet Union and the Soviet Union is a friend of Indonesia. Therefore PKI should be taken care of."[19]

Many U.S. policymakers were by now convinced that China, not the USSR, constituted the greatest threat to American interests in Asia, a perception magnified by Beijing's explosion of a nuclear device in September 1964. Sukarno compounded Washington's worries by making the utterly fantastic suggestion over the summer that Indonesia might explode an atomic device itself in the next year, presumably with the assistance of Beijing.[20] The U.S. press played its role, spilling rivers of ink on Jakarta's "nightmare alliance" with Beijing and declaring that "Indonesia has become the most dangerous threat to the peace and stability of Southeast Asia outside of China itself."[21] But not everyone was so alarmed. To the anger of administration officials, Japan continued to trade, offer aid, and explore investment opportunities in Jakarta, just as it did in China and Vietnam, becoming Indonesia's largest trading partner and aid donor by the end of 1965.[22]

To complicate matters, Sukarno's declining health raised the explosive question of presidential succession, sparking an intense behind-the-scenes struggle among possible contenders. Both Western and Indonesian observers believed that Sukarno was more likely to be felled by illness than by a putsch. "The fate of 100,000,000 people appears to hang on one non-functioning kidney and one endangered kidney," James Thomson only half-joked to McGeorge Bundy.[23] Neither armed forces chief of staff Yani nor Defense Minister Nasution appeared capable of uniting the fractured army, and all the civilian front runners (Chaerul Saleh, Adam Malik, and Subandrio) relied on either the army (in Malik's and Saleh's case) or the PKI (in Subandrio's case) for support. British officials were equally sanguine, concluding that Sukarno's likely successor would "postpone rather than avert the ultimate struggle for power between the Army and the PKI." The CIA observed that "to many politically aware Indonesians, this is now a major and perhaps the primary national political problem."[24]

The Johnson administration struggled vainly to formulate a response that offered some hope of stemming the tide. The steady cutoff of U.S. aid and targeting of U.S. interests by Indonesian radicals drastically narrowed the range of available options, increasing the appeal of covert action, despite its obvious risks. From his new post as ambassador to Malaysia, former director of the Office of Southwest Pacific Affairs James Bell began pushing the coup option more forcefully, suggesting that fear of a British attack might be restraining the army from moving against Sukarno. If this was the case, he asked, why not "reach completely reliable Indo military with assurances that GOM [Government of Malaysia] and commonwealth would refrain from interference" in an army move "unless it becomes apparent PKI [is] going to come out on top?"[25]

Jones disagreed, arguing that army reluctance to act stemmed from a lack of internal unity. The United States should refrain from such moves "unless certain [the] Army would be receptive to our initiative," he concluded. Jones insisted that "there are other things we can and should try first." Writing to McGeorge Bundy (who sided with Bell), NSC staffer Chester Cooper said, "I have brooded and checked around and agree with Jones."[26] Jones reported a few days later that high-ranking military sources had offered assurances not only that the army was "developing specific plans for takeover of government moment Sukarno steps off stage," but also that an "important segment" of the military leadership favored moving sooner, perhaps in one or two months if the PKI's political offensive continued.[27]

Despite mounting pressure in Washington and a behind-the-scenes campaign mounted by embassy staff and CIA employees in Jakarta to write off Sukarno entirely, Howard Jones continued to push for a last-ditch meeting between Lyndon Johnson and the Indonesian president. Jones's persistence reflected his belief that personal diplomacy was "perhaps [the] only hope" of reversing the tide in Jakarta, as well as his recognition that Sukarno retained significant mass support and was unlikely to be dislodged.[28] Surprisingly,

Dean Rusk drafted a letter from President Johnson to British prime minister Wilson suggesting a visit from the Indonesian president and Japanese mediation of an Afro-Asian conference concerning Malaysia; this marked a curious about-face for a president who generally disdained meeting with foreign leaders and reviled Sukarno. What Johnson might have expected from such an encounter is unclear, as is why Rusk—increasingly critical of continued aid to Jakarta—signed off on the request in the first place. It is possible that the overture reflected the White House's sensitivity to its increasing international isolation on Vietnam in January 1965 and a desire to suggest to allies that it was not opposed in principle to talks with adversaries. In any case Prime Minister Wilson reacted with predictable disdain, as did hardliners in the administration. A presidential meeting "would be sheer folly" and "an invitation for others to act the same," Marshall Green wrote William Bundy.[29] As a nod toward Jones, McGeorge Bundy had NSC staffer Michael Forrestal stop over in Indonesia while on a tour of Southeast Asia, but Forrestal, one of Jones's last defenders, departed Jakarta advocating a drawdown of the U.S. presence.[30]

The Anti-American Period and the Bunker Mission

Within weeks of Forrestal's departure, U.S. ties with Jakarta hovered on the brink of ruin. The PKI-led and government-tolerated offensive against American installations and property continued to intensify. Simultaneously, Indonesia's confrontation with Malaysia flared following new attacks against Malaysian territory. The rapidly deteriorating relations with Indonesia undercut Ambassador Jones's credibility and strengthened the hand of those calling for a low-posture policy to accompany ongoing covert operations. On February 15 Sukarno announced the seizure of the USIA library in Jakarta after 17,000 demonstrators besieged the building.[31] Three days later, protestors entered and partially ransacked the U.S. consulate in Medan. U.S. Information Agency (USIA) director Carl Rowan angrily called for the cutoff of all remaining aid and Jones's recall.[32] The United States had reached a "critical watershed" in its relations with Indonesia, Dean Rusk warned. Jones resisted calls for a harsh response (even as he delivered one to Sukarno), arguing that the United States "has no real capacity for retaliation against Indonesia, while they can hit us hard."[33] Shortly after meeting with Jones, however, Sukarno banned *Time, Life, U.S. News and World Report*, and *Newsweek* magazines from Indonesia and ordered the closure of remaining USIA facilities.

The PKI, heady with success and emboldened by the tacit encouragement of Subandrio and Sukarno, threw down a far greater challenge when estate workers with the party-affiliated union Sarbupri attempted to seize 160,000 acres of plantations in North Sumatra owned by U.S. Rubber. As demonstrators stormed the U.S. consulate in Medan, Estates Minister Frans Seda, Chaerul Saleh, and President Sukarno called in U.S. Rubber and Goodyear representatives to announce that the government was taking temporary "administrative control" of their estates, which would now be managed by Indonesian "supervisory teams."[34] Seda called the move a preventive measure designed to stave off demands for outright nationalization; he offered assurances that the government would exercise only nominal control. Two weeks later, however, Chaerul Saleh told Howard Jones and Francis Galbraith that events were moving so rapidly that "it would be impossible for Americans to be in field" and that negotiations over the future of the estates "should begin as soon as possible."[35] The companies were in a weak position—Indonesians could run the estates and market the rubber without a serious loss of production—leaving administration officials with few choices short of invoking the Hickenlooper amendment or cutting off rubber imports. Moreover, the CIA reported that Sukarno's KOTI, with Subandrio in the lead, had endorsed the takeover of Western properties. "We are several inches further down the slippery slope," James Thomson glumly wrote McGeorge Bundy, "and prospects for improvement are minimal."[36]

When Caltex officials awoke March 3 to find their headquarters in Sumatra covered with graffiti, they feared the slippery slope would be greased with oil seized from Western companies. "Its been made clear to Sukarno and key military commanders," Jones tried to reassure Washington, "that the moment anything happens indicating interference with control of Caltex . . . [the] lift of oil from Indonesia will be halted," causing the economy to implode.[37] Even the *Indonesian Herald* editorialized on the need to ensure the flow of oil, and Julius Tahija of Caltex predicted that army leaders would move against Subandrio and the PKI if company takeovers halted production, a move that would immediately cripple their forces, who were heavily reliant on air and sea transport.[38] On March 19 oil company representatives were summoned into Chaerul Saleh's office, where Saleh's deputy read a letter stating that the Indonesian government was placing all oil companies under "direct government control and temporary custody."[39] "In the long run," Ball fretted to McGeorge Bundy, "this may be more important than South Vietnam"—neither the first nor the last time that U.S. officials made such statements regarding the position of Western capital in Indonesia.[40]

To compound the dilemma facing policymakers in Washington, Indonesian forces continued to infiltrate and launch attacks inside Malaysia, albeit at a level seemingly designed not to provoke a major British retaliatory response. The Johnson administration was by now disinclined to look for shades of gray in Indonesia's behavior and began to view Jakarta as a real threat to its regional interests. Secretary of State Rusk told former British secretary of state for foreign affairs Patrick Gordon Walker during talks in March that "President Johnson has come increasingly to the conclusion that, at the end of the day, should it become necessary, he would be ready for major war against Indonesia." Rusk assured Walker that the United States would "back you to the hilt if necessary and hope for your support on Vietnam."[41]

The continued deterioration of relations with Jakarta convinced the State Department that it was time to "reduce [the] American presence in Indonesia."[42] The embassy recognized that some reduction was inevitable and proposed phasing out AID, the Military Assistance Advisory Group (MAAG), and USIA programs—while maintaining a smaller defense liaison staff and a full complement of CIA officers—to keep the mission "more water tight and storm worthy."[43] At the U.S. Chiefs of Mission conference in the Philippines in mid-March, however, Jones argued that "every inch of withdrawal hands that much more of a victory to the Communists"; he insisted that "we ought to stand fast with the maximum American presence it is possible to preserve" so that the United States could respond quickly to changing political circumstances.[44] President Johnson detested Sukarno and opposed further aid for Indonesia, but he was acutely sensitive to congressional criticism that he was not doing enough to counter Chinese power in the region. The last thing he needed was to get blamed for losing Indonesia to Communism. George Ball tried to reassure Johnson that "the reduction or even removal of our presence would *not* mean turning the country over to the Communists." "On the contrary," he argued, "it is more likely to mean a sharpened confrontation between the Communist Party and anti-Communists in the country."[45]

To provide the administration with political cover, Ball suggested that the president send an emissary to Jakarta for one last attempt at repairing relations with Washington.[46] The White House chose future ambassador to Vietnam Ellsworth Bunker, whose role in brokering the West Irian agreement had earned the respect of many Indonesians. It was expected that Bunker would resolve the dispute in Washington "as to Sukarno's intentions, Indonesia's power balance, and what [the] U.S. can do."[47] Bunker traveled to Jakarta at the end of March, accompanied by hard-liner David Cuthell of the State Department's Office of Southwest Pacific Affairs. For two weeks he spoke to Indonesian officials across the political spectrum and held extensive discussions with the U.S. embassy. Bunker also met four times with Sukarno, who repeatedly expressed his desire for better relations with Washington and an end to *Konfrontasi* but who made it clear that the Indonesian revolution would continue on its present course. As Bunker arrived, Sukarno announced a cabinet shuffle. He demoted Third Deputy Premier Chaerul Saleh from his position as minister of basic industries and mining and stripped Adam Malik of his portfolio as trade minister, shifting control of the ministry to Subandrio.[48] Two days later the government announced the takeover of the National Cash Register Company, one of the oldest American investors in Indonesia. As Bunker left Jakarta, the president signed a decree ordering the management takeover of all foreign enterprises in Indonesia, prompting workers to seize the headquarters of Singer Sewing Machine Company. After months of harassment Indonesia's Peace Corps contingent of physical education instructors also decided to pack up and withdraw.[49]

Bunker returned to Washington convinced that U.S.-Indonesian relations were "unlikely [to] improve [in the] near future." He cited Sukarno's ambition "to solidify [the] Afro-Asian bloc against the OLDEFOS," his near fanatical opposition to neocolonialism and imperialism, commitment to socialism, insistence that he could bend the PKI to his will, and a "mystical belief in his own destiny."[50] Moreover, Indonesians were as divided as their counterparts in Washington over what to do. Adam Malik strongly urged Bunker to resist a reduction in U.S. aid, which he thought would only encourage Subandrio and the PKI to further radicalism. On the other hand, General Nasution and other army officers thought that the American presence had become a political liability for the military and a lightning rod for the PKI and other radical forces.[51] Bunker's report to President Johnson was a clear but not unequivocal endorsement of Nasution's position. Although calling for programs that had become the target of recent protests to be phased out, he recommended maintenance of a skeletal AID staff, a small military advisory group, and completion of the army's fixed communication system. He argued that the United States should play for the long haul and maintain contact with elements of strength, such as the military, and otherwise reduce its visibility "so that those opposed to the Communists and extremists may be free to handle a confrontation . . . without being attacked as defenders [of the] U.S." "Indonesia will have to save itself," Bunker concluded, but the United States could help by "creating conditions which will give the elements of potential strength the most favorable conditions for confrontation." In other words, Bunker had sided with the CIA position in favor of a military takeover in Indonesia as the best way of advancing U.S. interests.[52]

For several months at least, the Bunker mission eased the strain in U.S.-Indonesian relations, giving the Johnson administration breathing space to find a replacement for the retiring Howard Jones, who was leaving to head up the East West Center at the University of Hawaii. The timing of Jones's departure—as a policy for which he had been the most ardent spokesman collapsed around him—was apt, as was Dean Rusk's selection of Assistant Secretary of State Marshall Green to replace him. Before his appointment as assistant secretary, Green was U.S. ambassador to Seoul when Park Chung Hee took power in a military coup. A hungry rumor mill fed on tidbits that Green's arrival in Jakarta portended similar activities. Many Indonesians viewed Green's appointment as a sign that Washington had written off the prospects of any improvement in its relations with Jakarta so long as Sukarno survived.[53] With Francis Galbraith running things in Jakarta until Green's arrival, the embassy began phasing out the U.S. aid presence and shedding all but essential staff.

The Bunker mission report omitted any mention of covert operations in Indonesia, but the Johnson administration had not given up on "creating conditions" to provoke a violent clash between the PKI and the army, or even a coup. In late February the 303 Committee reviewed the progress of its covert operations in Indonesia. (The interdepartmental 303 Committee was established in 1955 as the Special Group and was renamed in 1964; its mission was to review and authorize covert operations. Members included the national security adviser, the deputy secretary of defense, the deputy undersecretary of state for political affairs, and the director of Central Intelligence.) It also proposed an operational program for future activities, including "covert liaison with and support for existing anti-Communist groups, black letter operations, media operations, including [the] possibility [of] black radio, and political action within existing Indonesian institutions and organizations" aimed at "exploiting PKI factionalism." The operational program enjoyed the support of William Bundy and Howard Jones and was approved by the committee in early March.[54] At the Baguio Chiefs of Mission Conference a few days later, Jones mused that "from our viewpoint, of course, an unsuccessful coup attempt by the PKI might be the most effective development to start a reversal of political trends in Indonesia."[55]

Because the CIA refuses to declassify any of its operational files for Indonesia, we can only speculate about the scope of its covert operations in 1964 and 1965. However, repeated and similar statements by U.S., British, Australian, and New Zealand officials indicate that high priority was given to psychological warfare and other deceptive activities aimed at creating a climate of fear and confusion in Indonesia about the intentions of the army and the PKI in the hopes that the PKI might launch a premature coup attempt. We do know that Sukarno became convinced around this time—and rightly so—that the CIA had accelerated its operations in Indonesia. He complained to Jones and others that the CIA was "out of control." On a visit to Jakarta Michael Forrestal told Sukarno that he was "reading the wrong books," but the administration took the issue seriously enough to issue a public denial that the United States was not trying to overthrow or kill the Indonesian president, a not unreasonable suspicion in light of later revelations of CIA plots to assassinate foreign leaders—including Sukarno.[56]

Recently declassified British files reveal that in the winter of 1965 the United Kingdom had also decided to expand both military and covert operations against Indonesia. In January 1964 the British Chiefs of Staff (COS) and the office of the Commander in Chief for the Far East (CINC/FE) formed a committee "to examine deception activities" against Indonesia, refining proposals for media, military, and political activities over the course of the next twelve months. A year later the Defense and Overseas Policy Committee and the COS authorized an expansion of both "deniable" military operations, including raids up to 10,000 yards into Kalimantan, and "undeniable" operations, such as "attacks on Indonesian guerrilla camps in Borneo" and "seaborne attacks on Indonesian transit camps in Sumatra."[57] Shortly before the 303 Committee met to review the progress of its action program in February, the CINC/FE also proposed an intensified "war of nerves" against Indonesia involving both overt and covert activities, and they created a Southeast Asian monitoring unit in Singapore to coordinate propaganda operations. On March 23 U.K. ambassador to Indonesia Andrew Gilchrist and the CINC/FE called for the appointment of a "director of political warfare against Indonesia," to be based at the Information Research Department in Singapore. Gilchrist hoped that a dedicated political operative would be better placed to "act at a moment's notice to take advantage of sudden Indonesian misfortune and current events," such as a recent naval mutiny in Surabaya.[58] Three months later the Foreign Office appointed Norman Reddaway to the post, which he was scheduled to take up in early October—a bit of fortuitous timing, as it would turn out.[59]

Sukarno's fears were magnified by a welter of coup plotting and rumors that swept Jakarta in the spring of 1965, some of them probably spread by U.S. and British intelligence. A rise in bitter and often violent clashes between the PKI and anti-Communist forces throughout Java, Sumatra, and Bali lent a degree of credibility to such worries. Although sparked by the PKI's unilateral action campaign and disputes over land, the clashes took on an increasingly religious tone as NU and former Masjumi activists accused Communists and their supporters in the party's peasant organization (Barisan Tani Indonesia, or BTI) of attacking Islam.[60] One Muslim student activist who regularly visited the U.S. embassy reported a "vast amount of rebel activity and training" by antiregime elements in Sulawesi and East Java.[61] British intelligence observed that PKI officials were now "directing their efforts to subverting and penetrating the Armed forces," while army leaders claimed that the party was plotting a takeover.[62]

In April more than 200 army officers gathered to formulate the army's official doctrine, the *Tri Ubaya Cakti* (Three Sacred Promises), which called for deepening their already substantial political and economic role in Indonesian life. At about the same time General Suharto began grouping around him conservative officers, including KOSTRAD intelligence chief Ali Murtopo and General Yogi Sugama, to discuss how to counter PKI influence.[63]

Separately, the Washington-based journalistic duo Evans and Novak reported that the army had set up an "advisory commission on PKI activity," this one without Suharto.[64] After getting wind of these efforts, the PKI announced that an army "council of generals" had formed and was plotting against the government, prompting Sukarno to confront Lieutenant General Achmad Yani and demand an explanation. On April 23 Howard Jones wrote William Bundy that army leaders were preparing a coup against Sukarno the next time he left the country. While warning his army contact that the United States could not get involved, Jones "conveyed clearly my own sympathy with his objectives." The coup did not materialize, but army leaders could have no doubts about where Washington stood in the event they moved against either the PKI or Sukarno.[65]

Even as the embassy began phasing out remaining U.S. aid programs, officials in Washington and Jakarta sought to retain their contacts with military leaders. In May the Office of Public Safety program for the Indonesian Police departed, followed shortly by Colonel George Benson, who had headed the civic action program and who had the best contacts with the army. But the White House tried to move forward on a long-standing U.S. commitment to help the army build an advanced fixed telecommunications network despite widespread opposition. Generals Yani and Nasution considered such a network vital to their plans for modernizing the armed forces. In 1965 the army still had no secure means of communicating with the outer islands, much less with units in Java, leaving it dependent on an unreliable commercial network run by leftist communications workers. After the Lubis landings in September the State Department scaled back the original plan for a twelve-site network traversing the archipelago to three sites in Java and later deferred delivery for even those sites, "the bitterest pill the Indonesian Army has had to swallow in its long relationship with the American government," according to General Yani.[66]

Michael Forrestal and Ellsworth Bunker recommended moving forward with the project, using either backlogged MAP funds or selling the equipment on a commercial basis. The State Department, although conscious of the need to maintain military ties and bolster anti-Communist forces, worried that such a move would lead "to public debate which damages [the] Army and publicizes that [the] reason for [the] aid is to strengthen [the] Army against [the] PKI."[67] British officials, who had spent the last two years attempting to block weapons sales from Western nations to Indonesia, strongly opposed the sale of equipment that might enhance Indonesia's military capabilities against Malaysia and disrupt their signals intelligence interception activities.[68] Press coverage also ran strongly against providing assistance while William Broomfield led the charge in Congress, where the administration once again had to beat back amendments that would have imposed an outright ban on aid to Indonesia.[69] But House and Senate leaders quietly signaled their approval after State Department officials assured them that the network was for internal security and could be useful in helping the army to repress the PKI. Moreover, with U.S. personnel installing and maintaining such a network, its "intelligence value would be obvious."[70]

The Foreign Office watched the discussion over military assistance to Jakarta with dismay. In few other parts of the world did British and U.S. interests conflict as openly as in Indonesia, a point Whitehall referred to when it was criticized for trading with China, Cuba, and the Soviet Union.[71] Despite Johnson's tough talk and his tacit quid pro quo with Prime Minister Douglas Home, Washington was still trying to restrain the British in the interest of its larger regional policies. By early 1965 the Far East Command had deployed more than 60,000 troops in the region, "placing enormous strain on the British economy and, increasingly, on its ability to meet its obligations to NATO"—just as the Treasury was considering steep spending cuts and the gradual withdrawal of its forces from Southeast Asia. Compounding these difficulties, in January President Johnson asked Australia and New Zealand to provide forces for Vietnam, which would preclude them from sending more than a token deployment to Borneo. The British dilemma was acute. Their short-term goal was to maintain their presence in Southeast Asia until Indonesia backed down, unlikely if their plans to withdraw from east of the Suez became known. Washington, however, now *opposed* London taking decisive military action to end the conflict, further narrowing Whitehall's options.[72]

Indonesian military operations against the Malaysian mainland and in Kalimantan continued at a steady clip throughout the spring and summer of 1965, as U.S. army intelligence officers in Singapore knew from their regular briefings with British intelligence.[73] Yet Marshall Green and other U.S. officials urged their British counterparts to "resist confrontation only to [the] minimum extent necessary [to] prevent escalation."[74] Andrew Gilchrist suggested "that we ought to encourage the break-up of Indonesia as perhaps the only means of securing a respite from Confrontation," dismissing Washington's calls for restraint and support for Indonesian "moderates" such as Adam Malik and General Yani as unlikely to "contribute to such an explosion." The two nations' often divergent regional aims extended to their covert operations. British covert actions aimed "to this end and for its own sake, to spread alarm and despondency in Indonesia and aggravate and prolong the current crisis" as a way of destroying the military's ability to prosecute *Konfrontasi*. The CIA, in contrast, sought to preserve the political cohesion of the armed forces while pursuing the relatively limited objective of encouraging a move against Sukarno or drawing the PKI into a clash with the army.[75]

British fears that Indonesia intended to continue *Konfrontasi* indefinitely and U.S. concerns about the PKI's growing strength prompted renewed discussions in both London and Washington about the possibility of dismembering Indonesia, a startling development that has received little attention from historians. It is crucial to recognize the lineage of such discussions, which represented the revival of formerly discredited rollback proposals from the late 1950s. The Eisenhower administration in May 1957 first broached the subject of supporting the dissolution of Indonesia as a response to the outbreak of the PRRI revolt.[76] As early as February 1963 Lord Douglas Home expressed interest in supporting internal opposition in Sumatra or Sulawesi, telling U.S. officials that "it should be pretty easy to stir up revolt against Sukarno there" and that "Sumatra could be pinched off quite easily." In Washington it was Dean Rusk—not hard-liners in the CIA waxing nostalgic about the PRRI rebellion—who resurrected such talk. At Kennedy's funeral the secretary of state suggested to the prime minister that "it would be much better to avoid getting entangled in an area of Sukarno's own choosing. Why could not something be done in Sumatra?" In April 1964, when Foreign Minister Butler outlined British contingency plans for Malaysia, Rusk suggested that "a little war planning for other areas might usefully be done behind the scenes."[77]

The U.S. embassy in Jakarta and the consulate in Medan kept close tabs on armed unrest in South Sulawesi and North Sumatra, where British and Malaysian officials had initiated covert assistance to regional dissident forces in Sumatra, Celebes, and Kalimantan.[78] In 1965 the embassy also monitored

Malaysia's "infiltration [of] agents into Sumatra" for countersubversion, a policy long advocated by the Tunku.[79] Scattered evidence demonstrates persuasively that as hopes of working with Sukarno evaporated, officials in Washington and Jakarta gave more consideration to contingency planning aimed at possibly splitting off Sumatra and its wealth of oil and other resources from the rest of Indonesia, especially in the event of a PKI takeover or a continued escalation of *Konfrontasi*.[80]

In July 1964 Defense Secretary Denis Healey suggested that the British COS consider "subversive action on a large scale to disintegrate Indonesia." Simultaneously, embassy political officer Robert Martens argued that if the most pessimistic analyses of Sukarno were true—that he was consciously leading Indonesia toward Communism out of an ideological affinity toward the PKI—then the United States should give much greater consideration to "establishing a more friendly government or for fostering separatism in the outer islands." Martens urged that "active contingency planning should be initiated, to the extent that this may not have already been done, to decide how far the U.S. should go in supporting renewed outer island dissidence in the event of a Communist victory at the Jakarta level."[81] It is almost certain that British and U.S. officials were sharing their thoughts with each other on this matter.

A few months later James Thomson wrote to McGeorge Bundy that "we have pressed State Department to do some thinking and planning re U.S. moves or responses in the event that Sukarno's death creates fragmenting tendencies in Indonesia."[82] In March 1965 an unsigned memo to Bundy regarding possible retaliatory measures against Indonesia proposed that continued attacks against Malaysia might lead to U.S. military strikes against Indonesian supply lines and support for "independence movements in outer islands."[83] The Bunker mission, apparently responding to such currents, argued that "because the ideal of national unity is an overriding obsession with practically all Indonesians, stronger by far than any real divisive regional feeling, we should avoid becoming involved in efforts to split off Sumatra or other areas from Indonesia."[84] Discussions of this sort continued among top administration officials and their British counterparts until at least the end of 1965, nearly three months after the September 30th Movement. The Foreign and Commonwealth Relations Offices concluded in September that Britain should consider "making a determined effort to break up Indonesia because, however chaotic and unstable the consequences, this would be preferable to a strong and menacing communist state of 100 million people."[85] There is little doubt that the Johnson administration, far from being resigned to failure, was actively considering attempts to break up Indonesia should its covert operations fail and the PKI ascend to power, the same disastrous strategy it pursued during the failed PRRI-Permesta rebellions just seven years earlier.

The Hot Season in Jakarta

Over the summer of 1965 Washington evinced a deepening pessimism about the left's momentum in Jakarta and the countryside. In May Chaerul Saleh announced that Indonesia would no longer permit foreign investment and, while refraining from the confiscation of foreign enterprise, would replace foreign with Indonesian managers, few even remotely qualified for the task, accelerating the country's economic disintegration.[86] The PKI continued to demand the retooling of the Murba Party and the PNI, the Nasakomization of all levels of government, and the creation of a "fifth force" of armed peasants and workers. Sukarno's tacit embrace of Beijing continued as well, with the Indonesian news service Antara reporting on seven separate Indonesian delegations to China in the month of May alone.[87] More ominously, public discourse in Jakarta shifted sharply to the left as Subandrio and Sukarno attacked their opponents as counterrevolutionaries and hinted at further political purges. In July the government suspended participant training for Indonesian civilians at U.S. universities, shelving another crucial tool for acculturating Indonesian elites to the West. As a final indignity against Indonesian youth, on July 12 the police chief of Jakarta banned possession of records by the Beatles and the Rolling Stones. Francis Galbraith, who served as acting ambassador until Marshall Green's arrival, noted the "virtual impossibility of any overt GOI policy at this juncture deviating markedly from PKI wishes."[88] He recommended that the White House "energetically though quietly tool up for [an] effective counter-propaganda effort and other counter-actions against Sukarno's policies."[89]

Despite its rapid gains, the PKI was paying a heavy price for its radicalism. Through late 1964, organized anti-PKI efforts had been confined largely to

Jakarta and to urban elites. As the PKI political offensive continued in 1965, it generated a more widespread and violent response throughout the archipelago. The CIA reported an "expanding campaign of violence developing between PKI and Muslim organizations" in North Sumatra, East Java, and Central Java. In East Java "Muslim groups have sought to disrupt almost any Communist activity" and operated with the "sympathy and partial support of significant elements of the army and police." PKI chairman Aidit had recognized early on that the party's turn toward class struggle in the countryside, a departure from its previous emphasis on united front politics, would spark bitter opposition. But recognition that "in the village sphere at least, the party's offensives could be blunted" and even repelled encouraged anti-Communists of all stripes.[90]

At times Sukarno seemed to realize how dangerously destabilized Indonesian society had become, and he suggested that he would take steps to restore the domestic balance of power. In May he reinstated the Murba Party and dispatched General Nasution to Moscow to invite Soviet premier Aleksey Kosygin to visit Indonesia, a nod toward the army's fear of deepening Chinese influence. He also hinted at a cabinet shuffle that might bring in more moderates and perhaps restore Chaerul Saleh and Adam Malik, both PKI opponents, to their former positions.[91] British intelligence, however, dismissed suggestions of any balancing act, arguing that the PKI "has become less and less dependent upon Sukarno." One scholar of the PKI contends that by 1965 "party leaders had concluded that their movement was too large to repress" and that "its very size was a deterrent against a military strike by the Army since this was likely to ignite a civil war."[92]

Economic crisis, meanwhile, was an engine of political polarization. At the beginning of 1965 the black market exchange rate stood at 9,000 rupiah to the dollar, against a formal exchange rate of 45 rupiah to the dollar, creating enormous incentives for corruption. Although Indonesia's foreign debt had recently passed the $1 billion mark, the Bank of Indonesia was running a $300 million foreign exchange deficit. Industrial production neared collapse as foreign commercial credits dried up and spare parts and raw materials became unobtainable, spurring massive capital flight as everyone who was able to, especially Chinese entrepreneurs, moved their assets out of the country. Smuggling between Sumatra and Singapore exploded, with rubber and other commodity exports nearing levels comparable to the period before

Indonesia's severing of trade relations.[93] State-owned corporations proved particularly vulnerable, because most were regarded by their largely military managers not so much as sites of production but "as vehicles for appropriating public wealth and securing a share of the surplus of private profits." Corruption among military elites fed resentment not only among Indonesian radicals but also among lower-level officers and soldiers left to fend for themselves amid the chaos.[94] As the formal economy disintegrated, civil servants and industrial workers in urban areas took second and third jobs in the informal sector in a wild scramble to make ends meet. Economic planning became impossible, and the government "abandoned [any] effort to even formulate a budget for 1965."[95]

U.S. officials were by turns mystified and mortified at the Indonesian army's unwillingness in the face of such profound economic and political dislocation to act against Sukarno or the PKI, despite clear American encouragement. Military leaders continued to assure the U.S. mission in Jakarta that the PKI would never be allowed to take power, and over the summer coup rumors crested and fell with the regularity of the tide. Ambassador to Malaysia James Bell cited "credible sources" who suggested that there was "a strong possibility of move against the PKI and Sukarno in the near future," perhaps while Sukarno was out of town. Francis Galbraith concluded after checking around that Bell was "reading into [the] situation more than is warranted." Four days later, however, he cryptically told Bell to refrain from raising the issue of army coup plans with his sources, noting that the United States was "aware of [a] good deal of maneuvering going on beneath surface" and that Indonesians were "past masters [of] intrigue and may be deliberately trying create [the] opposite impression for [their] own reasons."[96]

The CIA's analyses betrayed the same sense of confusion over the volatile political situation as well as an inability to distinguish between the PKI's actual strength and that afforded by Sukarno's protection. A National Intelligence Estimate in July suggested that the PKI's gains were to some extent ephemeral and dependent on army leaders' reluctance—for the moment—to force a genuine test of power. The PKI had no weapons, thin support outside Java, and shallow loyalty among the peasantry. Although firmly on China's side in the Sino-Soviet split, the PKI remained a thoroughly "revisionist" party. The CIA accurately observed that the PKI "has only limited potential for armed insurgency and would almost certainly not wish to provoke the military into open opposition" but that the army was unwilling "to risk a civil war by initiating rollback of the Communists." As a result, the CIA concluded, the PKI's opponents "are discouraged and intimidated" and "even the military has all but lost the will to resist." The long-term prognosis was for both stalemate and continued PKI gains, with virtually no hope (if Langley's analysts are to be believed) for improvement so long as Sukarno lived.[97]

This was Marshall Green's bequest when he arrived in Jakarta in late July 1965. On the road from the airport to the ambassador's residence he could read the signs on which "Green Go Home!" graffiti had been scrawled.[98] At the presentation of Green's credentials a few days later, Sukarno bitterly criticized U.S. policy toward Vietnam and *Konfrontasi*, a "clear signal to Indonesians," Green wrote, "that [the] change [in] U.S. ambassadors does not rpt not mean any change in Indo opposition [to] U.S. policies." The PKI and other radical groups stepped up their regular protests in front of the embassy and other U.S. installations as Green arrived, leading the new ambassador to wonder whether the low-posture policy Washington had adopted in the wake of the Bunker mission was low enough.[99]

The day after Green's installation, demonstrators stoned the U.S. consulate in Medan after a series of rowdy protests. In early August Subandrio rejected a request by a U.S. research vessel to use the Banda Sea, implicitly challenging the right of U.S. ships to transit international waters. Green viewed the moves as signs that Sukarno might be preparing to break diplomatic ties, setting off a flurry of discussions about possible retaliatory measures. James Thomson fretted to McGeorge Bundy about the "disturbing views that are circulating on the seventh floor at State" and warned of the need to "move gently some feet away from the panic button."[100] Thomson and Chester Cooper called in Ambassador Palar and urged that Sukarno take some concrete measure to show he disapproved of recent actions, pointing to the pressure building in Congress for a break in relations.[101]

Two weeks after arriving in Jakarta, Marshall Green delivered his assessment. Sukarno was "deliberately promoting communism's cause in Indonesia," and while not a Communist himself, he saw the PKI's agenda as compatible with his own. Moreover, the Indonesian president identified anti-Communism with anti-Sukarnoism, putting political opponents at serious risk. Embassy officials reported that their contacts were wary of being seen with Americans and reluctant to talk openly about the deteriorating political scene. Indonesia, Green concluded, "has become an almost completely closed society."[102]

Sukarno's Independence Day speech on August 17 reinforced these perceptions, criticizing the U.N. at length and bitterly attacking the U.S. war against Vietnam. "Those who come from halfway around the world call themselves 'defenders of peace,'" he thundered, "while Vietnamese people who stay in their own country and mind their own affairs . . . these Vietnamese people are called aggressors. One of them must be insane, either Vietnam or the U.S. government." For the first time Sukarno identified Indonesia as part of a "Jakarta–Phnom Penh–Hanoi–Peiping–Pyongyang axis," a "natural axis forged by the course of history." He also denounced "false revolutionaries" and "capitalist bureaucrats" for undermining the economy—using the PKI's derogatory labels for army officers in charge of state enterprises—and attacked the PKI's opponents as traitorous, warning that "yesterday's revolutionaries could be today's counter-revolutionaries" (a none too subtle swipe at the army).[103]

Sukarno "has clearly identified [the] U.S. as [the] enemy," the embassy later wrote. There was little the United States could do at this point, Green suggested, except maintain ties with the military, keep as much of a diplomatic presence as possible, and continue intelligence reporting, covert operations, and propaganda activities.[104] In Washington, George Ball, Chester Cooper, James Thomson, and Robert Komer met to review U.S. policy options. As William Bundy recalls, Ball asked the group, "Isn't Indonesia as important as all Indochina?" Yes, they replied. "Wasn't it inexorably going Communist?" Again, yes. "Can we do something to slow or counter the trend?" No, they answered. How are the CIA's assets? Ball asked. Not good, was the response. In Bundy's account the meeting broke up with no resolution.[105] A week later, the CIA produced a rather muted National Intelligence Estimate on the implications of a Communist takeover in Indonesia. Surprisingly, the CIA concluded that although countries such as Malaysia and Australia would be deeply worried, given its small armed forces, "a Commie Indonesia would pose only a potential threat to [the] western position in Indonesia and to important sea and air lanes." Not only would Indonesia pose little threat, but it "would be more liability than asset" to Beijing and Moscow as it focused on internal consolidation.[106]

The Johnson administration's mounting anxiety was magnified by the Tunku's unexpected announcement on August 10 that Malaysia was expelling Singapore from the Malaysian Federation. The expulsion capped a months-long campaign by Lee Kwan Yew and his Peoples Action Party (PAP) during which he called for a "Malaysian Malaysia," enraging Malay leaders who argued that Lee had broken a PAP pledge not to intervene in mainland politics. The underlying concern of Malaysian officials was Lee's challenge to the Alliance Party and the dominance of the United Malay's National Organization (UNMO) in Malaysian politics and Malayan fears of the electoral threat posed by Singapore's Chinese majority.[107]

U.S. officials rightly speculated that Indonesia would view Singapore's independence as a vindication of its policy of *Konfrontasi* and characterization of Malaysia as a neocolonial construct.[108] More important than its impact in Jakarta, however, was the effect of Singapore's expulsion on British policy in the region. Lee Kwan Yew was unlikely to support British military bases in Singapore for the indefinite future, and bases in Malaysia were out of the question, raising the likelihood that Whitehall might now feel pressure to seek a negotiated solution to *Konfrontasi*. The head of the British Foreign Office's Committee on Malaysia sought to allay such concerns, assuring the U.S. ambassador in London that the Treasury "would maintain and if necessary increase defense expenditures at least through 1970 for costs [of] confrontation." The embassy in Kuala Lumpur chimed in that there was "no indication" British policy would change and that it was "unlikely that Singapore government wants to get British out in a hurry."[109]

In fact, Singapore's expulsion from Malaysia changed the entire calculus of British policy. With the sagging value of the British pound acting as an albatross around its neck, at the end of August the Overseas Policy and Defense Committee concluded that the country's long-term fiscal crisis made it "impossible to envision" British forces staying in either Malaysia or Singapore after 1970 and that the United Kingdom should resume diplomatic initiatives aimed at ending *Konfrontasi*, a position anathema to the Foreign Office just months before. Whitehall sprang the idea on stunned U.S., Australian, and New Zealand officials at quadripartite talks held in London in early September.[110] Johnson administration officials were outraged that Britain was even contemplating a withdrawal from Singapore, a move they predicted would undermine Western credibility throughout the region and sabotage the U.S. war in Vietnam. President Johnson quickly dispatched George Ball to London to meet with Prime Minister Harold Wilson, where for two days he spelled out Washington's opposition to British withdrawal from the region and to negotiations with Indonesia. London could not unilaterally make decisions that would undermine U.S. policies in Southeast Asia without consequences, the undersecretary warned. Ball bluntly told Wilson that "it would be a great mistake if the U.K. government failed to understand that the American effort to relieve sterling was inextricably related to the commitments of the U.K. government to maintain its commitments around the world."[111]

At the beginning of September, Marshall Green held his first meeting with Sukarno at the presidential palace, having already written off any possibility of dealing productively with the Indonesian president. They would not meet again.[112] Outside the palace Indonesian politics began to take on a surreal cast. Sukarno forged ahead with what the embassy described as a "general purge of anti-Communists." At the urging of the president, PNI head Ali Sastroamidjojo continued a massive purge of party leaders down to the provincial level throughout Java. In Medan a PKI-supported mayor was installed despite army-backed student protesters, whom Minister of Internal Affairs Sumarno denounced as "counter-revolutionaries."[113] Political consul Ed Masters, observing fear and intimidation among anti-Communists, wistfully described the situation just four months before as a comparative "golden age."[114] He cabled the State Department that "anti-U.S. propaganda . . . is daily mounting both in volume and viciousness," and he urged "the launching of psychological war against Indonesia" involving Voice of America broadcasts and the distribution of unattributable news items aimed at "discrediting the government."[115]

Meanwhile, PKI-led protests at the embassy and the U.S. consulates in Medan and Surabaya continued, as they had nearly every day since Green's arrival. On September 6 a crowd of 4,000 demonstrators sacked and destroyed the Indian embassy in Jakarta, followed the next day by a similarly large protest after which participants attacked and damaged the U.S. consulate in Surabaya. Embassy officials viewed the protests as the culmination of a "concerted campaign by [the] PKI" to shut down the U.S. presence in Indonesia. Dean Rusk began to consider just that, calling in Indonesian ambassador Palar to threaten a break in relations and retaliation against Indonesian installations in the United States.[116] Officials at Langley dashed off a protest against the possible closure of the consulate in Surabaya, reminding the White House and State Department of its value as a listening post.[117] Rusk also ordered Marshall Green to begin destroying classified documents in preparation for a possible assault on the beleaguered embassy.

Renewed fears about Sukarno's health added to the tensions in Jakarta. On August 4 Sukarno collapsed at a public function, and later in the month he canceled a trip to northern Sumatra after doctors warned that his continuous exertions had put his life in danger. The president's security forces warned of a different health threat, detecting "several plots to assassinate him" if he traveled to the overwhelmingly Muslim and anti-Communist region.[118] Uncertainty about Sukarno's longevity helped fuel rumors of subversion and plotting by both Communist and anti-Communist forces. In late August the PKI central committee warned all its branches of an impending coup by the army's Council of Generals. It issued another warning in mid-September of an alleged coup set for September 21.[119] Deputy Chief of Mission Francis Galbraith recalled that "we had rumors and reports almost every day of some kind of coup, and this became such a flood of things it was very hard to separate truth from fiction."[120] Fueling speculation, the army began to mass thousands of troops in the capital in preparation for the Armed Forces Day celebration on October 5. As coup rumors swirled and tensions rose, the chiefs of the Indonesian General Staff, a group including Generals Yani, Parman, and Suprapto, met on the night of September 30. Having received reports that night that the president was very sick, they discussed responses to Sukarno's incapacitation but left without making a decision.[121] A few hours later, their discussion, and many others that night in Jakarta, was rendered moot.

CHAPTER 7

The September 30th Movement
and the Destruction of the PKI

> I have never concealed from you my belief that a little shooting in Indonesia
> would be an essential preliminary to effective change . . . but it makes me sad
> to think that they have begun with the wrong people.
>
> —British Ambassador Andrew Gilchrist, in a letter
> to the Foreign Office, October 5, 1965

> Pressure for removing foreigners from direct control [of] extractive raw
> material production had been building for years. . . . If the September 30
> movement had not been launched or had not been aborted, removal of
> foreign oil companies would have been certainty.
>
> —Telegram from the U.S. Embassy in Jakarta
> to Washington, December 8, 1965

> If our struggle is only against Communists, and not against all those for
> whom torture, slavery, massacre and war are permissible methods of politics,
> if we welcome this slaughter or remain silent, do we deserve to survive?
>
> —Letter to the *New York Times*, January 17, 1966

On the morning of October 1, 1965, a breathless CIA officer burst into a
nondescript office in a nondescript building in Singapore that housed agents
of Britain's Information Research Department (IRD). The IRD was a propaganda arm of the Foreign Office linked to the British Foreign Intelligence
Service MI6 and connected to a network of media assets around the world.
The CIA officer had just heard the first radio broadcast of the September
30th Movement, which claimed to have forestalled a coup against President

Sukarno by a CIA-backed "council of generals," allegedly planned for October 5. As a teletype in the White House relayed the outlines of the still murky events taking place on the other side of the globe, the CIA officer in Singapore proposed the creation of "black radio" broadcasts into Indonesia, having already begun recruiting Indonesian speakers.[1] In Jakarta the movement, which had begun the night before under the alleged leadership of Lieutenant Colonel Untung with the kidnapping and killing of six generals of the Indonesian Army High Command, was already unraveling. The September 30th Movement was a relatively small-scale affair. It was poorly planned and so clumsily executed that it seemed almost preordained to fail. Major General Suharto, the commander of the army's Strategic Reserve Command (KOSTRAD) rapidly routed the meager forces under Untung's command, took control of the army, and blamed what he labeled a "coup attempt" entirely on the PKI. Within two weeks a much more momentous army-led and U.S.-backed movement to exterminate the PKI and its supporters was under way. Working with anti-Muslim organizations, student groups, and other anti-Communist organizations, the army proceeded over the next five months to murder hundreds of thousands of unarmed, alleged PKI members. The slaughter paved the way for the army's ouster of Sukarno in March 1966, its ascension to power, and the reconfiguration of Indonesian politics and foreign policy.[2]

The liquidation of the PKI in Indonesia was "perhaps the greatest setback for Communism in the Third World in the 1960s" and an event with enormous implications for each of the Great Powers. For the United States the PKI's destruction changed the political calculus of the Vietnam War and decreased by an order of magnitude the possible regional consequences of victory by Hanoi and the NLF (National Liberation Front), although ironically it was too late to affect the course of the Johnson administration's escalation of the war. For the Soviet Union and China the destruction of the left in Indonesia increased the importance that each attached to holding firm in Vietnam lest their credibility as revolutionary powers in the region be further undermined. Britain saw Sukarno's ouster and the PKI's demise as the first step toward ending *Konfrontasi* and beginning Britain's gradual retrenchment from Southeast Asia, a policy to which Washington was unalterably opposed as its military commitment to the region intensified.[3]

Domestically, the PKI's annihilation destroyed the political balance of power, dramatically undermining Sukarno and removing the only mass-based alternative to army rule. However, the emergence of the Indonesian army as the dominant political force and the military's pressing need to address the country's deep-rooted economic crisis also provided the United States and other Western powers with unusual leverage to shape the conditions under which the army would consolidate its power and legitimize its role in a military modernizing regime. U.S. officials acknowledged that the basic forces in Indonesia "are far beyond our capability to control," as Marshall Green put it. But Washington was also confident that "the next few days, weeks, and months may offer unprecedented opportunities for us to begin to influence people and events, as the military begin to understand problems and dilemmas in which they find themselves."[4]

The September 30th Movement and its bloody aftermath are central events in postwar Indonesian history, and competing interpretations of their roots, meaning, and legacy have become a cottage industry.[5] Much of the debate has centered on the precise role of the PKI, the degree of Sukarno's and/or Suharto's foreknowledge of the "coup attempt," and the local circumstances of the mass killings that followed. (Although I use the phrase *coup attempt* without quotes in the rest of this chapter, I do so with some degree of discomfort because I do not believe the history books are closed on the question of whether or not the September 30th Movement was planning a coup.) American historians in particular have spilled much ink on the question of Washington's involvement in these events. Until the fall of Suharto in 1998, one's position could reasonably be inferred from one's political sympathy to the New Order: Regime supporters blamed the PKI and rejected any American role, whereas critics viewed the "PKI as *dalang* (puppet master)" thesis with derision and charged Washington with varying degrees of complicity in the coup attempt and the mass killings.[6] Non-U.S. scholars have tended to downplay the U.S. role in recent years, rightfully concerning themselves with uncovering local histories of the September 30th Movement and its bloody aftermath.[7] The most recent and careful analysis of Indonesian sources has concluded that two leading members of the PKI—Chairman Aidit and head of the Special Bureau Sjam—conceived of and led the movement and that its aims are more properly seen as an attempted purge of the armed forces and not a coup attempt against Sukarno. Because most movement participants were summarily executed in the fall of 1965, historians have been forced to rely on flawed transcripts from army-organized show trials to debate these issues.[8]

More important than the September 30th Movement itself was the use to which Suharto, the Indonesian army, and its international supporters put the movement to justify the annihilation of the PKI. Here the recent partial declassification of U.S. and British materials has made it possible to evaluate competing claims on the role of the United States, the United Kingdom, and other nations with greater precision (and, since Suharto's fall, less ideological baggage) and to come to a few tentative conclusions. First, although the available evidence does not directly implicate the United States in the September 30th Movement or in Sukarno's ouster, quests for Washington's hidden hand are beside the point. The United States and Britain unquestionably sought to entice the PKI into a coup attempt or some other rash action in the hopes of provoking a violent response by the army and organized covert operations and propaganda efforts to this end for the better part of a year, a fact unmitigated by Washington and London's surprise at the actual timing of events. Second, U.S. encouragement of and support for the mass killings of alleged PKI supporters was greater than historians have heretofore acknowledged, as was that of other Western countries, in particular the United Kingdom. But U.S. involvement in mass murder is only part of the story, and it is less illustrative of Washington's long-range goals for Jakarta than the manner in which it engaged with the Indonesian army at the time of its greatest need to help midwife a parallel state apparatus, a strand of the story historians have accorded much less attention.

"This Business Has a Very Bad Smell to It"

The events of October 1, 1965, were a predictable, if unanticipated, result of months of bitter political combat in Indonesia between the PKI, the army, and other anti-Communist forces. What was unusual about the September 30th Movement was that the generals were killed rather than kidnapped (as were Sukarno and Hatta in August 1945 by militant students seeking to force them to declare Indonesia's independence). Each was seized from his home by small groups of soldiers and taken to Halim Air Force Base on the outskirts of Jakarta, where those not killed immediately were dispatched and dumped in a well on the edge of the base. The home of General Nasution was also raided, but Nasution managed to escape by jumping over his backyard wall into the yard of the Iraqi ambassador's residence. In the confusion Nasution's daughter was mortally wounded and the general's aide was seized in his place and later shot. Untung's meager forces haphazardly seized a number of strategic points in Jakarta, placing two battalions on three sides of Merdeka Square. Suharto—the highest ranking combat officer in the Indonesian army—was not targeted, according to Colonel Latief, because he had been forewarned of the night's events and judged agnostic or supportive of the September 30th Movement's actions. Untung's men correspondingly ignored the headquarters of the army's KOSTRAD, which stood across the square from the presidential palace on the fourth side of the square.[9]

A few hours after the broadcast, Sukarno went to Halim Air Force Base while Vice Marshall Omar Dhani flew to East Java. PKI chairman Aidit also spent the night at the base, where Pemuda Rakjat and Gerwani members had been receiving basic paramilitary training over the summer. That afternoon the movement announced the formation of a "Revolutionary Council" composed of forty-five people representing the armed forces and the major political parties, including the PKI. Sukarno's name was notable for its absence, and in fact the president refused to publicly endorse the movement, probably destroying its slim chances for success. By this time Suharto had swung into action, routing or co-opting Untung's forces in Jakarta and taking control of the army and ignoring Sukarno's orders to place the more pliable General Pranoto in command.

That evening, army paracommando troops (RPKAD) under the leadership of Lieutenant Colonel Sarwo Edhie surrounded Halim and issued an ultimatum for Dhani to surrender the base or face attack. Sukarno left Halim in his helicopter for Bogor Palace, while Lieutenant Colonel Untung, Omar Dhani, and Aidit fled to Central Java. Edhie took control of the air force base the next morning, and the September 30th Movement was basically finished in Jakarta. It took several more weeks to establish army control in East and Central Java, where support for both Sukarno and the PKI was strong and elements of the Diponegoro division had supported the September 30th Movement.[10] By October 2 Suharto was firmly in command of all strategic points in Jakarta and the army had ordered all media outlets in the city to cease publishing. All did, with the single exception of the PKI paper *Harian Rakjat*, which published an edition endorsing the September 30th Movement on the night of October 1.[11]

The U.S., British, Japanese, Australian, and other embassies initially reacted to the events of October 1 with surprise and confusion. Speculation about responsibility for the September 30th Movement centered quickly on the PKI, although the U.S. embassy admitted that the "situation in Jakarta is far from clear."[12] Nor did anyone seem to have much information about Suharto, an appalling intelligence failure considering the general had led the military campaigns for West Irian and Malaysia and headed KOSTRAD.[13] Sukarno's status was also unknown—on October 2 Marshall Green told the State Department that the president was "either dead, incapacitated, in hiding waiting for dust to settle, or masterminded [the] whole affair."[14]

Revealingly, administration officials were also uncertain about the degree of U.S. involvement. As the first reports came in from Jakarta, George Ball called CIA director Richard Helms. "Can we categorically deny this involvement of CIA operations in Indonesia situation?" After checking around, Helms replied that he could go on the record saying the CIA "had absolutely nothing to do with it."[15] Ball, guessing that the PKI leadership had orchestrated events, asked Defense Secretary McNamara to send any ships in the area steaming for Jakarta in case it became necessary to evacuate dependents or to directly intervene. Three days later, with Suharto firmly in control, William Bundy convinced McNamara to order the ships to turn around.[16]

On October 3 the bodies of the six murdered generals were discovered. Their exhumation became a major public event, and army-controlled newspapers luridly reported on their condition and printed grisly photos purportedly showing that several of the generals had been tortured, slashed with razor blades, and had their eyes gouged out and genitals cut off by bloodthirsty PKI activists from Pemuda Rakjat and the PKI Women's Front Gerwani. The army paper *Angkatan Bersendjata* on October 5 reported "barbarous deeds in the form of tortures executed beyond the bounds of human feeling," descriptions picked up and amplified by *Berita Yudha* and other publications in the ensuing months.[17] Claims about the alleged torture and mutilation of the generals became staples of a well-organized and unusually gendered Indonesian and Western propaganda campaign aimed at whipping up public frenzy in support of attacks on the PKI, and they became staples of U.S. reporting on the September 30th Movement and its aftermath for years after.[18] The descriptions, however, were deliberate fabrications—the official autopsies conducted on the bodies immediately after they were exhumed showed no signs of torture.[19]

Sukarno realized that the political forces unleashed on October 1 posed a threat to his rule, and he immediately sought to bring the army to heel. The president was also anxious to shield the air force—his strongest military ally—from the army's wrath and to prevent a crackdown on the PKI that might upend the delicate balance of power. In radio addresses Sukarno appealed for calm, denied air force involvement in the movement, and warned "we must remain on guard so that the Army and Air Force are not pitted against each other with beneficial results for the Nekolim and others."[20] Suharto and other army leaders, however, were determined to use the murder of the generals to move against the PKI and seize power, and in this task they had willing allies both locally and abroad. "Regardless of whether the Army really believes that the PKI was solely responsible," the CIA later reported, "it is presenting this as the case and is acting accordingly."[21] Army leaders quickly contacted anti-Communist groups, including Muslim organizations that had been mobilizing for months to counter the PKI in Java and Sumatra, and urged them into action. On October 2 KOTI's political chief, Brigadier General Sutjipto, called a meeting of anti-Communist leaders, who formed the Action Front to Crush the Thirtieth of September Movement (KAP-Gestapu). Two days later KAP-Gestapu held its first rally denouncing the PKI and Chairman Aidit. The Armed Forces Day parade planned for October 5 instead turned into a massive funeral march for the slain generals, punctuated by calls for revenge against the PKI. Sukarno was as conspicuous by his absence as Marshall Green was by his presence near the front of the reviewing stand—the U.S. ambassador was "much impressed," according to British ambassador Gilchrist, at the American training the slain generals had received.[22]

Army leaders also reestablished contact with the U.S. embassy, thereafter maintaining frequent, often daily communications.[23] In Washington, officials assembled an ad hoc Indonesia working group, recognizing that a major opportunity to crush the PKI was at hand but fearing the army might not go all the way.[24] "This is a critical time for the Army," George Ball told columnist James Reston. "If the Army does move they have strength to wipe up earth with PKI and if they don't they may not have another chance."[25]

The British embassy likewise complained that the army might "be letting this opportunity slip through their fingers as Sukarno attempts to exercise restraint."[26] Because no Western intelligence agencies were arguing that PKI involvement in the September 30th Movement extended to the rank and file, one can only conclude that the greatest fear of the U.S. and other governments was that the army might *refrain* from mass violence against the party's unarmed members and supporters, who by all accounts were unaware of and uninvolved in the movement. Andrew Gilchrist called for "early and carefully [planned] propaganda and psywar activity to exacerbate internal strife" and ensure "the destruction and putting to flight of the PKI by the Indonesian Army." "It's now or never," Marshall Green cabled Washington.[27]

The immediate dilemma facing the Johnson administration was how best to encourage the army to such violence. The State Department was understandably wary of overt U.S. assistance to the military, fearing that disclosure of any aid would prove embarrassing and play into the hands of Sukarno and the PKI, undermining its longer-term goals. George Ball warned the embassy in Jakarta to "exercise extreme caution in our contacts with the Army."[28] Green shared the State Department's concern, recommending that the United States hold off on aid but quietly assure Suharto and Nasution of Washington's readiness to covertly assist if needed. In the meantime the ambassador urged clandestine propaganda efforts to "spread the story of the PKI's guilt, treachery and brutality" as the "most needed immediate assistance we can give army."[29]

The United States and Britain were well positioned to provide such help. As early as 1963 the British had set up shop in Singapore for agents from the IRD. There they worked with army psychological warfare officers conducting "black propaganda operations" against Indonesia in an attempt to undermine its ability to wage *Konfrontasi*.[30] Norman Reddaway, the British coordinator of political warfare against Indonesia, who had been slated to arrive in Singapore in November, was instead rushed to his post on October 15 to take advantage of the changed circumstances in Jakarta.[31] By the time Reddaway arrived in Singapore, the Indonesian army had complete control over print media and radio and was, according to Australia's Ministry for External Affairs, "using its control . . . to discredit the PKI and limit the president's field of action by manipulation of public opinion."[32] Over the next two weeks a sophisticated, multinational propaganda operation unfolded. Reddaway and

U.S. officials received regular updates from intelligence officials and the U.S. embassy in Jakarta as well as, apparently, from listening in on the radio broadcasts of Indonesian military units. They would then distribute "strictly unattributable" news conforming to British and American propaganda aims to the *Singapore Straits Times*, the *Daily Telegraph*, the *Observer*, and the *Daily Mail* and to Western journalists who had been kicked out of Jakarta and were reporting from Bangkok, Hong Kong, or Singapore.[33] In their articles the reporters would cite "western sources" or "sources in Bangkok" who were among the few people with hard information on what was happening inside Indonesia.[34] Other press materials were doctored to make them appear as though they had originated in the Philippines or Pakistan. The Voice of America and the State Department duly circulated stories "playing up brutality of Sept. 30 rebels" from the army-controlled newspapers *Angkatan Bersendjata* and *Berita Yudha*—the only newspapers publishing in Jakarta for the first week in October—amplifying the army's own propaganda activities for international consumption.[35]

Major networks such as ABC expressed interest in exploiting the "film and tape possibilities" of the generals' exhumation and funerals. The army's propaganda themes and calls for destroying the PKI were "the sort of thing which interests the Americans," the British embassy in Washington wrote the Foreign Office. The Foreign Office instructed officials in Phoenix Park, headquarters of the British Far Eastern Command in Singapore, to "not exclude any unattributable propaganda or psywar activities" that might help the anti-PKI campaign, including a list of "suitable propaganda themes" similar to those recommended at the same time by the U.S. embassy in Jakarta.[36] Near the end of December Reddaway proudly surveyed his handiwork for the Foreign Office, noting that the Indonesian army's own propaganda often contained information drawn from printed IRD materials and that "anything which we here can have carried by a newspaper will find its way quickly into Indonesia."[37] Although it is unclear just how much British and U.S. officials kept Australian intelligence and Foreign Ministry officials apprised of their covert operations, Australian media coverage and propaganda themes mirrored those of their Anglo-American colleagues.[38]

U.S. officials were particularly interested in linking the September 30th plotters to Beijing. They helped to spread stories about China's alleged involvement and reported on caches of weapons purportedly "discovered" by the Indonesian army with the hammer and sickle conveniently stamped on them. "We have bonanza chance to nail chicoms on disastrous events in Indonesia," Green wrote the State Department. He urged a "continuation [of] covert propaganda" as one of the "best means of spreading [the] idea of chicom complicity," an allegation still being put forth by former U.S. officials forty years later.[39] Such efforts, intended or not, also encouraged attacks against Indonesia's indigenous Chinese minority and businessmen. Army leaders were actually worried by the strident tone of British and U.S. efforts and urged the U.S. embassy "not to unduly emphasize that [it] is seeking revenge," arguing that the military had its "hands full restoring order and stability without creating [the] impression it [is] going to massacre Communists."[40]

What Nasution and Suharto did want were assurances that British forces would not attack in Borneo or North Sumatra if they diverted combat units from those areas to go after the PKI and dissident army units in Central Java.[41] The U.S. embassy was reluctant to offer assurances about British goals, which included both destroying the PKI and crippling the army's ability to wage *Konfrontasi*.[42] Whitehall was likewise worried about taking any action that might strengthen the military while attacks against Malaysia continued, because both British and U.S. intelligence concluded that the army was likely to continue with *Konfrontasi*.[43] In a top secret message from Whitehall to the embassy in Washington, the Foreign Office noted the "conflict of aims in trying to build up the Generals against the PKI and bargaining with them over an end to Confrontation." British officials in both London and Jakarta worried that the White House might actually be willing to allow *Konfrontasi* to continue in the interests of bolstering the Indonesian army and forcing them to retain a strong military presence in Southeast Asia. But after consulting with Washington, the Foreign Office admitted that the army's short-term predicament outweighed London's and offered the needed assurances, noting that Suharto and other army leaders' positions on Malaysia would "continue to be our acid test for discriminating between one Indonesian faction and another."[44]

Over the next few weeks the army swiftly consolidated its gains and encouraged anti-Communist and religious groups to move against the PKI while building a public case that the party represented a mortal alien threat to Indonesian society, a cancer to be cut out of the body politic. (When asked later by the Pakistani military attaché—a man respected for his excellent intelligence ties—how he could engage in the close killing of unarmed civilians, an Indonesian military interrogator said he considered it "a duty to exterminate what he called 'less than animals.'") The CIA reported that senior Indonesian generals met after the funeral for the slain generals and agreed to implement plans to "crush the PKI."[45] Three days later KAP-Gestapu held a second rally in Jakarta, this one drawing tens of thousands, after which protestors sacked and burned the PKI's new headquarters. Signs and graffiti declaring "*Ganjang PKI*" (Hang the PKI) and "Hang Aidit" sprang up around the city.[46] On October 10, Suharto established the Operations Command for the Restoration of Order and Security (KOPKAMTIB), which he used to launch a massive purge of the government apparatus and arrest thousands of PKI activists in Jakarta.

Meanwhile, Ali Murtopo, chief of the Indonesian Army Special Operations Command (OSPUS), expanded the army's own propaganda operations. Sordid accounts and photos of the generals' murder and alleged mutilation circulated throughout the country, and army newspapers reported the discovery of PKI death lists, mass graves, and documents detailing the party's purported plans for the annihilation of its opponents. Sukarno railed publicly and privately against the army campaign, telling a gathering of military officers and journalists at Bogor Palace in November, "Over and over it's the same thing. . . . It's always Gestapu, Gestapu, Gestapu, Gestapu, Gestapu, razors, razors, razors, razors, razors, a grave for a thousand people, a grave for a thousand people, a grave for a thousand people, electric chair, electric chair, electric chair—over and over again, the same thing!" One scholar of the post–coup attempt massacres has concluded that "in the highly charged atmosphere of the time these 'revelations' were sufficient to make the party in general appear to be a demonic force whose destruction would be a service to the nation."[47] Although we still lack access to many of the relevant classified U.S. and British materials, it is highly likely that a key element of U.S. and British covert operations in this period involved the creation of such "black" propaganda inside Indonesia itself.[48]

With the exception of Medan, where KOSTRAD forces under the command of Brigadier General Kemal Idris immediately began slaughtering alleged PKI members—mainly rubber plantation workers—on a large scale after October 1, Suharto appears initially to have issued few direct orders for military commanders in the provinces to take specific actions against the party.[49] The army was far from monolithic, and in significant swaths of Central and East Java local commanders remained loyal to Sukarno, and some initially were even sympathetic to the September 30th Movement. But the OSPUS propaganda campaign, encouragement of KAP-Gestapu actions, and public statements by Suharto sent clear signals of the new leadership's intention to move violently against the PKI. When local army units hesitated or Suharto judged local officers insufficiently anti-Communist, he purged them and sent loyal RPKAD units to organize the killings, often working through local civilian forces. In East Java members of the NU (Nahdlatul Ulama) youth wing Ansor led attacks on PKI members and Chinese businessmen, with the first mass killings reported in mid-October. In Aceh, Muslim leaders again took the lead, initiating "what amounted to a holy war of extermination" in early October against PKI members and often their extended families, killing thousands over the next two months and reportedly wiping out entire villages.[50]

On October 13 Dean Rusk cabled Jakarta that the time had come "to give some indication to military of our attitudes toward recent and current developments." The army's campaign against the PKI was picking up steam, and "if [the] army's willingness to follow though against the PKI is in any way contingent upon or subject to influence by U.S., we do not wish [to] miss opportunity for U.S. action."[51] The State Department still had great reservations about substantially aiding the army, because it was not yet clear who was in charge or what the army's longer-range intentions were. Moreover, Sukarno still wielded substantial authority and commanded the loyalty of significant elements of the military. The risks of revelation with covert aid were great, and the administration considered it "essential not [to] give Subandrio and PKI citable evidence that U.S. supports Army against Sukarno."[52]

The next day, Sukarno was forced to name General Suharto commander of the armed forces. Most army leaders were anxious to avoid confronting Sukarno and hoped that he would bow to political realities and condemn the PKI and the September 30th Movement. The Great Leader's persistent refusal to do so deeply frustrated the army, prompting some to call for his overthrow.[53] "There are now two power centers in Indonesia, and not one," the embassy cabled Foggy Bottom. It was important to let the army know which side the United States was on. (The Indonesian army, for its part, thought it was dealing with *three* power centers: the State Department, the Pentagon, and the CIA.)[54] General Nasution provided an opportunity when his aide approached Marshall Green to request portable communications equipment for use by the Army High Command. It was just the sort of request the embassy could easily—and discreetly—meet, the State Department noted with approval, observing that the army was still keen to hide U.S. support and that "for [the] short run our assistance to them would probably have to be on covert or semi-covert basis related [to] specific, small, ad hoc needs."[55] The move toward covert U.S. assistance for the Indonesian military signaled Washington's tacit withdrawal of recognition of Sukarno as the legitimate leader of Indonesia.

Other countries had the same idea, especially Japan and West Germany. Late in October, in response to Indonesian army overtures, the Japanese Foreign Ministry shifted its support from Sukarno to Suharto and began making quiet preparations to covertly channel rice and textile assistance through the army.[56] Japanese ambassador Saito told Marshall Green that the time had come "for other countries to do something extra in the field of economic assistance for Indonesia," suggesting that Washington discreetly finance economic assistance through third parties. He later explained to British officials that "An Army dominated government is so much better than any other prospect that we cannot allow it to be ruined in public esteem by an accumulation of public misery in the form of a rice famine."[57] The Japanese embassy apparently also cooperated with its American and British counterparts in spreading unattributable propaganda about the PKI. Johnson administration officials emphasized the need to establish a "close liaison with Japanese," because Tokyo was the "only major free world country able to exert substantial influence in Indonesia."[58]

The embassy's political reporting during these weeks wavered between optimism at every indication of Sukarno and the PKI's decline and anxiety at every suggestion that the army might blow its opportunity to exterminate Communism in Indonesia and deal Sukarno a fatal blow in the process. The CIA warned in early October of the danger that the army might only "settle for action against those directly involved in the murder of the generals and permit Sukarno to get much of his power back," a concern shared by the Foreign Office. A few weeks later Green fretted that the army "seems to be moving toward a 'political settlement'" and might "hush up evidence of [Sukarno's] involvement in September 30" in order to preserve national unity, perhaps to the point of permitting a rehabilitated Communist Party to reemerge.[59] The army's destruction of the PKI, the ambassador cabled Washington, "will not be successful unless it is willing to attack communism as such," which meant going after Sukarno and the entire PKI apparatus, including unarmed rank-and-file members and affiliates. Despite his worries, Green observed that the army "has nevertheless been working hard at destroying PKI and I, for one, have increasing respect for its determination and organization in carrying out this crucial assignment."[60]

The Post–September 30 Massacres and the U.S. Response

U.S. officials initially thought that the struggle against Sukarno and the PKI would be bitter and protracted. But evidence reaching the embassy in Jakarta by the end of October indicated that the army was moving decisively to break the back of the PKI and defying or ignoring President Sukarno's efforts to restrain it. Local military commanders were taking the initiative to ban the PKI and its affiliates, whereas weak PKI branches simply dissolved in a desperate attempt to stave off annihilation. Only a month after the murder of the generals, the PKI had been banned or dissolved in almost all of Java and Sulawesi, and despite his maneuvering, cajoling, and threats, Sukarno was proving unable to shield his political allies from attack.[61] The army was especially keen to get Subandrio (whom the political correspondent of the army newspaper *Berita Yudha* described to Australian embassy officials in Jakarta as "a bastard who will get what's coming to him"), in part because it could not challenge Sukarno directly. In late October army leaders convinced the president to remove Subandrio from his position as foreign minister, later placing him under house arrest when he attempted to leave the country.[62]

As the welcome returns on the army's campaign against the PKI poured in, Marshall Green's anxiety dissipated and he prodded Foggy Bottom to "explore [the] possibility of short-term one shot aid on covert, non-attributable basis" as a sign of U.S. support.[63] The State Department replied with a lengthy assessment approved by Dean Rusk. The PKI was "in headlong retreat in [the] face [of] mass attacks encouraged by Army," which was "already making top policy decisions independently of Sukarno and is more and more acting as a de facto government." Moreover, as Indonesia's economic and political crisis deepened, the military would have to turn to the West for assistance, with the United States and Japan in particular poised to help. The army would need food, raw materials, access to credit, and "small weapons and equipment . . . to deal with the PKI." As a result, "the next few days, weeks, and months may offer unprecedented opportunities for us to begin to influence people and events, as the military begin to understand problems and dilemmas in which they find themselves."[64] This meant, in the short run, signaling to army leaders the need to halt *Konfrontasi*, cease political attacks against U.S. policy, and end the harassment of U.S. oil companies.[65]

At the end of October, White House officials established an interagency working group to plan for covert aid to the Indonesian military to meet its needs in fighting the PKI. Many initial reports reaching the embassy couched PKI resistance to Muslim and army-led attacks as the opening salvos of a possible guerrilla campaign.[66] Although in most regions the PKI—which had never organized itself for armed struggle—was unprepared for the attacks against it, the party was putting up stiff resistance in Central Java. A few days before the working group met, the embassy received "multiple reports of increasing insecurity and bloodshed in Central Java, particularly around Solo, Semarang and Jogja." Later reports told of fierce clashes between PKI youth and Ansor members, with dozens of casualties on both sides.[67] On October 18 Suharto authorized the deployment of several RPKAD battalions under the command of Lieutenant Colonel Edhie to the provincial capital of Semarang in Central Java, after which mass killings of PKI supporters commenced. Shortly after, the commander of the Central Java military area declared a state of war.[68]

The Indonesia working group instructed the embassy to inventory the army's needs for waging war against the PKI. The most pressing need was for tactical communications equipment for both army headquarters and field units, which the working group thought the administration should provide covertly through a third country, such as Thailand, using untraceable existing stocks rather than attempting to resume MAP shipments. In late October a CIA communications specialist traveled to Jakarta to consult with the embassy and conduct an on-site investigation of the army's needs. Two days after the working group met, General Sukendro made the first high-level approach to the embassy, requesting rice, communications equipment, medicines, and small arms. Ambassador Green recommended that the administration move forward with assistance, noting approvingly that the army was "moving relentlessly to exterminate the PKI."[69]

Washington agreed, but the administration was split over whether to tie the provision of short-term covert aid to larger questions concerning relations with Jakarta. White House and Pentagon officials thought that the United States should attach no strings to covert aid, arguing "it is important to assure the Army of our full support of its efforts to crush the PKI." The State Department disagreed, arguing that now was the time to open up a broader political dialogue with Suharto and Nasution and to make clear that Washington expected Indonesia to reverse course on policies inimical to U.S. interests as a condition of aid.[70] A few days later Francis Galbraith met with Nasution's contact for a discussion along these lines. Although the United States was "generally sympathetic with and admiring of what [the] army [is] doing," Galbraith said, serious disagreements between the two countries remained, especially with regard to U.S. oil interests, which if not resolved could preclude the extension of aid.[71]

The White House and the CIA still worried about the risks of exposure as they moved to covertly aid the army, which they had functionally recognized as Indonesia's new government, in overthrowing Sukarno and destroying the PKI.[72] The administration set up contact with General Sukendro (who had studied at the University of Pittsburgh and was one of the CIA's highest level contacts in the army) and a designated liaison in Bangkok, with whom it discussed the army's requests for communications equipment, small arms, and other supplies totaling more than $1 million. Sukendro cut short a visit to Beijing and stopped by the CIA station in Bangkok upon hearing of the September 30th Movement, before returning to Jakarta.[73] The 303 Committee approved the provision of medical supplies on November 5 and established covert mechanisms for delivery, which began two weeks later. The White House also authorized the CIA station in Bangkok to provide small arms to Sukendro in order to "arm Muslim and nationalist youth in Central Java for use against the PKI." The CIA was not yet convinced of the army's need for the weapons and was anxious about its ability to control the use and distribution of arms, which were being given to poorly trained Muslim militias and student groups, such as the Indonesian Student Action Front (KAMI), and thus was at risk of exposure. But it concluded that "these risks . . . must be weighed against the greater risk that failure to provide such aid which the Army claims it needs" would weaken Washington's influence down the road.[74]

The 303 Committee met again two weeks later to discuss the army's "urgent need for communications equipment." Suharto and Nasution were expressing grave concerns about their ability to communicate not just with regional military commanders in outlying provinces but with army leaders in Jakarta, hampering the coordination of anti-PKI military operations. To this end General Sukendro requested portable voice radios for the general staff in Jakarta; an army voice circuit linking Jakarta with military commands in Sumatra, Java, and Sulawesi; and tactical communications equipment for army units operating in Central Java.[75] The embassy team in Jakarta recommended approval of Sukendro's request as "critical" in the army's struggle against Sukarno and the PKI and argued that the equipment's importance "far outweighs [its] relatively minor cost."[76] The 303 Committee approved the aid but urged that "extreme care" be taken to prevent disclosure of its origins, delaying delivery for several weeks. In early December the CIA located and purchased mobile antennae and the first installment of the radio equipment on a commercial basis, arranging for its covert delivery from Clark Air Force Base in the Philippines to KOSTRAD headquarters in Jakarta.[77] According to the British embassy in Washington, the transaction— which Ambassador Gilchrist estimated was worth nearly $1 million—was "so covert that it is not intended to show up in Congress at all."[78] CIA technicians trained army communications officers and tuned their radios to frequencies known in advance by the National Security Agency (NSA). Afterward the NSA monitored army transmissions, providing U.S. intelligence officials with detailed information about army operations, including specific orders to kill individual PKI members.[79]

The Johnson administration's decisions to extend aid were made after it had become clear that the United States would be directly assisting the army, Muslim organizations, student groups, and other anti-Communist forces in a campaign of mass murder against unarmed civilians—alleged members of the PKI and its affiliate organizations. Moreover, U.S. officials knew and expected that the covert assistance they provided would further this campaign.

Army contacts informed the embassy that 150 PKI members had been executed in Jakarta during the first week of October alone by forces under the leadership of West Java military commander General Adjie and that firing squads had been formed elsewhere for this purpose.[80] At the end of October reports reached the embassy of mass attacks against PKI supporters in East, Central, and West Java. A U.S. military adviser just returned from Bandung reported that villagers were "clearing out PKI members and affiliates and turning them over to Army" for arrest or execution.[81]

The day before the 303 Committee approved the shipment of medicines to the army, the embassy cabled the State Department that RPKAD forces in Central Java under Edhie's command were "providing Muslim youth with training and arms and 'will keep them out in front' against PKI." While army leaders arrested higher-level PKI leaders for interrogation, "smaller fry" were "being systematically arrested and jailed or executed."[82] In North Sumatra and Aceh a few days later, "IP-KI [*sic*] Youth Organization [the Ikatan Pendukung Kemerdekaan Indonesia, or League of Upholders of Indonesian Independence, was an army-affiliated party], and other anti-Com elements" were engaged in a "systematic drive to destroy PKI . . . with wholesale killings reported"; the "specific message" from the army "is that it is seeking to 'finish off' the PKI."[83] On November 13 police information chief Colonel Budi Juwono reported that "from 50–100 PKI members are being killed every night in east and central Java by civilian anti-Communist groups with blessing of Army." Three days later "bloodthirsty" Pemuda Pantjasila members informed the consulate in Medan that the organization "intends to kill every PKI member they can get their hands on." Other sources told the consulate that "much indiscriminate killing is taking place." Consular officials concluded that, even accounting for exaggerations, a "real reign of terror" was taking place.[84] The CIA reported late in the month that former PKI members in Central Java were being "shot on sight by Army." Missionaries in East Java told the consulate in Surabaya that 15,000 Communists had reportedly been killed in the East Javanese city of Tulungagung alone. Again, even discounting for exaggerations, the consulate reported that a "widespread slaughter" was taking place.[85] An Indonesian intelligence officer in East Java described several mass killings of PKI activists and supporters in Kediri (where 300 peasant farmers were killed, apparently by mistake), Wates

(1,200 killed), and Ponggok (about 300 killed), with "many of those being killed . . . followers who do not know much."[86] It was still November.

The U.S. response to mass murder in Indonesia was enthusiastic—and instructive. Former U.S. officials such as CIA station chief Hugh Tovar (whose delight at the killings is exceeded only by the tendentiousness of his account of the U.S. role) and some historians have argued that Washington was either unaware of the killings when covert aid began or was "taken aback . . . by the violence of the purge."[87] Both claims are patently false. They ignore voluminous contemporary accounts of the slaughter that were reaching the U.S. and other embassies and the crucial fact that Washington continued its assistance long after it was clear that mass killings were taking place and in the expectation that U.S. aid would contribute to this end. Not a single U.S. official, however, ever expressed concern in public or private about the slaughter, although even cursory readers of the U.S. press understood what was happening.[88] "Our policy was silence," Walt Rostow later wrote President Johnson, a good thing "in light of the wholesale killings that have accompanied the transition" from Sukarno to Suharto.[89] In fact, Washington was so effusive in its support for Suharto and his allies that army officials told the embassy "to lay off praising it" for fear of tarnishing their nationalist credentials, a point British officials also made.[90] The CIA argued that "we should avoid being too cynical about [the army's] motives and its self interest, or too hesitant about the propriety of extending . . . assistance *provided* we can do so covertly" and without being embarrassed. "No one cared," recalled Howard Federspiel, the State Department's INR staffer for Indonesia in 1965, "as long as they were Communists, that they were being butchered."[91]

The United States and Britain were hardly alone in this disgraceful performance. Thailand offered rice on the condition that the army destroy both the PKI and Sukarno. The Soviet Union, while denouncing the slaughter in Indonesia, continued to ship weapons in an effort to maintain proper relations with the military and further undermine Chinese influence, "letting it be known to the Generals that if it comes down to a choice between the PKI or no PKI, the USSR would prefer the latter." (Nasution, still suspicious of the United States, remained on friendly terms with the USSR, a stance that may help to explain Suharto's increasing marginalization of him as he forged closer ties with Washington.) Before long, Soviet officials were privately blaming the September 30th Movement and the destruction of the PKI on Chinese-inspired adventurism, having long since abandoned the party to its fate.[92]

At the height of the massacres the Johnson administration continued to extend covert assistance directly to the forces carrying out the killings, apparently including small arms delivered to the army through the CIA station in Bangkok.[93] In early December the State Department also approved a covert payment of 50 million rupiah to finance the activities of KAP-Gestapu. Marshall Green noted approvingly that KAP-Gestapu's activities "have been an important factor in the Army's program," especially in Central Java, where it was leading the attack on the PKI. The ambassador considered the risks of revelation in this case to be "as minimal as any black bag operation can be."[94] Harry Kern, stalwart of the Japan lobby, set up a meeting between embassy officials and associates of former Japanese prime minister Kishi to discuss funneling additional U.S. assistance through Japanese intermediaries.[95] At about this time General Achmad, the newly appointed chief of KOTI's economic staff, told military attaché Willis Ethel that he estimated that more than 100,000 people had been killed in North Sumatra and East and Central Java alone. If accurate, Ethel noted, this meant that "far more communists have been killed in Indonesia over past two months than even in Vietnam."[96]

The embassy also turned over lists identifying thousands of PKI leaders and cadres to Indonesian army intermediaries.[97] For several years U.S. officials had considered the Indonesian army's intelligence gathering on the PKI to be woefully inadequate, especially at the local level. Marshall Green cabled the State Department in 1966 that Indonesian authorities still "seem to lack even the simplest information on PKI leadership."[98] Political officer Robert Martens and CIA analysts in the embassy compiled the lists, using published sources, to create detailed profiles of the PKI and its affiliate organizations from the national leadership down to regional, provincial, and local cadres. Martens handed the lists to Tirta Kentjana Adhyatman, an aide to Adam Malik who in turn passed them on to Suharto, who used them to track down PKI members for arrest and execution.[99] Embassy officials subsequently denied that they had drawn up assassination lists, as did the major media in numerous exculpatory articles. But the embassy's actions were hardly without precedent. In both Guatemala and Iraq the CIA turned over similar lists of Communists, government officials, and others "to eliminate immediately in event of [a] successful anti-Communist coup," going so far as to compile how-to manuals on political assassination.[100]

The postcoup massacres in Indonesia varied widely according to regional circumstances, as numerous local studies have shown, although much research remains to be done.[101] In East Java and North Sumatra, for example, fragmentary evidence suggests that local Muslim groups might have launched the first attacks against PKI supporters, encouraged and often assisted by local army units acting with relative caution until reinforcements arrived from Jakarta. In Central Java and Bali arriving RPKAD forces initiated the massacres when they arrived in early December, first hastily arming and training Muslim youth and other anti-Communist groups and then conducting village sweeps in which local PKI members were identified and either arrested or executed. This was close killing, often conducted with bamboo spears, machetes, or army-supplied weapons against one's neighbors. In the village of Pasuruan in East Java, a British engineer named Ross Taylor who was working at the Gratit Cotton Spinning Factory described the massacres of workers at the nearby Nebritex textile factory. Using lists of known or suspected members of the PKI, the trade union SOBSI, or PKI-affiliated groups, the local army commander placed victims in one of five categories, killing those in the first three and arresting the rest. Taylor estimated that 2,000 people had been killed in the vicinity of the factory since late November, with army units working from the main roads and radiating outward.[102]

The most intense killings generally took place where the PKI and its affiliates were strongest and where PKI activities, particularly in the area of land reform and labor activism, posed the greatest threat to existing social relations. As one scholar of the postcoup massacres put it, "The PKI was attacked because it proposed a full-scale restructuring of Indonesian society and in doing so had already created its own victims amongst those it saw as the beneficiaries and upholders of the established social order."[103] The army's opposition to the PKI was, the CIA noted, "far more complicated than simple anti-communism." This was a war of position—army leaders viewed their campaign to eliminate the PKI leadership and destroy its infrastructure in strategic terms, as "a power struggle, not an ideological struggle," with a rival power center in Indonesia that posed the chief obstacle to their vision of military-led modernization. The British consul at Medan framed the army-PKI struggle in Sumatra over control of local ports and rubber and tin estates as one "for the commanding heights of the Indonesian economy" and for the foreign exchange reserves and access to resources that such control conveyed. Not surprisingly, the tin and rubber estates in Northern Sumatra were the scene of some of the bloodiest attacks against PKI supporters, with the army "arresting, converting or otherwise disposing of some 3,000 PKI members a week."[104] The army, however, had to balance its desire to eliminate the PKI as a political force with its eventual need to restore political stability. By mid-December army leaders were expressing concern that the indiscriminate nature of the slaughter might exacerbate the breakdown in state power and unleash "monster[s] largely of its own creation," such as political Islam and the student movement that could emerge as rival power centers and complicate the consolidation of their rule.[105] Unevenly, the army began taking steps to bring the killings more directly under their control, although the murder of PKI supporters and prisoners continued on a smaller scale well into 1966.

"The savagery and scale of the killings" in Indonesia, the Australian embassy observed in 1966, "is probably unique."[106] Estimates of the death toll from the massacres vary widely, ranging from the 78,000 cited by Sukarno in December 1965, well before the killings had ended, to 1 million, the conclusion of a survey conducted by "university graduates" at the behest of KOPKAMTIB in 1966. At least 1 million more were arrested, with many tens of thousands kept in prison well into the 1970s.[107] U.S. and British officials were certainly aware by early 1966 that hundreds of thousands had been killed. In mid-January, armed forces liaison Colonel Stamboul told British military attachés attending a briefing at army headquarters that half a million people had been killed. Australian officials claimed to have an Indonesian police report putting the death toll "in Bali alone at 28,000."[108] Ambassador Gilchrist told Marshall Green a month later he thought the total toll was closer to 400,000, a figure that the Swedish ambassador found "quite incredible" and a serious underestimate based on his recent travels in the countryside.[109] Walt Rostow cited even lower figures of 300,000 dead in briefings for President Johnson.[110] Journalist Stanley Karnow, after a tour of Central and East Java and Bali, told political consul Edward Masters that press estimates based on Western diplomatic sources were "way too low" and that he thought 400,000 a minimum figure. Appropriately, Masters had just met with an assistant to Adam Malik—who also thought U.S.-cited figures of 300,000 were far too conservative—to discuss "the desirability of downplaying the extent of the carnage," remarking that "we believe it wiser to err on the side of lower estimates, especially when questioned by the press."[111]

General Suharto and the Indonesian army must bear primary responsibility for the slaughter following the September 30th Movement, in addition to the NU, PNI, and other civilian groups that made up the bulk of the civilian militias engaged in the killings. Although the roots of the massacres lay in long-standing local grievances against the PKI, as Harold Crouch and other scholars have concluded, "the huge scale of the massacre was possible only because of the encouragement given by the army."[112] The extermination of the PKI was a military campaign, planned and directed by the armed forces to clear away the chief barrier to its own ascension to power. The killings did not, as the U.S. embassy, Western journalists, and many Indonesia scholars argued, stem from "that strange Malay streak, that inner, frenzied blood-lust" rooted in pathologies of Indonesian culture that produced "a kind of mass running amok."[113]

Perpetrators of mass violence in the twentieth century, however, usually have accomplices, and the passive or direct involvement of external powers. The killings in Indonesia were no different. Indonesia's international supporters could have pressured it to limit the scope and scale of the violence— had they considered it in their interests to do so. The United States, however, viewed the wholesale annihilation of the PKI and its civilian backers as an indispensable prerequisite to Indonesia's reintegration into the regional political economy, the ascendance of a military modernizing regime, and the crippling or overthrow of Sukarno. Indeed, Washington did everything in its power to encourage and facilitate the army-led massacre of alleged PKI members, and U.S. officials worried only that the killing of the party's unarmed supporters might not go far enough, permitting Sukarno to return to power and frustrate the administration's emerging plans for a post-Sukarno Indonesia.[114] This was efficacious terror, an essential building block of the neoliberal policies that the West would attempt to impose on Indonesia after Sukarno's ouster. U.S. officials have always denied that Washington offered meaningful covert assistance to the army as it carried out these killings and have ignored the question of covert operations before September 30 entirely.[115] Many scholars of U.S.-Indonesian relations, lacking access to significant CIA materials, have largely accepted this interpretation.[116] But declassification of just a fraction of the CIA's records demonstrates that the agency's covert operations in Indonesia were more widespread and insidious than previously acknowledged. These records also reveal that the Johnson administration was a direct and willing accomplice to one of the great bloodbaths of twentieth-century history—the Cold War equivalent of aiding and abetting the Hutu genocide in Rwanda. The performance of Washington's allies in London and Tokyo, and its adversaries in Moscow for that matter, was hardly less disgraceful, with each maneuvering for advantage amid the carnage. The major media did their part as well, crudely cheering the "boiling bloodbath" in Indonesia as "the West's best news for years in Asia." The last word might be left to C. L. Sulzberger of the *New York Times*, who observed approvingly with the crude yet unremarkable racism of the day that "the killing attained a volume impressive even in violent Asia, where life is cheap."[117]

The Price of Aid

The Johnson administration remained deeply ambivalent about the Indonesian military even as it cooperated with the army to annihilate the PKI and seize control of the country. This ambivalence stemmed partly from the army's oft-wavering stance on removing President Sukarno and his supporters from power and partly from concern that they would resist Western demands for a restructuring of Indonesia's economy and foreign policy. Suharto recognized that Sukarno still commanded broad civilian and military support and was content to chip away at his power gradually rather than risk a frontal assault that might lead to civil war or undermine the legitimacy of military rule. Had Sukarno been willing to condemn or ban the PKI, accept a purge of September 30th Movement supporters, and tack toward the military, Suharto and other army leaders might have been forced to seek an accommodation allowing him to remain president with diminished authority, almost certainly reducing the death toll among low-level PKI supporters. But Sukarno's obstinacy on all counts alienated the military, Muslim groups, and restive students, and Indonesia's continued economic crisis eroded his remaining support and made Suharto's slow-motion coup against him easier.

Officials in Washington, London, Canberra, and other capitals were aghast at the prospects of any accommodation and insisted that the military must not only destroy the PKI but also get rid of Sukarno and his supporters. The U.S. embassy fretted that the army was "not yet willing to really challenge Sukarno and will continue to make concessions to preserve unity."[118] Marshall Green pressed the State Department to explore the "possibility of breaking up or restructuring of Indo state and courses of action open to us under varying conditions" should Sukarno reverse the army's gains.[119] A month later, Green suggested that the indiscriminate slaughter of PKI supporters and Suharto's strengthened internal position had mitigated the need for such planning. U.S., British, Australian, and New Zealand officials attending an ANZUS meeting agreed that "a radically new situation in Indonesia is developing"; they decided that for the time being "a policy of deliberately attempting to dismember Indonesia should be excluded." But so long as Sukarno remained in power, it would be difficult, if not impossible, for the United States to resume substantial assistance.[120]

More important, as David Cuthell reminded William Bundy, the army was "still strongly nationalistic and crushing the PKI won't change this."[121] U.S. officials anticipated that relations with Jakarta were unlikely to improve in the short run even if Sukarno were removed from the scene, because the armed forces had their own institutional interests to protect. They also recognized, however, that the army desperately needed foreign aid, investment, and capital to consolidate its power and address the country's economic crisis, giving the United States and the international community more generally substantial leverage. Although reluctant to push too hard too fast, the Johnson administration was determined to use this leverage to press for basic changes in the country's foreign and economic policies as they helped the armed forces ascend to power, changes they expected the military to resist.

Within forty-eight hours of the coup attempt, McGeorge Bundy and Walt Rostow outlined for George Ball the army's need for short-term credit and commodity assistance if it took power. Washington's help in supplying this "critically needed margin of resources" could have a big payoff, they wrote, and they urged Ball to develop detailed contingency plans with these considerations in mind.[122] A week later the generals began approaching the U.S. and other Western embassies, beginning with West Germany, seeking assistance in procuring weapons, spare parts, cotton, rice, and other supplies. "People we haven't heard from in years, including PSI and PRRI-Permesta [supporters], are coming out of woodwork," Green cabled Washington. Many of these officers, whom George Ball derisively termed the "international fast-buck fraternity," were "given fishing licenses by Suharto" as a form of patronage and sent in search of aid "to see if anything sticks."[123] By late October they were approaching prominent Texas cotton brokers, including heavyweights such as former assistant secretary of state Will Clayton and associates of right-wing oil billionaire H. L. Hunt, pressing them to apply for export licenses and guarantees for worthless Bank of Indonesia letters of credit so they could export cotton to Indonesia.[124]

Others came seeking rice. As hyperinflation wiped out the rupiah's value, farmers began hoarding their crops, causing shortages and skyrocketing prices in the midst of above average harvests. General Sukendro, concerned about the political implications of rice shortages, quickly bought 70,000 tons from Thailand and injected it into the market. But army leaders still worried about how to bring prices under control, especially when they lacked access to foreign exchange. The provision of even rice aid carried risks. Australian and New Zealand Foreign Ministry officials, who like others acknowledged Indonesia's need for "political" rice, worried that pro-Communist forces would use any Western assistance to attack the nationalist credentials of the armed forces.[125] When KOTI economic head General Achmad alerted the Pentagon and U.S. Navy to the Indonesian army's desire for the covert delivery of 50,000 tons of rice, the White House dismissed the request as a "practical impossibility." State Department officials argued that the United States "should be in no hurry to get such aid, and when we do there should be definite strings attached to it." They instructed the embassy to rebuff such approaches until Nasution or Suharto sent direct word and provided some concrete indication of the army's future political and economic plans.[126] Through his aide Nasution sent similarly cautious signals.[127]

Although it was too early to resume overt aid, it was not too early to begin making plans. As covert aid began to flow and the massacre of PKI supporters commenced, Washington began detailed discussions with the embassy and its allies to clarify the conditions under which they might resume economic assistance to Indonesia and the broader policy goals to which aid would be tied.[128] At quadripartite talks held in London in early December, U.S., British, Australian, and New Zealand officials agreed on the need to refrain from aiding Indonesia until the military's broad intentions were clearer. The administration needs to "begin letting [the army] know what the U.S. expects . . . in return for assistance," Dean Rusk wrote.[129] The out-lines of U.S. thinking were falling into place, to be endlessly reiterated in the coming months. Merely smashing the PKI was not enough. Sukarno would have to go, *Konfrontasi* would have to end, and attacks on U.S. policy and investments would have to cease before significant aid would be resumed. Once resumed, aid would be tied to Indonesia's willingness "to tackle some of the structural problems which have prevented economic development"; aid would also be directly linked to U.S.- and IMF-approved economic plans and would be disbursed on a multilateral basis, preferably with the Japanese taking the lead.[130]

U.S. officials expressed repeated frustration that Suharto and other military officers wanted to put off these issues and "treat [the] aid question in isolation from [the] broader politico-economic context [of] U.S.-Indo relations." All army leaders seemed to want to know, as one group put it to Marshall Green, was "how much is it worth to us that PKI be smashed and trend here reversed, thereby saving big part [of Southeast Asia] from communism?"[131] The U.S. frustration was misplaced. Australian embassy officials noted in mid-October that the army was already "seeking advice from the University of Indonesia's Economic Faculty" about "putting order into the economy."[132] Army leaders were reasonably clear about their strategy—to extort as much Western assistance as they could to consolidate their power while avoiding the conditions on aid that Washington hoped to impose as the price of support for military rule. As part of Washington's efforts to open up a more wide-ranging dialogue with Indonesian officials, the embassy approached civilians such as Adam Malik, who also bemoaned the army's focus on short-term security issues, so much so that he began briefing Suharto's mystics in an effort to broaden the general's political thinking.[133]

The position of U.S. oil companies in Indonesia was unquestionably the most important of these broader concerns.[134] Just before the coup attempt, U.S. officials learned that Sukarno had instructed Third Deputy Prime Minister Chaerul Saleh to complete the management takeover of U.S. oil companies and accelerate the purchase of their refining assets by the end of the year. At the end of October Stanvac and Caltex officials reported that the government's position had not changed.[135] The U.S. mission recognized that the army could ill-afford to take actions that suggested it was turning to the West, and Suharto's ally, Ibnu Sutowo—then battling Chaerul Saleh for control of oil policy—planned to push ahead with nationalization. It would "take time to develop [a] meaningful dialogue on oil matters with [the] Army," the embassy concluded, and applying pressure carried real political risks.[136]

But the risks of inaction were even greater, and time was short. Stanvac executives told the State Department that the company was backed into a corner and was considering pulling out if negotiations failed, charging Indonesia with expropriation and bringing into effect the Hickenlooper amendment. "This would be a disaster and destroy chances of being able [to] aid Indo Army," Dean Rusk wrote the embassy, instructing Marshall Green to do "anything which can be done to get into heads of new Indo leadership" the dire consequences of forcing the oil companies out.[137] The problem, as the embassy indelicately put it, was that "even most anti-communist Army leadership are strongly imbued with [the] conviction that Indonesians must control their own natural resources" and have "control over [their] own affairs."[138]

U.S. officials bluntly and repeatedly warned the emerging Indonesian leadership that Washington's support and their grip on power were at stake. These extraordinary overtures occurred at the very moment the Johnson administration was providing whatever assistance it could to facilitate the slaughter of PKI supporters and suggest how inseparable the wider position of foreign capital was in the White House's considerations. The Indonesian army was not yet in control and was "especially short of financing," Galbraith told General Nasution's aide in early November. A precipitous move against the oil companies would "profoundly affect both U.S.-Indo future relations and [the] Indo economic situation," crippling not just the economy but also the armed forces.[139] Backing off from the nationalization of oil refining capacity, on the other hand, would "permit companies to give all-out support to Army's and the country's needs"—that is, to channel desperately needed resources away from Sukarno to Suharto and the generals.[140] After a month of such warnings the embassy reported that the Supreme Operations Command (KOTI) and Generals Nasution and Suharto had the situation "very much in mind." Ibnu Sutowo, however, continued to insist that Indonesia might go ahead with nationalization, and the CIA reported that Permina officials had traveled to Hong Kong to explore distribution possibilities, such as the chartering of foreign tankers, in the event of Caltex's nationalization. Ibnu Sutowo and the army are "working together on this," Marshall Green observed.[141]

On December 9 Sutowo presented Julius Tahija of Caltex with a proposal for the sale of Caltex's remaining assets and the immediate transfer of management authority to the Indonesian government. Indonesia "appears to be determined to get control of foreign holdings by one means or another," George Ball wrote President Johnson. Again, the State Department instructed Green to warn Jakarta that its actions would make it impossible to resume aid and repair U.S.-Indonesian relations and would lead to a cutoff of foreign exchange earnings, the halting of production, and the destruction of the economy.[142] The White House apparently convinced Australian and Japanese officials to intervene as well. Julius Tahija told army leaders that Australia and Japan had also decided to refuse future aid if Indonesia took over the oil companies.[143] The Johnson administration's blunt threats had their intended effect. On December 16 a group of high-level Indonesian officials met to discuss a proposal by Chaerul Saleh concerning the takeover of Caltex and Stanvac. As the meeting got under way, Suharto arrived dramatically by helicopter, strode into the room, and "made it crystal clear to all assembled that [the] military would not stand for precipitous moves against oil companies." He then turned around and walked out. Chaerul Saleh tabled the proposal.[144] The oil companies would continue their often bitter negotiations with the Indonesian government through the spring of 1966, but a major crisis had been averted. Aside from demonstrating the extraordinary leverage that the United States held over Indonesia when the Johnson administration chose to exercise it, this episode highlights the broader economic concerns through which Washington filtered its considerations of Indonesia's future, even at the moment of the army's greatest political vulnerability.

Sukarno: Resurgence and Decline

By the beginning of 1966, the CIA concluded, Indonesia had reached a "major turning point in its history. The era of Sukarno's dominance has ended." The PKI was destroyed, and its leaders had been arrested, killed, or driven into hiding.[145] The army had substantially reduced Sukarno's power, forcing the reorganization of the Supreme Operations Command (KOTI) into a three-person triumvirate composed of General Nasution, Sultan Hamengku Buwono, governor of Yogyakarta, and Information Minister Ruslan Abdulgani, a Sukarno holdover. Subandrio was effectively stripped of his power, and his intelligence service, the BPI (Biro Pusat Intelijen, Indonesian Intelligence Bureau), had been disbanded. Suharto announced that trials would soon begin for high-ranking officials who had allegedly been involved in the September 30th Movement, offering new opportunities to publicly undercut Sukarno. And as the intensity of anti-American demonstrations, public rhetoric, banners, and billboards momentarily ebbed, embassy contacts began resurfacing in greater numbers, mainly to ask for aid.

Although Sukarno's power had waned considerably since September 30, the president was still a formidable political opponent commanding substantial support, and the army remained reluctant to force a decisive confrontation, much to the dismay of U.S. officials. On December 18, at the conclusion of the KOTI meeting that led to its reorganization, Sukarno refused to ban the PKI or to meet other demands put to him by Nasution, making it clear that he was "not going to concede one inch."[146] Nasution backed down, emboldening the president and disillusioning Sukarno's civilian opponents, especially student groups such as KAMI, which launched a series of army-backed demonstrations against price hikes, culminating in a massive protest at Bogor Palace on January 15. The British embassy complained that despite their support for the student protests, the generals "seem reluctant to take over the direct administration of the country." An official in the Joint Malaysian/Indonesian Department of the Foreign Office wrote that "the military administration is governing most of the country, so far as it is being governed at all, but they have not yet taken a grip on foreign or economic policy. In fact, there are indications that they may be trying to pin responsibility for extricating Indonesia from its economic and foreign policy difficulties on the parallel civilian administration."[147] Marshall Green appreciated the army's reasoning in continuing to chip away at Sukarno's power but considered the chances fifty-fifty that the president would still outflank his opponents, concluding that "U.S. capabilities to shape events are very slight."[148]

So long as the political stalemate between Sukarno and the army continued, the Johnson administration was reluctant to consider resuming aid, fearing it would merely reinforce Sukarno and discourage the army from making tough choices about Indonesia's future policies.[149] Emergency aid would come "when the time is right," Marshall Green told Helmi, the North

American head of Indonesia's Foreign Office, after he was approached with a request for emergency shipments of rice and cloth. Other Indonesian generals approached the governments of Japan and Thailand with similar requests. Back at the White House Robert Komer grew frustrated with the State Department's caution, which he thought was spooking Germany and Japan from resuming aid as well.[150]

Sensing the army's caution and confident that Suharto would not move directly against him, Sukarno went on the political offensive. On January 11 the president expelled all U.S. correspondents from Indonesia. Four days later, as thousands of KAMI members demonstrated outside, he held a cabinet meeting in which he angrily denounced student protestors and called on his supporters to gather themselves into *Barisan Sukarno* (Sukarno's ranks) to defend the president, prompting scores of groups to enlist their support and hold rallies across Java. Suharto and other army leaders, momentarily thrown off balance, declared their loyalty to Sukarno while simultaneously scurrying to dilute the *Barisan Sukarno* by banning them or bringing them under their control.[151] In early February Sukarno countered Suharto's earlier reorganization of KOTI by changing the command's mandate and limiting its authority to *Konfrontasi* against Malaysia. As the army prepared to open the first special military tribunal (*Mahmillub*) against PKI politburo member Njono, Sukarno gave an inflammatory speech to a National Front rally in which he praised the PKI's contribution to the Indonesian revolution and reiterated his call for the formation of *Barisan Sukarno*, throwing down a direct challenge to Suharto and his allies.

Johnson administration officials worried that Sukarno was poised to reverse many of the army's gains and that Suharto through his caution had "bought unity at the expense of further action." Indonesia faced a "virtual paralysis of administration," the CIA reported, "with two distinct power centers, neither of which has the ability to impose its will on the other."[152] So what, if anything, could the administration do to resolve the stalemate in the army's favor? In mid-February Marshall Green returned to Washington to meet with the president and other top officials in an attempt to answer this question. Robert Komer urged President Johnson to consider "giving a bit more quiet support" to army leaders as a means of helping them blunt Sukarno's political offensive, specifically by underwriting rice purchases, a position backed by Averell Harriman and Vice President Humphrey.[153]

Dean Rusk, on the other hand, was unconvinced that the army's situation was so dire and determined to tie rice and other assistance to a broad package of political and economic reforms, beginning with *Konfrontasi* and the treatment of U.S. oil companies. Marshall Green urged that the United States "maintain a low profile and preserve its options." Johnson was noncommittal and seemingly uninterested, ending the meeting by saying he would let Green decide when and how to resume aid.[154]

President Sukarno's efforts to recoup his power culminated on February 21, 1966, when he announced a major cabinet reshuffle aimed at rolling back the army's gains. General Nasution, Vice Admiral Martadinata, and eight other anti-PKI cabinet members were dismissed and replaced by Sukarno loyalists, several of whom the embassy judged as pro-PKI. The next day Sukarno stripped KOTI of most of its duties and renamed it the Crush Malaysia Command (KOGAM), although it remained formally under Suharto's control. U.S. officials worried about the army's public silence and especially about General Nasution's acceptance of the decision. Unless the army resisted Sukarno's actions, McGeorge Bundy wrote President Johnson, the cabinet purge would reverse the military's political gains since October and restore Sukarno to full power. There was little that the United States could do publicly, although U.S. and British covert propaganda efforts aimed at undermining Sukarno and the PKI continued. Foreign reporters bluntly complained to U.S. officials in Singapore that British operatives "are planting stories apparently designed to increase pressure on Suharto to remove Sukarno." The fabrications were so outrageous, however, that correspondents thought they had no choice but to report them, prompting the U.S. embassy to ask "if tacit complicity in this U.K. psywar is in our interests."[155]

Sukarno's dramatic defiance of the army and his continued defense of the PKI and September 30th Movement participants had convinced many army leaders that he must be confronted more directly.[156] The challenge for Suharto was to "reject the cabinet changes without taking action that would force members of the Armed forces to choose" between him and the president.[157] Suharto responded by authorizing KOSTRAD commander Kemal Idris, RPKAD commander Sarwo Edhie, and OSPUS chief Ali Murtopo to encourage the resumption of student protests. Once Sukarno realized that he could not control or halt the demonstrations, Suharto calculated, he would be forced to turn to the army to restore order, providing it with a "pretext for declaring martial law and reversing Sukarno's decisions."[158]

Two days after Sukarno's announcement, the Indonesian Student Action Front held a large and rowdy demonstration in Jakarta, demanding the banning of the PKI, the dismissal of Subandrio, and a reduction of prices for basic goods. Meanwhile, PNI demonstrators supporting Sukarno attacked the U.S. embassy across town, breaking windows and burning several cars. On February 24, students surrounded the presidential palace in an attempt to prevent the newly installed cabinet from meeting, letting the air out of the tires of all the cars in the area and forcing the ministers to fly in by helicopter. Inside, Sukarno angrily denounced the protestors. When the demonstrators attempted to storm police lines, Sukarno's Cakrabirawa guard opened fire, killing a university student and a high school girl and giving the student movement its first martyrs. The next day a massive funeral procession for Arief Rachman Hakim, the slain university student, snaked its way through the capital. Sukarno responded by banning demonstrations and dissolving KAMI. Hydralike, two new organizations sprung up to replace it, the Indonesian Student and Youth Action Front (KAPPI) and Laksar Arief Rachman Hakim. KAMI moved its offices from the University of Indonesia campus to KOSTRAD command headquarters, and the demonstrations continued.

As the student protests resumed, the Indonesian economy hovered on the brink of collapse. In mid-January Indonesia notified Washington and other governments that it was defaulting on its commercial loans, crossing "the great divide," as the embassy put it, and "completing the ruin of its international credit standing."[159] Spiraling inflation had already forced Chaerul Saleh and General Ibnu Sutowo to drastically raise the price of basic commodities and public services, prompting the first major student protests against the nascent New Order. Now army leaders sought to distance themselves from Sukarno's economic policies, permitting the Indonesian government to "stew in its own juices" until economic crisis gave the generals "adequate reason for taking full control early in the New Year." General Nasution sent word to the U.S. and other embassies that they "should give no rpt no econ assistance to Indonesia, including to [the] Indonesian Army."[160]

Far from simply dissociating themselves from Sukarno's economic policies, however, army leaders actively sought to promote Indonesia's economic collapse by diverting funds from the government and Central Bank to create a parallel government.[161] Just as important, the U.S. and British governments recognized and approved of what was happening—the creation of an army-controlled state within a state. The consulate in Medan reported that army commanders in Northern Sumatra "are collecting large sums of money from merchants, rice and rubber millers and cigarette makers in what amounts to virtual protection payments," using the funds to supply their units and to pay for the upkeep of tens of thousands of PKI prisoners.[162] In early February General Suharto and Ibnu Sutowo told Julius Tahija of Caltex that the military "desperately needed funds" to import basic commodities and supplies for its own needs—in other words, a separate budget and independent sources of income. Suharto and Sutowo instructed Caltex to immediately begin paying the Indonesian government's 60 percent share of oil revenues "into an unnamed bank account in Holland rather than to the Indonesian central bank." Plantation Minister Frans Seda made similar arrangements with Goodyear and U.S. Rubber to divert their revenues from the Central Bank and explored doing so for tin as well. "Indonesia's need for foreign exchange," David Cuthell wrote approvingly, "is now a greater influence than the GOI's desire to nationalize."[163] The diversion of Indonesia's three largest sources of foreign exchange was a mortal blow to Sukarno's rule, effectively stripping the government of access to hard currency. As Indonesia's economy hovered on the verge of collapse and austerity loomed, the army was securing for itself the resources needed to continue repressing the PKI, maintain the loyalty of its soldiers, and demonstrate the powerlessness of the Sukarno government to feed and clothe the populace. U.S. and British officials clearly saw what was happening, and, as they had at every stage since early October, tacitly or directly encouraged the army's gradual seizure of state power.

Meanwhile, as a rising tide of student protest swept Jakarta, Suharto and other army leaders prepared to move against Sukarno. Sarwo Edhie and Kemal Idris proposed to keep student groups out front and in the streets, hoping to simultaneously create disorder in the capital and keep the students from moving before the army was ready. Embassy officials admired the courage and discipline of the young students acting at the army's behest but complained that "KAMI-KAPPI . . . demonstrations are unlikely to bring Sukarno down, lacking active support of a hesitant army."[164] Despite the growing threat to public order and his own rule, Sukarno appeared confident to the last that he could outmaneuver his opponents. Hoping once again to force civilian and military leaders to declare their loyalty to him, the president called a series of meetings with various political forces from March 9 to March 11. U.S. officials, army leaders, student organizations, and the president's allies all recognized that the weekend might be a turning point. The day before the meetings began, thousands of KAPPI supporters stormed the Foreign Ministry building demanding the dismissal and arrest of Subandrio. Coup rumors swept the capital. "The situation is explosive," the embassy reported, "with [the] Army prepared to move at any time."[165]

Three days later Sukarno convened a cabinet meeting at the presidential palace, as student demonstrators again deflated car tires throughout the area, forcing cabinet members to arrive by helicopter and, in one case, by bicycle. As the meeting got under way, KOSTRAD troops under the command of Sarwo Edhie and Kemal Idris—their trademark red berets and insignia removed—took up positions outside. A Sukarno aide entered to inform him that unknown troops had surrounded the building, prompting the president, Subandrio, and Chaerul Saleh to immediately leave the meeting and flee by helicopter to the presidential palace at Bogor. Suharto sent several loyal generals to inform Sukarno that the armed forces chief could bring the situation under control if only the president would empower him. After tense negotiations President Sukarno signed a letter, later known as the *Supersemar*, ostensibly ordering Suharto "to take all measures considered necessary to guarantee security" and restore order.[166]

Suharto quickly exploited his newly won powers, banning the PKI and its affiliates in Sukarno's name and dealing the president's authority "a shattering blow."[167] Two days later Suharto gave a speech calling on the army to step up its campaign to "remove all traces" of the party. Newspapers and diplomatic sources reported that the execution of PKI prisoners "continued on [a] systematic basis"; according to the embassy, KOSTRAD raiders in Bali were still "killing Communists like hell."[168] On March 18, as students protested and Sukarno refused to dismiss his new cabinet members, Suharto simply arrested more than a dozen of them. Although Sukarno remained president and continued to wield substantial, if declining, influence, power had decisively shifted to Suharto and his allies.

Administration officials could scarcely hide their delight with what Marshall Green described as a "courteous constitutional coup" by "responsible

moderates," who, as the State Department and CIA knew, were still executing unarmed PKI supporters and had imprisoned tens of thousands in make-
shift concentration camps. "Things are so much brighter in almost every
way that I can hardly believe it is the same country," CIA station chief Hugh
Tovar gushed in a letter to RAND analyst Guy Pauker.[169] "It is hard to over-
estimate the potential significance of the Army's apparent victory over
Sukarno," Robert Komer wrote President Johnson. But the administration
had quick decisions to make. Army leaders would soon be approaching with
requests for assistance in rescuing Indonesia's shattered economy and consolidating their power. How would Washington respond? Komer characteristically urged President Johnson to shore up Suharto by swiftly resuming
U.S. assistance.[170] The State Department counseled caution. Aside from
their shared commitment to destroying the PKI, U.S. and Indonesian interests continued to diverge on a wide range of issues. The army had yet to signal its intentions or demonstrate its commitment to the sort of far-reaching
economic and political reforms that Washington and other Western powers
considered vital to Jakarta's rehabilitation.[171] As *The Economist* put it, "Even
if the generals get their way, they will not have won," for the challenge of
consolidating their New Order was just beginning.[172]

CHAPTER 8

Economists with Guns

Washington Embraces the New Order

Capitalists come back!
—Editorial, *The Economist*, August 19, 1967

It is almost impossible for a U.S. businessman who comes in contact with this vast area, and its people, not to feel a deep sense of involvement in the great economic and political experiment that is being played out there.
—James H. Gross V, General Electric, Gallatin Special Report, December 1967

The annihilation of the PKI and the steady diminution of Sukarno's power shifted the terrain of U.S.-Indonesian relations. Having realized its most important short-term goals—ending the threat to Western interests posed by Indonesian Communism and neutering Sukarno—Washington shifted its attention from anti-Communism to helping the Indonesian army consolidate a "moderate, responsible, and economic minded regime" in Jakarta. For General Suharto and his military allies the most important tasks were primarily political: purging Sukarnoists from the government, ending *Konfrontasi* with Malaysia, continuing the attack against the remnants of the PKI, and solidifying the army's hold on power. U.S. officials, on the other hand, contended that Indonesia's crucial tasks were now primarily economic: resuming aid; rescuing, stabilizing, and rehabilitating the Indonesian economy; regaining the confidence of creditors and investors; and re-enmeshing Indonesia in webs of Western influence. Washington's priorities in Indonesia starkly underlined the intimate connections between its anti-Communism and its broader political and economic concerns.

The Johnson administration was deeply reluctant to take the lead in this process, with the Vietnam War sharply constraining American options. It hoped instead to convince Japan and multilateral institutions such as the IMF to shoulder the political and economic burdens of dragging Indonesia "back into the real world," as the State Department put it.[1] The Kennedy administration's failed attempt to push an IMF stabilization package on Indonesia loomed large in the thinking of policymakers. "Even at the height of intimacy . . . in 1962–1963," Marshall Green reminded Washington, "our influence on decision making here was never great. . . . It would be a mistake to over-estimate the leverage we may have now" should the United States again seek to direct Indonesian recovery.[2]

Administration officials also recognized, however, that only Washington possessed the power and credibility needed to mobilize the international community behind a rescue and rehabilitation program large enough to meet Indonesia's enormous needs. William P. Bundy recalls that President Johnson was determined that the United States should quietly do whatever it could to help Indonesia, having "very quickly grasped the *inner meaning* of what happened after 1965" (emphasis added).[3] That's a good phrase, capturing the unspoken assumptions about Indonesia's place in the fabric of American hegemony and the opportunities that Sukarno's ouster presented to the international community. Years of U.S. assistance to and training of the armed forces had generated intimate relationships and mutual respect but also expectations among Indonesian military officers and technocrats that could only be ignored at Washington's peril. As such, the United States had both greater responsibility and greater leverage than other countries to press the army to undertake the far-reaching economic reforms it considered essential to Indonesia's recovery, and thus it was the United States that should help cobble together the military-technocratic alliance it expected to dominate the political and economic landscape. In this task U.S. officials sought to nurture and protect their strongest allies, civilians such as Adam Malik and the economists at the University of Indonesia, who emerged as Suharto's key advisers and the leading advocates of economic stabilization and market-oriented reform.

As the Johnson administration began underwriting the Suharto regime, it once again cast its task in the discourse of military modernization. The appointment of Walt Rostow as national security adviser in April 1966 ensured that the new regime, which took its legitimacy from its publicly professed desire for modernization, would receive a sympathetic hearing at the White House.[4] Washington rationalized Indonesia's authoritarianism as "the right mixture" for the country at its stage of development and army rule as the midwife of political stability and economic development.[5] By annihilating the PKI and cementing its hold on power, the military had cleared away a basic obstacle to the harsh measures that Washington saw as necessary for economic recovery and to the armed forces' emergence as Indonesia's dominant political force. But U.S. ambitions were initially less grand than in 1962–1963, a caution dictated by the dramatic deterioration of the Indonesian economy in the intervening years, a changed foreign aid climate, and recognition of Washington's limited leverage in the face of its massive economic and military commitment to Vietnam. The Johnson administration's more limited strategy for Indonesia's modernization correspondingly emphasized working with U.S. allies to spread the burden of aid. Washington promoted the IMF, the World Bank, and the Asian Development Bank (ABD) as partners in Indonesian stabilization and development, deemphasizing public assistance, and maximizing the role of private investment and self-help. U.S. officials still hoped, however, that they could return to the long-term—and now multilateral—challenge of setting Jakarta on the road to modernization.

Rescue

In the weeks following Sukarno's transfer of power to Suharto, Johnson administration officials cautiously appraised the political and economic landscape and mulled over the resumption of assistance. The State Department was in no hurry, arguing that "U.S. help depends on some showing that a constructive Indonesian government is establishing itself firmly in power, desiring to pull [the] country out of its present economic shambles."[6] The resumption of aid raised a host of tactical questions, especially with Congress, as well as broader strategic questions about the kind of regime likely to emerge in Jakarta and how U.S. assistance could maximize the pressure for economic (if not political) liberalization.

The administration had begun considering these questions on October 2, when McGeorge Bundy and Walt Rostow encouraged George Ball to begin planning for the resumption of U.S. aid.[7] The task fell to the State Department's Policy Planning Council, which over the next five months drafted a lengthy and detailed contingency plan.[8] The Council plan, representing the broad consensus in Washington, was circulated just as Sukarno transferred power to Suharto and offered an unusually incisive analysis of U.S. assistance possibilities and the Suharto regime's prospects.

U.S. policy options, the Council argued, were constrained not just by the depth of Indonesia's economic decay but also by the pervasive corruption that characterized political and economic life. The Indonesian state was "truly a clientele state," an oligarchic system structured since independence to serve elite interests while "the welfare of the masses has been grossly neglected." The elite groups that dominated government (politicians, civil servants, the military, and businessmen), of which the military was by far the most powerful, viewed the budget not as a tool for advancing the national interest but as a means of personal enrichment.[9] This was not going to change in the wake of Sukarno's ouster—corruption and nepotism were too deeply embedded in the social structure of the Indonesian state. The best Washington could do was "learn to live with these features of the system, and, if possible, use them to get our own goals achieved."[10]

From this perspective the ideal scenario would be a government dominated by "modernizers," such as Adam Malik, who would drag the country away from statism and toward economic liberalism. This highly unlikely outcome, however, would require a cultural revolution and the adoption of attitudes wholly alien to Indonesia. The most likely scenario was a mixed state-market economy and a clientelistic regime dominated by the army in which the modernizers were permitted to shape economic policy—that is, a military modernizing regime.[11] Over time, the Council suggested, external aid could be used as a lever to press for greater economic liberalization, as Washington was attempting to do in Latin America. Gone were the optimistic assessments of the possibilities for democratic development that informed U.S. policy during the 1950s. Given the alternatives, Washington had an "active political interest" in supporting a military-dominated government in Jakarta.[12]

In the short run the White House thought it should focus on providing basic commodities and spare parts and emphasize infrastructure rehabilitation. Rescue and rehabilitation of the Indonesian economy would of necessity be an international effort "because of the large size and broad international scope of its debt and because of the heavy involvement of Indonesia in the international economy." Given Washington's limited resources, long-term aid would have to be organized under a multilateral umbrella, including the IMF and the International Bank for Reconstruction and Development (IBRD), preferably with Japan in the lead, although the United States would likely be the largest aid donor. Most important, the United States would avoid attempting to formulate comprehensive aid programs that exaggerated Washington's ability to spur Indonesian development. It would take a herculean effort just to return the Indonesian economy to the level of 1963 when Kennedy administration officials last hewed to such visions. "We should have no preconceptions about constructing a plateau for economic take-off," Marshall Green urged, reflecting Washington's diminished ambitions.[13]

The Policy Planning Council concluded that Washington should move cautiously because "gradual movement will make such leverage as we possess more effective . . . by increasing awareness that we, not they, are in the stronger bargaining position." U.S. officials, however, also had to consider the global implications of their aid decisions for prospective client states in other parts of the world. If the United States refused or gave inadequate levels of aid to the army after its wholesale slaughter of PKI supporters and the ouster of Sukarno, it "could sow seeds of resentment which would bear bitter fruit for years to come," carrying "unforgettable lessons for those who may be faced by similar internal political challenges in the future."[14]

As Johnson administration officials met at the end of March to discuss the Policy Planning Council report, Sukarno announced the formation of a new six-member cabinet, with the triumvirate of Suharto (holding the positions of defense minister, army chief of staff, and KOTI chief of staff), Adam Malik (foreign minister), and the Sultan of Yogyakarta (in charge of economic affairs) wielding effective control.[15] Adam Malik approached the U.S. embassy in Jakarta at the same time seeking "urgent help in procuring rice," needed, he argued, to prevent looming shortfalls and ensure government stability. After months of recommending against the resumption of public assistance, Ambassador Green urged the administration to meet the request. The White House and Secretary of State Rusk immediately approved, but on hard terms that highlighted their continued caution. Congressional leaders, delighted at the turnaround in Jakarta, were uniformly supportive of the deal.[16]

British officials, still on the lookout for signs that the new triumvirate was prepared to end *Konfrontasi*, worried that the White House was "determined to rush ahead with aid the moment they can get an official request on the record." Two days later Japan announced it would provide rice and cotton aid worth $30 million.[17]

The Johnson administration considered it particularly important for Japan to take a leading role in providing emergency aid for Jakarta and in organizing the international community to tackle Indonesia's mammoth debt crisis. Robert McMahon correctly argues that by this point Japanese economic recovery "figured far less prominently in U.S. thinking about Southeast Asia," with Tokyo posting some of the highest sustained growth rates in recorded history. But by 1965 the United States was much more concerned with enlisting Japan's help in underwriting Asian development; Vietnam and congressional budget constraints forced Washington to shift its emphasis "to development assistance through advice, loans and help from the private sector, international agencies, and Japanese burden sharing, i.e. aid on the cheap."[18] U.S. officials still saw integration with Japan and the regional economy as the logical goal of Indonesian development and consequently desired that Tokyo carve out a role commensurate with its interests. They observed that "the economies of Japan and Indonesia are complementary" and that Japan depended more than any other country on Indonesian raw materials, especially oil. Foreign Minister Miki accordingly announced in January that "Japan should play a leading role in constructing the Indonesian economy" and that Tokyo would give aid to Indonesia "a high priority" in its regional plans. The *Economist* observed approvingly that Japan, whose exports to Indonesia rose 70 percent from 1965 to 1966, "sees trade and aid as its means of becoming the patron of a benign Asian co-prosperity sphere." "Clearly the Japanese are being set up as our front men," James Thomson wrote to Robert Komer, "and I suppose that makes sense."[19]

Suharto and his advisers recognized the need to quickly secure international backing for the new regime, both to consolidate their power and to gain access to aid that could help rescue the economy and restore a modicum of stability, thereby preventing a leftist resurgence. As Marshall Green told President Johnson while in Washington, Indonesia had as yet "offered no signs of being willing to talk to creditors as a group or to demonstrate it is prepared to tackle its problems in a rational manner to induce capital export-ing countries to be able to be of any assistance." At every opportunity the em-bassy drove this point home to officials in Jakarta, making it clear that aid would march in tandem with Indonesia's efforts to reverse Sukarno's policies, restore its economic credibility, and stabilize the economy in accordance with policies approved by Western creditors and international institutions.[20]

In early April 1966 the emerging regime offered the first real signals of its intentions. In two widely reported speeches the Sultan of Yogyakarta admit-ted the failures of past economic policies and declared that Indonesia would rehabilitate its infrastructure, reform state enterprises, simplify the tax sys-tem, petition creditor nations to reschedule its debts, and welcome back for-eign investors.[21] The State Department welcomed the sultan's pronounce-ments—drafted with the help of University of Indonesia economists—but continued to express caution. "The basic fact is that [the] Indonesian econ-omy is in ruins and [the] central bank is bankrupt," Dean Rusk wrote the embassy.[22] The sultan still did not even control government finances; Ibnu Sutowo and Frans Seda were still stashing foreign exchange receipts in over-seas bank accounts for the army's private use and, according to the U.S. em-bassy in Jakarta, demanding kickbacks even on emergency rice aid. Indonesia needed to "commit itself publicly to rationalization of the economy and out-line to creditors some steps it proposes to take in this regard."[23] A month later the sultan dispatched a series of economic missions to Western capitals to re-quest debt rescheduling and new credit arrangements from the IMF and the World Bank. They were not impressed. Japanese treasury and trade ministry officials told their Australian counterparts that they were "appalled by the In-donesian aid presentation of their aid requests, their skimpy and faulty eco-nomic statistics, and their lack of a realistic economic plan." Finance Minister Sumarno told embassy officials that Indonesia had $530 million in debt coming due in 1966 and would need at least a three-year moratorium on payments.[24]

In late May the embassies of creditor nations, with the notable exception of the Soviet Union, began informal discussions in Jakarta aimed at defining a common position on Indonesia's debt crisis.[25] Japanese and U.S. officials for months had discussed the need for some sort of international consortium, but Washington and Tokyo had split on the issue of whether debt renegotiations could proceed so long as Sukarno remained in power. Now with Sukarno's ouster the question was moot. Japanese foreign minister Nishiyama proposed to hold a preliminary meeting of creditor nations in Tokyo in July.[26] The Indonesian Ministry of Finance hoped that the creditors might agree to a rescheduling of debt and arrange a series of bilateral deals then and there, but they were disappointed. The IMF mission, which had just left Jakarta after their first return visit, described Indonesia's plight as "extremely unusual—a debt probably worse than any other case in recent history," with more than half of it incurred for military equipment. Creditors agreed that debt negotiations must be multilateral and tied to a resumption of IMF stabilization measures. But decisions on a debt payments moratorium and rescheduling terms were put off until September.[27]

As the Sultan of Yogyakarta declared Indonesia's intention to address its deep-seated economic problems, Adam Malik began moving cautiously but decisively to roll back the legacy of Sukarno's foreign policy. In early April he announced that Indonesia would return to a policy of "genuine non-alignment," seek a peaceful solution to *Konfrontasi*, rejoin the U.N. and other international bodies, and welcome economic and financial assistance from other nations. Malik also quietly broadened discussions with British, Malaysian, and Philippine officials, initiated by Ali Murtopo in 1965, to end *Konfrontasi*.[28] Officials in London and Kuala Lumpur expressed skepticism, citing Sukarno's public insistence that *Konfrontasi* would continue. The Tunku told a Philippine negotiator that Malaysia saw "little hope [of] any settlement as long as Sukarno wields as much influence as he still does." Marshall Green, however, was convinced that Indonesian officials were "genuinely searching for means to end Confrontation," mainly because their access to U.S. and international aid depended on it.[29]

Negotiations between Indonesian and Malaysian officials picked up steam in May 1966 after Malik and Suharto indicated that Indonesia would stop insisting on a referendum for the Borneo territories and would drop objections to the continued presence of British troops in Singapore.[30] Malaysian foreign minister Ghazali suggested that Sabah and Sarawak might be given a chance to "reaffirm" the popular will in upcoming elections, so long as Jakarta accepted it as a "foregone conclusion" that they would remain part of Malaysia (a useful precedent for West Irian). As part of what London frankly termed a buyout offer on *Konfrontasi*, the British government authorized the embassy in Jakarta to offer Indonesia £1 million in untied assistance as an incentive to move forward with negotiations.[31] London's motives were both strategic and pecuniary. Back in December, a high-ranking Foreign Office official had recommended to Prime Minister Harold Wilson that "if there is going to be a deal with Indonesia, as I think there will be, I think we ought to take an active part and try and secure a slice of the cake for ourselves," especially in light of the "great potential opportunities for British exporters" that a new government could be expected to provide.[32]

At the end of May a high-level delegation of Indonesian military officials traveled to Kuala Lumpur to give official notice of their desire to wind down the conflict with Malaysia. Suharto and Nasution likewise emphasized in public statements that *Konfrontasi* would continue using "socio-political rather than physical tactics."[33] Immediately afterward, Adam Malik met Tun Razak in Bangkok, where after three days of contentious talks they emerged with the Bangkok Accord, pledging both countries to end *Konfrontasi* but leaving the details to later negotiations.[34] Malik told U.S. officials that a formal agreement would have to wait until after the next session of the MPRS (Madjelis Permusyawaratan Rakyat Sementara, or Provisional People's Consultative Assembly) at the end of June, when Sukarno's power would hopefully be further circumscribed. In the meantime there would be a "major effort" to educate Sukarno, MPRS members, and recalcitrant military officials about the changed international situation.[35]

The task was delicate. Indonesia could not simply abandon a policy that it had so vigorously pursued for three years without a serious loss of face, especially with Sukarno still around, and military leaders insisted that Indonesia's credibility and dignity must be preserved in any agreement. Finally, on August 11, 1966, Indonesia and Malaysia signed the Bangkok Accord ending the conflict. The accord bound Malaysia to a "reaffirmation" of the will of the people in Sabah and Sarawak, called for the cessation of hostile acts between the two countries, and restored diplomatic relations. The CIA noted ironically that the settlement would likely increase Indonesia's influence over Malaysia because the last barrier to a reduction of the British presence in the region had now been removed.[36] The end of *Konfrontasi* also removed the last indigenous barrier to the pursuit of greater economic and political regionalism. Almost a year to the day after the Bangkok Accord, on August 8, 1967, Indonesia, Malaysia, the Philippines, Thailand, and Singapore formed the Association of Southeast Asian Nations (ASEAN), an ostensibly neutralist organization whose founders saw in increased regionalism a bulwark against growing Chinese power.[37]

As Suharto, Malik, and the Sultan of Yogyakarta demonstrated their commitment to rolling back Sukarnoism, the clamor grew for assistance to Jakarta. With U.S. rice shipments on the way, the focus now turned to cotton. Indonesian army officers had shrewdly approached high-profile Texas and Louisiana cotton brokers in late 1965 looking to cut deals, and now their appeals took on a life of their own. Former assistant secretary of state Will Clayton, Wall Street lawyer Max Kampelman, and other powerful Democrats stepped up their calls for cotton sales to Indonesia. Senator John Tower of Texas, who in 1965 had introduced an amendment to ban aid to Jakarta entirely, now complained to Dean Rusk that while the administration was offering rice, cotton brokers from his state could not "get a letter of guarantee to finalize sale of 40,000 tons of cotton to Indonesia."[38]

Tower's sudden conversion had less to do with his ideological support for the new regime in Jakarta than with his constituents: internationalist cotton brokers and independent midsize oil firms, both previously shut out of the Indonesian market but now anxious to secure a foothold with government help. He was not alone. In 1965 U.S. exports to Indonesia had declined to an all-time low of $41.5 million. The head of the American Indonesian Chamber of Commerce warned Secretary of State Rusk that Indonesian markets were "fast becoming eroded or lost to the competition of Japan or Europe where export financing and credit insurance facilities have been and are more liberal" than those being offered by Washington.[39] Alone among the major powers, Japan had maintained good relations with both Sukarno and the new triumvirate despite a dramatic trade slowdown since October 1. Now Japanese firms also were urging the government to extend low-interest loans and other forms of aid to preserve or enlarge their market shares.[40] Even Vice President Humphrey (a close friend of Max Kampelman) intervened, complaining to Walt Rostow and President Johnson that "once again it appears that we'll be letting the Japanese take a market away from us."[41]

Indonesian officials made similar appeals to the U.S. embassy, stressing the urgency of increased rice and textile assistance if political stability was to be maintained. Army leaders were frustrated with the Johnson administration's leisurely pace in resuming aid, having expected more concrete signs of American gratitude for their destruction of the PKI and ouster of Sukarno.

When Marshall Green met with Suharto for the first time at the end of May 1966, Suharto stressed that the "main danger the GOI faced is economic," and he pleaded for more aid. The ambassador finally weighed in. The "best possible way to strengthen [the] triumvirate's hand," Green wrote Dean Rusk, would be to approve Indonesia's request for 75,000 bales of cotton "as soon as possible" and on the "best possible terms."[42] Two weeks later the White House approved the deal, worth more than $10 million.[43]

In early June Walt Rostow outlined for President Johnson the challenges the administration would face in the coming months. The triumvirate was making incremental but steady progress toward economic recovery, seeking emergency aid from Japan and Germany, restoring control over foreign exchange receipts, and slowing the inflation of basic commodity prices. Anti-American activity had ground to a halt. Soon, however, the United States would have to make basic decisions about further emergency aid, debt rescheduling, long-term assistance, and the resumption of limited military aid. This would require more extensive discussions with Congress and eventually a presidential determination, which Johnson had been putting off now for two years.[44] Slowly but surely Washington was moving publicly to embrace the New Order. Other governments, notably Britain, Japan, and Australia, were doing the same: quietly committing to the resumption of overt economic assistance, sniffing out commercial opportunities, and spelling out to Indonesian officials their expectations of a transformation in Jakarta's economic and foreign policy.[45]

At the end of June the MPRS convened for the first time since September 30 to ratify some of the dramatic changes that had taken place over the last eight months. The assembly confirmed Sukarno's transfer of powers to Lt. General Suharto, selected General Nasution as head of the MPRS, and ordered presidential elections by the end of 1968. MPRS delegates also demanded that Sukarno provide a written explanation for his role in the events of September 30, an inconceivable request just months earlier. Political death by "a thousand cuts" was how *Newsweek* put it. However, the triumvirate still lacked the political strength to push through the Bangkok Accord over the objections of Sukarno loyalists in the Nahdlatul Ulama (NU) and the PNI. Malik delayed Indonesia's official reentry into the U.N. for similar reasons.[46]

Of far greater significance was the composition of the new cabinet. Malik predicted a "serious trial of strength" between Suharto and Sukarno, whom the MPRS had charged with the cabinet's formation, and was determined to ensure the dominance of ministers committed to economic recovery and an end to *Konfrontasi*. A Sukarnoist cabinet would almost certainly preclude the resumption of U.S. aid and assistance in debt rescheduling, undermining Suharto's chances of success.[47] After acrimonious negotiations the new Ampera Cabinet (Cabinet of the People's Suffering) was named on July 25. The State Department's Bureau of Intelligence and Research (INR) concluded that this "cabinet of technicians," removed entirely from Sukarno's day-to-day control, represented a "major step in [the] campaign to ease President Sukarno out of effective power." Suharto's economic advisers, however, thought that his choices for numerous slots had "compromised [the] chances for an effective approach to economic problems" in order to secure Sukarno's acquiescence, complaining that the generals had "no basic interest in economic affairs."[48]

The Technocrats

Washington had good reason to heed these concerns. The fate of Suharto's economic advisers was central to the Johnson administration's emerging plans for a post-Sukarno Indonesia and to the vision of military modernization that lay behind them. Although marginalized and under attack from Sukarno and leftist groups from late 1963 to late 1965, the technocrats— Widjojo Nitisastro, Mohammed Sadli, Subroto, Ali Wardhana, Emil Salim, and a handful of other U.S.-trained economists—continued to maintain ties with U.S. officials and sympathetic army figures such as SESKOAD (Army Staff and Command College) chief Suwarto, and they continued to engage in contingency planning aimed at rescuing and stabilizing the Indonesian economy.[49]

As they had during the Kennedy administration, policymakers in Washington set out to forge close ties with the technocrats, helping them to secure foundation study grants in the United States as conditions deteriorated under Sukarno and putting them out front as the New Order took shape. "At all stages of their considerations," Marshall Green reported, the technocrats "have been in close touch with Embassy and receptive to our comments."[50] Western embassies were keenly aware of the economists' political vulnerabilities and lack of a social base, agreeing with Adam Malik that "they are no match for [the] economically naïve but strongly entrenched vested interests" in the bureaucracy and military.[51] Indonesia's thin modernizing strata, Marshall Green observed, "rests precariously on an immense and restless mass of 'traditionalist' forces which will require years if not decades to change."[52]

When it came to reforming the economy, the technocrats realized that the army—corrupt, deeply entrenched in state enterprises, and only dimly aware of the magnitude of Indonesia's economic calamity—was simultaneously part of the problem and part of the solution. Suharto, however, was at least savvy enough to realize that he needed the technocrats' help if he was to have any hope of rescuing the economy, and he quickly put them to work. Widjojo, Salim, and Wardhana told Ed Masters that throughout the spring of 1966 they went "from one meeting to another—KOGAM, Bank Indonesia, the Sultan's office, etc.—with the same message: The economy is in really bad shape, and strong measures must be taken to rescue it." The embassy tried to help, sending clear signals to army leaders "that Indonesia would not get aid until they went the way the economists advised."[53]

U.S. and other Western officials invariably described the technocrats in glowing terms: "first rate," "capable," "energetic," "clear-headed," rational, and action-oriented. "These economists feel a sense of urgency," the U.S. embassy reported, in sharp contrast to the lethargy and stasis of Sukarno's ministers. "They want to see strong hands taken in cleaning out the bureaucracy." The technocrats described themselves and the process they were spearheading in similar terms, emphasizing that "modernization and rationality were closely associated." Their work, according to a contemporary scholar, was part of a "pragmatic effort by the regime to return sanity and rationality to Indonesia's economic life."[54] For Widjojo, perhaps the chief architect of New Order economic policy, this meant the creation of a free market economy and the dismantling of state controls, insofar as these were politically feasible. Behind the technocrats was the like-minded Adam Malik, "the most brilliant and dynamic man in Indonesia's government today," Marshall Green concluded, a person of "character, immense courage, an un-Indonesian capacity for action" according to one magazine, and a Catholic to boot.[55]

The embassy favorably contrasted Malik, a "direct, dynamic, intellectual," with Suharto, a "devious, slow-moving, mystical Javanese." Later profiles of Suharto characterized him as inscrutable (as Kennedy had concluded about

Sukarno before him), "a contradictory mixture of 'modernizer,' single minded military officer and Javanese traditionalist."⁵⁶ The *Wall Street Journal* dismissed the generals as fundamentally indifferent to economic realities, talking "glibly of economic development, throwing out such phrases as 'market forces' and 'production incentives' which they may even understand."⁵⁷ The dramatically different assessments of the technocrats and their army sponsors highlighted the fragile nature of the military-led regime taking shape in Jakarta. They would need tutoring, from the technocrats and from the United States, if they were going to serve as a modernizing military force.

The army took a crucial step in this direction in late August when SESKOAD commander Suwarto organized a now famous seminar in Bandung for the Army General Staff. The seminar's aim was to build a consensus among army leaders on Indonesia's political, economic, and foreign policies in the coming months. The University of Indonesia economists, many of whom moonlighted at SESKOAD and the affiliated National Institute for Social and Economic Analysis (*Leknas*), framed the overall discussion, stressing that "economic failure means failure [of the] whole regime" and issuing calls for tax reform, government austerity, civic action, and tough stabilization measures.⁵⁸ Following the gathering, where the economists' recommendations were accepted with little discussion, Suwarto assigned Mohammed Sadli to shadow Deputy Army Chief Panggabean and "convince him of the soundness of the political and economic ideas presented at the Seminar." Other army leaders announced that they were launching a "follow up program of indoctrination for other Indonesian leadership elements." Moreover, the technocrats dominated the various committees charged with economic planning, such as the National Development Planning Agency, the Inter-Department Stabilization Team, and the Foreign Investment Committee. U.S. embassy officials considered the Bandung seminar a "real turning point in evolution of the Army's political thinking," concluding that the new government now "knows action on stabilization is urgent and feels there is no alternative to vigorous prosecution."⁵⁹

Marshall Green wrote the White House shortly before the Bandung seminar to urge an official visit by Adam Malik and a presidential determination on the resumption of aid, citing progress in Jakarta on *Konfrontasi*, inflation, debt repayment, and stabilization. He recommended a limited program of civic action, student and participant training, raw materials, and spare parts assistance. Although it was important to continue with a low-profile U.S. approach, Green now argued that it was also necessary to demonstrate Washington's commitment to Suharto and his allies.[60] Walt Rostow thought that Green's recommendations "avoid involving us too deeply while laying the groundwork for subsequent assistance" and placed Indonesia on the NSC's agenda.

As the NSC met on August 4, Indonesian and Malaysian officials were negotiating in Bangkok. Army leaders were fulfilling their end of the bargain, and now they thought that they "ought to receive some tangible sign of U.S. assistance."[61] To be helpful, Adam Malik and the Sultan of Yogyakarta sent Dean Rusk a $500 million wish list of the government's most urgent needs. The secretary demurred, siding with Green on a more limited program of aid. Although political developments were almost uniformly favorable, Rusk maintained, there had been "only modest progress in dealing with the root causes of Indonesia's economic collapse," and an overenthusiastic U.S. response "could be the 'kiss of death' to the current leadership."[62] The top priority now was for the United States to move quickly and multilaterally. Walt Rostow, who had just replaced McGeorge Bundy as Johnson's national security adviser, took a special interest in Indonesian recovery and the prospects for a program of modernization whose burdens would be borne multilaterally. The now central role of the chief modernization theorist in Washington—and an inveterate hawk—symbolized the Johnson administration's embrace of military modernization and ensured that its advocates would have their views aired on favorable terms in the White House. Indonesia was "a pioneer case," Rostow told the NSC, an opportunity to "establish a new pattern of multilateral help in Asia" linked to the Asian Development Bank and patterned on the U.S. experience in Latin America. Including the anticipated U.S. contribution to an IMF-approved stabilization program, the proposed aid package would total some $100 million.[63]

President Johnson, who observed that just a year ago Indonesia had been on the verge of becoming "an out-and-out Communist state," was glad to have Jakarta back on the plus side of the foreign policy ledger. He supported the resumption of aid but wanted Rusk to make sure congressional leaders were on board before signing a presidential determination.[64] Over the course of August 1966 State Department officials canvassed opinion on Capitol

Hill, where they found widespread support for administration policy. The House Foreign Affairs Committee, previously a bastion of anti-Sukarno sentiment, was now "unanimously favorable" toward the resumption of aid. Senator William Fulbright, who shared the State Department's caution, told Dean Rusk there was now "no possible alternative to the proposed course of action."[65] It was a stunning turnaround. From Jakarta Ambassador Green reiterated his support for the administration's aid proposals. It was especially important to shore up Suharto's economic advisers, Green argued, warning that they "will drop out if they feel U.S. support for the new government is lacking." With wall-to-wall support, President Johnson at the end of August signed a presidential determination authorizing the resumption of U.S. assistance to Indonesia.[66] That same day the State Department cabled Jakarta that it would consider another PL 480 agreement for 150,000 bales of cotton, later expanded to include a $10 million loan for spare parts and raw materials. When the House voted on the administration's $3.09 billion foreign aid bill two weeks later, they deleted the ban on aid to Indonesia passed the previous year, allowing for the full resumption of assistance.[67]

In defending Washington's decision, Dean Rusk told a meeting of the Veterans of Foreign Wars that U.S. aid would help to maintain Indonesia as a "nonaligned bastion of freedom in Asia."[68] In private Rusk was more pessimistic, telling President Johnson that Suharto and his allies had "no major commitment to democratic freedoms as we know them." The State Department predicted that the army would continue to severely circumscribe individual liberties and use arbitrary arrest and imprisonment "as an established aspect of the exercise of state authority"[69] The embassy estimated that 250,000 political prisoners crowded Indonesian prisons and concentration camps (Amnesty International put the number at more than half a million) and that summary execution of jailed PKI members continued on a regular basis.[70] As Harry Goldberg, the AFL-CIO's representative in Indonesia, had noted earlier, such a regime was "hardly the soil for a rebirth and re-growth of a democratic trade union movement" along with other civil institutions that modernization theorists identified as prerequisites for political development.[71]

Marshall Green commented later, as he pitched for the resumption of military aid, that the "'new political order' in Indonesia will be army planned, army built and army sponsored. . . . It is the army which will be remain the dominant political force in Indonesia for a long time to come."[72] At the Bandung seminar in August army leaders outlined their plans for scrapping Sukarno's Guided Democracy in favor what they called Pantjasila Democracy, involving the replacement of proportional representation in the MPRS with a single-member constituency system, rehabilitation of several previously banned political parties, and an enlarged role for functional groups, of which the military would be the most powerful. Suharto made it clear that the military would control the process of political reorganization, citing its historical and indispensable role in preserving stability and public order. When combined with the army's dominant influence in the cabinet, crucial ministries, the provincial administrative apparatus, and state enterprises, "'Pantjasila Democracy,'" the embassy observed, "at quick glance looks suspiciously like a military dictatorship." It was more likely, however, to evolve into a stable authoritarianism dependent on key civilian groups, such as the technocrats and moderate Muslims, for support. Indonesia's postindependence politics had convinced most U.S. observers, and many Indonesian elites, that democracy was unlikely to take root in the country and that it would be counterproductive to push the army in this direction.[73] "For the military to withdraw from a major and active role in political life," Green later argued, "would be as disastrous for Indonesia as for the military to take over entirely." While lamenting the army's corruption and hostility to democracy, most technocrats agreed that the Indonesian population was too backward and saddled by traditional values, practices, and structures to effectively participate in politics. At Indonesia's current stage of economic and political development U.S. officials could see "no workable alternatives," and Washington had no choice but to support an army-controlled government "well into [the] 'new order.'"[74]

What counted for the Johnson administration was not adherence to democratic niceties, which it hardly championed elsewhere, but the restoration of political and economic stability. In Indonesia the New Order continued to make progress, although Sukarno retained a residual capacity for obstruction. In mid-August both the MPRS and the DPR (Dewan Perwakilan Rakyat, or People's Representative Council) ratified the Bangkok Accord ending *Konfrontasi* and approved Indonesia's reentry into the U.N. Sukarno would have none of it. In his last Independence Day address he denounced the Bangkok accords and declared that Indonesia would not return to the U.N., insisting it was the world body that had to change, not Jakarta. The president's speech, which Vice Speaker of Parliament Major General Sjarif Thajeb condemned as "a rallying cry for PKI remnants and radical leftists," sparked denunciations by anti-Communist groups and the military. Sukarno "can now be attacked without fear of reprisal," the embassy commented approvingly.[75] Although committed to the progressive denigration and eventual removal of Sukarno, army leaders, especially Suharto, still carried a healthy respect for the influence he wielded on Java. Most were content to undermine Sukarno indirectly through the ongoing trials of September 30th Movement participants, which highlighted the decadence and corruption of former government ministers such as Central Bank minister Jusuf Muda Dalam. Although there was little doubt about the eventual outcome, Sukarno's final ouster would be a "slow painful process."[76]

Shortly after President Johnson formally resumed aid to Indonesia, Jakarta's creditors traveled to Tokyo to discuss the rescheduling of what New Order officials were now terming the "Sukarno debt."[77] IMF officials, who had been in Indonesia since August working with Suharto's ministers on a possible stabilization package, painted a grim picture of the country's continued economic decline. It would be months before the IMF could accurately assess Indonesia's ills, much less come up with suitable recommendations for stabilization. Looming over the session was Jakarta's mammoth debt to the Soviet Union and the question of whether or not Moscow would accept the same terms as other creditors, without which no rescheduling agreement was possible. Indonesia's hopes for swift action were again dashed. The best that Indonesia's creditors could do was agree to a standstill on Indonesian debt servicing.[78]

In late September 1966 Foreign Minister Adam Malik traveled to the United States to plead Indonesia's case for aid, the first high-level visit since the September 30th Movement. Close on his heels came the Sultan of Yogyakarta, who led Indonesia's observer delegation to the annual meeting of the IMF and the World Bank.[79] Malik's schedule, which included meetings with top CIA and Department of Defense officials, House and Senate leaders, Vice President Humphrey, Secretary of State Rusk, and President Johnson, was a testimony to the importance that the administration attached to his visit.[80] He covered well-trod ground in stressing Jakarta's recent turnaround and the country's dire economic situation. Indonesia had largely wiped out Communism, something few recipients of U.S. aid could boast. What Indonesia needed now, Malik emphasized, was more emergency aid, lots of it, especially rice and cotton, "to keep the large numbers of troops in Indonesia satisfied and occupied." As Malik told President Johnson, "Indonesia's fundamental task is improvement of the economy," but he warned that unless economic conditions improved, the PKI could make a comeback.[81]

The Johnson administration, which considered Malik the most dynamic, intelligent, and pragmatic New Order official, was well aware of the need to strengthen his internal position back home where he lacked a social base and was vulnerable to attack by both the army and social forces critical of Indonesia's drift toward the West.[82] To make sure the foreign minister did not go back empty-handed, Dean Rusk authorized the provision of an additional 50,000 tons of rice and 150,000 bales of cotton to Jakarta on concessionary terms. Washington was sympathetic to Indonesia's needs, President Johnson told Malik, and the United States would do its part working with allies and the IMF to draw up plans for Indonesia's rehabilitation and development. But Rusk emphasized that "external resources could play only a marginal role in the development effort and that Indonesia itself must carry the main burden." Aid from Washington would act as a lever for change, not as a substitute for the transformation of Indonesian policies, values, and practices. As examples of the sort of long-run relationship to which Indonesia should aspire, Rusk cited the Alliance for Progress in Latin America and the U.S. aid program in India, two of Washington's most dramatic (and ultimately ineffective) attempts to use aid as a catalyst for modernization.[83]

With a presidential determination in hand, the White House resumed planning for the resumption of overt military aid to the Indonesian armed forces, but here it faced a dilemma. U.S. officials considered the consolidation of army power an imperative for the restoration of stability and the prevention of any comeback by Sukarno and other leftist forces. "Suharto must . . . produce some early and visible progress towards improving people's lot," Marshall Green wrote, "in order to retain their confidence and ensure his own dominant role" over those who advocated an outright military dictatorship. Considering that "government authority in the cities outside of Jakarta and in the outer islands is exercised exclusively by the military," the United States had little choice but to support the armed forces if it hoped to exercise any influence over New Order policies.[84]

The 300,000-strong Indonesian military, however, was an enormous drain on national resources, swallowing roughly two-thirds of the government budget since 1959. Suharto and his advisers, in the course of slashing government spending, claimed to have lowered that figure to 25 percent at the end of 1966, but this took no account of the military's vast off-budget activities, funneling of funds from state-owned enterprises, pervasive corruption, and smuggling. Military leaders resisted any attempts to pare back their lucrative economic activities, posing a direct challenge to technocrats' efforts to reform and streamline the economy and introduce market forces.[85] To the extent that the military was cutting spending, Adam Malik observed, it was doing so with the expectation that U.S. MAP funds would make up the difference. Army leaders spoke of military requirements "running into the hundreds of millions of dollars, which they hoped to obtain from the U.S."[86] During Malik's visit to Washington, General Jusuf, an associate of General Suharto, met with the deputy assistant secretary of defense for international security affairs to discuss the possible resumption of the Civic Action Program. Jusuf emerged from the meeting and announced that the Department of Defense had committed $500 million, forcing Pentagon officials to issue an embarrassing public denial.[87]

Throughout the summer of 1966 most U.S. officials opposed the resumption of anything but token assistance to the Indonesian armed forces, fearing that substantial aid would divert the military's attention from economic recovery and reduce the incentive to move forward with market-oriented reforms. Pentagon officials frankly admitted that there was "no military justification" for the resumption of MAP assistance and that any aid offered "would be largely for political and economic purposes."[88] The Indonesian military, the most well equipped in Southeast Asia (even if much of its arms came from the Soviet Union), was plenty strong enough to accomplish its primary goals: repressing internal dissent, enforcing economic austerity, and preventing the resurgence of the left. But by October Marshall Green was convinced of the need to resume a small program of military aid. The army was dominant everywhere, firmly entrenched, and deepening its hold on the regional administrative apparatus and key state enterprises, a state of affairs that Green said was "essentially [the] right mixture for Indonesia." What the military needed now was a "constructive role" to play in the New Order it had created, in part to distract army personnel from "corruption" and "hooliganism." Green proposed a resumption of spare parts shipments, noncombat equipment shipments, officer training, and civic action programs total-ing about $6 million.[89]

The Johnson administration emphasized programs of military and partic-ipant training and civic action not just to forge closer ties with army officials but to transmit doctrines, administrative and technical skills, and American values to Indonesia's ascendant elites. Official and scholarly discussions of the New Order leadership invariably noted the crucial role played by U.S.-edu-cated personnel and the modernizing impact of U.S. training. Robert McNa-mara pointed out to President Johnson that five of the generals killed on Oc-tober 1, 1965, had been U.S. trained and that "all thirteen top members of Suharto's staff received training in the U.S. under the MAP." The effective-ness of these training programs, Marshall Green wrote the State Depart-ment, could be gauged by the fact that "American trained elites were pre-dominantly in vanguard of moderate forces who are now in ascendancy."[90]

Johnson administration officials were particularly committed to military and participant training programs. They were also explicit about the pur-pose of such training: to enable the military to replace Sukarno and assume administrative control of Indonesia's political and economic institutions. Participant training was a crucial and underappreciated aspect of the U.S. civic action program in Indonesia before 1965, helping—along with other training and exchange programs—to create a nascent "state within a state" alongside the Sukarno regime. Under the auspices of CAP and AID pro-grams, hundreds of Indonesian army officers attended U.S. universities, such as Harvard, the University of Pittsburgh, and Syracuse, to take classes in in-dustrial enterprise management, business administration, personnel man-agement, and executive leadership.[91] The Ford Foundation had financed similar programs since 1955, providing most of the funding for a generation of University of Indonesia economists to study in the United States. "You cannot have a modernizing country without a modernizing elite," noted Frank Sutton, deputy vice president of the Ford Foundation's international division. In the early 1960s the University of Indonesia organized an Execu-tive Development Program modeled on its American counterparts to pro-vide management training for civilian and military leaders. "This training proved to be of great value when the Army assumed control of the govern-ment," Robert McNamara observed in 1966.[92]

At a time of surging unemployment and continued economic chaos, Indonesian officials looked to civic action programs to help restore economic stability. Suharto acknowledged the need to reduce the size of the armed forces but feared the political and social implications of a major military demobilization, as had General Nasution in 1962. General Soekoewati, deputy chief of staff for special operations, explained to the Australian military attaché that "whilst some demobilization is planned, the bulk of [troops] will be kept occupied on civic missions in addition to their normal training activities. 'Karya' (labour) projects, as well as the trans-Sumatran highway, were planned to come within the army sphere to keep the Army occupied and assist in the national recovery."[93] Such goals were, not coincidentally, "closely tied to the maintenance of internal security." Army leaders still believed that an expansion of their civic mission would "build an image of public service, national identification, managerial ability and heroic posture," in part by publicizing military-led modernization "as a popular goal, with political symbolism appropriate to the Army model."[94]

The Johnson administration shared these goals. The Indonesian army's doctrine of civic mission still resonated strongly with policymakers in Washington who asserted that the armed forces, trained and equipped by the United States, could serve as agents of modernization in the countryside, as they were attempting to do in Vietnam and Latin America. The embassy in Jakarta justified the resumption of civic action programs on the grounds that they would "provide for [the] efficient and active participation of Indonesian armed forces in the execution of GOI economic and development plans," activities for which they were uniquely suited. The army had the "clearest command channels, most equipment, most readily available manpower, the most experience and one of largest pools of technical expertise" for undertaking such projects. Moreover, the army's territorial command structure created a parallel administrative structure extending to the village level; this structure enabled a far greater degree of control over local political and economic affairs than had previously been possible. Washington could also expect the army, unlike other social groups that had not yet absorbed Western values, to be "direct, rational and tough" in dealing with Indonesia's pressing economic and social problems.[95]

In addition, with the PKI decimated, there were far fewer political obstacles to the armed forces playing a catalytic role in Indonesia. RAND scholar

Guy Pauker argued that the ouster of Sukarno and the army's subsequent takeover had already generated "a deep moral crisis" in Indonesia because military-led modernization challenged "traditional ways and values" among Indonesian peasants. Given the political and financial restraints on U.S. military aid, Pentagon officials argued, a civic action program in Indonesia "would have a politico-economic impact far out of proportion to its size" and "help us influence government decisions in every aspect of our relations." As Llewellyn Thompson wrote to Robert McNamara, "There is probably no other place in Asia where such a small investment can produce more significant long-range returns."[96]

Congress, however, had yet to include new money for Indonesia in its 1967 appropriations bill.[97] In the meantime Marshall Green urged army leaders to get their own projects under way, which U.S. aid could then supplement, but Suharto and the generals had expected a quicker response. A poor rice harvest and unexpectedly fierce student demonstrations against the continued economic crisis in October magnified their concern.[98] By December the embassy reported "unmistakable indications of growing frustration" at the slow pace of aid that threatened a real estrangement from Washington's erstwhile military allies. Part of the problem, observed embassy political analyst Jack Lydman, was that armed forces leaders were basing their budget projections on wholly unrealistic expectations of U.S. assistance. Indonesian officials were beginning to realize that much of the aid they needed from abroad would be slow in coming and that the political and economic benefits of such aid would be slower still. The administration's urgent task was to find "some low cost but visible gesture to [the] military with immediate impact," aid that would pacify army leaders yet not distract them from the more urgent task of economic recovery.[99]

The Return of Foreign Investors

By the end of 1966 Suharto and his ministers had taken important if preliminary steps to address the country's chaotic economic situation, restore a modicum of economic stability, and reassure their creditors that they were prepared to address the government's fiscal and monetary crisis. In early October the Central Bank dramatically raised interest rates and slashed imports for all but essential goods, the first in a series of austerity measures aimed at stemming inflation and recouping scarce foreign exchange. Indonesia was making progress on a stabilization plan, its creditors were meeting in Paris to discuss debt rescheduling, and the army had secured modest but politically significant infusions of emergency commodity assistance. But the international community's response was agonizingly slow and marked by what Indonesian officials thought was unreasonable caution.[100] The CIA estimated that Indonesia's economy would need two to three years to recover and that the pace of recovery would depend on the level of foreign aid and the creation of "a more stable environment for private enterprise."[101]

Suharto's economic ministers and U.S. officials agreed that the sluggish returns on multilateral and bilateral aid made it all the more important for Indonesia to encourage the return of foreign investors. The return of private investment to Indonesia was a central feature of the Johnson administration's planning for Indonesia's short-term recovery and long-term development and an increasing focus of its foreign and development assistance program more generally. The growing U.S. balance of payments deficit, which fired increasing congressional hostility to expanding foreign aid budgets, and skepticism about the impact of large-scale public investment programs led U.S. officials to place more emphasis on multilateralism, self-help, and the encouragement of private investment as the most effective path to development.[102]

"These people want to be friends of the U.S.," Hubert Humphrey enthused to President Johnson after meeting with one of Malik's advisers. "They are interested in encouraging U.S. private investment."[103] As Suharto took power, embassy officials began conveying to their Indonesian counterparts that Jakarta needed to restore the confidence not just of creditor nations but also of foreign investors. This would mean, for starters, reversing the takeover of U.S. and other companies and junking the April 1965 decree banning foreign investment. In his first meeting with General Suharto in May, Ambassador Green noted the limits of international aid in restoring Indonesia's economic health and emphasized the "advantages of assistance from foreign private capital in opening forest and other industries."[104]

Suharto's economic advisers pushed the same message for both ideological and practical reasons. The embassy later wrote that Indonesia's economic ministers "fully realize that foreign official assistance and debt rescheduling must be accompanied by substantial private investment if momentum is to be generated in the development process."[105] Richard Robison argued that "there is little doubt" that the technocrats were initially "convinced by the IMF/World Bank ideology of 'free market' economics, which limited the state to providing the fiscal and monetary conditions for capital accumulation, and trusted in the mechanisms of the market to generate maximum growth and efficiency."[106] They also bemoaned the army's reliance on "covert, illegal fund-raising organizations" and the notorious corruption and inefficiency of army-controlled state-run enterprises and import-export licensing boards.[107] Given Indonesia's desperate economic situation, most technocrats believed they had little choice but to push for market-friendly policies if they hoped to induce foreign, especially multinational, capital to return. When asked to describe the path they thought Indonesia should follow, however, these modernizing bureaucrats took Japan, Korea, Taiwan, and other developmental states as their models, not the United States, suggesting that their turn to the West was borne more by necessity than by principle. Other officials, notably Ibnu Sutowo and those linked to state-owned enterprises, agreed on the need to lure back foreign capital but insisted that Indonesia should do so on terms that would foster the growth of national industry, especially petroleum, resource extraction, and processing.[108]

The case of the New Orleans–based mining company Freeport Sulphur illustrates the weighty stakes involved. In 1959 Freeport geologists managed to get hold of promising old Dutch reports of copper-rich deposits in West Irian. For the next several years officials unsuccessfully negotiated with first Dutch and then Indonesian officials to gain access to the area. In April 1965 Freeport reportedly reached a preliminary arrangement with the Ministry of Mining to explore for copper and nickel, only to watch Sukarno close the door on foreign investment.[109] Freeport waited, biding its time and keeping in touch with high-ranking Indonesian and U.S. officials. In early September Freeport's ad and information director James Moyer, brother of White House assistant Bill Moyer, joined the White House staff. Two months later, as the army-led massacres of alleged PKI supporters commenced, Freeport officials opened negotiations with Indonesia's generals to reenter the country. Within days of Sukarno's March 11 transfer of power to Suharto, Freeport technicians were tromping through the jungles of West Irian sixty miles from its southern coast, racing against mining officials from the Japanese *zaibatsu* Mitsui. What Freeport officials found boggled the mind: a mountain rising 600 feet from the jungle floor literally filled with high-grade copper ore. The discovery of Ertsberg, as the mountain containing earth's largest copper mine would later be called, convinced them of the need to move swiftly to reach a concession agreement.[110]

In mid-April Forbes Wilson and Robert Duke of Freeport visited Washington and told the State Department they needed three things to move forward with their plans for Indonesia: an investment guarantee agreement (IGA), an acceptable investment climate, and clear concession rights with no production sharing. The system of production sharing as originally devised for oil companies and other extractive industries kept nominal management and control of resources in the hands of the Indonesian government while assigning day-to-day management and technical assistance to the company; it also allowed the government to take its share of royalties in the raw materials being extracted. It was Ibnu Sutowo's signal contribution to the world oil regime and extractive industries, providing a model that many developing states later used. Many Indonesian officials, even those who recognized the country's need for foreign capital, considered such an approach indispensable to the creation and strengthening of national industry.[111]

Both Indonesian and U.S. officials saw Freeport as a crucial test case. At Suharto's personal request, Minister of Oil, Mining, and Minerals Bratanata and Adam Malik visited West Irian to explore the proposed concession area. They returned "fired up by [the] need to have Freeport begin the project as soon as possible."[112] But Ali Budiardjo, an Indonesian official who later went to work for Freeport, recalled that "no one had any idea of how to proceed. There was no foreign investment office and . . . no foreign investment law." At a time when "Westerners with money" still reacted to Indonesia "like bulls to a red flag," however, this early foray by a prospective investor hinted at Jakarta's intentions.[113] The embassy characterized the start of talks between Freeport and Indonesian officials in mid-June as "the initial posing of the important question of whether Indonesia's negative attitude toward foreign investment is undergoing a change." In Freeport's wake a "small but nonetheless significant stream of potential U.S. investors" began to descend on Jakarta. The most significant of these was Lyndon Johnson's political patron, the construction firm Brown and Root, which approached Adam Malik in June through a prominent Indonesian businessman to propose a swap; Brown and Root would gain concession areas suitable for gold mining and export agriculture in exchange for a $30 million loan for road and harbor construction in Sumatra for which it hoped to be the builder. But with fiscally conservative technocrats in control of the budget, the government was "deferring grandiose public works projects," and the deal fell through. Brown and Root was not alone.[114]

The prospective return of oil companies highlighted differences not just among Indonesian officials but also between firms in various industrial sectors seeking access to Indonesia. The first U.S. companies to return to Jakarta were not integrated multinationals on the order of Caltex but midsize independent firms such as Union Oil of California and consortiums such as the Midwest-based Independent Indonesian American Petroleum Company (IIAPCO), which sought to break into international markets long dominated by the majors. As Freeport talks got under way in June, oil concession hunters from these smaller companies and from a handful of Japanese hopefuls arrived in the Indonesian capital. Like Freeport, they had begun and then halted negotiations with Indonesian officials in 1965 as more cautious investors were fleeing, and now they sought to return while the field was uncluttered.[115] As in 1963, the key issue was whether these companies would accept terms balked at by such giants as Caltex and Stanvac, a point recognized at the time by the *Wall Street Journal* but forgotten by historians. Marshall Green reported that the major oil companies generally opposed the production-sharing agreements Indonesian officials were insisting on, worrying that such contracts "might lead to a weakening of management relationships in other parts of the world, where, not incidentally, the majors produce vastly larger amounts of oil than in Indonesia." Not so the smaller independents.[116]

The initial scramble for oil also took place as a complex struggle unfolded between Permina head Ibnu Sutowo and Oil and Mining Minister Bratanata for control over Indonesian oil affairs. Bratanata sided with the majors (and the technocrats) and opposed production-sharing arrangements; he argued that Indonesia "should attract larger companies into the country" and leave management authority largely in foreign hands. Sutowo, on the other hand, favored the smaller companies, which were willing to accept production-sharing agreements and work with Permina. Army leaders generally favored Sutowo, who was close to Suharto and had diverted scarce foreign exchange their way in the months after the October 1 coup attempt (and according to many accounts still was).[117] Ibnu Sutowo won on both counts. On August 18 he signed a production-sharing contract with IIAPCO for a concession area off the coast of North Java, the first new foreign direct investment in nearly two years. When Bratanata tried to block the Presidium from considering the contract, Suharto intervened, stripping him of much of his portfolio and handing control of oil and gas matters over to Sutowo.[118]

As Freeport Sulphur officers arrived in Jakarta to begin negotiations with the Ministry of Mining, Dr. Jusuf Ismael, chief of the Multilateral Economic Cooperation Directorate, told the embassy's economic counselor that Indonesia was ready to seek an accommodation with foreign investors. Ismael sheepishly asked the embassy's help in providing publications and advice on "formulating ground rules for a new foreign investment policy." The ministers had almost no idea how to proceed. "This seems [an] excellent opportunity," the embassy wrote back to Washington, "especially in light [of the] current visit by Freeport Sulphur reps . . . to influence GOI thinking on foreign investment."[119] Two months later Adam Malik told Marshall Green that economic ministers led by Dr. Selo Sumardjan, a U.S.-educated economist and aide to the Sultan of Yogyakarta, had begun working on a new foreign investment law and were prepared to start talks on an investment guarantee agreement with Washington.[120]

The United States heavily influenced the drafting of Indonesia's foreign investment law. A consultant from the Denver-based Van Sickle Associates (which had just signed a production-sharing contract for the construction and operation of two Indonesian plywood factories) helped the economist Widjojo write the bill. When they completed the draft legislation in late September, Indonesian officials gave the embassy a copy and asked for comments on "possible improvements from [the] standpoint U.S. investors." State Department lawyers sent back line-by-line suggestions, complaining that the proposed legislation gave "too much discretionary authority" to the government and was "discouraging to potential investors" because the state sector included "a large area private foreign enterprises would want to enter," primarily in extractive enterprises. Widjojo revised the bill "in accordance with U.S. suggestions," seeking language that would ensure the "maximum liberalization" he also favored while placating economic nationalists on the lookout for signs that Jakarta was bowing to Western pressure. The episode was a stunning reminder of the structural power wielded by the Suharto regime's supporters over some of the most crucial decisions made by sovereign states.[121]

At the end of November, after months of negotiations, Indonesia finally reached a debt rescheduling agreement with the Soviet Union, meeting another demand of Western creditors. Soviet acceptance of a two-year debt moratorium and liberal repayment schedule cleared the way for Indonesia's creditors to reach an agreement at their upcoming meeting in Paris.[122] Johnson administration officials felt an increased sense of urgency. Sukarno was publicly declaring his defiance of the New Order regime, calling for the masses to "rise up and crush my enemies within the country." Moreover, the government was "suffering from serious loss [of] momentum," Adam Malik told embassy officials, to the point where he believed "immediate action must be taken to remove [the] President from office."[123]

To demonstrate Washington's concern, President Johnson sent Walt Rostow to Paris to head up the U.S. negotiating team, prompting everyone else to quickly upgrade their delegations. Robert Barnett, the administration's point man on Indonesian debt, wrote Averell Harriman (whose investment bank, Brown Brothers Harriman, previously financed cotton exports to Indonesia) that the other creditors "had not yet absorbed the extent of Indonesia's economic calamity."[124] For ten days before the meeting Walt Rostow worked closely with IMF officials and lobbied other creditors to offer Jakarta liberal terms. After two days of talks the group of creditors agreed to a four-year moratorium on payments and a lengthy repayment schedule. Just as important, the creditors acknowledged the central role to be played by the IMF and the World Bank and the need for greater multilateral assistance.[125]

The creditors meeting in Paris capped a month of decisions by the Suharto regime aimed at demonstrating Jakarta's commitment to the return of private, particularly American, investors. On December 12 Suharto reversed Sukarno's April 1965 decree banning foreign investment and ordered the return of all properties placed under government control the previous year. On Christmas Eve the Presidium approved the Foreign Investment Law, the New Order's first major piece of legislation.[126] Two weeks later Indonesia and the United States signed an investment guarantee agreement after Jakarta accepted without change the draft offered by Washington.[127]

Indonesia's efforts now began sparking the interest of major corporations, whose investment decisions would play a major role in determining the country's economic prospects. An official with the Garrett Corporation (an L.A.-based aerospace company), after speaking to the heads of some of the world's largest multinationals, proposed that major U.S.-based corporations might set up an "unofficial development consortium" for Indonesia.[128] At the end of 1966 James Linen, president of the Luce-owned Time Inc. (and a friend of Eugene Rostow), got the same idea after visiting Bali at the request of the Sultan of Yogyakarta. Upon his return to Washington, Linen met with State Department officials and proposed to organize a gathering "of major American companies which could help develop American interest in Indonesian economic development."[129] As Linen talked up private investment in Washington, a group of midsize mining firms, the U.S. Mineral Resources Trade Mission, was making the rounds in Jakarta to explore the possibilities for mining and other resource concessions.[130]

Sukarno's Ouster and the New Order

For Johnson administration officials the slow but steady trickle of foreign investors back to Jakarta offered confirmation of the wisdom of its policies in support of the Suharto regime. The New Order's "effort to eradicate [Sukarno's] policies has been systematic, continual and eminently successful," the embassy reported in early 1967, although Indonesia continued to face economic and political problems "of a magnitude to confound the mighty." There also remained the question of Sukarno. Although his power had been severely curtailed, U.S. officials worried that "as long as Sukarno is around . . . there is a direct threat to the realization of the fundamental aims of the New Order."[131] Conversely, a National Intelligence Estimate concluded, "the neutralization of Sukarno would greatly improve the outlook for political stability in Indonesia."[132] Army hawks and civilians such as Adam Malik had come to the same conclusion. In addition to publicly defying the military in December, Sukarno attempted to block passage of the Foreign Investment Law and to undermine the painful stabilization measures being implemented by Suharto's ministers. Moreover, until Suharto could restructure the MPRS, the "Old Order" PNI and NU parties could block New Order initiatives and prevent expansion of the body, which would bring it under army control. According to Marshall Green, "Suharto has now made basic decision that he must get rid of Sukarno within [the] next few months." Military officials came to the embassy and outlined their plans for a "deliberate buildup of pressure against Sukarno" in the coming weeks involving the MPRS, youth and other front groups, and the army leadership.[133]

By the end of December 1966 anti-Sukarno graffiti was once again appearing on walls and billboards in Jakarta as army-backed student demonstrations resumed. In meetings with foreign journalists Adam Malik bluntly called for Sukarno's ouster while privately suggesting that killing him might be the only way to ensure his removal.[134] Meanwhile, efforts to discredit the disgraced president continued. The trial of former air force marshal Omar Dhani was moved forward by nearly six weeks and was covered extensively by the Jakarta press. While insisting that he had acted to forestall an anti-Communist coup, Dhani offered damning testimony against Sukarno, alleging that he knew about the September 30th Movement and made no effort to prevent either it or the killing of the six generals. Following Dhani's conviction and death sentence, the Indonesian Lawyers Association demanded that Sukarno be dismissed from the presidency and put on trial.[135]

On January 30, 1967, Sukarno finally submitted a written explanation of his actions in connection with the events of October 1, 1965, as demanded by the MPRS in July. Unrepentant and evasive, Sukarno's explanation only outraged his opponents and provided the needed pretext for more aggressive action. In early February the MPRS passed a resolution demanding the dismissal of Sukarno and the creation of a special court to try him for his alleged role in the September 30th Movement. The Indonesian Supreme Court repeated the MPRS charges and also called for the president's trial. Sukarno had run out of room to maneuver; his options were limited to actions that would stave off a humiliating public trial and possible imprisonment. On February 20, on the eve of the MPRS session called to discuss his removal from office, Sukarno formally handed over authority to Suharto, who became acting president. The Provisional DPR delivered the final humiliating blow on March 12, when it confirmed the transfer of power and stripped Sukarno of his title. The man who had helped lead Indonesia to independence was defeated, broken, and powerless. Shortly after, he was placed under house arrest, "a pathetic old man," the State Department observed approvingly, "transformed . . . from the incarnation of the Indonesian state into a historical relic."[136]

The Johnson administration greeted Sukarno's final ouster with undisguised enthusiasm. Marshall Green praised Suharto, whose regime was still summarily executing and imprisoning alleged PKI members, for his "sincere dedication to democratic means."[137] Sukarno's ouster removed one of the last barriers to the full resumption of U.S. assistance to Indonesia. When

William Bundy and Marshall Green briefed House and Senate leaders on Indonesia's progress, they endorsed the administration's renewed commitment to Indonesia and its emphasis on multilateralism.[138] Washington was prepared to respond, but its proposed aid package for 1967 reflected the shift in U.S. priorities since the Kennedy administration had proposed a comprehensive program of more than $300 million in military, economic, and technical assistance five years earlier.

Now Walt Rostow urged President Johnson to foot the bill for one-third of the estimated $240 million in balance of payments assistance that Indonesia would need to finance the essential imports approved by the IMF as part of its stabilization program. The request consisted mostly of AID, PL 480, and commodity assistance, a $10 million spare parts loan, and $10–$20 million in support assistance. The embassy described the package as "lean and not lush," designed to "both push and sustain the new regime" until economic stabilization warranted consideration of longer-term development planning.[139] Johnson, whose interest in Indonesia increased in direct proportion to the deterioration of the U.S. position in Vietnam, was eager to demonstrate Washington's support. The Indonesian government was "working for the people," Rostow wrote the president, and "pursuing a pragmatic economic policy." Now was the time for U.S. aid to "jump start the process."[140]

Indonesia's creditors were getting ready to meet in Amsterdam, and the U.S. delegation wanted the authority to pledge $85 million. President Johnson told his national security adviser to canvass congressional opinion, scribbling on a memo to Rostow "OK on assumption Japan and Eur. 2/3 to U.S. 1/3." A few days later Rostow returned with the verdict: House and Senate leaders were unanimously in support.[141] In Amsterdam the Intergovernmental Group on Indonesia (IGGI) agreed to meet Indonesia's balance of payments needs as outlined by the IMF, with Japan and Europe each matching Washington's third of the total.[142] Much of the assistance would be allocated under the Bonus Export System, "a sharp departure from past foreign aid practices" and especially worrisome in light of Indonesia's rampant corruption.[143] The arrangement was formalized in mid-June at the second IGGI meeting in Scheveningen, Sweden, where Indonesia received a vote of confidence from its creditors and international organizations. Administration officials were encouraged not just by the contributions of other countries but also by the presentation of the Indonesian delegation, which left convinced of the "salutary consequences of IMF-supported move[s] toward reliance on free market forces for allocation [of] scarce resources."[144] As stabilization got under way and Western countries stepped in with credit, the IBRD prepared to return to Jakarta to survey Indonesia's longer range development needs. The Indonesian government had now achieved three of its broad goals for economic rescue: significant emergency assistance, debt rescheduling, and a resumption of international credit on terms that were not unfavorable to Jakarta. In return, Indonesia's leaders were steadily enmeshing the country in webs of Western aid and influence that, according to a National Intelligence Estimate, "virtually assures continuation of Indonesia's westward leading foreign policies."[145]

Despite their progress in securing Western financial backing, Indonesian military leaders were disappointed with the pace and scope of U.S. aid, especially to the armed forces. Relations with Moscow—Indonesia's leading military supplier—continued to deteriorate as the government moved to extirpate all remaining signs of PKI influence, including a ban on the teaching of Marxism-Leninism. Soviet leaders were correspondingly "suspicious and non-committal" regarding further assistance, demurring on Jakarta's request for desperately needed military equipment and spare parts.[146] Army leaders were thus bitter when the U.S. failed to respond quickly to requests for civic action assistance. As a result, Marshall Green's repeated attempts to secure an audience with Suharto were rebuffed, usually by generals bearing expansive army wish lists totaling hundreds of millions of dollars. Indonesian ambassador Suwito told William Bundy that the officers "had been led to expect substantial, unrestricted flows of U.S. aid" after 1965 and chafed at U.S. requests for close monitoring of aid loans to ensure that funds remained under the control of the technocrats.[147]

Marshall Green finally secured an audience with President Suharto in early July, spending much of the meeting "trying to dispel his concern over U.S. aid prospects during next two years."[148] When Suharto outlined Indonesia's continued need for more assistance, Green brusquely reminded him that the United States had already provided $160 million in aid, credits, and debt postponement in the last eighteen months, an extraordinary amount given the budgetary black hole that Vietnam represented for the aid budget. To assuage Suharto and the army, the State Department offered 72,000 sets of uniforms and 32,000 pairs of boots to equip military units involved in civic action activities. A few days later the first shipment of MAP-supplied spare parts for the navy arrived, significantly easing tensions.[149] Close on the heels of Green's meeting, Brigadier General Sudjono, a member of Suharto's economic team, flew to Washington and made the pitch for aid directly to Vice President Humphrey, Walt Rostow, and congressional leaders.[150]

Army leaders' frustration stemmed in part from the budget cuts imposed on them by the government's stabilization measures. In addition to slashing inflation, IMF officials admitted that tight credit policies, price hikes on basic goods, and reductions in government spending were slowing business activity, exacerbating unemployment, and inflicting enormous popular hardship. Groups such as the PSI (Indonesian Socialist Party), the Masjumi Party, and NU that opposed austerity measures and were unwilling to criticize Suharto directly instead turned their ire on Widjojo and other members of Suharto's economic team. Stabilization and its architects were "under mounting attack from many quarters," the embassy reported, making it all the more important for the United States to back them, because "they offer [the] only real hope of constructive change in [the] Indonesian economy."[151]

In early August the NSC met again to review U.S. policy toward Indonesia. Two days earlier Johnson and his advisers had gathered to discuss the military stalemate in Vietnam. General William Westmoreland's request for 200,000 additional troops hung over Washington like a cloud in July and August, and the president was deeply frustrated by the failure of U.S. bombing to turn the tide. Moreover, the continued expansion of the war was placing severe limits on the funds available to meet the White House's other foreign policy priorities. War funding constituted fully one-third of projected Defense Department budgets for FY 1968 and FY 1969, with no letup in sight. In addition, Congress was proposing to slash the foreign aid budget by nearly $800 million, reducing it to $2.5 billion, with more than one-third of the amount designated for Vietnam.[152] The turnaround in Jakarta, achieved with comparably little U.S. assistance, contrasted starkly with the administration's dismal showing in Vietnam, but there were more problems ahead. Washington faced two challenges. The first was to balance Indonesia's expectations with the limited U.S. ability to provide aid. Walt Rostow wrote President Johnson that "Indonesian expectations of U.S. aid vastly exceed anything we are going to be able to come up with." Yet many officials, led by Vice President Hubert Humphrey, argued that Johnson was not doing enough.

Administration officials were already having trouble coming up with the U.S. share of its commitment to Indonesian stabilization needs, and the proposed AID package for Jakarta included 100,000 tons of rice already vouched for by Vietnam. The State Department concluded that "it is almost certain that we will not be able to meet from anticipated resources [for] one-third of Indonesia's 1968 requirements."[153] The second and related challenge, as AID director William Gaud put it, was how to use the limited U.S. aid available "to help stimulate rapid enough developmental progress in Indonesia to sustain public and army support . . . without loosening the economic stabilization discipline which is essential to [the] long run solution of Indonesia's problems."[154] Here Marshall Green thought the key lay in continuing to "identify and support 'modernizing' elements in the national leadership" and in targeting aid in their direction because the fate of the other elements of Washington's strategy was bound up in their success.[155]

The worse things got in Vietnam, the more President Johnson wanted to invest in Indonesia's success, just as administration officials, the press, and Congress wanted to see Indonesia as a validation of the American stance in Indochina.[156] "Here is a country which has rejected communism and is pulling itself up by its bootstraps," Johnson told the NSC. Should not the administration be asking for more money? The consensus was that Congress would not appropriate more money for foreign aid for 1967. The president kept pressing. The United States should make Indonesia a showcase, he argued, because it was "one of the few places in the world that has moved in our direction." "We should take some of our ambitious plans which haven't been working in other countries," he said, perhaps referring to foundering schemes such as the Mekong Delta Development Authority, "and put them into action in Indonesia."[157] Administration officials recommended sticking to the one-third formula of financing Indonesian stabilization and rehabilitation that would commit Washington to roughly $110 million in aid for FY 1968. General Suharto asked Marshall Green for even more, warning that without additional aid "Indonesia's new order would be in serious trouble."[158] European nations were already balking at their share of the $300 million–plus that the IMF predicted Jakarta would need in 1968, and Green, who now supported a sizable aid package, returned to Washington in October to once again emphasize the importance of the U.S. commitment to Indonesia. "This is Indonesia's critical hour of need," he told a cabinet meeting in mid-October with

Rusk and Johnson present. "Our sacrifices in Vietnam avail little if we do not take strong and swift steps to foster [the] growth and strength which the new Indonesia can achieve."[159]

Johnson's remarks to the NSC reflected a widespread feeling within the administration that the U.S. war in Vietnam had in some way been responsible for the turnaround in Indonesia. New Order officials seeking aid from the White House encouraged this perception, as did White House officials themselves and supporters of the war, such as Australian prime minister Harold Holt. Meeting with Vice President Hubert Humphrey in September 1966, Adam Malik suggested that "General Suharto's success in defeating the Indonesian Communist Forces was directly influenced by the U.S. determination in South Vietnam."[160] More recently, historian Mark Moyar has argued that the Indonesian army would never have "resisted the Communists" in late 1965 had the U.S. withdrawn from Vietnam.[161] There is little evidence, however, to support such claims. The CIA, after an exhaustive search, concluded in May 1966 that the war in Vietnam had precisely "nothing to do" with stiffening the resolve of the generals in Jakarta. On the contrary, the CIA went on to observe, "most political groupings in Indonesia at present, even with a government following and anti-Chinese Communist foreign policy, view the U.S. presence in Vietnam as a continuation of the Western effort to control and dominate Asia."[162]

At the end of October 1967 Vice President Humphrey traveled to Southeast Asia to attend the inauguration of South Vietnamese President Thieu and stopped over in Jakarta to meet with Suharto and other officials. Upon his return, Humphrey made a strong pitch for increased aid to Jakarta, praising Suharto as "an honest, hard working man" whose aides were turning the economy around and bringing Indonesia into the Western fold. The vice president minced no words in characterizing the regime, observing that "the only real base of Suharto's government is the Army," but his enthusiasm for the New Order was unvarnished.[163] Johnson approved his aides' request to continue contributing one-third of Indonesia's aid requirements, telling Walt Rostow, "I want to do everything I can for Indonesia—as quickly as I can. Send me a program."[164]

The Johnson Administration Embraces the New Order

Indonesia's halting progress in restoring economic stability and the administration's struggle to find resources to meet its aid commitments merely highlighted the importance both countries attached to the return of foreign investors. The CIA concluded that Indonesia's prospects for a speedy recovery depended on the construction of "a more stable environment for private enterprise." But as former World Bank governor John J. McCloy observed, "Government capital can be directed . . . private capital has to be induced."[165] Jakarta had already taken significant steps in this direction: the passage of the Foreign Investment Law in December 1966, the signing of an investor guarantee agreement with Washington, the implementation of IMF-directed stabilization measures, and the rescheduling of its outstanding debt. Beginning in early 1967 Indonesian officials fanned out across the United States, Japan, and Western Europe, speaking before business forums and seeking to spread the word about the new welcome mat they had put out for foreign capital. Ambassador Suwito Kusomowidagdo, speaking at an American Indonesian Chamber of Commerce meeting in New York, insisted that the Suharto government had abandoned "rigid state control of the economy" for a greater reliance on market forces. In addition, he stressed the opportunities for investors "to cooperate with Indo under favorable terms in developing the nation's rich natural resources . . . now exploited at only one-tenth of their potential capacity."[166]

Following the lead of Freeport Sulphur and a handful of other companies, a steady stream of prospective foreign investors descended upon Indonesia. Scores of U.S. companies sent representatives to Jakarta during the first half of 1967, especially after Freeport signed a contract with the Ministry of Mining in April. The bulk of them were small or medium-size firms involved in raw materials extraction and production: mining, timber, independent oil, chemical and fertilizer companies, and the banks that financed them. These were firms historically tied to the nationalist-expansionist current of U.S. foreign policy and to the right wing of the Republican Party. The first bank to return to Jakarta, for example, was the Hearst-aligned First National City Bank, the largest U.S. bank in the Philippines and one closely tied to extractive industries there.[167] In early 1968 First National published a guide to investing in Indonesian timber, noting that it would likely soon replace the Philippines as the largest timber supplier in Asia. Chicago-based Continental Illinois National Bank and Trust likewise prepared a guide in early 1966 emphasizing investment in plantation agriculture, oil, and resource extraction, observing that "the industrial sector of the economy in terms of exports can be summed up in one word: petroleum."[168]

Most of these firms had bitterly opposed Sukarno and had sympathized with the covert action and rollback current in the CIA. As if on cue, nationalist oilman H. L. Hunt also returned, seeking concession areas off the coast of West Irian and complaining that the State Department and big oil companies were scheming against him. In a *Playboy* interview Hunt observed that Indonesia was the only place the United States was not losing the Cold War and that "the ousting of Sukarno, if successfully continued, is the greatest victory for Freedom since the last decisive battle of World War II."[169] One can usefully compare these companies with the historically internationalist, multinationally oriented, world-competitive firms that dominated the Indonesian market in the pre-independence and Sukarno periods: Stanvac and Caltex; Goodyear and U.S. Rubber; Morrison Knudson and Brown and Root; Singer Sewing Machine, Westinghouse Electrical, Morgan Guarantee Trust, General Motors, and Union Carbide.[170]

The first two U.S. trade missions arrived in Jakarta from Oregon and San Francisco in April 1967, representing midsize firms exploring concession possibilities in timber, plywood, chemicals, mining, and oil.[171] Trade missions from Belgium, the Netherlands, Australia, France, and North Korea soon followed, prompting the Dutch newspaper *De Volksrant* to observe that a "fierce international competitive struggle for a favorable position in the Indonesian market has broken out."[172] The embassy praised Suharto for accepting the "need for foreign investment as principal means for developing the outer islands" and taking steps to attract it, but technocrats worried that the large multinational firms they foresaw as engines of development had not yet taken the same initiative as smaller companies such as Freeport and IIAPCO had.[173]

In the latter half of 1967 this began to change. In August the Pacific-Indonesia Businessman's Association (PIBA) hosted a meeting in Jakarta sponsored by the Stanford Research Institute, a research and consulting firm whose analysts consulted on the Alliance for Progress. The meeting brought together 250 businessmen from the United States, Japan, Australia, and Western Europe to meet with Indonesian businessmen and a handful of Indonesian officials who outlined the steps the Suharto regime was taking to attract foreign capital. The embassy approvingly noted the speech of Manpower Minister Awaluddin Djamin, who described the new regime's repressive labor policies in a manner "designed to allay any fears prospective investors may harbor about possible trouble with trade unions."[174] Howard Jones called the gathering "most encouraging," noting that "it was the first time the American business community and, for that matter, the Indonesian business community had ever met with top government officials."[175]

Three months later in Geneva an even more important gathering took place. Scores of executives from dozens of the world's leading financial, manufacturing, and extractive firms met with Indonesia's top economic ministers to discuss investment opportunities under the New Order. Time-Life Inc. president James Linen, who organized the meeting, emphasized to President Suharto that "in order to attract the top potential investors it would be absolutely necessary to have someone of the caliber of the Sultan of Jogjakarta or the Foreign Minister" leading Indonesia's delegation. Suharto, who told Marshall Green in July that he "attached great importance to these meetings," made sure foreign investors got the right signal.[176] The Sultan, Malik, and virtually every important economic official attended the meeting, outlining sector by sector the incentives Indonesia was prepared to offer foreign investors and listening to investor concerns.[177] U.S. officials waxed enthusiastic about Suharto's courtship of multinational capital, especially Vice President Humphrey, whose visit to Indonesia coincided with the Geneva meeting. In a personal letter to Linen, President Johnson characterized the gathering as "a magnificent story of opportunity seen and promise awakened" and invited him to the White House for a visit.[178]

By the end of 1967 Jakarta's main hotel was "crowded with businessmen from the U.S., Western Europe, Japan and neighboring Asian countries" seeking investment opportunities.[179] Investment guides for Indonesia cooed that the Suharto regime was "prepared to go to the greatest lengths to attract foreign capital" and described the modernizing potential of foreign investment with the same optimistic faith and in much the same way as U.S. officials did.[180] The task of U.S. corporations, one guide suggested, was to help countries like Indonesia build the infrastructure of development, combining "a systems analysis and coordination of all . . . national development factors" with "old-fashioned Yankee ingenuity and free enterprise." The challenges posed by poverty, economic dislocation, corruption, political instability, and underdevelopment were daunting, but Indonesia and other developing nations had an advantage, namely, "the fact that, starting with a virtually clean economic slate, and with access to the latest in economic theory and expertise, far more rational and efficient planning is possible than ever before."[181] *Fortune* magazine similarly observed that Indonesia "is putting on trial what many observers have long considered to be model rules of behavior for backward nations." If successful, Indonesia could "point the way for many a floundering country in Asia, Africa, and Latin America." Upon returning from a study trip to Southeast Asia, Senator Joseph S. Clark of Pennsylvania agreed, writing that Indonesia had become "a testing ground for both free world, free enterprise concepts of development and the effectiveness of multilateral assistance."[182]

The continued, if wobbly, economic recovery in Indonesia and the mounting confidence and cohesion of the Suharto regime was one of the few bits of good news for the administration as it began what Walter LaFeber aptly calls "the year from hell." As Birch Bayh praised the situation in Jakarta, 80,000 North Vietnamese troops and NLF guerrillas were launching the Tet offensive, attacking a hundred cities across South Vietnam and shattering public confidence in White House claims that the U.S. war could be won anytime soon. The dismal situation in Vietnam only reinforced President Johnson's determination to do whatever he could to shore up the New Order. With administration prodding, Congress met his request to increase aid for Indonesia to $156 million, in stark contrast to the reductions other foreign aid recipients faced.[183] Robert McNamara, who had resigned from the administration and was now head of the World Bank, traveled to Indonesia in June and came home convinced that preservation of the New Order was an urgent necessity, establishing the Bank's first permanent mission in a developing country in Jakarta soon after.

In its policy assessment for 1968 the embassy in Jakarta offered an extraordinary analysis of past U.S. policy and the challenges Washington would face in achieving its goals for Indonesia in the coming years. The New Order regime faced myriad problems: inflation, unemployment, political infighting, capital shortages, a "desperate shortage" of skilled personnel, creeping militarism, endemic corruption, and rising expectations among the Indonesian population. Nevertheless, Marshall Green saw room for continued optimism because "things could easily have been far worse." Suharto had undergone a remarkable transformation, holding fast on economic stabilization measures while maintaining political stability and working to "civilianize" his image, even to the point of barnstorming around the country like an American politician.[184] Now U.S. policy and Indonesia itself were beginning the transition from the "relatively short-term task of economic stabilization" to the "long-term task of modernization." Washington had a heavy stake in helping the New Order succeed, the embassy observed, "because it is the latest test case of whether liberal economic policies combined with free world assistance offer a more solid path to modernization than communism or other totalitarian solutions."[185]

In this transition the Johnson administration faced two daunting challenges. The experience of the past fifteen years had convinced most policymakers of the continued need for a low-profile approach to Jakarta. Intrusive American aid programs and public diplomacy had done little but stoke the fires of Indonesian nationalism, providing fuel for Sukarno and his allies to mobilize Indonesians to oppose Western influence. Moreover, U.S. aid was often "rejected, deflected or transformed by basic features in the Indonesian social structure." But economic development alone would do little unless accompanied by such a transformation in Indonesian behavior, values, and attitudes. Because of this, the embassy now argued—ignoring the unbridgeable chasm between its vast ambitions and the meager resources and political capital it was bringing to bear—Washington should "regard our ultimate aim in Indonesia not as economic development alone but as modernization." Support for Jakarta's participation in ASEAN and other forums for regional cooperation would aid in this process by "interweav[ing] it inextricably in responsible regional activities" and encouraging Indonesia "to see itself as a partner and participant in a world-wide process of modernization." Foreign Minister Adam Malik shared this sentiment, contending that the "primary reason for regional cooperation is the necessity for modernization."[186]

In designing future aid programs, the embassy argued, the Johnson administration needed to take into account three broad features of Indonesian culture: "1) predominantly traditional (as contrasted to rational) modes of thought which resists change; 2) particularistic (or personalized) rather than universalistic values . . . or abstract codes of behavior, and 3) a decentralized and compartmentalized organization of society." The best way to ensure that U.S. aid had maximal impact with minimal intrusion was to continue working wherever possible through "so-called 'third culture'" Indonesians, such as the technocrats who could mediate between Indonesian and American culture and transmit modernizing attitudes to their more traditional fellow citizens, a role that coincided with the way the technocrats viewed themselves. Expanded U.S. participant training programs that concentrated on students, technical workers, and military officers would likewise expand the ranks of such third culture Indonesians, helping to move them "to an outside vantage point," which would "show them the deficiencies of their own social structure" and thereby stimulate a desire for change.[187] American educational aid programs, as one contemporary scholar put it, would help form students "who would shift from the folk image of man and society common to the mass of Indonesians and adopt a more or less 'scientific' attitude," instilling "a systematic, cause-effect approach to problems" and providing "a basis for a rational critique of Sukarno's Indonesia and the desire for rapid change."[188]

The embassy concluded by recommending that the Johnson administration treat its role in Indonesia "as a controlled experiment in modernization." "With a cooperative government, a classically traditionalist society, and a good measure of material resources, Indonesia constitutes a good test subject." Moreover, Washington was starting "with virtually a clean slate" on the aid front, providing a benchmark for evaluating the future success of its programs.[189] Aware of the limits of U.S. power but optimistic about the transformative potential of exposure to American aid, technical expertise, knowledge, and culture, the Johnson administration hoped to resume the ambitious project first envisioned by its predecessor: helping Indonesia to "set out on the long and probably torturous road to modernization."[190]

Conclusion

At the end of January 1968 Indiana senator Birch Bayh appeared on *The Joey Bishop Show*, a popular nationwide late-night television talk show, following his first visit to Indonesia. Bayh, previously a staunch opponent of U.S. aid to Jakarta, told Bishop:

> It is easy for me to get too enthusiastic about what is going on in Indonesia, because here you have a society that was strictly a socialist society, a state-controlled society, that was almost communistic, and now they have a group . . . most of them trained back here in the good old USA, and they have decided to implement a free enterprise system, and they are going to do it in a short period of time, and to see some of the evolution, if not revolution, that is taking place there now is extremely worthy.

"This belongs in the man bites dog category," Walt Rostow wrote the president, referring to the en masse conversion of Sukarno critics into Suharto boosters.[1]

Official optimism regarding Indonesia contrasted sharply with Washington's deepening pessimism—prompted in part by military and political stalemate in Vietnam—over its inability to effect similar political, economic, and social transformation in other postcolonial societies. U.S. officials viewed the Suharto regime in 1968 as one of the great successes of American foreign policy. Sukarno and the PKI were destroyed, political parties had been "neutralized," the regime was committed to economic reform and open to foreign capital, and the army—which the CIA argued was solely equipped for "the gigantic task of modernization"—was beyond effective political challenge. Moreover, Indonesia was playing a moderate, responsible political role in the region through its participation in ASEAN. Initially ASEAN was little more than a forum for periodic meetings of Southeast Asian foreign ministers (and it was hamstrung through 1968 by the Philippines' continued claim to the Malaysian island of Sabah), but U.S. officials viewed ASEAN as the first truly indigenous regional association of the Cold War era, one that could be expected to counter Beijing's influence and indirectly serve American interests.[2] Although Indonesia resolutely maintained its nonalignment in public, the government's utter dependence on foreign aid and investment and the military's bitter anti-Communism lent Indonesian neutralism a decidedly pro-Western cast.

The September 30th Movement and the ensuing mass murder of PKI supporters that paved the way for Suharto's ascendance made U.S. officials look prescient as well as lucky. McGeorge Bundy wrote President Johnson that the dramatic turnaround in Jakarta was "a striking vindication of our policy . . . of keeping our hand in the game for the long-term stakes despite recurrent pressures to pull out."[3] This policy was also a reflection of Washington's persistent conviction that Indonesia would prove unable to solve its manifold economic and political problems until the PKI was destroyed. The administration's enthusiastic support for the army-led slaughter was thus a predictable, if damnable, result of the United States's persistent linking of its own global credibility with the fortunes of indigenous radicalism and local military forces, a pattern repeated in Guatemala, Brazil, Chile, and countless other countries during the Cold War and one magnified in importance by escalation of the war in Vietnam.

Washington's fears about Indonesian Communism were intimately bound up with its commitment to Indonesian economic and political development.

The literature on U.S.-Indonesian relations during the Kennedy and John-son administrations—which focused on anti-Communism, geopolitics, and national security—has been almost wholly silent on this fusion of concerns, concerns so apparent, for example, in the scholarship on the Alliance for Progress in Latin America.[4] Historians have thus failed to recognize the un-derlying continuity of U.S. policy during the 1960s; instead, they have de-voted the bulk of their attention to what in retrospect should be regarded as an interregnum from 1964 to 1965 during which time U.S. officials were forced to abandon their ambitious agenda and focus on containing Sukarno and the PKI. An appreciation for the way U.S. officials and their Indonesian counterparts thought about and planned for Indonesian development, how-ever, is central to understanding U.S.-Indonesian relations in the 1960s and indeed throughout the postwar period. Indonesia was one of the few coun-tries where the United States and the Soviet Union competed directly for influence, a competition waged as much with technical and economic assis-tance as through military aid and training. Kennedy administration policy-makers recognized that they needed to respond to the "Soviet aid offensive" if they were going to present Indonesia with an alternative to the develop-mental model promoted by Soviet officials as the surest path to rapid indus-trialization. The administration's proposed comprehensive program of mil-itary aid, economic and technical assistance, and stabilization support was in part a response to this Soviet challenge. It coincided with Sukarno's launch-ing of an ambitious Eight-Year Plan that, if successful, would have given the state a leading role in economic development. U.S. officials throughout the period emphasized the links between the country's chronic economic crisis and the rising fortunes of the PKI, insisting that "actions to defeat commu-nism in Indonesia must be supplementary to long-range effective programs to improve the living standards of the masses."[5]

The economic underpinnings of American anti-Communism in Indonesia were most starkly revealed in the months following the collapse of the Sep-tember 30th Movement. William Bundy later wrote that historians "of the theorist and process-oriented persuasions" will find in this period "almost no formal papers seeking to define or describe the path that eventually led to a solid American relationship with the new regime in Indonesia and to a major American contribution to the economic and social recovery of this key na-tion."[6] But such a claim is not borne out either by Washington's actions or by the vast documentary trail that successive administrations left behind. By 1966, with the Cold War for all intents and purposes over inside Indonesia, the Johnson administration concluded, as had its predecessors, that the destruction of the PKI would matter little without a fundamental political and economic reorientation in Jakarta. Now it emphasized the short-term goal of rescuing and rehabilitating the Indonesian economy and the long-range goal of supporting a stable, politically moderate authoritarian regime in Jakarta, integrated into the regional economy. Such a regime could serve both as a counterweight to Chinese influence and as "a desirable market and source of raw materials" for Japan, Europe, and even the Soviet Union. U.S. officials were still cognizant of the potent force of Indonesian nationalism, which Sukarno had proved so adept at channeling, and thus insisted that their goals "must in the Indonesian's eyes appear as modernization, not westernization and least of all Americanization."[7]

Many Indonesians saw things differently, both from the United States and from each other. Like the military junta in Brazil, Suharto's New Order publicly based its legitimacy on the basis of its commitment to modernization and economic growth. But although U.S. officials and scholars shared a broad consensus on the definition of modernization, elites in Indonesia and many other countries "selectively appropriated its ideals to suit their own diverse needs and purposes."[8] Western-trained technicians, military officials, and Muslim groups, among others, all came to different conclusions as to the meaning of modernization and its implications for the country's political and economic development.

Indonesia's Western-educated technocrats described themselves and the process they were spearheading in terms that reflected their American training, emphasizing that modernization and rationality were closely associated. Their largely secular and Westernized vision of modernization was widely shared by other minority groups in Indonesia, including students, Catholics, and Protestants who saw Suharto as a "defender of Panca Sila principles of religious tolerance and political balance." Despite their receptiveness to American views on modernization, however, these economists, for the most part, did not take U.S.-style liberal capitalism as their model but instead looked to such countries as Japan, Taiwan, Korea, and India, in which the state took a leading role in the development process.[9]

Military officials likewise absorbed selected tenets of modernization theory and adapted them to their own ends. Under the auspices of the military and AID programs, hundreds of Indonesian army officers were brought to American universities, such as Harvard, the University of Pittsburgh, and Syracuse University, to take classes in industrial enterprise management, business administration, personnel management, and executive leadership. U.S. officials were explicit about the purpose of such training: to enable the military to replace Sukarno and assume administrative control of Indonesia's political and economic institutions. In the early 1960s the University of Indonesia organized an executive development program, modeled on the same programs at U.S. universities, to provide management training for civilian and military leaders. But rather than seeing their role in Indonesian political life as a transitory one on the road to modernization, army leaders proclaimed a "dual function" for the armed forces that envisioned them as permanent guardians of political and economic order, a role the military is still reluctant to discard forty years later, even after a nominal return to civilian rule.[10] In fact, Western-oriented Indonesian technocrats, unlike U.S. policymakers, presciently viewed the military as the primary obstacle to Indonesian democracy and modernization even as they hitched their wagons to the armed forces out of political expediency.

Finally, Indonesia's Muslim organizations and parties, although totally overlooked by U.S. officials as conveyors of modernizing values, also engaged in heated debates at the time about the nature of modernization and the stance Muslims ought to take toward it. Since independence, Indonesians have debated the relationship between Islam and the state and whether nationalism or religion ought to serve as the foundation of national identity. Having survived the political repression of the Guided Democracy period and having played a key role in the crushing of the PKI, Islamic organizations and parties in the late 1960s sought both political rehabilitation and an acknowledgment of their significant role in Indonesian religious and social life. They also hoped to demonstrate the compatibility of Islam with *Pancasila* and allay concerns that Islam was opposed to economic and political development. But the Suharto regime's commitment to modernization provoked serious divisions within the Muslim community. Modernist Muslims, such as members of the urban-oriented Muhammadiyah, generally displayed an openness to the West, a tolerance for religious and political pluralism, a belief in the divide between tradition and modernity, and an emphasis on the modernizing role of intellectual elites.[11] U.S. officials and the Ford Foundation actively courted these Muslims beginning in the 1950s, viewing them as possible counterweights to both the PKI and Islamic movements such as Darul Islam. Many openly espoused the views of modernization theorists such as Lucian Pye and Walt Rostow, leading one scholar to refer to them as "secular modernizers." In October 1966 modernist Muslim intellectual Deliar Noer offered an early reflection on Islam and the New Order in which he called for a "democratic modernization" that was not only forward thinking, rational, and dynamic but also committed to broad goals of social and economic equality consistent with *Pancasila*. Like many students and technocrats, however, Noer presciently worried that the regime would instead pursue a strategy of "undemocratic modernization."[12]

Traditional Muslim groups, on the other hand, especially those that still sought control of the state and the imposition of Islamic law in all or part of the archipelago, were deeply wary of the Suharto regime's commitment to what they viewed as a secular path to modernization. Muslim suspicion extended to the composition of the New Order state and its technocratic elite, which was disproportionately staffed by Christians, especially Catholics, and members of the Indonesian Socialist Party who espoused a Western vision of modernity. Traditionalist Muslims feared that the modernizers' emphasis on overcoming the alleged cultural obstacles to modernity and on the creation of a "new man" implied a secularization of the public sphere and political life.[13] A young Mohammed Amien Rais, future leader of the Muhammadiyah and later speaker of the Indonesian Parliament, expressed his concern in the early New Order period that Western-oriented modernization would weaken the role of Islam in Indonesian society. The Islamic scholar Hadji Abdul Malik Karim Abdullah (known as Hamka) declared more bluntly that "what is now called modernization is but camouflage for a big plan aimed at removing Islamic influences from our hearts so that we shall willingly become the tail-end of nations who are considered advanced."[14]

Some of those fears were well founded. Much of the Islamic community's concern with New Order modernization stemmed from the realization that the Suharto regime did not intend to rehabilitate Muslim organizations such as the Masjumi Party, which had been banned by Sukarno in 1960. Many army leaders still feared the potential power of political Islam and a revival of movements like Darul Islam, and they resented Masjumi Party support for the PRRI rebellions. When the regime allowed the formation under strict conditions of the more modernist Parmusi Party in 1967, party leaders tried to bring on board former Masjumi figures, prompting a crackdown that effectively gutted the organization. Continued repression forced Islamic leaders and intellectuals to reassess their stance toward national development goals, prompting scholar Nurcholish Madjid to begin grappling with the formulation of an Islamic "theology of development."[15] Tensions between the New Order regime and the Muslim community would continue into the 1980s, when Suharto attempted to patch up relations with traditionalist Islamic organizations as a way of bolstering his declining leverage vis-à-vis the army. As Juna Chandra Santosa suggests, political Islam's revival in Indonesia following the downfall of Suharto stemmed in part from this enduring tension between more traditional Islamic groups and the secular modernizing goals of the New Order, an experience shared in somewhat analogous fashion by Afghanistan and Iran through the 1970s, where similar modernizing projects led by repressive regimes helped spawn Islamic revolt.[16] In short, there was a plurality of Indonesian views on modernization in the late 1950s and early 1960s, and American views on the matter were rarely accepted by Indonesians wholesale but rather adapted to Indonesian circumstances, a reality that U.S. officials rarely acknowledged.

William O. Walker, surveying the wave of Washington-backed military regimes that swept Latin America during the 1960s in a sort of reverse domino effect, observes that by the end of the decade "the military had become the guardian of internal security and national development" nearly everywhere in the region, "which was exactly how the Kennedy and Johnson Administration wanted it."[17] The same can be said for Indonesia, where from the late 1950s Washington remained remarkably consistent in its support for authoritarianism and in its reliance on the armed forces as the guarantor of economic and political stability. After Sukarno dismantled parliamentary democracy with military support and returned to the 1945 constitution in the late 1950s, U.S. officials effectively abandoned talk of elections or representative government in Indonesia, rightly fearing that the PKI would thereby improve its position.

Following the army-led destruction of the PKI, however, the Johnson administration continued to oppose a return to democracy. Commenting on

Indonesia's prospects for political stability, embassy officials in late 1968 invoked Almond and Verba's model of "civic culture" to conclude that economic and political change should proceed at a pace "neither so slow as to cause irreversible disaffection among the modernizing elite nor so fast as to disturb the traditionalist masses."[18] While condemning Sukarno's authoritarianism, U.S. officials and commentators heaped praise on the exponentially more brutal authoritarianism of the Suharto regime, primarily because of its anti-Communism, openness to Western economic influence and investment, and willingness to accommodate U.S. policy in the region. As elsewhere, Washington's economic and strategic interests trumped any rhetorical concern with democratic practice, while social scientists provided a theoretical and scholarly patina to justify the U.S. alliance with the Indonesian armed forces. The antidemocratic bias of modernization theory, whose proponents claimed that developing nations would eventually converge on a liberal democratic modernity, was revealed in Indonesia in stark fashion.[19]

The foreign aid policies suggested by modernization theorists, although undoubtedly influencing U.S. policy, also generated fierce opposition. Historian Nils Gilman has characterized modernization theory as "the foreign policy analogue to 'social modernism' at home," represented in its ideal form by a fully realized, technocratic New Deal liberalism. Conservative and nationalist voices in Congress and elsewhere also saw things this way and rejected the Kennedy administration's aid policies for precisely this reason. They viewed Washington's support for public foreign investment in Indonesia, mild encouragement of state-owned enterprise, and the whole aid apparatus as an outward thrust of the New Deal. Social science thinking on development, at least with regard to Indonesia, thus buttressed a particular vision of political economy at home and abroad and the interests of identifiable political and social constituencies, an intersection of ideas and interests that deserves to be explored at much greater length.[20] The partial opening of Chinese and Russian archives should stimulate similar research into how Soviet and Chinese officials viewed modernization in the light of their own experience and the role they saw foreign assistance playing in accelerating this process in postcolonial states.

It is just as important to acknowledge the limits of modernization theory as an explanatory device, however, as it is to see the limits of anti-Communism as a guide to policy. As Michael Latham has accurately observed, social sci-

entific theories of modernization may have "shaped institutional understandings of the development process . . . and suggested specific ways in
which American policy might direct and accelerate global change," but they
"were not determinative or exclusive forces" and were nowhere the sole
cause of policy.[21] In trying to achieve their goals for Indonesia, the Kennedy
and Johnson administrations were just as hamstrung by the limits of American power as by their domestic opposition. The deepening U.S. military
commitment to Vietnam placed decisive constraints on Washington's ability
to devote the resources and political attention to Indonesia that its ambitions
and the country's strategic and economic importance warranted. Washington's commitment to integrating Jakarta more fully into the regional economy, while closely bound to its conceptions of Indonesian development,
owed more to policymakers' assessment of Indonesia's role in the fabric of
American hegemony and, in particular, its relationship with Japan. Historians might in this regard usefully compare scholarly and official discourses on
Indonesian modernization with those on Korea and Taiwan, which were directly within Washington's hegemonic reach and where U.S. officials were for
a time more indulgent of state-led developmental schemes than they were in
Jakarta and elsewhere.[22]

The consolidation of power by a largely U.S.-trained army and the crucial role of U.S.-trained economists and technical personnel in 1966–1967
appeared to confirm the hopes that Eisenhower and Kennedy administration
officials had placed in them and to validate the predictions of modernization
theorists. Washington's hopes, however, proved ephemeral. Western observers
noted almost immediately the simmering discontent inside Indonesia with
the corruption, repression, and authoritarianism of the Suharto regime. As
early as 1970 the U.S. embassy concluded that "resentment of military
power and privilege and the all-pervasive involvement of the military in government, business, education and politics and in the daily lives of the people" would continue for the foreseeable future, undermining Suharto's rule.
U.S. officials saw the handwriting on the wall yet dismissed the political and
economic implications of Washington's long-term reliance on the army as
the guarantor of stability in Indonesia. They argued that "we should judge
the political performance of the government on its contribution to long-
range growth and modernization, and not on its support for the parapher-
nalia or formal procedures of parliamentary democracy." Succeeding U.S.

administrations would largely keep to this script, to the great disservice of Indonesian prodemocracy, human rights, and civil society activists.[23]

Thirty-two years after he came to power Suharto was swept from it, ironically by the forces of economic collapse, popular mobilization, and a divided military that had crippled his predecessor.[24] The Indonesian crisis of 1997–1998 signaled not only the collapse of the Suharto regime but the failure of the thirty-two year experiment with the authoritarian developmental model it inaugurated upon coming to power. U.S. officials, multilateral institutions such as the World Bank, social scientists, and others who made their careers funding and cheering Indonesia's purported modernization while muting criticism of its appalling human rights record were suddenly forced to reckon with the ugly legacy of Suharto's rule. For more than three decades the New Order promised stability in the name of development, rationalizing state violence and the repression of civil society, the labor movement, and students— whose flowering modernization was supposed to enable—as the price of growth. But among the chief casualties of the New Order's collapse was the myth of its developmental success and alleged record of poverty reduction, which, when not made up out of whole cloth, masked growing inequality, the squandering or misallocation of tens of billions of dollars in development loans, and spectacular corruption, cronyism, and nepotism on a scale nearly unmatched in the postwar era. Ten years after the ouster of Suharto, nearly half of all Indonesians live near or below the government's official poverty line, a figure that is growing.[25] Moreover, the resource extraction and commodity export development model pushed by Western creditors under Suharto's rule, the riches of which flowed overwhelmingly to a tiny sliver of Indonesia's elite, has ravaged the country's environment, leading to the loss of more than half of Indonesia's tropical forests, some of the worst pollution in Asia, and, starting in the late 1990s, catastrophic forest fires.[26] As Richard Robison has argued, this oligarchic constellation of political and business interests that emerged and enriched themselves during the New Order has "largely survived the collapse of the Suharto regime."[27]

Many of the problems that plagued Indonesia in 1998 and after—endemic corruption, an attenuated civil society, environmental degradation, state violence in Aceh, East Timor, and West Papua, and the recrudescence of political Islam—were at least exacerbated by, if not finding their roots during, the New Order.[28] These lessons have not been well learned. In the years following Suharto's downfall, the army continues to play a destabilizing role in the country's political and economic life, and the Bush administration has renewed full-scale assistance to its armed forces in the name of fighting the so-called war on terror.[29] Indonesians who continue to put forward a different vision of their country's modernization—one rooted in pluralism, democracy, and balanced development—still wrestle with the bitter legacy of the choices forged in Jakarta and Washington during these fateful years.

Reference Matter

Abbreviations

ADB	Asian Development Bank
AID	Agency for International Development
CENIS	Center for International Studies, MIT
CO	Country
CWIHP	Cold War International History Project
DAC	Development Assistance Committee
DDRS	Declassified Documents Reference Service
DEF	Defense Ministry Files, U.K. National Archives
DH	Indonesia Subseries of FO-371, U.K. National Archives
DO	Dominions Office, Records of the Commonwealth Relations Office, U.K. National Archives
DOS	Department of State
FBIS	Foreign Broadcast Information Service
FCO	Records of the Foreign and Commonwealth Affairs Office (United Kingdom)
FFA	Ford Foundation Archives
FO	Records of the Foreign Office (United Kingdom)
FOIA	Freedom of Information Act
FRUS	Foreign Relations of the United States
HFAC	Foreign Affairs Committee, U.S. House of Representatives
HI	Hoover Institute, Stanford University
INR	State Department Bureau of Intelligence and Research
JFKL	John F. Kennedy Presidential Library

LBJL	Lyndon Baines Johnson Presidential Library
LOC	Manuscripts Division, Library of Congress
NA	National Archives and Records Administration (United States)
NIE	National Intelligence Estimate
NIES	National Intelligence Estimates
NSAM	National Security Action Memorandum
NSC	National Security Council
NSF	National Security Files
OCI	Office of Current Intelligence
PET	Petroleum Files, U.S. National Archives and Records Administration
POF	Presidential Office Files
POL	Politics Files
PPS	Policy Planning Staff
PREM	Records of the Prime Ministers Office, U.K. National Archives
RAC	Rockefeller Archives Center
RFA	Rockefeller Foundation Archives
RG	Record Group
SNF	Subject Numeric Files
SNIE	Special National Intelligence Estimate
UKNA	United Kingdom National Archives
WHCF	White House Central Files
WNG	West New Guinea

Notes

INTRODUCTION

1. Memo for Johnson, October 1, 1965, *Foreign Relations of the United States* [*FRUS*], *1964–1968*, v. 26, 300–301.

2. See McNamara, *In Retrospect*, 215, 270; Senate Committee on Foreign Relations, *Vietnam Hearings*, 140.

3. Anderson, *Violence and the State in Suharto's Indonesia*; Heryanto and Hadiz. "Post-Authoritarian Indonesia."

4. See also Notosusanto and Saleh, *Coup Attempt of the "September 30 Movement."*

5. "PKI Reinstated as 1965 Tragedy Culprit in School Textbooks," *Jakarta Post*, September 18, 2006.

6. "Forty Years on, Events of 1965 Remain a Mystery," *Jakarta Post*, September 30, 2005.

7. Zurbuchen, *Beginning to Remember*, 3.

8. McMahon, "Cold War in Asia"; Kahin and Kahin, *Subversion as Foreign Policy*; Subritzky, *Confronting Sukarno*; Matthew Jones, *Conflict and Confrontation in Southeast Asia*; Matthew Jones, "U.S. Relations with Indonesia"; Green, *Indonesia*, xii; Brands, "Limits of Manipulation"; Brands, *Wages of Globalism*, 155–183; McMahon, *Limits of Empire*; Kolko, *Confronting the Third World*, 173–191; Lu, "United States Relations with Indonesia"; Foo, "The U.S. and the Indonesian-Malaysia Dispute"; Bunnell, "Kennedy Initiatives in Indonesia"; Sullivan, "The United States and the 'New Order' in Indonesia"; Markin, "West Irian Dispute."

9. Borden, *Pacific Alliance*, 194.

10. Green, *Indonesia*, xii; Lu, "United States Relations with Indonesia," 340; Brands, "Limits of Manipulation," 789.

11. Memo from Joint Chiefs of Staff to McNamara, September 5, 1962, *FRUS*, *1961–1963*, 628; "U.S. Strategic Interest in Indonesia," JCSM-725-61, *FRUS*, 443; Guidelines of U.S. Policy in Indonesia, November 3, 1961, James Thomson Papers, Box 21, Indonesia, General, 1961–1963, John F. Kennedy Presidential Library (JFKL).

12. Westad, *Global Cold War*, 396.

13. Latham, *Modernization as Ideology*, 30; Cummings, "Boundary Displacement: Area Studies and International Studies During and After the Cold War," in his *Parallax Visions*; Cullather, "Development?"

14. Packenham, *Liberal America and the Third World*; Gendzier, *Managing Political Change*; Natal, "Road to Vietnam."

15. Michael Hunt, *Ideology and U.S. Foreign Policy*, 161; Gordon, "Alliance at Birth"; Rosenberg, *Financial Missionaries to World*.

16. Berger, "Decolonisation, Modernisation, and Nation-Building."

17. Simpson, *Universities and Empire*.

18. Latham, *Modernization as Ideology*, 15; Best, *Politics of Historical Vision*, 110–111. Foucault put it best: "We should admit that power produces knowledge; that there is no power relation without the correlative constitution of a field of knowledge, not any knowledge that does not at the same time presuppose and constitute power relations" (Foucault, *Discipline and Punish*, 28).

19. Wallerstein, "Rise and Future Demise of the World Capitalist System," 72–73.

20. Woo, *Race to the Swift*, 19–43; Kohl, *State-Directed Development*; Robison, *Indonesia*, 3–105; Dick et al., *Emergence of a National Economy*.

21. Robison, *Indonesia*, 108; Cooper and Packard, *International Development and the Social Sciences*, 3–4.

22. Memo from Rostow to Kennedy, "Critical Issues in Foreign Aid," February 28, 1961, Presidential Office Files (POF), Staff Memoranda, Rostow, JFKL.

23. Basic National Security Policy Draft, May 9, 1962, Thomson Papers, Box 6, Policy Planning Staff (PPS), 1962–1963, JFKL; Paul Rosenstein-Rodan, "International Aid for Underdeveloped Countries," National Security Files (NSF), Box 324, Staff Memos for Walt Rostow, Foreign Aid, January 1961, JFKL.

24. Quoted in Adas, *Dominance by Design*, 243.

25. Scott, *Seeing Like a State*; Ekbladh, "'Mr. TVA.'"

26. Latham, *Modernization as Ideology*, 30; Gilman, "Paving the World with Good Intentions"; Engerman et al., *Staging Growth*; Cullather, "Damming Afghanistan."

27. Merrill, *Bread and the Ballot*; Fifield, *Southeast Asia in United States Policy*, 7, 246–284; Basic National Security Policy Draft, May 9, 1962, Thomson Papers, Box 6, PPS, 1962–1963, JFKL; Rabe, *Most Dangerous Area in the World*.

28. Geoffrey Smith, "National Security and Personal Isolation"; Rosenberg, "'Foreign Affairs' After WWII."

29. Dean, *Imperial Brotherhood*, 169–179, 197.

30. Bowles, quoted in Telegram 910 from Jakarta to State, November 18, 1961, POF, Box 119, Indonesia, JFKL; Schaller, *American Occupation of Japan*, 141–163.

31. Draft Memo on East and Southeast Asia, March 20, 1962, Thomson Papers, Box 7, JFKL, 26–32.

32. Lu, "United States Relations with Indonesia," 340; McMahon, *Limits of Empire*, 106, 120; Brands, "Limits of Manipulation," 789.

33. Fifield, *Southeast Asia in United States Foreign Policy*, 383; McMahon, *Limits of Empire*, 106; Memo from Rusk to Johnson, August 1, 1966, Record Group (RG) 59, Central Files, 1964–1966, POL 23-9, Indon., National Archives (NA).

34. LaFeber, "Tension Between Democracy and Capitalism"; Schmitz, *Thank God They're on Our Side*; Tony Smith, *America's Mission*.

CHAPTER I

1. Goto, *Tensions of Empire*.

2. McMahon, *Colonialism and the Cold War*; Kahin, *Nationalism and Revolution in Indonesia*; quote from the CIA report, "Consequences of Dutch 'Police Action' in Indonesia," January 27, 1949, Declassified Documents Reference Service (DDRS).

3. Swift, *Road to Madiun*; Efimova, "Who Gave Instructions?"

4. Gouda, *American Visions of the Netherlands East Indies/Indonesia*.

5. McMahon, *Limits of Empire*, 49.

6. Legge, *Sukarno*, 317–361.

7. Hatta, "Colonial Society and the Ideals of Social Democracy," cited in Feith and Castles, *Indonesian Political Thinking*, 32–40; Hatta, *Portrait of a Patriot*.

8. Quoted in Berger, "Decolonisation, Modernisation, and Nation-Building," 429; Anderson, "Perspective and Method in American Research on Indonesia," 70.

9. Brands, *Specter of Neutralism*.

10. Kahin, *Nationalism and Revolution in Indonesia*; Robison, *Indonesia*, 108; Moon, "Takeoff or Self-Sufficiency."

11. Rotter, *Path to Vietnam*, 109–131; Borden, *Pacific Alliance*, 137–142.

12. Cumings, "Asian Crisis," 19–21.

13. McMahon, *Limits of Empire*, 222.

14. Gilman, *Mandarins of the Future*, 174.

15. *Newsweek*, April 25, 1955, 46–47.

16. Carlisle, "Changing Soviet Perspective"; Shinn, "The 'National Democratic State.'"

17. Memo of Conversation with the General Secretary of the CC CCP, Member of the Politburo of the CC CCP, Deng Xiaoping, May 17, 1960, Cold War International History Project (CWIHP), Virtual Archive (available at http://wilsoncenter .org/index.cfm?fuseaction=topics.home&topic_id=1409).

18. Sukarno speech, April 18, 1955, in Indonesian Ministry of Foreign Affairs, *Africa-Asia Speaks from Bandung*, 19–29.

19. Powell, quoted in Matthew Jones, "A 'Segregated' Asia?" 863; Parker, "Cold War II"; Fraser, "American Dilemma"; Wright, *Color Curtain*; Romulo, *Meaning of Bandung*.

20. Higgins and Pauker, "Economic Implications of the Asian-African Conference"; Iriye, *Global Community*, 78–79.

21. Berman, *Influence of the Carnegie, Ford, and Rockefeller Foundations*; Bruce Cumings, "Boundary Displacement"; Simpson, *Universities and Empire*.

22. Benda, *"The Decline of Constitutional Democracy in Indonesia*, by Herbert Feith," 449.

23. Agency for International Development briefing book for 1964, January 1, 1964, Jones Papers, Box 72, Subject File, Hoover Institute (HI), Stanford University.

24. Moon, "Takeoff or Self-Sufficiency," 203.

25. See Ford Foundation, *Celebrating Indonesia*; Bresnan, *At Home Abroad*. Bresnan was the Ford Foundation representative in Indonesia from 1961 to 1965.

26. See Sadli, "Recollections of My Career"; Salim, "Recollections of My Career"; and Subroto, "Recollections of My Career."

27. Parmar, "Building a Modernizing Knowledge Elite for Indonesia," 29, 31.

28. Subroto, "Recollections of My Career," 71–73.

29. Proposed action, Cornell University–University of Indonesia, School of Economics grant proposal, May 20, 1955, Record Group 1.2, Series 652, Indonesia, Box 7, Folder 81, Rockefeller Foundation Archives (RFA), Rockefeller Archives Center (RAC); Kahin and Kahin, *Subversion as Foreign Policy*, 105–106, 135–137; among representative publications see Djojohadikusumo, *Bahan ceramah tentang perspektif perkembangan dalam 30 tahun mendatang*.

30. Ransome, "The Berkeley Mafia and the Indonesian Massacre"; MacDougall, "Technocrats as Modernizers"; Bresnan, *Managing Indonesia*, 51–86.

31. "A Contingency Plan for Rescue, Stabilization, and Rehabilitation of the Indonesian Economy" [Johnson Report], March 25, 1966, RG 59, PPS, Subject and Country (CO) Files, 1965–1969, Box 319, NA, p. 15; MacDougall, "Technocrats as Modernizers," 360–364.

32. For the Ford Foundation and Cornell's Modern Indonesia Project, see materials related to Grant 52-00152, Cornell University Modern Indonesia Project, Ford Foundation Archives (FFA), New York.

33. Cornell Modern Indonesia Project bibliography, undated, Reel 408, Grant PA 54-6, FFA.

34. Memo from Shane McCune to Paul Hoffman, "Educational Aid to Indonesia," August 18, 1951, Reel 0696, Grant PA 56-248, FFA.

35. Kahin, *Southeast Asia*.

36. Cornell University grant proposal for the Study of Political Life in Indonesia, January 20, 1954, Reel 408, Grant PA 54-6, FFA; Cornell University Modern Indonesia Project report for period July 1, 1954–September 30, 1955, October 20, 1955, Reel 408, Grant PA 54-6, FFA.

37. For a detailed analysis of the MIT Center for International Studies, see Gilman, *Mandarins of the Future*, 155–203.

38. Engerman, "West Meets East."

39. Gilman, "Involution and Modernization," 6.

40. Materials related to Grant 53-00073, MIT Center for International Studies, Indonesia Field Project, FFA.

41. Materials related to Grant 53-00073, MIT Center for International Studies, Indonesia Field Project, FFA.

42. Heryanto, "Development of 'Development,'"; Millikan, *Fourth Annual Report, 1954–1955*, FFA.

43. From 1953 to 1955 the Indonesia project produced more than twenty monographs and articles, including Grasberg, "Indonesia's Investment Requirements"; Paauw, "Financing Economic Development in Indonesia"; and Pauker and Higgins, "Economic Implications of the Asian-African Conference."

44. Gilman, "Involution and Modernization," 6.

45. Geertz, "Religious Belief and Economic Behavior in a Central Javanese Town"; Geertz, "Development of the Javanese Economy"; Geertz, *Agricultural Involution*.

46. Geertz, *Agricultural Involution*, 90–103, 126–129; Gilman, "Involution and Modernization," 7–11.

47. White, "Rice Harvesting and Social Change in Java"; Hammar, "Philosophy of Shared Poverty."

48. Beers, *American Experience in Indonesia*; Moon, "Takeoff or Self-Sufficiency," 209.

49. On Indonesia, see Efimova, "Stalin and the Revival of the Communist Party."

50. Memo of Discussion at a Meeting of the National Security Council, November 15, 1955, *FRUS, 1955–1957*, v. 10, 28–31.

51. Abdulgani, *Foreign Minister's Report to Parliament on President Sukarno's Second Tour*, 45–47.

52. Joseph Burkholder Smith, *Portrait of a Cold Warrior*, 238–240. Smith worked on the CIA's Indonesia/Malaysia desk from 1956 to 1958 and was a major figure in pushing for covert support for the PRRI rebels.

53. Minutes of the Meeting of the CPSU CC Plenum on the State of Soviet Foreign Policy, June 24, 1957, CWIHP, Virtual Archive.

54. McMahon, *Limits of Empire*, 73.

55. Letter from J. Smits, Chairman of IPTP, to George Meany, October 24, 1957, RG 18-001, International Affairs Department, Country (CO) Files, 1945–1971, 27/3 Indonesia, 1950–1965, AFL-CIO Library and Archives.

56. Penders, *West New Guinea Debacle*, 39–160.

57. Lu, "United States Relations with Indonesia," 132–192; Robison, *Indonesia*, 478–530; Stoler, *Capitalism and Confrontation in Sumatra's Plantation Belt*, 125–162.

58. Derkach, "Soviet Policy Towards Indonesia."

59. Proposal for a Research Program in Economic Development and Political Stability, CENIS, no date, Reel 115, Grant 152-52, FFA.

60. Notes on a meeting of the Indonesian Embassy and the Center for International Studies, December 20–21, 1954, Washington, DC, Reel 116, Grant 54-88, FFA; Westad, *Global Cold War*, 154–155.

61. Dick et al., *Emergence of a National Economy*, 117–130; NSC 5518, "U.S. Policy on Indonesia," May 3, 1955, *FRUS, 1955–1957*, v. 22, 153.

62. Sutan Sjahrir, "Problems the Country Faces," *Atlantic Monthly*, October 1956; Chalmers and Hadiz, *Politics of Economic Development in Indonesia*, 13.

63. Higgins, *Indonesia's Economic Stabilization and Development*, 41–46; Anderson, "Perspective and Method in American Research on Indonesia," 76.

64. National Intelligence Estimate (NIE) 100-3-56, "Sino-Soviet Policy and Its Probable Effects in Underdeveloped Areas," April 24, 1956, CIA, Freedom of Information Act (FOIA) Electronic Reading Room (available at http://www.foia.cia.gov/).

65. Engerman, *Modernization from the Other Shore*.

66. CIA Memo, "The Nature and Problems of Soviet Economic Penetration of Underdeveloped Areas," March 14, 1956, CIA, FOIA Electronic Reading Room (available at http://www.foia.cia.gov/); Khrushchev, *Khrushchev's Tour of Asia*, 7.

67. Millikan, *Fourth Annual Report, 1954–1955*, FFA.

68. Adas, *Dominance by Design*, 239.

69. Liu, "'The China Metaphor,'" 10; Taylor, "Indonesian Views of China"; Hauswedell, "Anti-Imperialist United Front in Chinese and Indonesian Foreign Policy," 165–182.

70. Telegram 1024 from the Embassy in Indonesia to the Department of State, October 27, 1956, *FRUS, 1955–1957*, v. 22, 316–319; Hatta, quoted in Liu, "'The China Metaphor,'" 98.

71. Mortimer, *Indonesian Communism Under Sukarno*, 255; Engerman, "West Meets East," passim.

72. See Higgins, *All The Difference*, 47–95.

73. NIE 100-3-56, "Sino-Soviet Policy and Its Probable Effects in Underdeveloped Areas," April 24, 1956, CIA, FOIA Electronic Reading Room (available at http://www.foia.cia.gov/); Westad, *Global Cold War*, 166.

74. Adas, *Dominance by Design*, 247, 256.

75. Airgram A-263, December 24, 1966, NSF, CO Files, Indonesia, Box 248, Indonesia Cables, v. 6, November 1965–May 1966, Lyndon Baines Johnson Presidential Library (LBJL); CIA Current Support Brief, "Bloc Assistance or Agricultural Development in Underdeveloped Countries," March 16, 1961, CIA, FOIA Electronic Reading Room (available at http://www.foia.cia.gov/); Mahajani, *Soviet and American Aid to Indonesia*, 14.

76. Higgins, *Indonesia's Economic Stabilization and Development*, 41–46, 50.

77. Sarbini Sumawinata, "An Economist's View of Indonesian Socialism," *Indonesian Herald*, December 2, 1961; Howard P. Jones, *Indonesia*, 80; "Soviet Aid and Economic Development," *Indonesian Herald*, December 13, 1961.

78. Hauswedell, "Anti-Imperialist United Front in Chinese and Indonesian Foreign Policy," 178; Saunders, *Cultural Cold War*, 64–69.

79. Grant-in-Aid to the University of Indonesia, Technical Faculty at Bandung, April 2, 1956, RG 1.2, Series 652, Indonesia, Box 3, Folder 34, Bandung Institute of

Technology, Art, 1955–1958, RFA, RAC; Office Memo, USIA, October 14, 1955, RG 2, General Correspondence, 1955, Series 652, Box 66, Folder 421, RFA, RAC.

80. Memo, "Labor and Politic in Indonesia," by Harry Goldberg, July 1965, RG 18-001, International Affairs Department, CO Files, 1945–1971, 27/3 Indonesia, 1950–1965, AFL-CIO Library and Archives; RG 1.2, Series 652, Indonesia, Box 1, Folders 1–11, RFA, RAC; RG 1.2, Series 652, Indonesia, Box 3, Folder 37, Bisri Mambaudin, RFA, RAC.

81. Belmonte, "Selling Capitalism," 117; Frey, "Tools of Empire," 543, 565.

82. Editorial Note, NSC Meeting on April 5, 1956, *FRUS, 1955–1957*, v. 22, 254.

83. Lev, "Memory, Knowledge, and Reform."

84. Berger, "Decolonisation, Modernisation, and Nation-Building," 426, 429.

85. Materials related to Grant 53-00073, MIT Center for International Studies, Indonesia Field Project, FFA.

86. Anderson, "Perspective and Method in American Research on Indonesia," 70; Kahin, "Indonesia's Strengths and Weaknesses."

87. NIE 65-56, August 7, 1956, *FRUS, 1955–1957*, v. 22, 290–291.

88. Feith, *Decline of Constitutional Democracy in Indonesia*, 414–462; Joseph B. Smith, *Portrait of a Cold Warrior*, 209–210.

89. Editorial Note, NSC Meeting on April 5, 1956, *FRUS, 1955–1957*, v. 22, 254.

90. Memo from the Director of the Office of Philippine and Southeast Asian Affairs to the Assistant Secretary of State for Far Eastern Affairs, January 3, 1956, *FRUS, 1955–1957*, v. 22, 222–225.

91. Telegram 942 from Jakarta to State, October 11, 1957, *FRUS, 1955–1957*, v. 22, 475–480.

92. Evans, "Influence of the U.S. Army," 39; transcript of David Ransom interview with Willis Ethel, undated, Bunnell Papers, in author's possession.

93. Lev, *Transition to Guided Democracy*.

94. *FRUS, 1958–1960*, v. 17; Kahin and Kahin, *Subversion as Foreign Policy*, 75–99, 143–165; Matthew Jones, "Maximum Disavowable Aid."

95. NIE 10-63, "Bloc Economic and Military Assistance Programs," January 10, 1963, CIA, FOIA Electronic Reading Room (available at http://www.foia.cia.gov/); CIA Intelligence Report, "Communist Military Assistance to Indonesia," October 1965, NSF, CO Files, Indonesia, Box 248, Indonesia Memos, v. 7, May 1966–June 1967, 2 of 2, LBJL.

96. Telegram 291 from Jakarta to State, December 3, 1960, *FRUS, 1958–1960*, v. 17, 567–568; Gilman, *Mandarins of the Future*, 186–188.

97. Young, "Age of Global Power," 277.

98. Telegram 272 from Singapore to the Foreign Office, April 25, 1958, Records of the Prime Minister's Office (PREM) 11-2370, U.K. National Archives (UKNA).

99. Mackie, "Indonesia's Government Estates and Their Masters"; Lev, "Political Role of the Army in Indonesia"; McVey, "Post-Revolutionary Transformation of the Indonesian Army."

100. "Political Implications of Afro-Asian Military Takeovers," May 1959, cited in Schmitz, *Thank God They're on Our Side*, 221–227.

101. Memo of Discussion at the 410th Meeting of the NSC, Washington, June 18, 1959, *FRUS, 1958–1960*, v. 16, 97–103.

102. Anderson, "Perspective and Method in American Research on Indonesia," 70.

CHAPTER 2

1. NSC 6023, "U.S. Policy on Indonesia," December 19, 1960, RG 59, NSC Files, NA.

2. Telegram from Jakarta to State, December 27, 1960, *FRUS 1958–1960*, v. 17, 586–588.

3. Pauker, "Soviet Challenge in Indonesia," 622–623; Neil Sheehan, "Sukarno's Style: Hostility to U.S.," *New York Times*, August 15, 1965; NSC 6023, "U.S. Policy on Indonesia," 7–9.

4. NSC 6023, "U.S. Policy on Indonesia," 27.

5. Telegram 2384 from Jakarta to State, February 18, 1961, RG 59, Central Files, 611.98/2-1861, NA.

6. See Thomas J. Noer, "New Frontier and African Neutralism"; Metz, "American Attitudes Toward Decolonization in Africa"; and Little, "New Frontier on the Nile." See also Document 118, Memo from Rostow to Kennedy, "Neutralism and Foreign Aid," October 4, 1961, *FRUS, 1961–63*, v. 9 (available at http://dosfan.lib.uic.edu/ERC/frus/frus61-63ix/index.html).

7. Telegram 2154 from Jakarta to State, January 25, 1961, RG 59, Central Files, 611.98/1-2561, NA.

8. Latham, *Modernization as Ideology*, 27–28.

9. Telegram 2154 from Jakarta to State, January 25, 1961, RG 59, Central Files, 611.98/1-2561, NA.

10. Memo from Rusk to Kennedy, February 14, 1961, POF, Box 119, JFKL; Telegram 2154, RG 59, Central Files, 611.98/1-2561, NA.

11. Bunnell, "The CIA-DPP 1961 Secret Memorandum on Indonesia," 134.

12. Bunnell, "The CIA-DPP 1961 Secret Memorandum on Indonesia," 137–141; Bunnell, "Kennedy Initiatives in Indonesia," 78–94; Joseph, *Cracks in the Empire*; Cumings, *Origins of the Korean War*.

13. Ferguson, *Golden Rule*.

14. Cumings, *Origins of the Korean War*.

15. Schlesinger, *A Thousand Days*, 533–534; Schurmann, *Logic of World Power*, 412–415.

16. Schurmann, *Logic of World Power*, 435, 444–445; Howard Jones, *Indonesia*, 199.

17. Letter from H. L. Hunt to Kennedy, April 22, 1961, Correspondence Files, Box 122, LBJL.

18. Telegram 7048 from Jakarta to State, May 28, 1968, RG 59, Central Files, 1967–1969, Petroleum Files (PET) 10-3, Indonesia, NA; Sampson, *Seven Sisters*, 172; Hunt, *HLH Columns*.

19. Howard Jones, *Indonesia*, 170, 203, 294–295; Hilsman, *To Move A Nation*, 376–378. On American investors, see Gould, *Americans in Sumatra*, which provides an excellent guide to layout of American investment in Sumatra in the pre-1960 period.

20. The group was an informal forum for interagency discussion composed of McGeorge Bundy (special assistant for national security), Rostow (deputy special assistant for national security), George McGhee (chairman of State Department Policy Planning), Paul Nitze (assistant secretary of defense for international security affairs), Robert Amory (deputy director of intelligence at the CIA), and Richard Bissell; "Development of Current WNG Crisis," undated, NSF, Box 423A, Komer Series, West New Guinea (WNG), 1961–1963, JFKL.

21. CIA Memo from Bissell to Bundy et al., March 22, 1961, NSF, Box 113, Indonesia, Attachment A, JFKL.

22. Letter from Komer to Bundy, March 27, 1961, NSF, Box 113, JFKL.

23. Robin, *Making of the Cold War Enemy*, 185–205.

24. Note from Komer to Kaysen, January 15, 1962, NSF, Box 423A, Komer Series, WNG, 1961–1963, JFKL.

25. Penders, *West New Guinea Debacle*, 179–196; record of the meeting between Kennedy and Dutch Foreign Minister Luns, Washington, April 10, 1961, *FRUS, 1961–1963*, v. 22, 345–350.

26. Telegram 2508 from Jakarta to State, March 3, 1961, *FRUS, 1961–1963*, v. 23, 316.

27. Zegwaard, "Headhunting Practices of the Asmat of Netherlands New Guinea"; Saulnier, *Headhunters of Papua*; Essai, *Papua and New Guinea*; Ryan, *Fear Drive My Feet*.

28. Tipps, "Modernization Theory and the Comparative Study of Societies"; Cooper, "Modernizing Bureaucrats, Backwards Africans, and the Development Concept," 64.

29. Van der Kroef, "Political Awakening in WNG," 71; McLeod, *Cannibals Are Human*, 8.

30. Gardner, *Shared Hopes, Separate Fears*, 193; Wick, *God's Invasion*; "Hunters of Art Vex New Guinea," *New York Times*, December 6, 1961.

31. See Howard Jones, *Indonesia*, 181; Memo from George McGhee to Rusk, "Possible United Nations Resolution on WNG," February 15, 1961, NSF, Box 113, CO Files, WNG, JFKL.

32. Memo of Conversation, "Subject: WNG," April 10, 1961, *FRUS, 1961–1963*, v. 23, 352–357; see also Lyons, "Keeping Africa Off the Agenda."

33. Note from Komer to Kaysen, January 15, 1962, NSF, Komer Papers, Box 423A, WNG, 1961–1963, White House Memo folder, JFKL.

34. Memo from Johnson to Rostow, April 18, 1961; and Memo from Komer to Rostow, April 5, 1961, both in NSF, CO Files, WNG, v. 1, April 16–30, 1961, JFKL.

35. Barclay, "In the Sticky Fly Paper."

36. Telegram 1332 from Hague to State, April 16, 1961, POF, Box 119, JFKL; Borden, "Defending Hegemony," 62.

37. *FRUS, 1961–1963*, v. 23, 343–364; Memo from Johnson to Bundy and Kaysen, January 4, 1962, White House Central Files (WHCF), Box 59, JFKL.

38. Sukarno Briefing Book, April 24–25, 1961, Tab F, "U.S. Military Assistance to Indonesia," NSF, Box 113, JFKL.

39. "U.S. Economic and Military Assistance to Indonesia," Sukarno Briefing Book, NSF, Box 113, JFKL.

40. Kahin and Kahin, *Subversion as Foreign Policy*, 207, 218; Telegram 2199 from Jakarta to State, April 20, 1964, RG 59, Central Files, 1964–1966, DEF 19-3, U.S.-Indonesia, NA.

41. Memo from Jones, "U.S. Objectives in Indonesia," December 6, 1961, Howard Jones files, Box 477, Harriman Papers, Library of Congress.

42. "Jakarta to Seek Arms," *New York Times*, December 23, 1960; "Indonesia Adds More Trappings of Red Dictatorship," *Wall Street Journal*, November 15, 1960; Telegram from Jakarta to State, December 3, 1960, *FRUS, 1958–1960*, v. 17, 567–568.

43. Telegram 2536 from Jakarta to State, March 7, 1961, RG 59, Central Files, 611.98/3-761, NA.

44. For parallels to Latin America, see Rabe, "Controlling Revolutions"; Schafer, *Deadly Paradigms*.

45. Memo from Carlisle Runge to Sargent Shriver, October 2, 1961, NSF, Box 412, Komer Series, Counterinsurgency/Civic Action, JFKL.

46. Evans, "The Influence of the United States Army," 34–41; Memo from Lansdale for Deputy Secretary Gilpatric, "Subject: U.S. Visit of Sukarno, Defense Actions," POF, Box 11, General, JFKL.

47. The criticism of civic action programs in Indonesia was part of a larger attack waged by rational choice theorists and other advocates of "coercive counterinsurgency." See Robin, *Making of the Cold War Enemy*, 185–205.

48. Editorial, "The Amused Indonesians," *Wall Street Journal*, March 2, 1960; CIA Memo from Bissell to Bundy et al., March 22, 1961, NSF, Box 113, Indonesia, JFKL; Pauker, "Recent Communist Tactics in Indonesia," August 15, 1960, NSF, Box 115, Indonesia, RAND Studies, JFKL.

49. Hindley, "Foreign Aid to Indonesia"; Cullather, "Damning Afghanistan."

50. Telegram 2384 from Jakarta to State, February 18, 1961, RG 59, Central Files, 611.98/2-1861, NA.

51. "Indonesia's Potholed Road Back," *Fortune*, June 1, 1968; Arndt, "PT Krakatau Steel." Scavenged for spare parts and shuttered in 1966 after Sukarno's ouster, the project eventually opened as PT Krakatau Steel in 1974. It became the largest inte-

grated steel plant in Southeast Asia, as well as a source of lucre for the military in the 1990s when owned by Sumitro's son Hashim, who funneled some profits to his brother, army general (and Suharto son-in-law) Prabowo.

52. Note to Joe Western of the *Wall Street Journal* from Rick Reuter, Special Assistant to President for Food for Peace, July 19, 1963, White House Subject Files, Box 234, PL 480, JFKL; Prasad, *Food for Peace*; Roberts, *Food for Peace*.

53. Telegram 2889 from Jakarta to State, April 10, 1961, RG 59, Central Files, 1961–1963, Political Files (POL) 1, Indonesia, Box 3940, NA.

54. Letter from Hilsman to Gallagher, July 12, 1963, RG 59, Central Foreign Policy Files, 1961–1963, POL 1, Indonesia, Box 3940, NA; Robison, *Indonesia*, 108; Higgins, *Indonesia*, 88.

55. Telegram 465 from Jakarta to State, September 8, 1963, NSF, Komer Series, Box 5, JFKL; Memo, "Economic Support for Indonesia," POF, Box 119, Sukarno Briefing Book, JFKL.

56. NIE 55-61, "Outlook in Indonesia with Special Reference to WNG," March 7, 1961, NSF, Komer Series, Box 423A, JFKL.

57. "American Aid Spurs Indonesian Socialism, Helps Some Workers," *Wall Street Journal*, December 2, 1960; "The Economics of Envy," *Wall Street Journal*, August 19, 1960; "Memo on President Sukarno's Impending Visit to Washington," Council on Foreign Relations, NSF, Box 119, Sukarno Briefing Book, JFKL.

58. Telegram 2384 from Jakarta to State, February 18, 1961, NSF, Komer Series, Box 5, Indonesia, General, 1961–1963, JFKL.

59. Penders, *West New Guinea Debacle*, 335; Schlesinger, *A Thousand Days*, 533.

60. Memo of Conversation, "Conversation Between Kennedy and President Sukarno of Indonesia," April 24, 1961, NSF, Box 113, Sukarno Visit, JFKL.

61. Gardner, *Shared Hopes, Separate Fears*, 175; Editorial Note, *FRUS, 1961–1963*, v. 23, 390; Howard Jones, *Indonesia*, 197.

62. NIE 55-62, "The Prospects for Indonesia," March 7, 1962, NSF, National Intelligence Estimates (NIES), Box 7, Malaysia/Indonesia, LBJL.

63. Howard Jones, *Indonesia*, 189.

64. McVey, "Post Revolutionary Transformation of the Indonesian Army," 12–15; Anderson, *Imagined Communities*, 177–178.

65. Bunnell, "Kennedy Initiatives in Indonesia," 76; Rostow, *Diffusion of Power*, 194.

66. Memo from Rostow to Johnson, May 12, 1961, *FRUS, 1961–1963*, v. 23, 391.

67. Memo from Johnson to Rostow, April 7, 1961, NSF, Komer Series, Box 423A, Indonesia and WNG, JFKL; Memo from Rusk to Kennedy, May 23, 1961, *FRUS, 1961–1963*, v. 23, 391; Memo from Rusk to Kennedy, September 9, 1961, *FRUS, 1961–1963*, v. 23, 422–423.

68. Maga, "New Frontier vs. Guided Democracy"; "Urgent Planning Problems," June 9, 1961, NSF, Komer Series, Box 438, JFKL.

69. Telegram from Jakarta to State, May 24, 1961; and Memo from Johnson to Rostow, September 2, 1961, both in POF, Box 119, JFKL.

70. Memo from Johnson to Rostow, September 14, 1961; and Memo from Rostow to Kennedy, September 10, 1961, both in *FRUS, 1961–1963*, v. 23, 423, 427–428; Telegram from U.N. Mission to State, September 16, 1961, *FRUS, 1961–1963*, v. 23, 429–433.

71. Telegram 910 from Jakarta to State, November 18, 1961, POF, Box 119, Indonesia, JFKL. On Rusk, see Halberstam, *Best and the Brightest*, 188–197, 398; Bird, *Color of Truth*, 275.

72. Memo from Johnson to Walt W. Rostow, November 6, 1961, *FRUS, 1961–1963*, v. 23, 447; Memo from Johnson to Rostow, November 15, 1961, POF, Box 119, JFKL.

73. Memo, Johnson to Rostow, November 15, 1961, POF, Box 119, JFKL; Howard Jones, *Indonesia*, 200–201; Memo from Rostow to Kennedy, November 30, 1961, NSF, CO Files, WNG, December 1–5, 1961, JFKL.

74. Telegram 1018 from Jakarta to State, December 8, 1961, RG 59, Central Files, 656.9813/12-961, NA; CIA information report, TDCS-3/494, "General Nasution's Attitude Towards the West Irian Problem," November 21, 1961, NSF, CO Files, WNG, December 1–5, 1961, JFKL; Memo from Battle to Bundy, undated, *FRUS, 1961–1963*, v. 23, 467.

75. On Harriman's arrival, see Howard Jones, *Indonesia*, 203; Hilsman, *To Move a Nation*, 378; Bird, *Color of Truth*, 249–252; Halberstam, *Best and the Brightest*, 190–200; Schlesinger, *A Thousand Days*, 533–534.

76. Schurmann, *Logic of World Power*, 164–190, passim.

77. Halberstam, *Best and the Brightest*, 197; Abramson, *Spanning the Century*, 585; Hilsman Oral History Interview, August 14, 1970, JFKL. On Laos, see Karabell, *Architects of Intervention*.

78. Halberstam, *Best and the Brightest*, 197.

79. Memo from Joint Chiefs of Staff to Secretary of Defense McNamara, "U.S. Strategic Interest in Indonesia," JCSM 725-61, October 13, 1961, *FRUS, 1961–1963*, v. 23, 443–444; "Guidelines of U.S. Policy in Indonesia," November 3, 1961, Thomson Papers, Box 21, JFKL.

80. Memo from Jakarta to State, "Economic Summary: Second Quarter 1962," July 19, 1962, Jones Papers, Box 93, Office Memos, HI.

81. Pauker, "Indonesia's Eight-Year Development Plan"; Telegram 333 from Jakarta to State, August 23, 1961, 898.2553/8-2361, NA; "Indonesia Decrees It Gets 60% of Profits Previously Split Evenly with Oil Concerns," *Wall Street Journal*, August 29, 1961.

82. Memo from Johnson to Bundy, November 6, 1961, NSF, CO Files, WNG, November 1–5, 1961, JFKL; Telegram 2939 from Foreign Office to Canberra and other posts, December 21, 1961, PREM 11-4309, UKNA.

83. Memo from Bundy to Kennedy, December 1, 1961; and Memo from Rostow to Kennedy, November 30, 1961, both in *FRUS, 1961–1963*, v. 23, 461–464.

84. Memo from Johnson to Rostow, December 8, 1961, NSF, CO Files, WNG, December 11–15, 1961, JFKL; Memo from State Executive Secretary to Bundy, undated, NSF, CO Files, WNG, December 16–20, 1961, JFKL; "Indonesia Favors Parley on Guinea," *New York Times*, January 5, 1962.

85. Attachment, "Some Fundamentals with Respect to WNG," December 18, 1961, WHCF, Box 59, JFKL.

86. Sukarno, "People's Command for the Liberation of West Irian"; "Resolution of the Political Bureau of the Communist Party of Indonesia on the Work of the Delegation of the Communist Party of Indonesia to the 22nd Congress of the Communist Party of the Soviet Union, Issued on December 15, 1961," in *Marxism's New Horizon*, 124–135; on D. N. Aidit, see Aidit, *Selected Works*.

87. Glen St. J. Barclay, "In the Sticky Fly Paper," 68–69; NIE 55-62, "The Prospects for Indonesia," March 7, 1962, NSF, NIES, Box 7, Malaysia/Indonesia, LBJL; van der Kroef, "Recent Developments in WNG," 286.

88. Telegram 679 from Commonwealth Relations Office to Wellington, November 20, 1960, PREM 11-4309, UKNA.

89. Telegram 852 from Foreign Office to Jakarta, December 16, 1961; and Telegram 636 from U.K. Mission to the U.N. to the Foreign Office, September 26, 1961, both in PREM 11-4309, UKNA.

90. Penders, *West New Guinea Debacle*, 301–328; Fifield, *Southeast Asia in United States Foreign Policy*, 351; Barclay, "In the Sticky Fly Paper," 68; Memo from State Department Executive Secretary to Bundy, undated, NSF, CO Files, WNG, December 16–20, 1961, JFKL; Memo of Conversation, March 31, 1961, NSF, Indonesia/Malaysia/Singapore, RAND Studies, JFKL; Telegram 602 from State to Jakarta, December 9, 1961, RG 59, Central Files, 656.9813/12-9-61, NA.

91. Penders, *West New Guinea Debacle*, 326; West, "New Guinea Question," 505; Memo from Johnson to Kennedy, November 30, 1961, NSF, CO Files, WNG, December 16–20, 1961, JFKL; Memo from Bundy to Kennedy, December 1, 1961, NSF, CO Files, WNG, December 1–6, 1961, JFKL.

92. Memo from Sterling Cottrell to Harriman, "Third Country Assistance to Vietnam," April 27, 1962, *FRUS, 1961–1963*, v. 2, 350–352; Barclay, "In the Sticky Fly Paper," 72–73.

93. Attachment, Memo from Kaysen to Bundy, January 12, 1962, *FRUS, 1961–1963*, v. 23, 505; Memo from Komer to Kaysen, February 2, 1962, NSF, Komer Series, Box 423A, Indonesia-WNG, 1961–1963, JFKL; Memo of Conversation of the 496th meeting of the NSC, January 18, 1962, *FRUS, 1961–1963*, 241; Barclay, "In the Sticky Fly Paper," 73.

94. Memo for the President from Komer, February 28, 1962, NSF, Komer Series, Box 423A, Indonesia-WNG, 1961–1963, JFKL.

95. Telegram 2343 from Jakarta to State, February 23, 1962, *FRUS 1961–1963*, v. 8, 538–541.

96. Memo of Conversation, "WNG," March 2, 1962, RG 59, Central Files, 656.9813/3-262, NA.

97. Memo, Conversation between the Secretary of State and the Netherlands Foreign Minister, March 14, 1961, PREM 11-4309, UKNA.

98. WNG Chronology, undated, WHCF, Box 59, Indonesia, JFKL; Telegram 1052 from State to Jakarta, March 21, 1962, RG 59, Central Files, 656.9813/3-262, NA.

99. Memo from Komer to Bundy, March 28, 1962, NSF, Komer Series, WNG, 1961–1963, JFKL.

100. Telegram 749 from The Hague to State, April 3, 1962, RG 59, Central Files, 656.9813/4-262, NA.

101. House Committee on Foreign Affairs, *Foreign Assistance Act of 1962*; Senate Committee on Foreign Relations, *Foreign Assistance Act of 1962*; text of release from Senator Thomas Dodd, April 18, 1962, United States Information Service, found in Jones Papers, Ambassadorial file, Box 92, HI.

102. Pauker, "Soviet Challenge in Indonesia."

103. NIE 55-62, "The Prospects for Indonesia," March 7, 1962, State Department, INR/EAP files, Lot 90 D 165, NA; Memo of Conversation, April 17, 1962, *FRUS, 1961–1963*, v. 23, 573–576; Memo from DCI Assistant Knoche to DCI John McCone, May 22, 1962, *FRUS, 1961–1963*, v. 23, 573–577, 595–596; Telegram from State to Athens, TOSEC 66, May 4, 1962, RG 59, Central Files, 656.9813/5-462, NA.

104. State Department Bureau of Intelligence and Research (INR), Memo RSB-96, April 27, 1962, NSF, CO Files, WNG, JFKL; "Russian Arms Pact Hailed By Indonesia," *New York Times*, May 9, 1962; "Background Summary on the Military Assistance Program for Indonesia," Attachment to NSAM 179, September 21, 1962, NSF, Komer Series, Box 423, NSAM 179, JFKL; Memo, July 16, 1962, NSF, Komer Series, Box 412, Counterinsurgency/Civic Action, JFKL.

105. Memo from Komer to Kaysen, May 22, 1962, NSF, Meetings and Memoranda, Staff Memos, Komer, May 1962, JFKL.

106. Crouch, *Army and Politics in Indonesia*, ch. 2; CIA Information Report TDCS-3/517, July 27, 1962; and CIA Information Report TDCS-3/524,504, October 5, 1962, both in POF, Box 119, General, JFKL.

107. Chronology, "Development of WNG Crisis," WHCF, Box 59, Indonesia, JFKL; Mackie, *Konfrontasi*, 83, 101.

108. Background summary of MAP, September 1962, National Security Action Memorandum (NSAM) 179 attachment, NSAM 179, JFKL.

109. Memo of conversation, "WNG," July 19, 1962, NSF, Komer Series, Box 423A, WNG, JFKL.

110. Komer cover memo to Bundy, August 1, 1962, and attachment, July 31, 1962, NSF, Komer Series, Staff Memos, July 1962, JFKL.

111. Chronology, "Development of WNG Crisis," WHCF, Box 59, Indonesia, JFKL.

112. Editorial, "New Guinea Settlement," *New York Times*, September 16, 1962; Arthur Krock, "Our Good Offices Sanction Aggression in the Pacific," *New York Times*, September 16, 1962; Memo from Mr. Selby to Lord Home, "Observations on the West New Guinea Settlement," September 7, 1962, PREM 11-4309, UKNA.

113. Mike Broomfield (MI) in *Congressional Record, Senate*, May 13, 1963, 8362; "GOP Attacks Kennedy on His Indonesia Policy," *New York Times*, October 18, 1962.

114. Saltford, "United Nations Involvement with the Act of Self-Determination in West Irian."

CHAPTER 3

1. Johnson, "Internal Defense and the Foreign Service," 22.

2. Marquis, "Other Warriors."

3. Bunnell, "Kennedy Initiatives in Indonesia," 208–210.

4. On Salant, see Borden, *Pacific Alliance*, 28, 40–42, 235; Borden, "Defending Hegemony," 74; Salant, *United States Balance of Payments in 1968*.

5. "Perspectives and Proposals for United States Economic Aid: Indonesia" (hereafter referred to as the Humphrey Report), foreword, NSF, Box 115, JFKL.

6. Humphrey Report, foreword.

7. Humphrey Report, 96–169.

8. Humphrey Report, 15; Dean, *Imperial Brotherhood*, 169–201.

9. House Committee on Foreign Affairs, *Foreign Assistance Act of 1963*; Cullather, "'Fuel for the Good Dragon.'"

10. Humphrey Report, 44, 32.

11. Rosenstein-Radan, cited in Latham, *Modernization as Ideology*, 85–86, 93.

12. "Economic Planning: Points of Success and Failure," Theodore Morgan, conference papers from "Conference on Economic Planning in SEA," February 1–5, 1965, Jones Papers, Box 75, HI.

13. Gilman, "Paving the World with Good Intentions," 254–255.

14. Salant, quoted in Borden, *Pacific Alliance*, 28, 40–42, 235; Rotter, *Path to Vietnam*, 20–23, 113–114, 209–210.

15. "Foreign Aid and the State of the U.S. Economy," remarks by H. R. Gross, June 11, 1963, *Congressional Record Appendix, 1963*, A3756–A3757.

16. Memo from Fowler Hamilton to Kennedy, May 25, 1962, NSF, Meetings and Memo Series, NSAM 159, JFKL.

17. Bienen, *The Military and Modernization*, 7; Pauker, "Southeast Asia as a Problem Area."

18. Fox, "Civil-Military Relations Research."

19. "To the Aid of Aid," *Time*, March 30, 1959.

20. *Report of the President's Committee to Study the United States Military Assistance Program* (Washington, DC: Government Printing Office, 1959), v. 2, 55. On CENIS, see Berger, "Decolonisation, Modernisation, and Nation-Building," 439.

21. Memo of Discussion at the 410th Meeting of the NSC, Washington, June 18, 1959, *FRUS, 1958–1960*, v. 16, 97–103.

22. Several of the papers at this conference were later published in a landmark book edited by John H. Johnson, *Role of the Military in Underdeveloped Countries*.

23. Senate Committee on Foreign Relations, *Economic, Social, and Political Change in the Underdeveloped Countries*; quote from Gilman, *Mandarins of the Future*, 183–191.

24. Examples include Gutteridge, *Armed Forces in the New States* and *Military Institutions and Power in the New States*; Huntington, *Soldier and the State* and *Changing Patterns of Military Politics*; Lissak, "Selected Literature of Revolutions and Coup d'Etat"; and McCalister, "Recent Research and Writing on the Role of the Military in Latin America."

25. Janowitz, *The Military in the Political Development of New Nations*, 44; Lissak, "Role of the Military."

26. Quoted in Levy, "Armed Forces Organizations," 73.

27. Janowitz, *The Military in the Political Development of New Nations*, 63–66; Shils, "The Military in the Political Development of the New States," 9.

28. Telegram 3439 from State to Jakarta, July 14, 1961, RG 286, Records of the AID, Office of Public Safety, Operations Division, East Asia Branch, Indonesia, Box 39, NA.

29. Proposal for a one-year extension of CENIS Indonesia program, May 26, 1953, Reel 116, Grant PA53-73, FFA; Berger, "Decolonisation, Modernisation, and Nation-Building," 432–441.

30. Pauker, "Role of the Military in Indonesia."

31. Ransom, "Ford Country," 95–98; Pauker, "Role of the Military in Indonesia"; Pauker, "Indonesian Doctrine of Territorial Warfare"; Pauker, "Southeast Asia as a Problem Area"; Bienen, *The Military and Modernization*, 8.

32. Perlmutter, "The Praetorian State and the Praetorian Army."

33. Bienen, *The Military and Modernization*, 9, 21.

34. "The Role of the Military in the Underdeveloped Areas," State Department Policy Planning Council, January 25, 1963, Thomson Papers, Box 6, JFKL.

35. Document 85, Letter from George Kennan to Rostow, May 15, 1962, *FRUS, 1961–1963*, v. 8, 285–294.

36. McClintock, *Instruments of Statecraft*; Hilsman, *To Move a Nation*, 413–415.

37. Paterson, *Contesting Castro*; Freedman, *Kennedy's Wars*; Summary of Kennedy's Remarks to the 496th Meeting of the NSC, January 19, 1962, *FRUS, 1961–1963*, v. 8, 238–242.

38. Michael Hunt, *Ideology and U.S. Foreign Policy*, ch. 4.

39. Memo from Kennedy to Defense Secretary McNamara, January 11, 1962, POF, Defense, January–March 1962, JFKL; NSAM 56, June 28, 1961, NSF, Meetings and Memo Series, NSAM 56, JFKL.

40. NSAM 88, September 5, 1961, NSF, Meetings and Memo Series, NSAM 88, JFKL; NSAM 114, November 22, 1961, NSF, Meetings and Memo Series, NSAM 114, JFKL; McClintock, *Instruments of Statecraft*, 157–165; Schmitz, *Thank God They're on Our Side*, 236–241.

41. NSAM 56, "Evaluation of Paramilitary Requirements," June 28, 1961, NSF, NSC Series, NSAM 56, JFKL; NSAM 57, "Responsibility for Paramilitary Operations," June 28, 1961, NSF, NSC Series, NSAM 57, JFKL.

42. Memo from General Maxwell Taylor to Members of the Special Group, "Establishment of the Special Group (Counterinsurgency)," January 2, 1962, NSF, NSC Series, Special Group, April 16, 1961, to June 7, 1962, JFKL; Draft of NSAM 124, January 2, 1962, NSF, NSC Series, Special Group, April 16, 1961, to June 7, 1962, JFKL.

43. Grandin, *Last Colonial Massacre*; Streeter, *Managing the Counterrevolution*.

44. McClintock, *American Connection*, 13 and ch. 2; "Summary Report, Military Counterinsurgency Accomplishments Since January 1961," July 21, 1962, NSF, NSC Special Group, Military Organization, JFKL.

45. Memo from Carlisle Runge to Sargent Shriver Jr., October 2, 1961, NSF, Box 412, Komer Series, Counterinsurgency/Civic Action, JFKL.

46. Pye, "Armies in the Process of Political Modernization," 78; Pauker, "Role of the Military in Indonesia"; Rabe, *Most Dangerous Area in the World*, 126–131; NSAM 179, Enclosure 10, "Civic Action Program," undated, Thomson Papers, Box 6, SEA-Indonesia "Plan of Action," JFKL.

47. The special group defined military civic action as "the use of preponderantly indigenous military forces on projects useful to local population at all levels in such fields as education, training, public works, agriculture, transportation, communications, health, sanitation and others contributing to economic and social development, which would also serve to improve the standing of the military forces with the population." Joint State Department/AID/USIA/Defense message, July 12, 1962, NSF, NSC Series, Special Group, July 3, 1962, to May 20, 1963, JFKL; Memo from Carlisle Runge to Sargent Shriver Jr., October 2, 1961, NSF, Box 412, Komer Series, Counterinsurgency/Civic Action, JFKL.

48. Memo from Saunders to Rostow, September 22, 1961, NSF, Box 412, Counterinsurgency/Civic Action, 1961–1963, JFKL; Pauker and Knorr, cited in Robin, *Making of the Cold War Enemy*, 188–189.

49. Memo from Saunders to Bundy, December 13, 1961; Memo for the President, "Military Contribution to Economic Development," December 13, 1961; and Draft of NSAM 119, "Civic Action," December 13, 1961, all in NSF, Box 412, Counterinsurgency/Civic Action, 1961–1963, JFKL.

50. CIA paper for the Special Group, December 11, 1961, and December 14, 1961, cited in *FRUS, 1964–1968*, v. 26, 234–235.

51. Letter from Bell to Jones, December 28, 1961, POF, Box 119, JFKL.

52. Memo from Komer to Bundy, April 10, 1962; Agenda for C-I Group Meeting, April 12, 1962; and Minutes of April 3, 1962, meeting, all in NSF, NSC, Special Group Meetings, JFKL.

53. Memo from Komer to Bundy, April 10, 1962, NSF, NSC, Special Group Meetings, JFKL.

54. See Telegram 1749, Jakarta to State, March 30, 1962; Telegram 1957, Jakarta to State, May 3, 1962; and Memo from Saunders to Davis, July 19, 1962, all in NSF, Box 412, Komer Series, Counterinsurgency/Civic Action, 1961–1963, JFKL.

55. The standard account remains Crouch, *Army and Politics in Indonesia*, esp. 24–69.

56. Nasution, *Fundamentals of Guerrilla Warfare*, 100; Nasution, *Kekaryaan ABRI*; Sundhaussen (with Penders), *Abdul Haris Nasution*.

57. Pauker, "Indonesian Doctrine of Territorial Warfare," 21–25.

58. For background, see Reid, *Verandah of Violence*; Robinson, "*Rawan* Is as *Rawan* Does."

59. Pauker, "Indonesian Doctrine of Territorial Warfare," 21–25.

60. Mortimer, *Indonesian Communism Under Sukarno*, 278–283; Van der Kroef, "Peasant and Land Reform in Indonesian Communism."

61. Quoted in Pauker, "Indonesian Doctrine of Territorial Warfare," 37–39; Evans, "Influence of the U.S. Army," 35; Lev, "Political Role of the Army in Indonesia"; Mrazek, *United States and the Indonesian Military*.

62. Memo from Komer to William Bundy, Frank Coffin, and Jeff Kitchen, May 7, 1962, NSF, Box 412, Komer Series, Counterinsurgency/Civic Action, JFKL.

63. Michael Forrestal recalls similar battles with the European desk and noted that "Harriman used to complain continuously that State [was] dominated by Europhiles, Eurocentrists, and [that it] was very difficult to get them to understand that Holland's interest in WI had very little to do with U.S. interests in world." Forrestal interview with Bunnell, January 1969, Bunnell Papers, author's collection.

64. Background summary of MAP, September 1962, NSF, Meetings and Memo Series, NSC, NSAM 179, JFKL.

65. Memo from Bundy to Maxwell Taylor, February 14, 1962, NSF, NSAM, NSAM 114, JFKL; NSAM 132, February 19, 1962, NSF, NSAM, NSAM 132, JFKL.

66. Letter, Francis Underhill to Bunnell, May 3, 1981, Francis Underhill folder, author's personal collection.

67. "ICA Work in Public Safety," March 1961, NSF, Box 413, Counterinsurgency Police Program, 1961–1963, JFKL.

68. Memo from Interagency Committee on Police Assistance Programs to Kennedy, July 20, 1962, *FRUS, 1961–1963*, v. 8, 345–346.

69. Klare and Arnson, *Supplying Repression*, 18; Memo for the Secretary of State and Secretary of Defense from Kennedy, April 17, 1962, NSF, Box 413, Counterinsurgency Police Program, 1961–1963, JFKL; NSAM 146, April 20, 1962, NSF, NSAM, JFKL.

70. Evans, "Influence of the U.S. Army," 30; McClintock, *Instruments of Statecraft*, 188.

71. Robert Amory Oral History, JFKL, 100.

72. On June 18, 1963, Leon Gavin (R-Penn.) inserted an article from *The Era* (Bradford, Pennsylvania) by Andrew Tully. The article argued that the "U.S. supports Gestapo" in Indonesia and that "just to make sure this junior grade Hitler maintains his grip on his CO, we have earmarked $2.7 million of that financial sop to train and equip a special unit of the Indonesian police to keep the Indonesians in their place. Apparently, you don't call that sort of special unit a Gestapo these days." *Congressional Record, House*, June 18, 1963.

73. "ICA Work in Public Safety," March 1961, NSF, Box 413, Counterinsurgency Police Program, 1961–1963; see Enclosure 9, "PL-480 Program," NSF, Box 423, NSAM 179, JFKL.

74. Memo from Saunders to Davis, July 19, 1962, NSF, Box 412, Komer Series, Counterinsurgency/Civil Action, 1961–1963, JFKL.

75. First Colonel Soetjipto Joedodihardjo had been to Fort Bragg, Quantico, Paris Island, and Fort Gordon, Georgia, and on a 1963 visit to the United States both he and Djojonegoro met with FBI officials.

76. "Military and Paramilitary Police Assistance," undated attachment to NSAM 179, NSF, Box 413, Counterinsurgency and Police Program, 1961–1963, JFKL; Memo for the Special Group (CI), Report of Civic Action team to Indonesia, November 1, 1962, NSF, Box 423, Indonesia, 1961–1963, JFKL.

77. Memo from Hilsman to Rusk, November 16, 1961, *FRUS, 1961–1963*, v. 1, 621.

78. AID General Notice, "Office of Public Safety," November 1, 1962, NSF, Box 413, Counterinsurgency Police Program, 1961–1963, JFKL; Klare and Arnson, *Supplying Repression*, ch. 2 and 4. As Francis Underhill recalled in 1981, "In both training and material, we had provided vastly more to Indonesian police. There was one period when George Benson was bringing in shovels, hoes, picks, rock crushers and steam rollers for the army civic action programs and AID was importing for the Mobile Brigade rifles, ammunition, recoilless rifles and armored cars." Letter, Francis Underhill to Bunnell, May 3, 1981, author's collection.

79. Robert Amory says of U.S. police training in Indonesia, "In some respects, the groundwork done there, in Indonesia, may have been responsible for the speed with which this coup of last September, or whenever it was, was wrapped up." Amory Oral History, JFKL.

80. Crouch, *The Army and Politics in Indonesia*, ch. 2.

81. Lev, "Political Role of the Army in Indonesia," 362; Memo from Saunders to BKS, May 17, 1962, NSF, Box 412, Komer Series, Counterinsurgency/Civil Action, 1961–1963, JFKL.

82. Memo from Komer to Frank Coffin, William Bundy, and Jeffrey Kitchen, July 16, 1962, NSF, Box 412, Komer Series, Counterinsurgency/Civil Action, 1961–1963, JFKL.

83. Memo for the President, August 15, 1962, NSF, Box 423, Komer Series, Indonesia, 1961–1963, JFKL.

84. Draft of NSAM 179, NSF, Meetings and Memo Series, NSAM 179, JFKL; Peterson Memo to Janow et al., August 30, 1962; and Memo, First Meeting of the Indonesian Working Group, September 4, 1962, both in NSF, Box 423A, Komer Series, Indonesia, 1962–1963, JFKL.

85. Draft Response to NSAM 179, September 10, 1962, NSF, Meetings and Memo Series, NSC, NSAM 179, JFKL.

86. "First Speculative Outline, Scope of Plan of Action Responsive to NSAM 179," August 30, 1962, NSF, Box 423, Komer Series, Indonesia, 1961–1963, JFKL.

87. Memo from Saunders to David Burgess of AID, September 10, 1962; and Memo from Saunders to Komer, "NSAM Review Papers," September 10, 1962, both in NSF, Box 423, Komer Series, Indonesia, 1961–1963, JFKL. For the AID response, see Joint Embassy/USAID telegram 769, Jakarta to AID, October 11, 1962, DDRS, 1982, fiche 2502.

88. See *New York Times*, September 23, 1962; *Washington Post*, September 24, 1962; *Indonesian Herald*, September 25, 1962; Bunnell, "Kennedy Initiatives in Indonesia," 211–216.

89. Weinstein, *Indonesian Foreign Policy*, 221–223; Memo from Ball to Kennedy, October 10, 1962, *FRUS, 1961–1963*, v. 23, 634; Memo from Saunders to David Burgess of AID, September 10, 1962, NSF, Box 423, Komer Series, Indonesia, 1961–1963, JFKL. For an exception, see Sadli, "Inflation," 297–299.

90. Telegram 441, Henderson to State, September 6, 1962, NSF, CO Files, Box 114, Indonesia, JFKL.

91. Background to Plan of Action for Indonesia, October 2, 1962, NSF, Meetings and Memo Series, NSC, NSAM 195, JFKL, 9.

92. Memo from Ball to Kennedy, October 10, 1962, NSF, Meetings and Memo Series, NSC, NSAM 195, JFKL; Memo of Conversation Between Kennedy and Jones, October 11, 1962; Memo from Forrestal to Harriman, September 24, 1962; and Memo from Forrestal to Kennedy, October 11, 1962, all in *FRUS, 1961–1963*, v. 23, 633–634, 643–646.

93. Memo from Forrestal to Harriman, September 24, 1962, *FRUS, 1961–1963*, v. 23, 633–634; Memo to David Burgess of AID from Harold Saunders, September 10, 1962, NSF, Meetings and Memo Series, NSC, NSAM 195, JFKL.

94. NSC 6023 (signed December 1960) listed the primary short-range U.S. objective in Indonesia as "Prevention [of] Communist Control of Indonesia" and the

long-range objective as a "viable stable nation friendly to West and able to resist Communists."

95. Fifield, *Southeast Asia in United States Foreign Policy*, 383–387; Hilsman, cited in Schaller, *Altered States*, 183.

96. Welfield, *Empire in Eclipse*, 212; Woo, *Race to the Swift*, 89; Nishihara, *The Japanese and Sukarno's Indonesia*, 80–126.

97. Background to Plan of Action for Indonesia, October 2, 1962, NSF, Meetings and Memo Series, NSC, NSAM 195, JFKL.

98. Background to Plan of Action for Indonesia, October 2, 1962, NSF, Meetings and Memo Series, NSC, NSAM 195, JFKL, p. 10.

99. Anderson, "Perspective and Method in American Research on Indonesia," 77; Higgins, Foreword, ix.

100. Telegram 696 from Jakarta to State, October 16, 1962, DDRS, 1982, Document 002503.

101. Memo from Forrestal to Kennedy, October 11, 1962, NSF, NSC, Meetings and Memo Series, NSAM 195, JFKL.

102. NSAM 195, October 22, 1962, *FRUS, 1961–1963*, v. 23, 649; Action Telegram 497 from State to Jakarta, October 26, 1962, DDRS, 1982, Document 002506.

103. See Attachment 8 to NSAM 179, "Summary of IMF Staff Report on Indonesian Consultations," NSF, Meetings and Memo Series, NSC, NSAM 195, JFKL; Letter from Hilsman to Cornelius Gallagher, July 12, 1963, RG 59, Central Foreign Policy Files, 1963, POL 1, Box 3940, NA.

CHAPTER 4

1. Memo from Mr. Selby to Lord Home, "Observations on the West New Guinea Settlement," September 7, 1962, PREM 11-4309, UKNA.

2. NSF, Meetings and Memo Series, NSC, NSAM 179, JFKL; Memo for the President, August 15, 1962, Komer Series, WNG (West New Guinea), 1961–1963, JFKL.

3. Memo from Mein to Parsons, September 10, 1959, *FRUS, 1958–1960*, v. 17, 434–435; Telegram 2889 from Jakarta to State, April 10, 1961, POF, Box 119, Indonesia Security, JFKL.

4. Attachment 8 to NSAM 179, "Summary of IMF Staff Report on Indonesian Consultations," NSF, Meetings and Memo Series, NSC, NSAM 195, JFKL.

5. Telegram 2103 from Jakarta to State, May 30, 1962, DDRS, Retrospective Collection, 560B.

6. Letter from Walter Salant to David S. Burgess, acting director of the Office of Burma-Indonesia Affairs, AID, May 25, 1962, Bunnell Papers, author's collection; Jones Comments, March 5, 1962, handwritten notes, Bunnell Papers, author's collection; Telegram 696 from Jakarta to State, October 16, 1962, DDRS, 1982, Document 002503.

7. Memo for the President from Ball, October 10, 1962, NSF, Meetings and Memo Series, NSC, NSAM 195, JFKL.

8. Robison, *Indonesia*, 63.

9. Howard Jones, *Indonesia*, 195; letter from Bernard Bell to Don Humphrey and Walter Salant, undated, Bunnell Papers, ESP/DAC/IMF Folders, author's collection; Bunnell interview with Jones, undated, Bunnell Papers, author's collection; Bunnell interview with Sutikno Slamet, October 16, 1969, Bunnell Papers, author's collection.

10. Memo from Saunders to Burgess, "Comments on Draft Response to NSAM 179," September 10, 1962, NSF, Meetings and Memo Series, NSC, NSAM 195, JFKL; Bunnell interview with Sutikno Slamet, October 16, 1969, Bunnell Papers, author's collection. See "Cabinet Discussed Selection of Foreign Credit Offers," *Antara*, November 21, 1962; Weinstein, *Indonesian Foreign Policy*, 223–224.

11. Bunnell interview with Jones, undated, Bunnell Papers, author's collection; Bernard Bell, "A Program of Economic Action for Indonesia," November 24, 1962, Bunnell Papers, ESP/DAC/IMF Folders, author's collection; Bunnell, "Kennedy Initiatives in Indonesia," 214–215.

12. "Program of Economic Stabilization," January 15, 1963; and Bunnell interview with Sutikno Slamet, October 16, 1969, both in Bunnell Papers, author's collection; Weinstein, *Indonesian Foreign Policy*, 223–224.

13. Memo from Forrestal of the NSC Staff to Kennedy, November 23, 1962; and Memo from Seymour Janow, AID Assistant Administrator for the Far East, to Harriman, November 16, 1962, both in NSF, CO Files, Indonesia, v. 3, November–December 1962, JFKL. Indonesia's innovation of production-sharing agreements, in which extractive firms act as a contractor to the state—which takes part or all of its royalties in kind—has since become a standard contractual arrangement for extractive industries in dozens of developing countries.

14. Quoted in Cumings, "Asian Crisis," 24; Kolko, *Confronting the Third World*, 232.

15. Seymour Janow testimony, Briefing on Indonesia: Hearings Before the Committee on Foreign Affairs, House of Representatives, Subcommittee on the Far East and the Pacific, August 8, 1963; Bunnell, "Kennedy Initiatives in Indonesia," 216, 222, 372–374; Background Papers for Development Assistance Committee (DAC) Far East Regional Meeting Scheduled to Be Held in Paris, December 11–13, November 10, 1962, Bunnell Papers, author's collection; Development Assistance Committee, Summary Conclusions of the 12th meeting in Paris, December 21, 1962, Bunnell Papers, author's collection.

16. Memo for the President from Forrestal, December 17, 1962; and Memo from Forrestal to Secretary of State Rusk, December 18, 1962, both in *FRUS, 1961–1963*, v. 23, 652–654.

17. Bunnell, "Kennedy Initiatives in Indonesia," 278–280, citing the *Indonesian Herald* from December 1962–January 1963; Winters, *Power in Motion*, ch. 1.

18. Mortimer, *Indonesian Communism Under Sukarno*, 264.

19. *Indonesian Observer*, January 17, 1963.

20. Telegram 1118 from Jakarta to State, January 20, 1963, RG 59, Central Files, 101.2/1-2063, NA.

21. Telegram 1121 from Jakarta to State, January 22, 1963, RG 59, Central Files, 101.2/1-2263, NA; Chetwynd, "Indonesian Stabilization Attempt of 1963," 41–42; Sutikno Slamet interview with Bunnell, October 16, 1969, author's collection.

22. Chetwynd, "Indonesian Stabilization Attempt of 1963," 39, 48; "Indonesia Explores Aid from IMF," *Christian Science Monitor*, March 1, 1963.

23. Bernard Bell, "A Program of Economic Stabilization," January 15, 1963, Bunnell Papers, ESP/DAC/IMF Folders, author's collection.

24. Memo Prepared by Fund Staff, "Points for Further Consideration Between Indonesia and the Fund on Plans for Stabilization," March 8, 1963, Records of the Foreign Office (FO) 371-172369, UKNA; *Indonesian Observer*, March 9, 1963; *Antara*, March 9, 1963.

25. "The Economic Declaration: Basic Economic Strategy," March 28, 1963, cited in Chetwynd, "Indonesian Stabilization Attempt of 1963," appendix; Mackie, *Problems of Indonesian Inflation*, 38.

26. Telegram 1333 from Jakarta to State, March 1, 1963, *FRUS, 1961–1963*, v. 23, 659–661.

27. Memo from Forrestal to Kennedy, May 10, 1963, *FRUS, 1961–1963*, v. 23, 666–667.

28. "The Soviet and Sukarno: U.S. Gets Some Comfort from Signs Indonesia Is Cooling to Russian Aid," *New York Times*, April 4, 1963; "Chinese Reds Head of State in Indonesia for Nine-Day Visit," *New York Times*, April 13, 1963; Telegram 368 from Peking to Foreign Office, May 23, 1963, FO 371-169684, UKNA.

29. Office of Current Intelligence Special Report, "Growth of Chinese Influence Among World Communists," May 17, 1963; and CIA Research Staff Intelligence Memo, November 23, 1962, both available at CIA, FOIA Electronic Reading Room (available at http://www.foia.cia.gov/); quote from Letter from Frank Brewer, China and Korea Section, Research Department, to Mr. Boyd, Far East Department, January 21, 1969, Records of the Foreign and Commonwealth Affairs Office (FCO) 21-461, UKNA; Hindley, "Indonesian Communist Party."

30. INR Research Memo, "Moscow and Peiping Differ in Treatment of Brunei and Malaysia," March 1, 1963, NSF, Box 432, Komer Series, Malaysia, 1961–1963, JFKL; INR Research Memo, "The Soviet Attitude Toward WNG," April 27, 1962, NSC, Box 423A, Komer Series, JFKL; Kochavi, "Washington's View of the Sino-Soviet Split," 50–79.

31. Mozingo, "China's Policy Toward Indonesia," 195–205.

32. Feith, "President Sukarno," 971; "Anti Chinese Rioting Flares in 3 Regions of Indonesia," *New York Times*, May 12, 1963.

33. Memo from Bell to Komer, May 1, 1963, Thomson Papers, Box 22, JFKL.

34. James C. Thomson handwritten notes, June 1963, Thomson Papers, Box 5, Foreign Affairs Committee, House of Representatives (HFAC), General, JFKL;

"Foreign Aid and the State of the U.S. Economy," Remarks by H. R. Gross, June 11, 1963, *Congressional Record Appendix, 1963*.

35. Nils Gilman astutely points out that "modernization theory defined a healthy modernity as a fully realized New Deal America: a God-fearing but secular society in which race and gender were of little import; a privately run, full-employment economy of well-paid workers, all of whom owned a house and a car; a formal democratic system in which widespread agreement existed about societal goals, the details of which would be worked out by technically trained service elites" (Gilman, "Modernization Theory," 56). But he does not follow the logic of his observation to explore the opposition in any detail or the political economy of their worldview.

36. "The Third World War: On the Southern Flank," *National Review*, February 23, 1965.

37. *Congressional Record, 1963*, Senate, 21,348, 22,503; Robert Smith, *Tiger in the Senate*.

38. "Headless Foreign Aid Horsemen," Remarks by Hon. O. C. Fisher (D-Tex.), May 23, 1963, *Congressional Record Appendix, 1963*; remarks by William Broomfield (R-Mich.), H. R. Gross (R-Iowa), Charles Mathias (R-Md.), Paul Findley (R-Ill.), May 13, 1963, *Congressional Record, 1963*, 7884–7886; "Sukarno: Front for a Red Takeover?" Newsletter Backgrounder, Thomson Papers, Box 5, HFAC, General, JFKL.

39. Bunnell, "Kennedy Initiatives in Indonesia," 317; House Committee on Foreign Affairs, Subcommittee on the Far East and the Pacific, Briefing on Indonesia, August 8, 1963, 88th Congr., 55.

40. *Report of the Citizens Committee to Strengthen the Security of the Free World* (Clay Report); Schlesinger, *A Thousand Days*, 597–598.

41. *Who's Who in America, 1962–1963*, passim; Burch, *Elites in American History*, 195.

42. "The Clay Committee Recommendations Regarding the Scope and Distribution of U.S. Military and Economic Assistance Programs: Report to President from Committee to Strengthen the Security of the Free World," March 20, 1963, *American Foreign Policy, Current Documents, 1963* (Washington, DC, 1967), 1148–1164, passim; *Wall Street Journal*, March 26, 1963.

43. Quoted in Heath, *John F. Kennedy and the Business Community*, 110, and more generally 105–113; Passman, "Report of the Clay Committee"; Mahajani, "Kennedy and the Strategy of AID"; see also Collado, "Economic Development Through Private Enterprise."

44. See *Congressional Record, House, 1963*, 15,448–15,450; Collins, *More*, 40–98.

45. Clay Report, 1150.

46. "Clay on Target," editorial, *Christian Science Monitor*, February 4, 1963; "Less Aid, Better Spent," *Christian Science Monitor*, February 28, 1963; "Sukarno Imperialism," *St. Paul Dispatch*, May 16, 1963.

47. House Foreign Affairs Committee Hearings, 84th Congr., 1st sess., April 5, 1963, 81; "McNamara Warns of Peril in Reducing Military Aid," *New York Times*, April 9, 1963; "Indonesia: Another Cuba?" *Business Week*, April 27, 1963.

48. *Congressional Record, House, 1963,* 8363, 10,313; *Congressional Record, Senate, 1963,* 769–770; *Congressional Record, Appendix, 1963,* A3928, A2351, A3755; House Foreign Affairs Committee, *Hearings,* April 5, 1963, 21; *Congressional Record, House, 1963,* 8362–8363.

49. "Position Paper: Assistance to Indonesia," no author, June 23, 1963; and Memo, "U.S. Aid to Indonesia," June 1963, Briefing on Indonesia, both in Thomson Papers, Box 5, HFAC, General, June–November 1963, JFKL; Hearings before the Committee on Foreign Affairs, House of Representatives, Subcommittee on the Far East and the Pacific, August 8, 1963, 4–5; *HFAC Hearings,* April 10, 1963, 165–166; and May 14, 1963, 798.

50. Memo, Rusk to Kennedy, July 22, 1963, *FRUS, 1961–1963,* v. 23, 680; Memo from Bell to Hilsman, May 11, 1963, Hilsman Papers, Box 2, Indonesia, 1963–1964, JFKL.

51. *HFAC Hearings,* May 7, 1963, 606.

52. Telegram 501 from Foreign Office to United Kingdom delegation to OECD in Paris, July 22, 1963, DO (Records of the Commonwealth Relations Office) 169–70, UKNA.

53. Telegram 3896 from Foreign Office to Washington, July 30, 1963, DO 169–70, UKNA.

54. Briefing on Indonesia, *HFAC Hearings,* August 8, 1963, 6–7; *HFAC Hearings,* May 14, 1963, 797.

55. Aden, "Oil and Politics in Indonesia," 14–40.

56. Irvine Anderson, *Standard-Vacuum Oil Company.*

57. Embassy Petroleum Report, 1959–1960, July 8, 1960, RG 59, 898.2553/10-2761, NA; "Caltex in Central Sumatra," Memo from Medan to State, September 27, 1960, RG 59, 898.2553/9-2760, NA; "Oil and Nationalism Mix Beautifully in Indonesia," *Fortune,* July 1973. For analogous claims concerning Saudi Arabia, see Vitalis, *America's Kingdom.*

58. Embassy Petroleum Report, 1959–1960, 11–12; Telegram from Jakarta to State, August 9, 1960, RG 59, 898.2553/8-960, NA.

59. Memo, "Stanvac's Problems in Indonesia," February 2, 1961, RG 59, 898.2553/2-261, NA.

60. "Bigger Role Ahead for State Companies," *Oil and Gas Journal,* May 21, 1962, 107–110; Telegrams G-97 and G-98 from Jakarta to State, September 16, 1960, RG 59, 898.2553/9-1660, NA; Aden, "Oil and Politics in Indonesia," 198–205; on the history of Pertamina, see Bartlett et al., *Pertamina.*

61. "Indonesia May Cancel Foreign Firms' Oil Rights," *Wall Street Journal,* October 24, 1960; "Indonesia Moves to Take Over Oil," *New York Times,* November 2, 1960; "Indonesia's Sukarno Adds More Trappings of Red Dictatorship," *Wall Street Journal,* November 15, 1960; "Nationalization Is Threatened by Indonesia," *Oil and Gas Journal,* October 31, 1960, 73; "Expropriation Fears Soothed by Indonesia," *Oil and Gas Journal,* November 7, 1960, 115.

62. "Indonesian Oil in Transition," *Petroleum News Service*, June 1963, 218.

63. Telegram 1991 from Jakarta to State, January 7, 1961, RG 59, 898.2553/1-761, NA; Memo, February 7, 1961, RG 59, 898.2553/2-761, NA; Memo from F. A. Warner to Prime Minister Macmillan, "Indonesian Oil," May 27, 1963, FO 371-169941, UKNA.

64. Blair, *Control of Oil*, 70–98; Sampson, *Seven Sisters*, 175.

65. Sampson, *Seven Sisters*, 181; "Drilling of Oil Starts," *Indonesian Herald*, December 2, 1961.

66. "Esso Pushes into New Territory After Stanvac Split," *Oil and Gas Journal*, April 9, 1962; "How to Set Up a New Oil Company—Quickly," *Oil and Gas Journal*, May 28, 1962.

67. Telegram 1622 from Jakarta to State, March 13, 1962, RG 59, 898.2553/3-1362, NA; Action Memo 1219 from State to Jakarta, April 20, 1962, RG 59, 898.2553/4-2062, NA; Telegram 2914 from Jakarta to State, June 22, 1962, RG 59, 898.2553/6-2262, NA; Bush, "Oil and Politics in Indonesia," 225–226.

68. "Summary of IMF Staff Report on Indonesia," August 14, 1962, PPS, Staff Files, 1962, Lot File 69-D 121, Indonesia, NA; Memo, "Political Strategy for Indonesia," September 26, 1962, RG 59, 898.2553/9-2662, NA; Telegram 688 from C. E. Chalmers to Sir David Ormsby Gore, March 5, 1963, FO 371-169941, UKNA.

69. Telegram A-450 Jakarta to State, November 14, 1962, RG 59, 898.2553/11-1462, NA.

70. Bunnell, "Kennedy Initiatives in Indonesia," 274, 313; Telegram 970 from Jakarta to State, December 20, 1962, RG 59, 898.2553/12-2062, NA; Telegram 1281 from Jakarta to State, February 21, 1963, Central Files, PET 6, Indonesia, Box 3621, NA.

71. Telegram 1281 from Jakarta to State, February 19, 1963, RG 59, 898.2553/2-1963, NA; Memo, "Meeting with American Oil Company Representatives," March 1, 1963, Central Files, PET 6, Indonesia, Box 3621, NA.

72. Telegram 1345 from Jakarta to State, March 6, 1963, Central Files, PET 6, Indonesia, XR, and PET 15, Indo-Chi Coms Folder, NA; Telegram 811 from Jakarta to State, March 4, 1963, Central Files, PET 6, Indonesia, NA; Telegram 823 from Jakarta to State, March 6, 1963, Central Files, PET 6, Indonesia, XR, and PET 13, Indonesia, NA.

73. Memo, "Western Oil Companies' Negotiations: Indonesia," March 4, 1963, Central Files, PET 10-2, Indonesia, NA; Telegram 1345 from Jakarta to State, March 6, 1963, PET 6, Indonesia, and PET 15, Indo-Chi Coms Folder, NA; Memo, "Oil Company Negotiations in Indonesia," March 7, 1963, PET 6, Indonesia, NA; Memo from Jakarta to Foreign Office, "Possibility of Chinese Oil Purchases from Indonesia," March 29, 1963, FO 371-170708, UKNA.

74. Memo, "Oil Negotiations in Indonesia," March 7, 1963, Central Files, PET, Indonesia, NA.

75. Memo from F. A. Warner to Prime Minister Macmillan, "Indonesian Oil," May 27, 1963, FO 371-169941, UKNA.

76. On corporatism, see Painter, *Oil and the American Century*.

77. Telephone conversation, John McCone and Harriman, March 7, 1963; and telephone conversation, Gwyn Follis and Harriman, March 7, 1963, both in Harriman Papers. I am indebted to Kai Bird for these phone records concerning petroleum, which were purged from the Harriman Papers stored in the Library of Congress.

78. Telegram 1370 from Jakarta to State, March 9, 1963; and Telegram 1316 from Jakarta to State, February 27, 1963, both in Central Files, PET 6, Indonesia, NA. For Pan Am's identical pledge, see Telegram 1390, March 12, 1963; and Memo of Conversation, "Caltex Negotiations with the Indonesian Government," March 29, 1963, both in Central Files, PET 6, Indonesia, NA.

79. Action Memo 860, March 18, 1963, Central Files, 1961–1963, PET 6, Indonesia, NA.

80. Telegram 1700 from Jakarta to State, May 3, 1963, RG 59, Central Files, PET 6, Indonesia, XR Aid (U.S.), Indonesia, NA.

81. Telegram 1731 from Jakarta to State, May 7, 1963, Central Files, 1961–1963, PET 6, Indonesia, NA; State Department Action Memo 1013, May 11, 1963, Central Files, 1961–1963, PET 15-2, Indonesia, NA.

82. Bush, "Oil and Politics in Indonesia," 230–231.

83. Memo of Conversation, "Caltex Petroleum Negotiations: Indonesia," May 9, 1963, RG 59, Central Files, PET 6, Indonesia, NA; Hilsman to Jones, State Department Action Memo 1013, May 11, 1963, RG 59, Central Files, PET 15-2, Indonesia, NA.

84. Telephone conversation, Harriman and Robert Barnett, May 24, 1963; and telephone conversation, Harriman and Fred Dutton, May 24, 1963, both in Harriman Papers, Telephone Conversations, May 17–30, 1963, Library of Congress; Memo, Forrestal to Kennedy, May 10, 1963; and Memo, Forrestal to Kennedy, undated, both in *FRUS, 1961–1963*, v. 23, 666–667.

85. Telegram 1787 from Jakarta to State, May 16, 1963, Central Files, PET 6, Indonesia, NA.

86. Memo from Harriman to Jones, May 17, 1963, Central Files, 1961–1963, PET 6, Indonesia, NA.

87. Telegram 4575 from London to State, May 16, 1963, Central Files, PET 6, Indonesia, NA; Memo from Forrestal to Kennedy, May 20, 1963, *FRUS, 1961–1963*, v. 23, 668–669; telephone conversation, Harriman and Ball, May 17, 1963; telephone conversation, Harriman and Levy, May 17, 1963; telephone conversation, Harriman and Forrestal, May 20, 1963, all three in Harriman Papers, Telephone Conversations, May 17–30, 1963, Library of Congress Manuscript Division (LOC); Action Memo from Harriman to Jones, May 17, 1963, Central Files, PET 6, Indonesia, NA; Telegram 1845 Jones to State, May 24, 1963, Central Files, PET 6, Indonesia, NA.

88. Memo from Harriman to Jones, May 21, 1963, Central Files, PET 6, Indonesia, NA; Action Memo 1060, May 23, 1963; and Memo of Conversation, "Indonesian Oil Negotiations," May 25, 1963, both in Central Files, PET 6, Indonesia, NA; telephone conversation, Harriman and Sir David Ormsby-Gore, May 24, 1963, Harriman Papers, Telephone Conversations, 1963, Library of Congress.

89. Memo from Harriman to Jones, May 21, 1963, Central Files, PET 6, Indonesia, XR, POL 7, Indonesia, NA; Action Memo from Harriman to Jones, May 17, 1963; and Action Memo 1060, May 23, 1963, both in Central Files, PET 6, Indonesia, NA; Telegram 1832 from Jakarta to State, May 20, 1963, Central Files, PET 6, Indonesia, NA; on Shell, see Telegram 471 from Djakarta to Foreign Office, May 17, 1963, FO 371-169941, UKNA.

90. Memo of Conversation, "Clarification of the Legal Issue in the Companies' Indonesia Negotiation," May 22, 1963, Central Files, PET 10-3, Indonesia, NA.

91. "Oil Firms Face Showdown in Indonesia," *Oil and Gas Journal*, May 27, 1963; "U.S. Takes Active Role in Indonesian Fuss," *Oil and Gas Journal*, June 3, 1963; "U.S. Urges Sukarno to End Threat on Oil," *New York Times*, May 29, 1963; "Crossroads for Sukarno," Editorial, *New York Times*, May 30, 1963.

92. Telegram 2845 from Jakarta to State, May 28, 1963; and Telegram 1064 from Jakarta to State, May 24, 1963, both in Central Files, 1961–1963, PET 6, Indonesia, NA.

93. House Committee on Foreign Affairs, *Foreign Assistance Act of 1963: Hearings*, pt. 8, 1569–1590; "Report on Meeting Between Mr. Wyatt and President Sukarno," May 31, 1963, Central Files, PET 10, Indonesia, XR, and PET 15-2, Indonesia, NA; Walter Levy, "The Mission of the Presidential Emissary to President Sukarno of Indonesia, May–June, 1963: A Review of the Issues Affecting Oil," Harriman Papers, personal collection of Kai Bird; Bunnell, "Kennedy Initiatives in Indonesia," 367.

94. *HFAC Hearings*; Levy, Appendix B, "Summary of the Oil Presentation as the Meeting with President Sukarno," Harriman Papers, personal collection of Kai Bird.

95. Information Memo 1115 from Jakarta to State, June 4, 1963, Central Files, PET 6, Indonesia, NA.

96. "A Complete Draw," *Fortune*, August 1963, 79; "Indonesian Oil Pact," *New York Times*, June 2, 1963; "U.S. Diplomatic Triumph in Indonesia," *Business Week*, June 22, 1963, 72; "Showdown Brings Indonesia Small Gain," *Oil and Gas Journal*, June 10, 1963.

97. Memo from Forrestal to Kennedy, June 10, 1963, *FRUS, 1961–1963*, v. 23, 672; Letter from A. L. Nickerson to Harriman, June 13, 1963, Indonesian Oil Negotiations, Box 472, Harriman Papers, Library of Congress.

98. Telegram 1333 from Jakarta to State, March 1, 1963, *FRUS, 1961–1963*, v. 23, 659–661; Memo from James D. Bell to Komer, "Assessment of Political and Politico-Military Factors Involved in Indonesian Stabilization," May 1, 1963, NSF, Komer Papers, Box 423, Indonesian Stabilization Folder, JFKL.

99. Howard Dick, "Formation of the Nation-State," 190.

100. Chetwynd, "Indonesian Stabilization Attempt of 1963," 69–72; Bunnell, "Kennedy Initiatives in Indonesia," 380–383.

101. Robison, *Indonesia*, 83–84.

102. "Sukarno Returns, Facing Anger over Price Rises," *New York Times*, June 28, 1963.

103. *Harian Rakjat*, May 29, 1963; Feith, "President Sukarno, the Army, and the Communists."

104. Chetwynd, "Indonesian Stabilization Attempt of 1963," 77–78; Bunnell, "Kennedy Initiatives in Indonesia," 405; "Austerity in Jakarta," *New York Times*, July 20, 1963.

105. Slamet Sutikno interview, October 16, 1969, Bunnell Papers, author's collection; Weinstein, *Indonesian Foreign Policy*, 311, 315–316.

106. Telegram 126 from Jakarta to State, July 21, 1963, NSF, Indonesia, v. 4, June–August 1963, JFKL.

107. Weinstein, *Indonesian Foreign Policy*, 315–318; Chetwynd, "Indonesian Stabilization Attempt of 1963," 82–92; Bunnell, "Kennedy Initiatives in Indonesia," 410–442; Slamet Sutikno interview, October 16, 1969, Bunnell Papers, author's collection.

108. Telegram 2113 from Jakarta to State, June 27, 1963, NSF, Indonesia, v. 4, June–August 1963, JFKL.

109. Background to Plan of Action for Indonesia, October 2, 1962; and Memo to Burgess of AID from Saunders, September 10, 1962, both in NSF, Meetings and Memo Series, NSC, NSAM 195, JFKL.

110. Pauker, "The Strategic Implications of Soviet Military Aid to Indonesia"; Memo from Jones to Forrestal, February 8, 1963, NSF, Komer Series, Box 423, JFKL.

111. "Soviet Union Agrees to Prolong Repayment Period of Credits to Indonesia," *Antara*, July 5, 1963. See also Telegram 2 from Jakarta to State, July 1, 1963, NSF, Indonesia, v. 4, June–August 1963, JFKL.

112. "Indonesia Seen Turning to West," *New York Times*, July 7, 1963.

113. Memo from Forrestal to Komer, July 19, 1963; and Memo for the President from Komer, July 23, 1963, both in NSF, Indonesia, v. 4, June–August 1963, JFKL.

114. "Indonesian Economy Shows Some Improvement," *New York Times*, August 13, 1963; "Indonesia Needs 50 Million Now," *New York Times*, August 15, 1963.

115. Editorial, "Is Sukarno Shifting Policy?" *New York Times*, July 8, 1963.

CHAPTER 5

1. See Pauker, "Strategic Implications of Soviet Military Aid to Indonesia"; Brackman, *Southeast Asia's Second Front*; Subritzky, *Confronting Sukarno*, 42–45.

2. Memo from James D. Bell to Komer, "Assessment of Political and Politico-Military Factors Involved in Indonesian Stabilization," May 1, 1963, *FRUS, 1961–1963*, v. 23, 659–661; "Rich Indonesia in Deep Trouble Economically," *Washington Post*,

February 28, 1963; Memo from Komer to Bundy, January 16, 1963, *FRUS, 1961–1963*, v. 23, 656–658; NIE 55-63, "Indonesia's International Orientation," April 10, 1963, NSF, NIES, Indonesia, Box 7, LBJL.

3. For a comprehensive documentary collection, see Stockwell, *British Documents on the End of Empire.*

4. Mackie, *Konfrontasi*, 29; Telegram 4 from Jakarta to State, July 1, 1963, NSF, CO Files, Indonesia, v. 4, June–August 1963, LBJL; Matthew Jones, "'Maximum Disavowable Aid.'"

5. Crouch, *Army and Politics in Indonesia*, 38–40.

6. Matthew Jones, "Creating Malaysia," 88.

7. Subritzky, *Confronting Sukarno*, 28, 41; Foo, "The U.S. and the Indonesia-Malaysia Dispute," 49.

8. Mackie, *Konfrontasi*, 105; Foo, "The U.S. and the Indonesia-Malaysia Dispute," 21.

9. Pamela Sodhy, "Malaysian-American Relations During Indonesia's Confrontation Against Malaysia."

10. Matthew Jones, "Creating Malaysia," passim; Mackie, *Konfrontasi*, 111–144.

11. Telegram 1118 from Jakarta to State, January 20, 1963, RG 59, Central Files, 101.2/1-2063, NA.

12. Memo from Bell to Harriman, "General Nasution's Position on the Role of the Indonesian Armed Forces," *FRUS, 1961–1963*, v. 23, 655–666; Mackie, *Konfrontasi*, 124–128; Memo for Bundy from Lord Home, January 16, 1963, NSF, Box 432, Komer Series, Malaysia 1961–1963, JFKL.

13. Bunnell interview with Sutikno Slamet, October 16, 1969, Bunnell Papers, ESP/DAC/IMF Folder, author's collection; Komer to Bundy, January 16, 1963, NSF, CO Files, Indonesia, v. 3, January–February 1963, JFKL.

14. Foo, "The U.S. and the Indonesia-Malaysia Dispute," 59; State Department Action Telegram 615 to Jones, December 19, 1962; and Memo, Edward C. Ingraham (SPA) to David Cuthell (SPA), "Synopsis of U.S.-Indonesian Exchanges on Borneo Situation," undated, both in State Department Central Files, POL Malaysia and Singapore, 1961–1963, NA.

15. Bunnell, "Kennedy Initiatives in Indonesia," 13–14; Howard Jones, *Indonesia*, 272; Attachment 6, Political Assessment, NSAM 179, NSF, Box 423, Komer Series, Indonesia, 1961–1963, JFKL; Kahin, "Malaysia and Indonesia."

16. Fetzer, "Clinging to Containment," 183, 359; Bunnell interview with Sutikno Slamet, October 16, 1969, Bunnell Papers, ESP/DAC/IMF Folder, author's collection.

17. Hindley, "Indonesia's Confrontation of Malaysia," 406–407; Howard Jones, *Indonesia*, 270–271; NIE 55-63, "Indonesia's International Orientation," April 10, 1963, and NIE 54/55-63, NSF, NIES, Malaysia/Indonesia, Box 7, LBJL; Telegram 1039 from Jakarta to State, January 9, 1963; and Telegram 98 from Jakarta to State, July 17, 1963, both in NSF, CO Files, Indonesia, v. 4, June–August 1963, JFKL.

18. Kochavi, "Washington's View of the Sino-Soviet Split," 64–70; Policy Planning Council, "U.S. Policy Toward Communist China," November 30, 1962, *FRUS 1961–1963*, v. 22, 325–332.

19. Foo, "The U.S. and the Indonesia-Malaysia Dispute," 25–26; Mackie, *The Chinese in Indonesia*; Mozingo, *Sino-Indonesian Relations*.

20. Memo from Edward Ingraham to David Cuthell, undated, RG 59, POL 32, Brunei Revolt, NA; Memo, Robert Barnett to Harriman, July 2, 1963, POF, Box 119, General, JFKL.

21. Bunnell, "Kennedy Initiatives in Indonesia," 294–298.

22. Memo for Bundy from Lord Home, January 16, 1963, NSF, Box 432, Komer Series, Malaysia 1961–1963, JFKL; Subritzky, *Confronting Sukarno*, 43, 50–52; Telegram 1242 from Jakarta to State, February 12, 1963, NSF, Box 432, Komer Series, Malaysia 1961–1963, JFKL; Howard Jones, *Indonesia*, 274.

23. "Attack of Borneo Rebels Erupts Within Sarawak," *New York Times*, April 13, 1963; Howard Jones, *Indonesia*, 277.

24. Mackie, *Konfrontasi*, 149; "West Reassesses Sukarno Stance," *Christian Science Monitor*, June 13, 1963; Editorial, "Stroke of Sanity," *Washington Post*, June 4, 1963; Memo, Hilsman to Forrestal, July 8, 1963, NSF, Box 242, President's Proposed Far East Trip, JFKL.

25. Subritzky, *Confronting Sukarno*, 61–62; Telegram 98 from Jakarta to State, July 17, 1963, NSF, CO Files, Indonesia, v. 4, June–August 1963, LBJL.

26. ANZUS Council Meeting, Agenda Position Paper, Subject Indonesia, May 21, 1963, RG 59, Central Files, 1961–1963, Political Affairs and Relations, General Background, NA; Subritzky, *Confronting Sukarno*, 61–62; Memo from Forrestal to Chayes/Hilsman, July 15, 1963, Harriman Papers, Box 538, Trips and Missions Folder, Library of Congress.

27. Clay Report, 1150; *HFAC Hearings*, June 4, 1963, 1575; Telephone conversation between Hilsman and Congressman J. L. Pilcher, June 25, 1963, Hilsman Papers, Box 2, Indonesia 1963–1964, JFKL.

28. Memo from Bell to Hilsman, June 12, 1963; and Memo for Bundy from Executive Secretary William H. Brubeck, July 10, 1963, both in Hilsman Papers, Box 2, Indonesia, 1963–1964, JFKL; Bunnell, "Kennedy Initiatives in Indonesia," 333–334; Memo from Ben E. Brown to Hilsman, June 10, 1963; and Memo from Bell to Hilsman, June 12, 1963, both in Hilsman Papers, Box 2, Indonesia, 1963–1964, JFKL.

29. Telegram 295 from Jakarta to State, August 14, 1963, NSF, Indonesia, v. 4, June–August 1963, JFKL.

30. Howard Jones, *Indonesia*, 278; Telegram 98 from Jakarta to State, July 17, 1963, NSF, CO Files, Indonesia, v. 4, June–August 1963, LBJL; Memo, Rusk to Kennedy, undated, *FRUS, 1961–1963*, v. 23, 678–680; Hilsman, *To Move a Nation*, 393.

31. CIA information report, July 17, 1963, NSF, Box 114, CO Files, Indonesia, June–August 1963, JFKL; "House Unit Votes Jakarta Aid Curb," *New York Times*,

July 26, 1963; Telegram 98 from Jakarta to State, July 17, 1963, NSF, CO Files, Indonesia, v. 4, June–August 1963, JFKL; Memo from Rusk to Kennedy, undated, *FRUS, 1961–1963*, v. 23, 678–680.

32. "House Committee Rejects Restriction on Aid to Indonesia," *New York Times*, July 19, 1963.

33. "Showing Sukarno," editorial, *Washington Post*, July 28, 1963; Telegram 205 from Jakarta to State, July 31, 1963, NSF, CO Files, Indonesia, v. 4, June–August 1963, JFKL.

34. Bunnell, "Kennedy Initiatives in Indonesia," 485–492.

35. Memo from Robert Barnett to Harriman, July 2, 1963, POF, Box 119, JFKL.

36. "IMF Delegates to Help Stabilize Economy," *Indonesian Observer*, June 13, 1963; "IMF Report May Decide Aid Policy on Indonesia," *Washington Post*, July 7, 1963; Letter from Djuanda to Frank Southard, managing director of the IMF, July 4, 1963, Bunnell Papers, ESP/DAC/IMF Folder, author's collection.

37. "U.S. and Fund Ready to Gamble Aid Money to Help Out Sukarno," *Washington Post*, August 1, 1963; Memo from Forrestal to Komer, July 19, 1963, NSF, Indonesia, v. 4, June–August 1963, JFKL; Memo from Rusk to Kennedy, undated, *FRUS, 1961–1963*, v. 23, 678–680.

38. *HFAC Briefing on Indonesia*, August 8, 1963, 7–8, 25, 69; "Threat of Aid Cut Keyed to Kashmir," *New York Times*, August 10, 1963.

39. Cordier and Harrelson, *Public Papers of the Secretaries General*, 401–402.

40. Telegram 590 from Jakarta to State, September 19, 1963, *FRUS, 1961–1963*, v. 23, 683–685.

41. Telegram 637 from Jakarta to State, September 21, 1963; and Decree of the Minister of Basic Industry and Mining, No. 635, September 21, 1963, both in RG 59, PET 6, Indonesia, NA; Bunnell interview with Sutikno Slamet, October 16, 1969, Bunnell Papers, author's collection.

42. "Malaysia Dispute to Cost Indonesia New Aid from U.S.," *New York Times*, September 25, 1963. In 1962 Malaysia imported $374 million in goods and services from Indonesia and exported $114 million.

43. Telegram 357 from State to Jakarta, September 23, 1963, Central Files, PET 6, Indonesia, NA; Memo of Conversation, "Petroleum: Indonesia," September 27, 1963, Department of State (DOS), Central Files, Box 3621, PET 13, Indonesia, Marketing and Distribution, NA; Economic Summary, Third Quarter 1963, October 30, 1963, RG 84, Indonesia: Jakarta General Records, 1962–1963, Economic Reporting 1962–1963, NA.

44. Bunnell, "Kennedy Initiatives in Indonesia," 688; Record of a Meeting of the Foreign Ministers of the Central Treaty Organization held in the U.S. Mission in New York, September 26, 1963, FO 371-181524, UKNA.

45. Memo from Barnett to Hilsman and Irving Janow, September 21, 1963, Hilsman Papers, Box 2, Week of September 17, JFKL.

46. Bunnell interview with Michael Forrestal, January 1969, Bunnell Papers, author's collection; extract from Record of Conversation Between Kennedy and Lord Home at the White House, October 4, 1963, FO 371-181524, UKNA.

47. "Indonesian Aggression," editorial, *Washington Post*, September 19, 1963; *Congressional Record, Appendix*, September 19, 1963, A5915; *Congressional Record, House*, September 30, 1963, 18,294–19,295; Telegram 363 from State to Jakarta, September 24, 1963, *FRUS, 1961–1963*, v. 23, 688–689.

48. "Slamet Sees No Hope for Indo Stabilization Program," DCS/61, September 25, 1963, NSF, Komer Series, Box 423, Discussion of Indonesian Stabilization, JFKL; "Stabilization Plan Halted," *New York Times*, September 25, 1963; Economic Summary, Third Quarter, 1963, October 30, 1963, Central Files, RG 84, Indonesia: Jakarta General Records 1962–1963, Economic Reporting 1962–1963, NA.

49. Telegram 353 from State to Jakarta, September 22, 1963, Central Files, RG 84, Indonesia: Jakarta General Records 1962–1963, Economic Reporting 1962–1963, NA.

50. Telegram 355 from Anderson for Winkler via State, September 23, 1963, Central Files, PET 6, Indonesia, NA; Horne, *Harold Macmillan*, 414–415.

51. Telegram 1485 from London to State, September 24, 1963, Central Files, POL 1, Indonesia-Malaysia, NA; Telegram 343 from State to Jakarta, September 20, 1963, Central Files, PET 6, Indonesia, NA.

52. Horne, *Harold Macmillan*, 414–415; Memo from C. L. Alexander to Bundy, September 25, 1963, NSF, Box 432, Komer Series, Malaysia 1961–1963, White House Memos, JFKL; Telegram 391 from State to Jakarta, September 27, 1963, Central Files, PET 6, Indonesia, NA.

53. Telegram 363 from State to Jakarta, September 24, 1963, Central Files, AID (U.S.), Indonesia, NA.

54. Rostow, *Diffusion of Power*, 195; Mackie, *Konfrontasi*, 179.

55. Logevall, *Choosing War*; Kaiser, *American Tragedy*.

56. Telegram from Jakarta to State, September 28, 1963, *FRUS, 1961–1963*, v. 23, 689.

57. CIA Intelligence Memo, October 25, 1963, NSF, CO Files, Malaysia, General, Box 140, JFKL; Subritzky, *Confronting Sukarno*, 76.

58. Notes from Quadripartite Talks on Malaysia and Indonesia, Summary of First Meeting, October 16, 1963, Hilsman Papers, Box 2, JFKL; "The Malaysian-Indonesian Conflict," NIE 54/55-63, October 30, 1963, NSF, Malaysia, v. 1, LBJL.

59. Quadripartite Talks on Malaysia and Indonesia, Summary of First Meeting, October 16, 1963, Hilsman Papers, Box 2, JFKL; Subritzky, *Confronting Sukarno*, 83–85.

60. Telegram 503 from State to Embassy in Indonesia, October 24, 1963, RG 59, Central Files, POL, Indonesia-Malaysia, NA; "Current Status of U.S. Aid Program in Indonesia," prepared for Senator William Proxmire by AID, November 8, 1963, NSF, CO Files, Indonesia, v. 1, Box 246, LBJL.

61. House Foreign Affairs Committee, *Report of the Special Study Mission to Southeast Asia*; *Congressional Record*, 88th Congr., 2nd sess., November 7, 1963, 21,340.

62. *Congressional Record*, November 7, 1963, 20,903, 21,339–21,349; "Aid to Indonesia and UAR Curbed," *New York Times*, November 7, 1963; "Conferees Kill a Ban on Red Aid," *New York Times*, November 28, 1963.

63. Telegram 1012 from Jakarta to State, November 4, 1963, RG 59, Central Files, POL 15-1, Indonesia, NA; Memo of Conversation, November 19, 1963, *FRUS, 1961–1963*, v. 23, 694–696; Handwritten notes, November 19, 1963, Jones Papers, Ambassadorial Files, Box 92, Miscellaneous Meeting Notes, HI.

64. Memo from Hilsman to Rusk, Hilsman Papers, Presidential Far Eastern Trip Plans, Box 5, JFKL; see also Maga, *John F. Kennedy and the New Pacific Community*.

65. Michael Forrestal interview with Bunnell, January 1969, in author's possession.

66. Telegram 1846 from Jakarta to State, March 6, 1964, NSF, CO Files, Indonesia, v. 1, December 1963–March 1964, LBJL.

67. Gardner, *Pay Any Price*, 86–87; Memo of Conversation, "The South Vietnam Situation," November 24, 1963, *FRUS, 1961–1963*, v. 4.

68. Telegram 1053 from Jakarta to State, November 9, 1963, RG 59, Central Files, POL 7, Indonesia, NA; "Indonesia's General Nasution," CIA Special Report, SC 00618/63C, November 15, 1963, NSF, CO Files, Indonesia, v. 5, October–November 1963, JFKL.

69. Memo from Rusk to Johnson, December 12, 1963; attachment, "Proposed Presidential Letter to President Sukarno," no date; and Memo of Conversation," Call on the President by Ambassador Jones," December 18, 1963, all in NSF, CO Files, Indonesia, v. 1, November 1963–April 1964, Box 246, LBJL. See also Howard Jones's notes for the meeting with Johnson, December 18, 1963, Jones Ambassadorial Files, Box 92, Miscellaneous Meeting Notes, HI.

70. Michael Forrestal interview with Bunnell, January 1969, in author's possession; Telephone conversation between Johnson and McNamara, January 2, 1964, *FRUS, 1964–1968*, v. 26, 1–2.

71. Memo from Forrestal to Bundy, December 27, 1963; and Telephone conversation between Johnson and McNamara, January 2, 1964, both in NSF, CO Files, Indonesia, Box 246, LBJL; Hilsman, *To Move a Nation*, 407.

72. Telegram 564 from Kuala Lumpur to State, January 1, 1964, NSF, Malaysia, v. 1, LBJL; Telegram 727 from State to Jakarta, January 4, 1963, RG 59, Central Files, 1964–1966, POL-15-1, Indonesia, NA.

73. Memo for the President from Rusk, January 6, 1964, NSC Meeting Files, v. 1, NSC Meeting, January 7, 1964, LBJL.

74. Memo on Indonesia, January 7, 1964, NSC Meeting Files, v. 1, NSC Meeting, January 7, 1964, LBJL; notes on NSC Meeting, January 7, 1964, LBJL.

75. Foo, "The U.S. and the Indonesia-Malaysia Dispute," 131; Beschloss, *Taking Charge*, 110–115; Notes on NSC Meeting, January 7, 1964, NSC Meeting Files, v. 1, NSC Meeting, January 7, 1964, LBJL.

76. Memo from Benjamin Read to Bundy, January 13, 1964, *FRUS, 1964–1968,* v. 26, 29; Memo from Komer to Bundy and Forrestal, October 9, 1963, NSF, Name File, Komer Memos, v. 1, LBJL; Beschloss, *Taking Charge,* 156–158.

77. Memo from Benjamin Read to Bundy, January 13, 1964, RG 59, Central Files, 1964–1966, ORG 7, U.S., NA; Schlesinger, *Robert F. Kennedy and His Times,* 579–562, 633; Telegram 1829 from State to Tokyo, January 17, 1964, RG 59, Central Files, 1964–1966, POL 32-1, Indonesia-Malaysia, NA.

78. Memo from Komer to Bundy, January 15, 1964, NSF, Name File, Komer Memos, v. 1, LBJL; Telegram 1048 from Manila to State, January 18, 1964, NSF, CO Files, Malaysia, v. 1, November 1963–March 1964, LBJL.

79. Memos from Komer to Johnson, January 22 and 25, 1964, NSF, Komer Series, Malaysia, December 1963–March 1966, LBJL.

80. Schlesinger, *Robert F. Kennedy and His Times,* 635; Theodore White, *Making of the President,* 261; Geyelin, *Lyndon B. Johnson and the World,* 135.

81. Telegram 635 from State to Kuala Lumpur, January 31, 1964, RG 59, Central Files, 1964–1966, POL 32-1, Indonesia-Malaysia, NA; Telegram 2295 from Jakarta to State, May 4, 1964, NSF, CO Files, Malaysia, v. 2, May–September 1964, LBJL.

82. Letter from British Foreign Secretary Butler to Rusk, January 22, 1964, *FRUS, 1964–1968,* v. 26, 49–51; Telegram 308 from Wellington to State, February 7, 1964, RG 59, Central Files, 1964–1966, POL 31-2, Indonesia-Malaysia, NA.

83. Memo, "American Aid to Indonesia and British Trade with Cuba, China, and the Soviet Union," February 2, 1964, FO 371-175288, UKNA.

84. Subritzky, *Confronting Sukarno,* 97–102.

85. Subritzky, *Confronting Sukarno,* 98; NIE 55-63, "The Malaysia-Indonesia Conflict," October 30, 1963, NSF, NIE 55, Indonesia, LBJL; NIE 55-64, "Prospects for Indonesia," July 22, 1964, NSF, NIE 55, Indonesia, LBJL; Summary of Discussions on Indonesia and Malaysia, Notes from Quadripartite Talks on the Far East, Washington, February 10–11, 1964, Hilsman Papers, Box 2, Malaysia-Indonesia Quadripartite Talks, JFKL.

86. Joseph, *Cracks in the Empire,* 99; Hilsman, *To Move a Nation,* 534–536.

87. Halberstam, *Best and the Brightest,* 375–376; Bird, *Color of Truth,* 275; Abramson, *Spanning the Century,* 627–635.

88. Foo, "The U.S. and the Indonesia-Malaysia Dispute," 109–114; Seymour Irving Janow letter to Bunnell, October 7, 1970, Bunnell Papers, ESP/DAC/IMF Folder, author's collection.

89. Memo for the Record, Daily White House Staff Meeting, March 4, 1964, *FRUS, 1964–1968,* v. 26, 67–68; Telegram 946 from State to Jakarta, March 3, 1964, NSF, CO Files, Indonesia, v. 1, Box 246, LBJL.

90. Telegram 946 from State to Jakarta, March 3, 1964; and Telegram 733 from Kuala Lumpur to State, February 23, 1964, both in NSF, CO Files, Indonesia, v. 1, November 1963–April 1964, Box 246, LBJL; Telegram 787, Kuala Lumpur to State, March 3, 1964, NSF, CO Files, Malaysia, v. 1, LBJL.

91. Memo for Members of the Inter-Agency Working Group on the Indonesia Policy Paper, March 31, 1964, Hilsman Papers, CO Files, Box 2, Malaysia-Indonesia, 1963–1964, JFKL.

92. Telegram 1890 from Jakarta to State, March 12, 1964, NSF, CO Files, Malaysia, v. 1, November 1963–April 1964, LBJL; CIA intelligence cable, "Indo Plans and Intentions on Malaysia and SEA," February 28, 1964, NSF, CO Files, Malaysia, v. 1, LBJL.

93. Telegram 1854 from Jakarta to State, March 6, 1964; Telegram 1890 from Jakarta to State, March 12, 1964; and Telegram 1943 from Jakarta to State, March 19, 1964, NSF, CO Files, Malaysia, v. 1, LBJL.

94. Memo from Forrestal to Bundy, February 6, 1964, NSF, CO Files, Indonesia, v. 1, LBJL.

95. Telegram 2000 from Jakarta to State, March 27, 1964, RG 59, Central Files, 1964–1966, AID (U.S.), Indonesia, Box 559, NA; "Sukarno Tells U.S., 'To Hell with Your Aid,'" *New York Times*, March 26, 1964; Letter from Congressman Harold Ryan to Lyndon Johnson, March 28, 1964, Central Files, 1964–1966, AID (U.S.), Indonesia, Box 559, NA; Tarpley and Chaitkin, *George Bush*, ch. 9, passim.

96. Telegram 1802 from Jakarta to State, April 2, 1964, NSF, CO Files, Indonesia, v. 1, LBJL; "Keating Protests Aid to Indonesians," *New York Times*, April 27, 1964.

97. Memo of Conversation, March 13, 1964, Thomson Papers, Box 6, JFKL; Memo for the Record, Daily White House Staff Meeting, March 4, 1964, *FRUS, 1964–1968*, v. 26, 67–68.

98. Telegram 2067 from Jakarta to State, April 3, 1964, NSF, CO Files, Indonesia, v. 2, LBJL; Telegram 2119 Jakarta to State, April 10, 1964, RG 59, Central Files, 1964–1966, POL 32-1, Indonesia-Malaysia; Mackie, *Konfrontasi*, 229–230.

99. Telegram 1609 from Manila to State, April 17, 1964; and Telegram 1609 from Manila to State, April 17, 1964, both in *FRUS, 1964–1968*, v. 26, 84–91.

100. Memo for Bundy from Forrestal, April 27, 1964, NSF, CO Files, Malaysia, v. 2, LBJL; "Malaysia's Internal Problems," CIA Special Report SC 00612/64B, March 27, 1964, NSF, CO Files, Malaysia, v. 1, LBJL.

101. Crouch, *Army and Politics in Indonesia*, 61, 70; Telegram 2289 from Jakarta to State, May 4, 1964, NSF, CO Files, Malaysia, v. 2, LBJL; Action Telegram 1238 from State to Jakarta, May 16, 1964, NSF, CO Files, Indonesia, v. 2, LBJL.

102. "Indonesia's Food Problem," CIA Office of Current Intelligence (OCI), Report 1108/64, April 7, 1964, NSF, CO Files, Indonesia, v. 1, November 1963–April 1964, LBJL; "Jakarta's Best Troops Seek Celebes Rebels," *New York Times*, April 11, 1964.

103. Telegram 1366 from State to Jakarta, June 24, 1964, *FRUS, 1964–1968*, v. 26, 112–114.

104. Telephone conversation between Johnson and Bundy, May 1, 1964, NSF, CO Files, Indonesia, v. 2, LBJL.

105. Memo from Rusk to Johnson, June 29, 1964, RG 59, Central Files, 1964–1966, AID (U.S.), Indonesia, NA; NSAM 309, July 6, 1964, *FRUS, 1964–1968*, v. 26,

119; "Prospects for Indonesia," NIE 55-64, July 22, 1964, NSF, CO Files, Indonesia, v. 2, LBJL.

106. Memo from Komer to Johnson, May 14, 1964; and Memo from Ball to Johnson, May 12, 1964, both in NSF, CO Files, Malaysia, Tunku Visit, May 1964, LBJL; Note from William Bundy to Rusk, May 15, 1964, *FRUS, 1964–1968*, v. 26, 110.

107. Subritzky, *Confronting Sukarno*, 94–115.

108. Circular Telegram 182 from State to Various Embassies, July 30, 1964, NSF, CO Files, Malaysia, Tunku Visit, LBJL.

109. For background on Australia, New Zealand, and Vietnam, see Doyle et al., *Australia's Vietnam War*; Murphy, *Harvest of Fear*; and Rabel, *New Zealand and the Vietnam War*.

110. Action Telegram 77 from State to Jakarta, July 22, 1964; Telegram 32 from Singapore to State, July 22, 1964; and "Communal Riots in Malaysia," INR Intelligence Note, July 22, 1964, all in NSF, CO Files, Malaysia, v. 2, LBJL.

111. Mackie, *Konfrontasi*, 258–259; Telegram 226 from State to Embassy in Thailand, August 13, 1964, *FRUS, 1964–1968*, v. 26, 128–129.

112. Memo from Thomson to Bundy, August 25, 1964, NSF, Bundy Files, Box 18, LBJL.

113. Telegram 94 from Jakarta to State, July 14, 1964, NSF, CO Files, Malaysia, v. 2, LBJL.

114. John Prados, ed., "Tonkin Gulf Intelligence 'Skewed' According to Official History and Intercepts," NSA Briefing Book 132 (available at http://www.gwu.edu/~nsarchiv/NSAEBB/NSAEBB132/press20051201.htm).

115. Telephone conversation between Harriman and Robert Kennedy, August 3, 1964, Harriman Papers, Box 582, Library of Congress.

116. *Congressional Record, Senate*, 88th Congr., 2nd sess., August 13, 1964, 19,422–19,428, 22,035–22,038; "Aid for Indonesia Barred in Senate," *New York Times*, August 14, 1964; "Indonesians Shut U.S.-Run Library," *New York Times*, August 16, 1964.

117. Memo from Bundy to Johnson, August 31, 1964, *FRUS, 1964–1968*, v. 26, 144.

118. Memo from Komer to Johnson, August 19, 1964, DDRS, RC 908A; Telephone conversation between Ball and Johnson, August 17, 1964, 5:45 pm, Ball Papers, Box 4, Indonesia, April 1964–November 1965, LBJL.

119. Telegram 317 from Jakarta to State, August 18, 1964, RG 59, Central Files, 1964–1966, POL 15-1, Indonesia, NA; Current Intelligence Memo, OCI 2217/64, August 20, 1964, NSF, CO Files, Indonesia, v. 2, Cables and Memos, LBJL.

120. Memo from Green to Rusk, August 19, 1964, RG 59, Central Files, 1964–1966, AID (U.S.), Indonesia, XR ORGS, NA.

121. Note from Komer to Bundy, August 24, 1964, NSF, Bundy Files, Box 18, LBJL; Memo from Thomson to Bundy, August 26, 1964, NSF, CO Files, Indonesia, v. 2, May–August 1964, Box 246, LBJL; Memo from Joint Chiefs of Staff to Secretary of Defense McNamara, JCSM-734-64, August 26, 1964, *FRUS, 1964–1968*, v.

26, 141–142; Telegram 359 from Jakarta to State, August 24, 1964, RG 59, Central Files, 1964–1966, POL 1, Indonesia-U.S., NA.

122. Memo from Bundy to Johnson, August 31, 1964; and Attachment, Memo from Rusk to Johnson, August 30, 1964, both in NSF, CO Files, Indonesia, v. 2, Cables and Memos, LBJL.

123. Mackie, *Konfrontasi*, 258–264; Subritzky, *Confronting Sukarno*, 116–117.

124. Telegram 1590 from State to London, September 2, 1964, *FRUS, 1964–1968*, v. 26, 149–150.

125. Matthew Jones, *Conflict and Confrontation in Southeast Asia*, 208.

126. DIA Intelligence Memo, September 3, 1964, DDRS, 1975, Fiche 154C; Subritzky, *Confronting Sukarno*, 119–120.

127. Foo, "The U.S. and the Indonesia-Malaysia Dispute," 217.

128. Telegram 278 from State to Jakarta, September 12, 1964, RG 59, Central Files, 1964–1966, POL 32-1, Indonesia-Malaysia, NA.

129. Memo from Green to Harlan Cleveland, September 8, 1964, Green Papers, Box 11, HI; Telephone conversation between Harriman and Senator Thomas Dodd, September 24, 1964, Harriman Papers, Box 582, Library of Congress; Airgram A-375 from U.S. Mission to the United Nations (USUN) to State, September 22, 1964, RG 59, Central Files, 1964–1966, POL 32-1, Indonesia-Malaysia, NA; United Nations, *Verbatim Record of the 1144th Meeting of the Security Council*; United Nations, *Verbatim Record of the 1145th Meeting of the Security Council*; United Nations, *Verbatim Record of the 1152th Meeting of the Security Council*.

130. See CIA Intelligence Information, Cable DB-315/00846-64, NSF, CO Files, Indonesia, v. 3, Cables, LBJL; Telegram 513 from Jakarta to State, September 11, 1964, NSF, CO Files, Indonesia, v. 3, Cables, LBJL; Subritzky, *Confronting Sukarno*, 121.

131. "Short-Term Prospects in the Malaysia-Indonesia Conflict," Special National Intelligence Estimate (SNIE) 54/55-64, September 16, 1964, NSF, NIES 54/55, Malaysia-Indonesia, Box 7, LBJL; Circular Telegram 714 from State to Certain Posts, October 22, 1964, *FRUS, 1964–1968*, v. 26, 167–170.

132. Circular Telegram 715 from State to Certain Posts, October 22, 1964, RG 59, Central Files, 1964–1966, POL 1, Indonesia, NA; Letter from Komer to Bundy, October 21, 1964, NSF, CO Files, Malaysia, v. 3, LBJL.

133. "Sukarno and the Communists," CIA Office of Current Intelligence, Report 00642/64A, NSF, NIES 55, Indonesia, Box 7, LBJL.

134. Memo from CIA Office of National Estimates to Bundy, "Trends in World Situation," June 1, 1964, NSF-CIA, v. 1, LBJL.

135. "Prospects for Covert Action," Memo prepared in CIA for State, September 18, 1964, *FRUS, 1964–1968*, v. 26, 161–164. The proposal almost certainly originated in Jakarta with Francis Galbraith and Hugh Tovar, the CIA station chief (replacing Joe Smith, who returned to Washington to become William Colby's deputy on Indonesia in the Deputy Directorate of Plans).

136. "Prospects for Covert Action," Memo prepared in CIA for State, September 18, 1964, *FRUS, 1964–1968*, v. 26, 161–164. The memo was first prepared by William Colby and sent to William Bundy on September 5.

137. Bunnell, "American 'Low-Posture' Policy Toward Indonesia," 34.

138. NSC 5901, "U.S. Policy on Indonesia," January 16, 1959, RG 59, NSC Files, NA.

139. Telegram 1846 from Jakarta to State, March 6, 1964; and "The Succession Problem in Indonesia," DOS/INR Research Memo RFE-16, March 9, 1964, both in NSF, CO Files, Indonesia, v. 1, LBJL.

140. "Indonesia's General Nasution," CIA Special Report, SC 00618/63C, November 15, 1963, NSF, CO Files, Indonesia, v. 5, LBJL; Telegram 1854 from Jakarta to State, March 6, 1964, NSF, CO Files, Malaysia, v. 1, LBJL.

141. Bunnell, "American 'Low-Posture' Policy Toward Indonesia," 33–36; Letter from Komer to Bundy, January 15, 1964, NSF, CO Files, Indonesia, v. 1, LBJL; Telegram 2154 from Jakarta to State, January 25, 1961, RG 59, Central Files, 611.98/1-2561, NA.

142. "Political Action Paper," Central Intelligence Agency, DO Files, Job 78-00597R, Far East/State Department Meetings, 1964, November 19, 1964, *FRUS, 1964–1968*, v. 26, 181–184.

143. "Political Action Paper," Central Intelligence Agency, DO Files, Job 78-00597R, Far East/State Department Meetings, 1964, November 19, 1964, *FRUS, 1964–1968*, v. 26, 181–184. See also Note from Komer to Bundy, November 19, 1964, *FRUS, 1964–1968*, v. 26, 184.

144. Telegram 487 from State to Jakarta, November 19, 1964, RG 59, Central Files, 1964–1966, POL 1, Indonesia, NA.

145. State Department, Top Secret Cable from Rio De Janiero, "Brazil Marks 40th Anniversary of Military Coup," March 27, 1964, NSA Electronic Briefing Book 118, March 31, 2004 (available at http://www.gwu.edu/~nsarchiv/NSAEBB/NSAEBB118/index.htm#3).

146. Sikkink, *Ideas and Institutions*; Weis, "Twilight of Pan-Americanism."

147. See generally *FRUS, 1964–1968*, v. 31.

148. Transcript, George W. Ball Oral History Interview 2, July 9, 1971, 39–40, LBJL.

149. Easter, "British and Malaysian Covert Support," 202; Easter, "British Intelligence and Propaganda," 94–95.

150. Subritzky, *Confronting Sukarno*, 125–129.

151. Memo from M. J. C. Templeton to Edward Peck, December 19, 1964, Foreign Office General Correspondence Files, FO 371-15251, DH 1015/112, UKNA. Although the extent to which U.S. and British encouragement of a premature coup attempt by the PKI is unclear (and must remain so until more records are declassified), there is no doubt that the coup was a goal of U.S and British covert operations and was on the minds of many officials. More tantalizing is a letter from a British

researcher, Neville Maxwell, who, while conducting research in Pakistan on the background of the 1965 Indonesian-Pakistani conflict, came across a letter to Foreign Minister Bhutto from one of his ambassadors in Europe; the letter reported a conversation between a Dutch intelligence officer and a NATO official. According to Maxwell, the Dutch officer in the letter told the Pakistani ambassador that Indonesia was "ready to fall into Western lap like a rotten apple." Western intelligence agencies, he said, would stimulate a "premature communist coup . . . which would be foredoomed to fail, providing a legitimate and welcome opportunity to army to crush the Communists and make Sukarno a prisoner of the Army's good will." The letter, like the New Zealand high commissioner's remarks, was dated December 1964; letter from Neville Maxwell, Senior Research Officer, Institute of Commonwealth Studies to *New York Review of Books*, June 5, 1978.

CHAPTER 6

1. Telegram 1358 from Jakarta to State, January 14, 1965, NSF, CO Files, Indonesia, v. 3, LBJL.

2. Notes prepared for Jones meeting with Kennedy, November 19, 1963, Jones Papers, Ambassadorial Files, Box 92, Miscellaneous Meeting Notes, HI.

3. CIA Special Memo, Office of National Estimates, January 26, 1965; and Telegram 1358 from Jakarta to State, January 14, 1965, both in NSF, NIES 55, Box 7, LBJL.

4. Telegram 1358 from Jakarta to State, January 14, 1965, NSF, CO Files, Indonesia, v. 3, LBJL.

5. Bunnell, "American 'Low-Posture' Policy Toward Indonesia," 31.

6. McMahon, *Limits of Empire*, 123.

7. Crouch, *Army and Politics in Indonesia*, 95.

8. Mortimer, *Indonesian Communism Under Sukarno*, 277–278; Mortimer, *The Indonesian Communist Party and Land Reform*; Utrecht, "Land Reform in Indonesia."

9. Sullivan, "The United States and the 'New Order' in Indonesia," 122.

10. van der Kroef, "Indonesian Communism's 'Revolutionary Gymnastics,'" 226–227.

11. Pauker, "Indonesia in 1964," 92–94; Telegram 1091 from Jakarta to State, December 10, 1964, DDRS, RC, 908 E.

12. Telegram 962 from Jakarta to State, November 25, 1964, *FRUS, 1964–1968*, v. 26, 185; note from Komer to Bundy, November 14, 1965; and CIA/OCI Intelligence Memo 2057/64, "Rallying of Communist Forces in Indonesia," December 2, 1964, both in NSF, CO Files, Indonesia, v. 3, LBJL.

13. van der Kroef, "Indonesian Communism's 'Revolutionary Gymnastics,'" 229; Telegram 1358 from Jakarta to State, January 14, 1965, NSF, CO Files, Indonesia, v. 3, LBJL; CIA Intelligence Information Special Report, NSF, CO Files, Indonesia, Box 249, Indonesia Cables, v. 9, September–November 1968, LBJL.

14. Subritzky, *Confronting Sukarno*, 132.

15. Special Memo of Office of National Estimates of CIA, January 26, 1965, NSF, NIE 55, Box 7, LBJL; Telegram 194 from Jakarta to Foreign Office, January 19, 1965, FO 371-180333, UKNA; Editorial, *Indonesian Herald*, January 21, 1965.

16. CIA Intelligence Information, Cable 314/00496-65, January 13, 1965, NSF, CO Files, Indonesia, v. 3, LBJL.

17. Letter from Frank Brewer, China and Korea Section, Research Department, to Mr. Boyd, Far East Department, January 21, 1969, FCO 21-461, UKNA; Mozingo, *China's Policy Toward Indonesia*, 219.

18. Chen, *Mao's China and the Cold War*, ch. 8; Memo of Conversation between Zhou Enlai and the Indonesian First Prime Minister Subandrio, May 28, 1965, CWIHP Virtual Archive (available at http://wilsoncenter.org/index).

19. Gilbert, "Wars of Liberation"; quoted in Westad, *Global Cold War*, 187; Suraputra, *Role of America and Soviet Aid to Indonesia*.

20. Memo from Deputy Assistant Secretary of Defense for ISA to Assistant Secretary of Defense, August 11, 1965, *FRUS, 1964–1968*, v. 26, 281–283; Cornejo, "When Sukarno Sought the Bomb."

21. See "Sukarno Moves Toward Peking," *New York Times*, January 16, 1965; Editorial, "Peking Seeks a New Role," *New York Times*, January 29, 1965; "Bond with Red China Cited by Sukarno," *New York Times*, February 3, 1965; "Indonesia: Looking Toward China," *New York Times*, February 6, 1965; "Sukarno: The Other Asian Problem," *Readers Digest*, May 1965.

22. Welfield, *Empire in Eclipse*, 218; LaFeber, *The Clash*, 330.

23. Special Memo of Office of National Estimates of CIA, January 26, 1965, NSF, NIES 55, Box 7, LBJL; Memo from Thomson to Bundy, December 9, 1964, Thomson Papers, Box 11, JFKL.

24. Guidance No. 7, "Indonesia: The Coming Struggle for Power," January 6, 1965, FO 371-180311, UKNA; CIA/OCI Intelligence Memo 2860/64, "The Succession Problem in Indonesia," December 1964, NSF, CO Files, Indonesia, v. 3, LBJL.

25. Telegram 836 from Kuala Lumpur to State, January 9, 1965, NSF, CO Files, Indonesia, v. 3, LBJL.

26. Telegram 1227 from Jakarta to State, January 13, 1965; and Note from Chet Cooper to Bundy, undated, both in NSF, CO Files, Indonesia, v. 3, LBJL.

27. Telegram 1435 from Jakarta to State, January 21, 1965, NSF, CO Files, Indonesia, v. 3, LBJL. George Benson reported similar army contingency plans in October 1962; Telegram from Army Attaché to State, October 19, 1962, RG 59, 798.00/10-1962, NA.

28. Telegram 1358 from Jakarta to State, January 14, 1965, NSF, CO Files, Indonesia, v. 3, LBJL.

29. Note from Green to William Bundy, January 20, 1965, *FRUS, 1964–1968*, v. 26, 212–213; Letter from President Lyndon Johnson to Prime Minister Harold Wilson, January 26, 1965, PREM 13-2718, UKNA; Record of a conversation between

the Prime Minister and Rusk at No. 10 Downing St., January 29, 1965, PREM 13-2718, UKNA; on the administration's isolation in early 1965, see Logevall, *Choosing War*, 300–305.

30. Memo from Thomson to Bundy, January 16, 1965; Telegram 1583 from Jakarta to State, February 13, 1965; and Letter from Forrestal to Jones, February 19, 1965, all in NSF, CO Files, Indonesia, v. 3, LBJL.

31. "Indonesia May Halt Activities of USIS," *New York Times*, December 18, 1964; Sullivan, "The United States and the 'New Order' in Indonesia," 99–104; Hughes, *Indonesian Upheaval*, 97–100.

32. Memo from Carl Rowan to Rusk, February 18, 1965, *FRUS, 1964–1968*, v. 26, 223.

33. Telegram 727 from State to Jakarta, February 20, 1965; Telegram 1658 from Jakarta to State, February 24, 1965; and Telegram 1730 from Jakarta to State, March 3, 1965, all in RG 59, Central Files, 1964–1966, POL, Indonesia-U.S., NA.

34. Telegram 1642 from Jakarta to State, February 22, 1965, NSF, CO Files, Indonesia, Box 246, v. 3, LBJL.

35. Memo from Robert Morris to David Cuthell, February 25, 1965, RG 59, Central Files, 1964–1966, INCO Rubber Indonesia, NA; Telegram 1760 from Jakarta to State, March 5, 1965, NSF, CO Files, Indonesia, v. 4, LBJL.

36. Telegram 1694 from Jakarta to State, February 27, 1965, NSF, CO Files, Indonesia, Box 246, v. 3, LBJL; CIA Intelligence Cable 315/00716-65, March 2, 1965, NSF, CO Files, Indonesia, Memos, v. 4, LBJL; Memo from Thomson to Bundy, March 1, 1965, Thomson Papers, Box 12, JFKL.

37. Telegram 1718 from Jakarta to State, March 3, 1965; see also Airgram A-595 from Jakarta to State, February 9, 1965, both in RG 59, Central Files, 1964–1966, PET, Indonesia-U.S., NA.

38. Telegram 1844 from Jakarta to State, March 13, 1965, RG 59, Central Files, 1964–1966, PET, Indonesia-U.S., NA; Editorial, "Ensuring Oil Flow," *Indonesian Herald*, March 23, 1965.

39. Telegram 629 from Jakarta to Foreign Office, March 19, 1965, FO 371-180361, UKNA; Telegram 1942 from Jakarta to State, March 20, 1965, NSF, CO Files, Indonesia, Cables, v. 4, LBJL.

40. Airgram A-908 from Jakarta to State, May 28, 1965, RG 59, Central Files, 1964–1966, PET 15-2, Indonesia, NA; Memo of Conversation, "Indonesian Actions Against U.S. Official and Private Establishment," March 25, 1965, RG 59, Central Files, 1964–1966, POL, Indonesia-U.S., NA; Burch, *Elites in American History*, 201; Telephone conversation between Ball and Bundy, March 15, 1965, Ball Papers, Box 4, LBJL.

41. Telegram 285 from Foreign Office to Jakarta, February 11, 1965, FO 371-181490, UKNA; Subritzky, *Confronting Sukarno*, 144.

42. Telegram 795 from State to Jakarta, March 5, 1965, NSF, CO Files, Indonesia, v. 4, LBJL.

43. Telegram from Jakarta to State, March 8, 1965, RG 59, Central Files, 1964–1966, POL, Indonesia-U.S., NA.

44. Presentation by Howard Jones at the 1965 Chief of Mission Conference, "American-Indonesian Relations," Jones Papers, Box 22, HI.

45. Memo for the President from Ball, undated, NSF, Indonesia, v. 4, LBJL; Memo from Harriman to Ball, March 18, 1965, Harriman Papers, Box 451, Library of Congress.

46. Memo from Ball to Johnson, March 18, 1965, *FRUS, 1964–1968*, v. 26, 251–252.

47. Memo from Thomson to Johnson, March 24, 1965, NSF, Indonesia, v. 4, LBJL.

48. "Sukarno Demotes 2 Anti-Red Aides," *New York Times*, April 1, 1965.

49. Telegram 2350 from Jakarta to State, April 28, 1965, RG 59, Central Files, 1964–1966, POL 23-8, Indonesia, NA.

50. Report from Ellsworth Bunker to Johnson, Part 1, General Conclusions, April 23, 1965, NSF, Indonesia, v. 4, LBJL.

51. Telegram 2360 from Jakarta to State, April 29, 1965, RG 59, Central Files, 1964–1966, DEF 19-3, U.S.-Indonesia; Howard Jones, *Indonesia*, 363.

52. Bunker Report, Part 1, General Conclusions, April 23, 1965, NSF, Indonesia, v. 4, LBJL; Subritzky, *Confronting Sukarno*, 143; Editorial, "Bung Karno and the United States," *Indonesian Herald*, April 2, 1965.

53. Hilsman Oral History, 4, JFKL.

54. Memo prepared for the 303 Committee, February 23, 1965, *FRUS, 1964–1968*, v. 26, 234.

55. Howard Jones Presentation at 1965 Chief of Mission Conference, "American-Indonesian Relations," Jones Papers, Box 22, HI.

56. Telegram 1583 from Jakarta to State, February 13, 1965, NSF, CO Files, Indonesia, Box 246, v. 3, LBJL; "U.S. Denies It Supports Any Anti-Sukarno Group," *New York Times*, February 25, 1965; Telegram 1369 from Jakarta to State, March 16, 1965, RG 59, Central Files, 1964–1966, POL, Indonesia-U.S., NA; U.S. Congress, Senate, Select Committee to Study Governmental Operations with Respect to Intelligence Activities, Interim Report 94-465, *Alleged Assassination Plots Involving Foreign Leaders*, 94th Congr., 1st sess., 1975.

57. Memo from E. H. Peck to Lord Walston, "Political Preparations for Proposed Military Action," January 6, 1965, FO 371-181490, UKNA.

58. Memo, "War of Nerves: Indonesia," September 23, 1965, FO 1011-1, UKNA; Letter from Andrew Gilchrist to Norman Reddaway, August 11, 1965, FO 1011-1, UKNA; for an account of the mutiny see Telegram 425 from Jakarta to Foreign Office, February 23, 1965, FO 371-180311, UKNA.

59. Report by J. K. Drinkall, "Proposal for the Appointment of a Coordinator of Political Warfare Against Indonesia," June 7, 1965, FO 1011-1, UKNA.

60. Mortimer, *Indonesian Communism Under Sukarno*, 317; Airgram A-455 from Jakarta to State, "Background on Increasing Peasant Tensions in Java and Bali," December 18, 1964, RG 59, Central Files, 1964–1966, POL 23-8, Indonesia, NA.

61. Airgram A-825 from Jakarta to State, April 30, 1965, RG 59, Central Files, 1964–1966, POL 13-2, Indonesia, NA.

62. Memo from D. Tonkin to Foreign Office, May 26, 1965, FO 817-180515, UKNA.

63. Elson, *Suharto*, 93.

64. Crouch, *Army and Politics in Indonesia*, 81; David Challis, *In the Shadow of the Generals*, 76–77; Evans and Novak, cited in Peter Dale Scott, "The United States and the Overthrow of Sukarno," 258.

65. Letter from Jones to William Bundy, April 23, 1965, *FRUS, 1964–1968*, v. 26, 254.

66. Telegram 647 from Jakarta to State, October 3, 1964, NSF, CO Files, Indonesia, v. 3, LBJL; Telegram 368 from State to Jakarta, October 8, 1964; and Telegram 912 from Jakarta to State, November 18, 1964, both in RG 59, Central Files, 1964–1966, DEF 19, U.S.-Indonesia, NA.

67. Telegram 1197 from State to Jakarta, May 21, 1965; Telegram 2653 from Jakarta to State, June 8, 1965; and Telegram 2784 from Jakarta to State, June 28, 1965, all in RG 59, Central Files, 1964–1966, DEF 21, Indonesia, NA.

68. Memo of Conversation, "U.S. Communications Equipment for the Indonesian Army," July 20, 1965, NSF, CO Files, Indonesia, v. 4, LBJL; Easter, "British Intelligence and Propaganda," 85.

69. Letter from William Gibbons to Senator William J. Fulbright, June 22, 1965, RG 59, General Policy Plans and Coordination, Box 559, Indonesia Aid, July 1, 1966, NA; "Senate Rejects Aid Restrictions," *New York Times*, June 11, 1965.

70. Telegram 66 from State to Jakarta, July 22, 1965; and Telegram 2784 from Jakarta to State, June 28, 1965, both in RG 59, Central Files, 1964–1966, DEF 21, Indonesia, NA.

71. Memo, "American Aid to Indonesia and British Trade with Cuba, China, and the Soviet Union," February 3, 1964, FO 371-175288, UKNA; Department of State Memo of Conversation, "Sale of Communication Equipment to Indonesia," July 28, 1965, NSF, CO Files, Indonesia, v. 3, LBJL.

72. Subritzky, *Confronting Sukarno*, 137, 155–160.

73. Telegram CX-39-65 from U.S. Army Kuala Lumpur to Defense Intelligence Agency, June 4, 1965, RG 59, Central Files, 1964–1966, POL 32-1, Indonesia, Box 2325, NA.

74. Letter from M. Stewart to Sir B. Burrows, July 25, 1965, FO 371-181538, UKNA.

75. Memo from Ambassador Gilchrist to Mr. Peck in the Foreign Office, May 20, 1965, FO 817-180313, UKNA; Telegram 2679 from Commonwealth Relations Office to Canberra, October 12, 1965, FO 371-180175, UKNA.

76. Memo from the Deputy Director of the Office of Southwest Pacific Affairs (Mein) to the Assistant Secretary of State for Far Eastern Affairs, May 17, 1957, *FRUS, 1955–1957*, v. 22, 381–385.

77. Matthew Jones, *Conflict and Confrontation in Southeast Asia*, 128, 212, 227–228, 231, 263.

78. Telegram 1161 from State to Jakarta, April 15, 1964, RG 59, Central Files, 1964–1966, POL 23-9, Indonesia, Box 2317, NA.

79. Telegram 584 from Jakarta to State, November 25, 1965, RG 59, Central Files, 1964–1966, POL 32-1, Indonesia-Malaysia, NA.

80. The U.S. willingness to divide nations—whether Germany, Korea, Vietnam, or Indonesia—as a Cold War strategy and not as a response to conditions in individual nations is a topic worthy of further study.

81. Easter, "British and Malaysian Covert Support," 203; Airgram 1034 from Jakarta to State, May 8, 1964, RG 59, Central Files, 1964–1966, POL 12, Indonesia, NA.

82. Memo for Bundy, "The Week That Was," December 24, 1964, Thomson Papers, Box 11, JFKL.

83. Attachment to Memo from Chester Cooper to Bundy, March 13, 1965, *FRUS, 1964–1968*, v. 26, 250.

84. Bunker Report, Part 2, Recommendations, April 23, 1965, NSF, Indonesia, v. 4, LBJL.

85. Easter, "British and Malaysian Covert Support," 205.

86. "Foreign Investment Barred by Jakarta," *New York Times*, May 16, 1965.

87. Chinese Premier Zhou Enlai reportedly first raised the prospect of arming Indonesian peasants with Sukarno. Letter from Jakarta to Foreign Office, May 14, 1965, FO 371-180333, UKNA.

88. Telegram 72 from Jakarta to State, July 14, 1965, RG 59, Central Files, 1964–1966, AID (U.S.) 8-6, Indonesia, NA.

89. Telegram 2641 from Jakarta to State, June 5, 1965, *FRUS, 1964–1968*, v. 26, 267–269.

90. Office of Current Intelligence No. 0783/65, March 17, 1965, NSF, CO Files, Indonesia, Memos, v. 4, LBJL; Mortimer, *Indonesian Communism Under Sukarno*, 327; Aidit, "Dare, Dare, and Dare Again"; Aidit, "The Indonesian Revolution and the Immediate Tasks."

91. CIA Intelligence Cable 314/06624-65, May 14, 1965, NSF, CO Files, Indonesia, Memos, v. 4, LBJL.

92. Memo from D. Tonkin to Foreign Office, May 26, 1965, FO 817-180515, UKNA; Mozingo, *China's Policy Toward Indonesia*, 224.

93. KOSTRAD commander General Suharto played a key role in the army's smuggling operations in Northern Sumatra; Elson, *Suharto*, 88, 93.

94. Robison, *Indonesia*, 83–88; Telegram 447 from Jakarta to Foreign Office, February 25, 1965, FO 371-180311, UKNA.

95. Pauker, "Indonesia in 1964," 95.

96. Telegram 1520 from Kuala Lumpur to State, June 8, 1965; Telegram 1256 from Jakarta to State, June 12, 1965; and Telegram from State to Kuala Lumpur and

Jakarta, June 16, 1965, all in RG 59, Central Files, 1964–1966, POL 23-9, Indonesia, NA.

97. NIE 54/55-65, Prospects for Indonesia and Malaysia, July 1, 1965, NSF, NIES 54/55, Malaysia/Indonesia, Box 7, LBJL; CIA Intelligence Cable 314/06626-65, May 14, 1965, NSF, CO Files, Indonesia, Memos, v. 4, LBJL.

98. Green, *Indonesia*, 17–18.

99. Telegram 102 from State to Jakarta, July 30, 1965; and Telegram 188 from Jakarta to State, July 31, 1965, both in NSF, CO Files, Indonesia, v. 4, LBJL.

100. Memo from Director, Far Eastern Region (Blouin), to Assistant Secretary of Defense for International Security Affairs, August 3, 1965, *FRUS, 1964–1968*, v. 26, 275; Memo for Bundy from Thomson, August 3, 1965, Thomson Papers, Box 11–12, JFKL.

101. Memo for the Record, Meeting with Indonesian Ambassador Palar, August 12, 1965, NSF, Indonesia, v. 4, LBJL.

102. Telegram 264 from Jakarta to State, August 8, 1965, NSF, CO Files, Indonesia, v. 4, LBJL; Airgram A-242 from Jakarta to State, "A Comparison of Fear and Intimidation Levels in the Soviet Union and Indonesia," September 25, 1965, RG 59, Central Files, 1964–1966, POL 1, Indonesia, Box 2306, NA.

103. Telegram 353 from Jakarta to State, August 17, 1965, NSF, CO Files, Indonesia, v. 4, LBJL; "Jakarta Joining a Leftist 'Axis,'" *New York Times*, August 17, 1965.

104. Telegram 403 from Jakarta to State, August 23, 1965, NSF, CO Files, Indonesia, v. 4, LBJL.

105. Green, *Indonesia*, xi–xii.

106. SNIE 55-65, "Prospects for and Strategic Implications of a Communist Takeover in Indonesia," September 1, 1965, State Department, INR/EAP Files, Lot 90 D 165, SNIE 55-65, NA.

107. Mackie, *Konfrontasi*, 293–297.

108. Telegram 268 from Jakarta to State, August 9, 1965, RG 59, Central Files, 1964–1966, POL 16, Singapore, Box 2425, NA.

109. Telegram 606 from London to State, August 9, 1965, RG 59, Central Files, 1964–1966, DEF 1, U.K., Box 2325, NA; Telegram 159 from Kuala Lumpur to State, August 11, 1965, RG 59, Central Files, 1964–1966, POL 16, Singapore, Box 2325, NA.

110. Matthew Jones, *Conflict and Confrontation in Southeast Asia*, 275–277, 287–290; Subritzky, *Confronting Sukarno*, 160–162.

111. Matthew Jones, *Conflict and Confrontation in Southeast Asia*, 289.

112. Telegram 486 from Jakarta to State, September 1, 1965, *FRUS, 1964–1968*, v. 26, 292.

113. Telegram A-178, Joint Weekly no. 35, September 4, 1965; and Telegram A-197, Joint Weekly no. 36, September 11, 1965, both in RG 59, Central Files, 1964–1966, POL 2-1, Indonesia, NA.

114. Airgram A-242 from Jakarta to State, "A Comparison of Fear and Intimidation Levels in the Soviet Union and Indonesia," September 25, 1965, RG 59, Central Files, 1964–1966, POL 1, Indonesia, Box 2306, NA.

115. Airgram A-146 from Jakarta to State, "Urgent Need for Expanded Propaganda Program," August 25, 1965, RG 59, Central Files, 1964–1966, POL 1, Indonesia-U.S., NA.

116. Telegram 435 from State to Jakarta, September 10, 1965; and Memo of Conversation with Ambassador Palar, September 10, 1965, both in NSF, CO Files, Indonesia, v. 4, LBJL.

117. Unsigned Memo, "Possible Closure of U.S. Consulate in Surabaya," September 13, 1965; and attachment to Memo from Thomson to Bundy, September 16, 1965, both in Thomson Papers, Box 12, JFKL.

118. CIA Intelligence Cable 314/11666-65, August 27, 1965, NSF, CO Files, Indonesia, Memos, v. 4, LBJL.

119. Challis, *In the Shadow of the Generals*, 78–79.

120. Brands, "Limits of Manipulation," 801.

121. CIA information cable, TDCS 314/13575/65, October 2, 1965, NSF, CO Files, Indonesia, Memos, v. 5, LBJL.

CHAPTER 7

1. Memo for Johnson, October 1, 1965, *FRUS, 1964–1968*, v. 26, 300–301; Top Secret Telegram from the Political Adviser to CinCFE Singapore, October 1, 1965, FO 1011-2, UKNA.

2. Representative works include Holtzappel, "30 September Movement"; Central Intelligence Agency, *Indonesia—1965*; Hughes, *Indonesian Upheaval*; van der Kroef, "Interpretations of the 1965 Indonesian Coup"; Lev, "Indonesia 1965"; Peter Dale Scott, "The United States and the Overthrow of Sukarno"; May, *Indonesian Tragedy*; Elson, *Suharto*; and Wertheim, "Whose Plot?"

3. Westad, *Global Cold War*, 185; Telegram 868 from Jakarta to State, October 5, 1965, *FRUS, 1964–1968*, v. 26, 307.

4. Telegram 545 from State to Jakarta, October 29, 1965, RG 59, Central Files, 1964–1966, POL 23-9, Indonesia, NA.

5. "The Legacy of Violence in Indonesia," special edition of *Asian Survey* 42 (July–August 2002).

6. Anderson and McVey, *Preliminary Analysis of the October 1, 1965, Coup*; Brands, "Limits of Manipulation," 803; Tovar, "Sukarno's Apologists," 355; Gardner, *Shared Hopes, Separate Fears*, 202–240; Scott, "The United States and the Overthrow of Sukarno," 239–264; McGehee, "Indonesian Massacres and the CIA," 56–58; Robinson, *Dark Side of Paradise*, 280–286.

7. For a survey of recent literature see Cribb, "Unresolved Problems in the Indonesian Killings."

8. Roosa, *Pretext for Mass Murder*.

9. Colonel Latief, a September 30th Movement participant brought to trial only in 1978, insists that he told Suharto of the group's plans the night of September 30; "Latief: Suharto Knew Generals Would Be Murdered," *Agence France Presse*, May 24, 1998.

10. Crouch, *Army and Politics in Indonesia*, 97–101; CIA information cable, TDCS 314/13658/65, October 2, 1965, NSF, CO Files, Indonesia, v. 5, LBJL.

11. British officials guessed that, if legitimate, the editorial was an "ad hoc comment" and an "unauthorized comment" taken unilaterally by the editor; Memo from Gilchrist to Foreign Office, October 19, 1965, FO 371-180320, DH 1015/218, UKNA.

12. Telephone conversation between Ball and McNamara, October 1, 1965, Ball Papers, Box 4, Indonesia, April 1964–November 1965, LBJL; Telegram 800 from Jakarta to State, October 1, 1965, RG 59, Central Files, 1964–1966, POL 23-9, Indonesia, NA; Cabinet Joint Intelligence Committee, Special Assessment 796/65, Indonesia, October 4, 1965, PREM 13, 2718, UKNA. Two years later Australian officials were still unsure of the level of PKI involvement. See Memo from K. L. Wells to Secretary, Department of External Affairs, "30th of September 1965 Coup," October, 4, 1967, Series A1838/2, Item 3034/2/1/8 Pt. 15A, Indonesia—Coup d'Etat—1965 Folder, National Archives of Australia.

13. CIA Intel Memo OCI 2329/65, October 2, 1965, NSF, CO Files, Indonesia, Memos, v. 5, LBJL; Elson, *Suharto*, 80–92.

14. Jakarta teleconference with the State Department, October 2, 1965; and Memo from Francis Underhill to William Bundy, October 1, 1965, both in NSF, CO Files, Indonesia, v. 5, LBJL.

15. Telephone conversation between Ball and Richard Helms, October 1, 1965, *FRUS, 1964–1968*, v. 26, 300–301; Telephone conversation between Ball and Robert McCloskey, October 1, 1965, Ball Papers, Box 4, Indonesia, April 1964–November 1965, LBJL.

16. Telephone conversation between Ball and McNamara, October 1, 1965, Ball Papers, Box 4, Indonesia, April 1964–November 1965, LBJL; Gardner, *Shared Hopes, Separate Fears*, 215.

17. C. L. Sulzberger, "Foreign Affairs: When a Nation Runs Amok," *New York Times*, April 13, 1966; "Indonesia: Night of Terror, Dawn of Hope," *Readers Digest*, October 1966.

18. Wieringa, "Birth of the New Order State." Accounts repeating the army's propaganda claims include Brackman, *Communist Collapse in Indonesia*, 79; Hughes, *Indonesian Upheaval*, 43–57; and Gardner, *Shared Hopes, Separate Fears*, 221.

19. Anderson, "How Did the Generals Die?"

20. Crouch, *Army and Politics in Indonesia*, 138–139.

21. CIA Intel Memo OCI 2940/65, November 8, 1965, NSF, CO Files, Indonesia, Memos, v. 6, LBJL.

22. Telegram 2134 from Jakarta to Foreign Office, October 13, 1965, FO 371-180318, UKNA.

23. Bunnell, "American 'Low-Posture' Policy Toward Indonesia," 59. Military attaché Willis Ethel and Deputy CIA Station Chief Joe Lazarsky met on a near daily basis with aides of General Nasution and, apparently, Suharto as well.

24. Telegram 812 from Jakarta to State, October 2, 1965; Telegram 858 from Jakarta to State, October 5, 1965; and CIA Intel Memo OCI 2330/65, "The Up-

heaval in Indonesia," October 3, 1965, all in NSF, CO Files, Indonesia, v. 5, Memos, October–November 1965, LBJL.

25. Telephone conversation between Ball and James Reston, October 4, 1965, Ball Papers, Box 4, Indonesia, April 1964–November 1965, LBJL.

26. Telegram 671 from Singapore to Foreign Office, October 5, 1965, FO 371-180313, UKNA; CIA Intel Memo OCI 12857, October 6, 1965, NSF, CO Files, Indonesia, v. 5, LBJL.

27. Telegram 264 from the Political Adviser to CinCFE Singapore, October 5, 1965, FO 1011-2, UKNA; Telegram 858 from Jakarta to State, October 5, 1965, NSF, CO Files, Indonesia, v. 5, LBJL.

28. Telegram 400 from State to Jakarta, October 6, 1965, RG 59, Central Files, 1964–1966, POL 23-9, Indonesia, NA.

29. Telegram 868 from Jakarta to State, October 5, 1965; and Telegram 851 from Jakarta to State, October 5, 1965, both in RG 59, Central Files, 1964–1966, POL 23-9, Indonesia, NA; Ralph McGehee, "The CIA and the White Paper on El Salvador," *The Nation*, April 11, 1981.

30. Lashmar and Oliver, *Britain's Secret Propaganda War*, 1–10; Easter, "British Intelligence and Propaganda," passim; Challis, *Shadow of a Revolution*.

31. Top Secret Telegram from the Political Adviser to CinCFE Singapore, October 1, 1965, FO 1011-2, UKNA.

32. Memo for the Minister for External Affairs, "The Indonesian Situation," October 12, 1965, Series A1838/280, Item 3034/2/I/8/Pt. 2, Indonesia—Political—Coup d'Etat of October 1965, National Archives of Australia.

33. Telegram 1835 from Foreign Office to POLAD Singapore, October 6, 1965, FO 1011-2, UKNA.

34. Easter, "British Intelligence and Propaganda," 90–99. Ian Stewart, of the *New York Times*, writing from Singapore, cited "Western sources" who claimed that Sukarno "not only knew about the coup but was one of its prime movers" (Stewart, "Sukarno Seen Behind Coup," *New York Times*, October 5, 1965). Seth King cited "informed sources in Bangkok," speaking on "information reaching them through private channels" in Jakarta (King, "Indonesian Army Battles Rebels in Key Java City," *New York Times*, October 7, 1965).

35. Telegram 1835 from Foreign Office to POLAD Singapore, October 6, 1965, FO 1011-2, UKNA; Telegram 400 from State to Jakarta, October 6, 1965, NSF, CO Files, Indonesia, v. 5, LBJL; CIA Memo on Covert Assistance to Indonesian Armed Forces Leaders, November 9, 1965, *FRUS, 1964–1968*, v. 26, 361.

36. Letter from British Embassy in Washington to Southeast Asia Department of the Foreign Office, October 5, 1965, Indonesia subseries of FO 371 (DH) 1015.163, UKNA; Action Telegram 405 from State to Jakarta, October 6, 1965, RG 59, Central Files, 1965–1966, POL 23-8, Indonesia, NA; Letter from British Embassy in Washington to Southeast Asia Department of the Foreign Office, October 5, 1965, DH 1015.163, UKNA.

37. Memo, "Getting at Nasution," December 24, 1965, FO 1011-8, UKNA.

38. Cottle and Najjarine, "Department of External Affairs."

39. McGehee, "Indonesian Massacres and the CIA," 58; Foreign Broadcast Information Service (FBIS), "Counterrevolutionary Documents Uncovered," October 25, 1965, 12–13; Telegram 1086 from Jakarta to State, October 19, 1965, NSF, CO Files, Indonesia, v. 5, LBJL; Telegram 740 from Hong Kong to State, October 27, 1965, RG 59, Central Files, 1964–1966, XR POL 23-9, Indonesia, NA; Gardner, *Shared Hopes, Separate Fears*, 219.

40. Telegram 903 from Jakarta to State, October 7, 1965, RG 59, Central Files, 1964–1966, XR POL 23-9, Indonesia, NA.

41. Telegram from Jakarta to State, October 10, 1965, RG 59, Central Files, 1964–1966, POL, Indonesia-U.K., NA.

42. Letter from British Embassy in Washington to Southeast Asia Department of the Foreign Office, October 5, 1965, DH 1015.163, UKNA.

43. Telegram 678 from Singapore to Foreign Office, October 7, 1965, DH 1015/186/G, FO 371-180318, UKNA; Letter from J. E. Cable to U.K. Delegation to NATO, November 11, 1965, FO 371-180323, UKNA.

44. Top Secret Telegram 8775 from Foreign Office to Washington, "Short Term Policy Towards Indonesia," November 5, 1965, PREM 13, 2718, UKNA; Telegram 2314 from Jakarta to Foreign Office, October 25, 1965, FO 371-181519, UKNA; Telegram 8102 from Foreign Office to Washington, October 16, 1965, FO 377-180317, UKNA.

45. Letter from British Embassy Jakarta to Foreign Office, November 25, 1965, FO 371-181323, UKNA; CIA, OCI 13185, October 8, 1965, NSF, CO Files, Indonesia, v. 5, LBJL.

46. Telegram 910 from Jakarta to State, October 8, 1965, RG 59, Central Files, 1964–1966, POL 23-9, Indonesia, NA.

47. Sukarno, quoted in Roosa, *Pretext for Mass* Murder, 243; Michael van Langenberg, "Gestapu and State Power," and Robert Cribb, "Introduction," both in Cribb, ed., *Indonesian Killings of 1965–1966*, 29, 35, 47–49.

48. Telegram 1863 from Foreign Office to POLAD Singapore, October 9, 1965, FO 1011-2, UKNA.

49. Airgram A-82 from Jakarta to State, August 17, 1966, RG 59, Central Files, 1964–1966, POL 23-9, Indonesia, NA.

50. Crouch, *Army and Politics in Indonesia*, 142–148.

51. Telegram 452 from State to Jakarta, October 13, 1965, NSF, CO Files, Indonesia, v. 5, LBJL.

52. Telegram 400 from State to Jakarta, October 6, 1965, NSF, CO Files, Indonesia, v. 5, LBJL.

53. Telegram 971 from Jakarta to State, October 12, 1965, RG 59, Central Files, 1964–1966, POL 23-9, Indonesia, NA.

54. Telegram from Jakarta to State, October 14, 1965, RG 59, Central Files, 1964–1966, DEF 21, Indonesia, NA; Memo from David Cuthell to William Bundy, November 3, 1965, *FRUS, 1964–1968*, v. 26, 348–351.

55. Telegram 470 from State to Jakarta, October 14, 1965, NSF, CO Files, Indonesia, v. 5, LBJL; Telegram 508 from State to Jakarta, October 22, 1965, *FRUS, 1964–1968*, v. 26, 330–331.

56. Cablegram 832 from Australian Embassy Tokyo to Canberra, October 26, 1965, Series A1838/280, Item 3034/2/I/8/Pt. 3, Indonesia—Political—Coup d'Etat of October 1965, National Archives of Australia.

57. Saito, quoted in Telegram 1238 from Jakarta to State, October 28, 1965, RG 59, Central Files, 1964–1966, AID 1, Indonesia, NA; Welfield, *Empire in Eclipse*, 219; Saito, quoted in Telegram 2543 from Jakarta to Foreign Office, October 27, 1965, FO 371-181519, UKNA; Quadripartite Discussions on Indonesia, Brief for Australian Delegation, no date, Series A1838/280, Item 3034/2/I/8/Pt. 2, Indonesia—Political—Coup d'Etat of October 1965, National Archives of Australia.

58. Telegram 526 from Kuala Lumpur to POLAD Singapore, October 8, 1965, FO 1011-2, UKNA; Telegram 1304 from Jakarta to State, November 2, 1965, NSF, CO Files, Indonesia, v. 5, LBJL; Telegram 1623 from Tokyo to State, November 4, 1965, RG 59, Central Files, 1964–1966, POL 23-9, Indonesia, NA.

59. CIA Information Cable, OCI 13114, October 17, 1965, NSF, CO Files, Indonesia, v. 5, LBJL; Telegram 1047 from Jakarta to State, October 17, 1965, RG 59, Central Files, 1964–1966, POL 23-9, Indonesia, NA.

60. Telegram 1090 from Jakarta to State, October 20, 1965, RG 59, Central Files, 1964–1966, POL 12, Indonesia, NA.

61. Telegram 1195 from Jakarta to State, October 25, 1965, RG 59, Central Files, 1964–1966, POL 23-9, Indonesia, NA.

62. Telegram 1171 from Jakarta to State, October 23, 1965; and Telegram 1166 from Jakarta to State, October 23, 1965, both in NSF, CO Files, Indonesia, v. 5, LBJL; Australian Embassy, Jakarta Memo of Conversation with Mr. J. S. Hadie, October 13, 1965, Series A1838/280, Item 3034/2/I/8/Pt. 2, Indonesia—Political—Coup d'Etat of October 1965, National Archives of Australia; Telegram 1182 from Jakarta to State, October 25, 1965, RG 59, Central Files, 1964–1966, POL 23-9, Indonesia, NA.

63. Telegram 1228 from Jakarta to State, October 28, 1965, NSF, CO Files, Indonesia, v. 5, LBJL.

64. Telegram 545 from State to Jakarta, October 29, 1965, *FRUS, 1964–1968*, v. 26, 340–343.

65. Telegram 545 from State to Jakarta, October 29, 1965, *FRUS, 1964–1968*, v. 26, 340–343.

66. See Editorial Note, *FRUS, 1964–1968*, v. 26, 338–340.

67. Telegram 1215 from Jakarta to State, October 26, 1965, NSF, CO Files, Indonesia, v. 5, LBJL.

68. Telegram 1255 from Jakarta to State, October 28, 1965, RG 59, Central Files, 1964–1966, POL 23-9, Indonesia, NA.

69. Memo from Assistant for Indonesia to Deputy Assistant Secretary of Defense for ISA, October 30, 1965, *FRUS, 1964–1968*, v. 26, 343–345; Telegram 1288 from

Jakarta to State, November 1, 1965, RG 59, Central Files, 1964–1966, POL 23-9, Indonesia, NA.

70. Telegram 1304 from Jakarta to State, November 2, 1965, NSF, CO Files, Indonesia, v. 5, LBJL; Memo from Assistant for Indonesia to Deputy Assistant Secretary of Defense for ISA, October 30, 1965, *FRUS, 1964–1968*, v. 26, 351–353.

71. Telegram 1326 from Jakarta to State, November 4, 1965, RG 59, Central Files, 1964–1966, POL 23-9, Indonesia, NA.

72. Dean Rusk, for example, emphasized to Galbraith the need for a political channel with the army "as distinct from Indonesian Government"; Telegram 562 from State to Jakarta, November 1, 1965, RG 59, Central Files, 1964–1966, POL 23-9, Indonesia, NA.

73. Bunnell, "American 'Low Posture' Policy Toward Indonesia," 59; Telegram 2536 from Jakarta to Foreign Office, November 14, 1965, FO 371-181519, UKNA.

74. Telegram 920 from Jakarta to State, November 5, 1965, NSF, CO Files, Indonesia, v. 5, LBJL; Memo for the 303 Committee, November 17, 1965, *FRUS, 1964–1968*, v. 26, 367–371; Letter from M. H. Clapham to the Secretary, Department of External Affairs, "Arms Given to KAMI," June 24, 1966, Cablegram, Series A1838/2, Item 3034/2/1/8 Pt. 15, Indonesia—Political Coup 30-9-65 Folder, National Archives of Australia.

75. Telegram 951 from Bangkok to State, November 11, 1965, RG 59, Central Files, 1964–1966, POL 23-9, Indonesia, NA.

76. Telegram 1427 from Jakarta to State, November 12, 1965, RG 59, Central Files, 1964–1966, POL, Indonesia-U.S., NA.

77. Memo for the 303 Committee, November 17, 1965, *FRUS, 1964–1968*, v. 26, 367–371.

78. Top Secret Memo from the British Embassy in Washington to the Foreign Office, January 4, 1966, FO 371-187583, UKNA; Telegram 2536 from Jakarta to Foreign Office, November 14, 1965, FO 371-181519, UKNA.

79. Kathy Kadane, letter to Editor, *New York Review of Books*, April 10, 1997; "Ex-Agents Say CIA Compiled Death Lists for Indonesians," *States News Service*, May 19, 1990. The scant CIA documents that have thus far been released are consistent with Kadane's claims that the CIA set Indonesian army radio frequencies in advance for the purposes of gathering intelligence.

80. CIA, OCI 12857, October 5, 1965; and Indonesian Working Group, Situation Report 10, October 6, 1965, both in NSF, CO Files, Indonesia, v. 5, LBJL.

81. Telegram 545 from State to Jakarta, October 29, 1965, *FRUS, 1964–1968*, v. 26, 340–343; Telegram 1255 from Jakarta to State, October 28, 1965, RG 59, Central Files, 1964–1966, POL 23-9, Indonesia, NA.

82. Telegram 1326 from Jakarta to State, November 4, 1965, RG 59, Central Files, 1964–1966, POL 23-9, Indonesia, NA.

83. Telegram 1374 from Jakarta to State, November 8, 1965, NSF, CO Files, Indonesia, v. 5, LBJL; Telegram 1401 from Jakarta to State, November 10, 1965, RG 59, Central Files, 1964–1966, POL 23-9, Indonesia, NA.

84. Telegram 1438 from Jakarta to State, November 13, 1965; and Telegram 65 from Consulate in Medan to State, November 16, 1965, both in RG 59, Central Files, 1964–1966, POL 23-9, Indonesia, NA.

85. CIA Intel Memo, OCI 2943/65, "Indonesian Army Attitudes Toward Communism," November 22, 1965, NSF, CO Files, Indonesia, v. 6, LBJL; Telegram 41 from Surabaya to State, November 27, 1965, RG 59, Central Files, 1964–1966, POL 23-8, Indonesia, NA; Telegram 32 from Surabaya to State, November 14, 1965, NSF, CO Files, Indonesia, v. 5, LBJL.

86. "Report from East Java," *Indonesia* 41 (April 1986), 145–146; see also Sulistyo, "The Forgotten Years," 188–214.

87. Quoted in Brands, "Limits of Manipulation," 803; see also Tovar, "Sukarno's Apologists," 355; Gardner, *Shared Hopes, Separate Fears*, 230–233.

88. "Protest Awaited on Murder of Communists," letter to Editor, *New York Times*, January 17, 1966; "Our 'Anti-Communism,'" letter to Editor, *New York Times*, March 27, 1966; "Indonesia's Purge," letter to Editor, *New York Times*, May 22, 1966; "Indonesia's Genocide," letter to Editor, *New York Times*, June 19, 1966.

89. Memo with attachment from Rostow to Johnson, June 8, 1966, NSF, CO Files, Indonesia, v. 7, May 1966–June 1967, LBJL.

90. Telegram 1401 from Jakarta to State, November 10, 1965, RG 59, Central Files, 1964–1966, POL 23-9, Indonesia, NA; Confidential Memo from H. S. H. Stanley, October 13, 1965, FO 371-181455-1, UKNA.

91. Memo prepared in the CIA, November 9, 1965, *FRUS, 1964–1968*, v. 26, 361–363; Federspiel, quoted in Kadane, "Ex-Agents Say CIA Compiled Death Lists for Indonesians," *States News Service*, May 19, 1990. In a letter to biographer Kai Bird, William Bundy wrote, "I don't suppose that certain people would forgive what we did, but I thought that it was eminently justified" (Bird, *Color of Truth*, 353).

92. Memo for Mr. Bundy from Chet Cooper, October 16, 1965, NSF, Name File, Box 2, Chet Cooper Folder, LBJL; Telegram 2328 from Jakarta to Foreign Office, December 23, 1965, FO 371-180334, UKNA; Letter from British Embassy Moscow to Foreign Office, November 12, 1965, FO 371-180334, UKNA.

93. In interviews with Bunnell in 1981–1982, Sukendro confirmed that the CIA station in Bangkok did deliver the small arms; Bunnell, "American 'Low Posture' Policy Toward Indonesia," 59.

94. Telegram 1628 from Jakarta to State, December 2, 1965, *FRUS, 1964–1968*, v. 26, 379–380.

95. Telegram 931 from Jakarta to State, January 13, 1966, NSF, Komer Series, November 1963–March 1966, LBJL. Kern, primarily concerned with the health of the Japanese economy, later came to Jakarta for discussions with Indonesian officials on increasing oil exports to Tokyo; Indonesia Bi-Weekly Economic Summary, March 18–31, 1967, RG 59, Subject Numeric Files (SNF), 1967–1969, E 2-2, Indonesia, NA.

96. Telegram 1651 from Jakarta to State, December 4, 1965, RG 59, Central Files, 1964–1966, POL 23-9, Indonesia, NA.

97. CIA officials helped their Guatemalan intelligence counterparts compile similar lists (of more than 70,000 people), and for similar purposes, after the U.S.-sponsored overthrow of the Arbenz regime in 1954. See Streeter, *Managing the Counterrevolution*, 38–41.

98. Airgram A-74 from Jakarta to State, August 10, 1966, RG 59, Central Files, 1964–1966, POL 12, Indonesia, NA.

99. Kadane, "Ex-Agents Say CIA Compiled Death Lists for Indonesians"; Michael Wines, "CIA Ties Asserted in Indonesia Purge," *New York Times*, July 12, 1990; Stephen Rosenfeld, editorial, *Washington Post*, July 12, 1990; Robert Barnett note to Green, Green Papers, Box 15, HI; Robert Martens, unpublished manuscript, Green Papers, Box 15, HI.

100. "CIA and Guatemala Assassination Proposals, 1952–1954," CIA History Staff Analysis by Gerald K. Haines, June 1995; "Guatemalan Communist Personnel to Be Disposed of During Military Operations of Calligeris," origin deleted, undated (available at http://www.gwu.edu/~nsarchiv/NSAEBB/ NSAEBB4/index.html); on Iraq see Roger Morris, "A Tyrant 40 Years in the Making," *New York Times*, March 14, 2003.

101. See Young, "Local and National Influences in the Violence of 1965," 63–101 and passim; on Bali see Robinson, *Dark Side of Paradise*, 273–304; Hefner, *Political Economy of Mountain Java*; Sudjatmiko, "Destruction of the Indonesian Communist Party"; Sulistyo, "Forgotten Years."

102. Letter from British Embassy Jakarta to Foreign Office, December 16, 1965, FO 371-181323, UKNA.

103. Cribb, *Indonesian Killings of 1965–1966*, 6; Cribb, "Unresolved Problems in the Indonesian Killings," 550–564.

104. See Airgram A-512 from Jakarta to State, February 11, 1966, RG 59, Central Files, 1964–1966, DEF 6, Indonesia, NA; Dispatch from Medan to Foreign Office, January 3, 1966, FO 371-186027, UKNA; Letter from British Consulate Medan to Jakarta, January 3, 1966, FO 371-186026, UKNA.

105. Letter from British Consulate Medan to Jakarta, December 14, 1965, FO 371-180333, UKNA; Guidance no. 26 from Foreign Office and Commonwealth Relations Office to Certain Missions, January 18, 1966, FO 371-186027, UKNA.

106. Draft, "Indonesia Internal Situation," undated, Series A1838/2, Item 3034/2/1/8/Pt. 15, Indonesia—Political Coup 30-9-65 Folder, National Archives of Australia.

107. See Cribb, *Indonesian Killings of 1965–1966*, 12 and 1–45, for a nuanced and detailed discussion of the historiography of the massacres.

108. Memo from Foreign Office and Commonwealth Relations Office to Certain Missions, January 18, 1966, DH 1015/280, FO 371-180024, UKNA; Letter from James Murray, Embassy Jakarta, to Foreign Office, January 13, 1966, FO 871-180325, UKNA; Memo 1011/66 from James Murray to A. J. de la Mare, January 13, 1966, FO 371-186027, UKNA.

109. Telegram 2347 from Jakarta to State, February 21, 1966, RG 59, Central Files, 1964–1966, POL 23-9, Indonesia, NA; Letter from British Embassy in Jakarta to Foreign Office, February 23, 1966, DH 1015/80, FO 371-186028, UKNA.

110. Memo from Rostow to Johnson, June 8, 1966, NSF, CO Files, Indonesia, v. 7, May 1966–June 1967, LBJL.

111. Airgram A-641 from Jakarta to State, April 15, 1966, RG 59, Central Files, 1964–1966, POL 2, Indonesia, NA.

112. CIA Intel Memo, OCI 2943/65, "Indonesian Army Attitudes Toward Communism," November 22, 1965, NSF, CO Files, Indonesia, v. 6, LBJL; Crouch, *Army and Politics in Indonesia*, 152–155.

113. Airgram A-263, December 24, 1966, NSF, CO Files, Indonesia, Box 248, Indonesia Cables, v. 6, November 1965–May 1966, LBJL; C. L. Sulzberger, "When a Nation Runs Amok," *New York Times*, April 13, 1966, 40.

114. Memo of Conversation, February 14, 1966, RG 59, Central Files, 1964–1966, POL 2, Indonesia, NA. Cribb ("Unresolved Problems in the Indonesian Killings"), argues that there is no evidence that Washington's assistance led to greater levels of killing.

115. Gardner, *Shared Hopes, Separate Fears*, 227; Green, *Indonesia*, 69; Tovar and Collins, "Sukarno's Apologists," 356; Tovar, "Indonesian Crisis of 1965–1966."

116. McMahon, *Limits of Empire*, 123–124; Brands, *Wages of Globalism*, 176; Subritzky, *Confronting Sukarno*, 176; exceptions include Bunnell, "American 'Low Posture' Policy Toward Indonesia," 58–60; and Bird, *Color of Truth*, 352–354.

117. "Vengeance with a Smile," *Time*, July 15, 1966; C. L. Sulzberger, "Foreign Affairs: When a Nation Runs Amok," *New York Times*, April 13, 1966.

118. Telegram 1304 from Jakarta to State, November 2, 1965, NSF, CO Files, Indonesia, v. 5, LBJL.

119. Telegram 1495 from Jakarta to State, November 18, 1965, RG 59, Central Files, 1964–1966, POL 23-9, Indonesia, NA.

120. Telegram 1843 from Jakarta to State, December 22, 1965, *FRUS, 1964–1968*, v. 26, 388–390; Short-Term Policy Toward Indonesia, Summary of Pointers from Discussions on December 1–2, 1965, Amongst Australian, British, New Zealand, and U.S. Officials, undated, Harriman Papers, Box 451, Library of Congress.

121. Memo from David Cuthell to William Bundy, November 3, 1965, *FRUS, 1964–1968*, v. 26, 348–351.

122. Memo from Bundy and Rostow to Ball, October 2, 1965, RG 59, PPS Subject and CO Files, 1965–1969, Box 319, NA.

123. Telegram 1497 from State to Tokyo, November 19, 1965, RG 59, Central Files, 1964–1966, POL 23-9, Indonesia, NA.

124. Letter to Rusk, November 3, 1965, RG 59, Central Files, 1964–1966, INCO, Indonesia, Cotton, NA; Letter from Harry McPherson, Special Assistant to President, to Arthur Stehling of Security State Bank and Trust, October 22, 1965, White House Confidential Files, TA 4/CO 122, Box 91, LBJL; Meeting at State with Thomas Coyne of Southwest International Trading Company in Amarillo, November 3, 1965, RG 59, Central Files, 1964–1966, INCO-Cotton 17, Indonesia-U.S., NA.

125. Memo for the Minister, "The Rice Position in Indonesia," October 25, 1965, Series A1838/280, Item 3034/2/I/8/Pt. 3, Indonesia—Political—Coup d'Etat of October 1965, National Archives of Australia.

126. Telegram 1113 from Jakarta to State, October 22, 1965; and Telegram 741 from State to Jakarta, December 8, 1965, both in RG 59, Central Files, 1964–1966, POL 23-9, Indonesia, NA; Memo from Director of the Far East Region (Blouin) to Deputy Assistant Secretary of Defense for ISA (Friedman), December 13, 1965, *FRUS, 1964–1968*, v. 26, 383–385.

127. Telegram 926 from Jakarta to State, October 8, 1965; and Telegram 433 from State to Jakarta, October 9, 1965, both in NSF, CO Files, Indonesia, v. 5, LBJL; Second meeting of the Indonesia Working Group, November 4, 1965, *FRUS, 1964–1968*, v. 26, 351–353.

128. Telegram 1712 from Jakarta to State, December 10, 1965, RG 59, Central Files, 1964–1966, POL 23-9, Indonesia, NA.

129. Top Secret Telegram 9645 from Foreign Office to Washington, "Short Term Policy Towards Indonesia," December 3, 1965, PREM 13, 2718, UKNA; Telegram 562 from State to Jakarta, November 1, 1965, RG 59, Central Files, 1964–1966, POL 23-9, Indonesia, NA; Quadripartite Discussions on Indonesia, Brief for Australian Delegation, no date, Series A1838/280, Item 3034/2/I/8/Pt. 2, Indonesia—Political—Coup d'Etat of October 1965, National Archives of Australia.

130. Airgram A-317 from Jakarta to State, November 9, 1965, RG 59, Central Files, 1964–1966, AID (U.S.), Indonesia, NA.

131. Telegram 741 from State to Jakarta, December 8, 1965; and Telegram 1605 from Jakarta to State, December 1, 1965, both in RG 59, Central Files, 1964–1966, POL 23-9, Indonesia, NA.

132. Australian Embassy Jakarta, Record of Conversation with Dr. Pang Lay Kim, October 14, 1965, Series A1838/280, Item 3034/2/I/8/Pt. 2, Indonesia—Political—Coup d'Etat of October 1965, National Archives of Australia.

133. Telegram 1509 from Jakarta to State, November 19, 1965, NSF, CO Files, Indonesia, v. 5, LBJL; Telegram 1542 from Jakarta to State, November 23, 1965, RG 59, Central Files, 1964–1966, POL 23-9, Indonesia, NA.

134. Gabriel Kolko is alone in appreciating the significance of this issue to U.S. policymakers in late 1965; Kolko, *Confronting the Third World*, 182–183.

135. Telegram 696 from Jakarta to State, September 20, 1965; and Telegram 538 from State to Jakarta, October 23, 1965, both in RG 59, Central Files, 1964–1966, PET 15-2, Indonesia, NA; Aden, "Oil and Politics in Indonesia," 279–290.

136. Telegram 1271 from Jakarta to State, October 30, 1965, NSF, CO Files, Indonesia, v. 5, LBJL; Telegram 1358 from Jakarta to State, November 6, 1965, RG 59, Central Files, 1964–1966, PET 15-2, Indonesia, NA; Aden, "Oil and Politics in Indonesia," 274.

137. Telegram 546 from State to Jakarta, October 29, 1965, RG 59, Central Files, 1964–1966, PET 15-2, Indonesia, NA.

138. Telegram 1687 from Jakarta to State, December 8, 1965, RG 59, Central Files, 1964–1966, PET 15-2, Indonesia, NA.

139. Telegram 1401 from Jakarta to State, November 10, 1965, RG 59, Central Files, 1964–1966, POL 23-9, Indonesia, NA; Telegram 1509 from Jakarta to State, November 19, 1965, NSF, CO Files, Indonesia, v. 5, LBJL.

140. Telegram 545 from State to Jakarta, October 29, 1965, RG 59, Central Files, 1964–1966, POL 23-9, Indonesia, NA.

141. Telegram 1687 from Jakarta to State, December 8, 1965; and Memo from David Cuthell to Richard Barnett, November 5, 1965, both in RG 59, Central Files, 1964–1966, POL 23-9, Indonesia, NA.

142. Memo for the President from Ball—Items for evening reading, December 10, 1965, WHCF, Indonesia, Box 110, LBJL; Telegram 1642 from Jakarta to State, December 3, 1965; and Telegram 750 from State to Jakarta, December 11, 1965, both in RG 59, Central Files, 1964–1966, PET 15-2, Indonesia, NA.

143. Telegram 1720 from Jakarta to State, December 10, 1965, RG 59, Central Files, 1964–1966, PET 15-2, Indonesia, NA.

144. Telegram 1787 from Jakarta to State, December 16, 1965, RG 59, Central Files, 1964–1966, PET 15-2, Indonesia, NA.

145. CIA, OCI 0481/66, "The Changed Political Situation in Indonesia," January 3, 1966, NSF, CO Files, Indonesia, v. 6, LBJL. PKI chairman Aidit had been captured and summarily executed in Central Java on November 22.

146. Telegram 2204 from Jakarta to State, February 2, 1966, RG 59, Central Files, 1964–1966, POL 23-9, Indonesia, NA.

147. Memo from Foreign Office and Commonwealth Relations Office to Certain Missions, January 18, 1965, DH 1015/280, FO 371-180024, UKNA; Memo from H. S. H. Stanley of Joint Malaysian/Indonesian Department, January 7, 1966, FO 371-181519, UKNA.

148. Telegram 2204 from Jakarta to State, February 2, 1966, RG 59, Central Files, 1964–1966, POL 23-9, Indonesia, NA.

149. Telegram 1451 from State to Bangkok, February 15, 1966, RG 59, Central Files, 1964–1966, INCO-RICE 17, Indonesia-Thailand, NA.

150. Telegram 2092 from Jakarta to State, January 19, 1966, *FRUS, 1964–1968*, v. 26, 393; Telegram 2022 from Jakarta to State, January 12, 1965, RG 59, Central Files, 1964–1966, POL 23-9, Indonesia, NA.

151. Crouch, *Army and Politics in Indonesia*, 167–170.

152. CIA, OCI 0494/66, "Paralysis in Indonesia," February 6, 1966, NSF, CO Files, Indonesia, v. 6, LBJL.

153. Memo from Komer to Johnson, February 15, 1966; and Briefing Notes for Johnson, February 15, 1966, both in Robert W. Komer Files, Indonesia, November 1963–March 1966, LBJL; Telegram 604 from Canberra to State, February 18, 1966, RG 59, Central Files, 1964–1966, INCO-RICE 17, Indonesia-Thailand, NA.

154. Memo of Conversation with Secretary Rusk, February 14, 1966, RG 59, Central Files, 1964–1966, POL 2, Indonesia, NA; Memo of Conversation with the President, February 15, 1966, RG 59, Central Files, 1964–1966, POL, Indonesia-U.S., NA.

155. Memo from Bundy and Chester Cooper to Johnson, February 21, 1966, NSF, CO Files, Indonesia, v. 6, LBJL; Telegram 595 from Singapore to State, March 17, 1966, RG 59, Central Files, 1964–1966, POL 15-1, Indonesia, NA.

156. Elson, *Suharto*, 133.

157. Crouch, *Army and Politics in Indonesia*, 180.

158. Memo from Bundy and Chester Cooper to Johnson, February 21, 1966, NSF, CO Files, Indonesia, v. 6, LBJL.

159. Airgram A-528 Biweekly Economic Review, February 22, 1966, RG 59, Central Files, 1964–1966, E 2-2, Indonesia, NA.

160. Telegram 2370 from Jakarta to State, February 23, 1966, RG 59, Central Files, 1964–1966, POL 23-9, Indonesia, NA; Letter from Murray in Jakarta to Foreign Office, November 9, 1965; and Telegram 2515 from Jakarta to State, March 9, 1966, both in FO 371-181519, UKNA.

161. Memo from J. O. Moreton to Minister of State, February 16, 1966; and Telegram 235 from Jakarta to Foreign Office, February 10, 1966, both in DO 169 416, UKNA.

162. Telegram 88 from Medan to State, February 14, 1966, RG 59, Central Files, 1964–1966, DEF 6, Indonesia, NA.

163. Telegram 2255 from Jakarta to State, February 6, 1966; and Memo from David Cuthell to Samuel Berger, March 28, 1966, both in RG 59, Central Files, 1964–1966, PET 15-2, Indonesia, NA.

164. Telegram 2469 from Jakarta to State, March 4, 1966; and Telegram 2515 from Jakarta to State, March 9, 1966, both in RG 59, Central Files, 1964–1966, POL 23-9, Indonesia, NA.

165. Telegram 2536 from Jakarta to State, March 10, 1966, RG 59, Central Files, 1964–1966, POL 23-9, Indonesia, NA.

166. "General Denies Report on Sukarno Hand Over of Power to Suharto," *Agence France Presse*, September 4, 1999.

167. Elson, *Suharto*, 138; Crouch, *Army and Politics in Indonesia*, 192.

168. "Indonesian Army Told to Wipe Out Communist Party," *New York Times*, March 14, 1966; "Indonesian Reds Are Still Slain Despite the Ouster of Sukarno," *New York Times*, March 15, 1966; Airgram A-641 from Jakarta to State, April 15, 1966, RG 59, Central Files, 1964–1966, POL 2, Indonesia, NA; Airgram A-512 from Jakarta to State, February 11, 1966, RG 59, Central Files, 1964–1966, DEF 6, Indonesia, NA.

169. Telegram 2682 from Jakarta to State, March 19, 1966, RG 59, Central Files, 1964–1966, AID 1, Indonesia, NA; Letter from Hugh Tovar to Guy Pauker, March 28, 1966, Pauker Papers, Box 1, Correspondence, HI.

170. Memo for the President from White House Situation Room, March 11, 1966, NSF, CO Files, Indonesia, v. 6, Memos, November 1965–May 1966, LBJL; Memo from Komer to Johnson, March 12, 1966, NSF Memos to President, Bundy Papers, v. 21, LBJL.

171. Telegram 1173 from Jakarta to State, March 17, 1966, RG 59, Central Files, 1964–1966, AID (U.S.), Indonesia, NA.

172. "Economists with Guns," *The Economist*, March 19, 1966.

CHAPTER 8

1. Telegram 1182 from State to Jakarta, March 22, 1966, RG 59, Central Files, 1964–1966, POL 1, Indonesia, NA.

2. Telegram 2704 from Jakarta to State, March 23, 1966, RG 59, Central Files, 1964–1966, FN 1-1, Indonesia, NA.

3. William P. Bundy Oral History, LBJL.

4. Gilman, *Mandarins of the Future*, 199.

5. Telegram 2007 from Jakarta to State, October 27, 1966, RG 59, Central Files, 1964–1966, DEF 19, U.S.-Indonesia, NA.

6. Telegram 1173 from Jakarta to State, March 17, 1966, RG 59, Central Files, 1964–1966, AID (U.S.), Indonesia, NA.

7. Memo from Bundy and Rostow to Ball, October 2, 1965, RG 59, PPS Subject and CO Files, 1965–1969, Box 319, NA.

8. "A Contingency Plan for Rescue, Stabilization, and Rehabilitation of the Indonesian Economy," March 25, 1966, RG 59, PPS, Subject and CO Files, 1965–1969, Box 319, NA (hereafter the Johnson Report).

9. Johnson Report, 16, 114–115; see also Airgram A-244 from Jakarta to State, November 30, 1966, RG 59, Central Files, 1964–1966, POL 2, Indonesia, NA.

10. Airgram A-301, "Year-End Analysis: Current and Prospective Problems," January 4, 1967, RG 59, Central Files, 1964–1966, POL 2, Indonesia, NA.

11. For an analysis of the early New Order, see Mas'oed, "Indonesian Economy and Political Structure During the Early New Order."

12. Johnson Report, 68.

13. Airgram A-719 from Jakarta to State, June 8, 1965, RG 59, Central Files, 1964–1966, E 1-1, Indonesia, NA.

14. Johnson Report, 39, 43, 57.

15. The other cabinet members were Leimena, Ruslan Abdulgani, and Idham Chalid.

16. Memo from Samuel Berger to Bill Moyers, March 31, 1966; and Memo from Douglas MacArthur, March 31, 1966, both in RG 59, Office of Executive Secretary, CO Files, 1963–1966, Box 8, NA; Telegram 1211 from State to Jakarta, March 31, 1966, RG 59, Central Files, 1964–1966, AID (U.S.) 15-1, Indonesia, NA.

17. "Japan to Rescue," *The Economist*," April 2, 1966; Telegram 495 from Jakarta to Foreign Office, March 16, 1966, IM 1042/30, FO 371-187561, UKNA.

18. McMahon, *Limits of Empire*, 107; Woo, *Race to the Swift*, 80; Report of the President's General Advisory Committee on Foreign Assistance Programs, October 25, 1968, *FRUS, 1964–1968*, v. 9 (available at http://www.state.gov/r/pa/ho/frus/johnsonlb/ix/).

19. Memo from Secretary of State Rusk to Johnson, August 1, 1966, *FRUS, 1964–1968*, v. 26, 449–457; Note from Thomson to Komer, March 18, 1966, *FRUS, 1964–1968*, v. 26, 422; Bresnan, *Managing Indonesia*, 69; "What Sukarno Wants," *The Economist*, April 16, 1966; Welfield, *Empire in Eclipse*, 219.

20. Memo of Conversation, February 14, 1966, RG 59, Central Files, 1964–1966, POL 2, Indonesia, NA.

21. Panglaykim and Thomas, "New Order and the Economy."

22. "Indonesian Economic Plans," Memo from State Department/INR, April 15, 1966, NSF, CO Files, Indonesia, Memos, v. 6, LBJL; Telegram 1336 from State to Jakarta, May 4, 1966, RG 59, Central Files, 1964–1966, AID 1, Indonesia, NA.

23. Telegram 2313 from Jakarta to State, February 16, 1966, NSF, CO Files, Indonesia, Box 248, Indonesia Cables, v. 6, November 1965–May 1966, LBJL; Telegram 2315 from State to Jakarta, May 24, 1966, RG 59, Central Files, 1964–1966, FN 14, Indonesia, NA.

24. Telegram 3116 from Jakarta to State, May 6, 1966, RG 59, Central Files, 1964–1966, AID 1, Indonesia, NA; Telegram 3413 from Jakarta to State, June 12, 1966, RG 59, Central Files, 1964–1966, AID 9, Indonesia, NA; Memo from H. N. Loveday to Canberra, "Future Aid to Indonesia," June 3, 1966, Series A1398/308, Item 2036/5/Pt. 8, Columbo Plan—Economic Aid—Indonesia General, National Archives of Australia.

25. The chief creditor nations were the United States, West Germany, France, the Netherlands, Japan, and the USSR.

26. Telegram 2315 from State to Jakarta, May 24, 1966, RG 59, Central Files, 1964–1966, FN 14, Indonesia, NA; Telegram 4333 from Tokyo to State, June 13, 1966, RG 59, Central Files, 1964–1966, AID 9, Indonesia, NA.

27. Telegram 501 from Tokyo to State, July 20, 1966, RG 59, Central Files, 1964–1966, FN 14, Indonesia, NA; Memo of Conversation, "Indonesian Economic Stabilization and Debt Rescheduling," July 26, 1966, RG 59, Central Files, 1964–1966, E 1, Indonesia, NA.

28. Telegram 757 from Jakarta to Foreign Office, April 20, 1966, IM 1042/44, FO 371-187562, UKNA; Airgram A-662 from Jakarta to State, May 2, 1966, RG 59, Central Files, 1964–1966, POL, Indonesia-Malaysia, NA.

29. Telegram 1162 from Kuala Lumpur to State, April 6, 1966; and Telegram 3120 from Jakarta to State, May 6, 1966, both in RG 59, Central Files, 1964–1966, POL 32-1, Indonesia-Malaysia, NA.

30. Ali Murtopo told Malaysian officials as late as April 27 that Suharto thought *Konfrontasi* could be solved by detaching Sabah and Sarawak and perhaps incorporating them into Indonesia. See Telegram 2410 from Canberra to London, Series A 2908/1, Item M120, Pt. 6, Malaysia/Indonesia Dispute Folder, National Archives of Australia.

31. Mackie, *Konfrontasi*, 318–320; Telegram 3161 from Jakarta to State, May 11, 1966, RG 59, Central Files, 1964–1966, POL 32-1, Indonesia-Malaysia, NA; Draft Memo, "British Policy Towards Indonesia," April 1, 1966, DO 169 406, UKNA; Telegram 24 from Jakarta to Foreign Office, May 5, 1966, IM 1051/74, FO 371-187543, UKNA.

32. Foreign Office Memo 65/168 to Prime Minister, December 6, 1965, PREM 13, 2718, UKNA.

33. Telegram 3300 from Jakarta to State, May 27, 1966; and Telegram 3272 from Jakarta to State, May 24, 1966, both in RG 59, Central Files, 1964–1966, POL 32-1, Indonesia-Malaysia, NA.

34. "An Uproar of Peace," *Time*, June 10, 1966.

35. Telegram 3357 from Jakarta to State, June 3, 1966, RG 59, Central Files, 1964–1966, POL 32-1, Indonesia-Malaysia, NA.

36. Intelligence Note from Thomas Hughes to Rusk, August 12, 1966; and CIA Office of National Intelligence, "The End of Confrontation: The Debit Side," August 16, 1966, both in NSF, CO Files, Indonesia, v. 7, LBJL.

37. Bangkok Declaration, August 8, 1967; Pollard, "ASA and ASEAN, 1961–1967"; Shee, "A Decade of ASEAN, 1967–1977."

38. Letter from Congressman James Morrison to Johnson, April 8, 1966; Memo of Conversation, April 25, 1966; and Letter from Senator John Tower to Rusk, April 21, 1966, all in RG 59, Central Files, 1964–1966, INCO Cotton 17, Indonesia-U.S., NA.

39. Letter from Ladd Johnson, Secretary of the American Indonesian Chamber of Commerce, to Rusk, May 20, 1966, RG 59, Central Files, 1964–1966, AID, U.S.-Indonesia, NA; *International Commerce*, July 18, 1966, 34.

40. "Indonesia Finds Trade with Japan Paralyzed Since Attempted Coup," *Wall Street Journal*, January 10, 1966; American Indonesian Chamber of Commerce, Bulletin 797, February 9, 1966; "Japan Planning Aid to Indonesia," *New York Times*, January 26, 1966; LaFeber, *The Clash*, 331.

41. Memo for the President from Hubert Humphrey, May 13, 1966, NSF, Name File, Box 4, Memos from Vice President, v. 2, LBJL; Memo from Hubert Humphrey to Rostow, May 1, 1966, RG 59, Central Files, 1964–1966, INCO Cotton 17, Indonesia-U.S., NA.

42. Telegram 3170 from Jakarta to State, May 12, 1966, RG 59, Central Files, 1964–1966, AID (U.S.), Indonesia, NA; Telegram 3294 from Jakarta to State, May 27, 1966; and Telegram 1366 from Jakarta to State, May 30, 1966, both in RG 59, Central Files, 1964–1966, POL, Indonesia-U.S., NA.

43. Memo of Conversation, June 16, 1966, RG 59, Central Files, 1964–1966, AID (U.S.) 15, Indonesia, NA.

44. Memo from Rostow to Johnson, June 8, 1966, NSF, CO Files, Indonesia, v. 7, May 1966–June 1967, LBJL.

45. Memo from H. N. Loveday to Canberra, "Future Aid to Indonesia," June 3, 1966, Series A1398/308, Item 2036/5/Pt. 8, Columbo Plan—Economic Aid—Indonesia General, National Archives of Australia.

46. "Indonesia: A Thousand Cuts," *Newsweek*, July 4, 1966; Telegram 127 from Jakarta to State, July 8, 1966, RG 59, Central Files, 1964–1966, POL 15-1, Indonesia, NA; Savingram 33 from Australian Embassy Jakarta to Department of External Affairs, July 7, 1966, Series A1838/2, Item 3034/2/1/8/Pt. 15, Indonesia—Political Coup 30-9-65 Folder, National Archives of Australia.

47. Telegram 127 from Jakarta to State, July 8, 1966, RG 59, Central Files, 1964–1966, POL 15-1, Indonesia, NA.

48. Intelligence Note from Thomas Hughes to Rusk, July 25, 1966; and CIA Intel Memo 1591/66, "Political Forces in Indonesia," July 23, 1966, both in NSF, CO Files, Indonesia, v. 7, May 1966–June 1967, LBJL; Telegram 435 from Jakarta to State, July 26, 1966; and Telegram 456 from Jakarta to State, July 28, 1966, both in RG 59, Central Files, 1964–1966, POL 15-1, Indonesia, NA.

49. For example, University of Indonesia economist Mohammed Sadli in February 1965 attended a "Conference on Economic Planning in SEA," where he presented the paper "National Goals and Development Strategies: The Role of Economists." Conference papers from "Conference on Economic Planning in SEA," February 1–5, 1965, Jones Papers, Box 75, HI.

50. Memo of Conversation with Ford Foundation, November 22, 1965, RG 59, Central Files, 1964–1966, AID (Ford Foundation), NA; Telegram 6221 from Jakarta to State, June 20, 1967, RG 59, SNF, 1967–1969, AID, US 8, Indonesia (Rockefeller and Indonesia 1967 folder), Box 477, NA.

51. Airgram A-223 from Jakarta to State, November 15, 1966, RG 59, Central Files, 1964–1966, POL 2, Indonesia, NA. Khouw Bian Tie likewise praised many of the economists but "bemoaned their lack [of] executive experience" in Telegram 3018 from Jakarta to State, December 30, 1966, RG 59, Central Files, 1964–1966, XE, Indonesia, NA. Cablegram 2403 from Australian Embassy Washington to Department of External Affairs, Series A1838/2, Item 3034/2/1/8/Pt. 15, Indonesia— Political Coup 30-9-65 Folder, National Archives of Australia.

52. Draft Airgram A-12 from Jakarta to State, July 21, 1967, Green Papers, Box 11, HI.

53. Sullivan, "The United States and the New Order in Indonesia," 522; MacDougall, "Technocrats as Modernizers," 266–267; see also Memo, "Indonesia: The Scope of United States Relations," November 1968, RG 59, SNF, 1967–1969, POL-US, Box 2212, NA.

54. Airgram 642 from Jakarta to State, April 27, 1966, RG 59, Central Files, 1964–1966, FN 1-1, Indonesia, NA; Memo, H. C. Hainsworth to Stewart, "First Impressions of Indonesia," December 10, 1968, OD 35-141, UKNA; MacDougall, "Technocrats as Modernizers," 205–206; Sullivan, "The United States and the New Order in Indonesia," 302–304.

55. Telegram 2652 from Jakarta to State, NSF, CO Files, Indonesia, Box 249, Indonesia Cables, v. 8, June 1967–June 1968, LBJL; Airgram A-139 from Jakarta to State, September 17, 1966, RG 59, Central Files, 1964–1966, POL 15, Indonesia, NA; "Indonesia's Unfinished Revolution," *The Reporter*, July 14, 1966.

56. Airgram A-203 from Jakarta to State, October 22, 1966, RG 59, Central Files, 1964–1966, POL 2, Indonesia, NA; Airgram A-176, September 27, 1967, NSF, CO Files, Indonesia, Box 248, Indonesia Cables, v. 7, May 1966–June 1967, LBJL; Seth King, "Suharto: New Man in Indonesia," *New York Times*, April 3, 1966.

57. "Post Sukarno Indonesia Still a Worry," *Wall Street Journal*, April 21, 1967.

58. Telegram 1063 from Jakarta to State, September 2, 1966; and Telegram 1095 from Jakarta to State, September 6, 1966, both in RG 59, Central Files, 1964–1966, POL 15-1, Indonesia, NA.

59. Airgram A-210 from Jakarta to State, "The Indonesian Army's Blueprint for the 'New Political Order,'" October 29, 1966; and Airgram A-203 from Jakarta to State, October 22, 1966, both in RG 59, Central Files, 1964–1966, POL 2, Indonesia, NA.

60. Memo from Donald Ropa of NSC to Rostow, July 9, 1966; and Memo from Donald Ropa to Rostow, July 11, 1966, both in NSF, CO Files, Indonesia, v. 7, May 1966–June 1967, LBJL.

61. Telegram 599 from Jakarta to State, August 4, 1966, RG 59, Central Files, 1964–1966, POL 15, Indonesia, NA.

62. Memo from Rusk to Johnson, August 1, 1966, RG 59, Central Files, 1964–1966, POL 23-9, Indonesia, NA.

63. Notes of the 563rd Meeting of the NSC, August 4, 1966, NSF, NSC Meetings, v. 4, Table 4, LBJL.

64. Memo for Rusk from William S. Gaud, "The Case for Interim Bilateral Aid to Indonesia," August 22, 1966, RG 59, Central Files, 1964–1966, AID 9, Indonesia, NA.

65. *Congressional Record*, 89th Congr., 2nd sess., Senate, July 21, 1966, 16,570–16,571; Memo for the President from Rusk, September 1, 1966, RG 59, Central Files, 1964–1966, DEF 19-8, U.S.-Indonesia, NA.

66. Telegram 749 from Jakarta to State, August 13, 1966, RG 59, Central Files, 1964–1966, AID (U.S.), Indonesia, NA; Memo for the President, August 18, 1966, RG 59, Central Files, 1964–1966, FE/INDO, NA; Memo from Rostow to Johnson, August 31, 1966, NSF, CO Files, Indonesia, v. 7, LBJL.

67. Telegram 38993 from State to Jakarta, August 31, 1966, RG 59, Central Files, 1964–1966, AID (U.S.), Indonesia, NA; "House Votes $3.09 Billion in Aid," *New York Times*, September 17, 1966.

68. Sullivan, "The United States and the New Order in Indonesia," 350.

69. Memo from Rusk to Johnson, August 1, 1966, RG 59, Central Files, 1964–1966, POL 23-9, Indonesia, NA; Memo from David Cuthell to William Bundy and Samuel Berger, January 7, 1966, RG 59, Central Files, 1964–1966, POL 2, General Reports and Statistics, NA.

70. "Slaughter of Reds Gives Indonesia a Grim New Legacy," *New York Times*, August 24, 1966; "Vengeance with a Smile," *Time*, July 15, 1966; "Indonesia's Night of Terror," *Saturday Review*, February 4, 1967; Airgram A-49, August 2, 1967, RG 59, SNF, 1967–1969, POL 29, Indonesia, NA.

71. Memo, "Labor and Politic in Indonesia," Harry Goldberg, July 1965, RG 18-001, International Affairs Department, CO Files, 1945–1971, 27/3 Indonesia, 1950–1965, AFL-CIO Library and Archives.

72. Telegram 2007 from Jakarta to State, October 27, 1966, RG 59, Central Files, 1964–1966, DEF 19, U.S.-Indonesia, NA.

73. Abu Bakar Lubis, Malik's chief de cabinet, told embassy officials that the "present government under Suharto is the best possible for Indonesia at this stage of development," in Airgram A-223 from Jakarta to State, November 15, 1966, RG 59, Central Files, 1964–1966, POL 2, Indonesia, NA; Paget, "The Military in Indonesian Politics," 303.

74. Airgram A-210 from Jakarta to State, "The Indonesian Army's Blueprint for the 'New Political Order,'" October 29, 1966; and Telegram 2007 from Jakarta to State, October 27, 1966, both in RG 59, Central Files, 1964–1966, POL 2, Indonesia, NA; MacDougall, "Technocrats as Modernizers," 272–275; Letter from Green to Samuel Berger, April 25, 1967, RG 59, Central Files, 1967–1969, POL 15, Indonesia, NA.

75. Telegram 893 from Jakarta to State, August 23, 1966; and Telegram 901 from Jakarta to State, August 23, 1966, both in RG 59, Central Files, 1964–1966, POL 15-1, Indonesia, NA.

76. "Indonesia: Who's on Trial?" *Newsweek*, September 9, 1966; Telegram 45 from Surabaya to Jakarta, September 13, 1966, RG 59, Central Files, 1964–1966, POL 15, Indonesia, NA.

77. "The Burned Moneymen Appraise Indonesia," *New York Times*, September 18, 1966.

78. Memo of Conversation, September 17, 1966, RG 59, Central Files, 1964–1966, POL 2, Indonesia, NA; Telegram 739 from Jakarta to State, September 16, 1966, RG 59, Central Files, 1964–1966, XE, Indonesia, NA.

79. Memo from Francis Underhill to William Bundy, September 22, 1966, RG 59, Central Files, 1964–1966, POL 7, Indonesia, NA.

80. Memo from Samuel Berger to William Bundy, September 23, 1966, RG 59, Central Files, 1964–1966, POL 7, Indonesia, NA.

81. Memo from Humphrey to Johnson, September 25, 1966, *FRUS, 1964–1968*, v. 26, 470–472; Memo of Conversation, September 27, 1966, *FRUS, 1964–1968*, v. 26, 474–476.

82. Airgram A-139 from Jakarta to State, September 17, 1966, RG 59, Central Files, 1964–1966, POL 15, Indonesia, NA; Cablegram 2403 from Australian Embassy Washington to Department of External Affairs, Series A1838/2, Item 3034/2/1/8/ Pt. 15, Indonesia—Political Coup 30-9-65 Folder, National Archives of Australia.

83. Memo from William Bundy to Rusk, September 24, 1966, RG 59, Central Files, 1964–1966, POL 7, Indonesia, NA; Memo of Conversation, September 27, 1966, *FRUS, 1964–1968*, v. 26, 472–474; on the Alliance for Progress, see Latham, *Modernization as Ideology*, ch. 2; on India, see Merrill, *Bread and the Ballot.*

84. Telegram 2007 from Jakarta to State, October 27, 1966; and Memo from Llewellyn Thompson to McNamara, October 19, 1966, both in RG 59, Central Files, 1964–1966, DEF 19, U.S.-Indonesia, NA.

85. Telegram 2486 from Jakarta to State, November 27, 1966; and Airgram A-259 from Jakarta to State, December 7, 1966, both in RG 59, Central Files, 1964–1966, POL 15, Indonesia, NA; Airgram A-244 from Jakarta to State, "Bapak-ism in Indonesia and Its Implications," November 30, 1966, RG 59, Central Files, 1964–1966, POL 2, Indonesia, NA.

86. Telegram 2486 from Jakarta to State, November 27, 1966, RG 59, Central Files, 1964–1966, POL 15, Indonesia, NA; Memo from Rusk to Johnson, August 1, 1966, *FRUS, 1964–1968*, v. 26, 455.

87. Telegram 7015 from State to Jakarta, October 21, 1966, RG 59, Central Files, 1964–1966, AID, U.S.-Indonesia, NA; Sullivan, "The U.S. and the New Order in Indonesia," 523–526.

88. Memo from John McNaughton to Defense Secretary McNamara, August 3, 1966, *FRUS, 1964–1968*, v. 26, 457–459.

89. CIA Intelligence Report, "Communist Military Assistance to Indonesia," October 1965, NSF, CO Files, Indonesia, Box 248, Indonesia Memos, v. 7, May 1966–June 1967, 2 of 2, LBJL; Telegram 2007 from Jakarta to State, October 27, 1966, RG 59, Central Files, 1964–1966, DEF 19, U.S.-Indonesia, NA.

90. Telegram 3136 from Jakarta to State, May 10, 1966, RG 59, Central Files, 1964–1966, AID 1, Indonesia, NA; Memo from McNamara to Johnson, March 1, 1967, *FRUS, 1964–1968*, v. 26, 497.

91. USAID/Jakarta, Briefing Book for the Ambassador, 1964, Jones Papers, Box 92, Ambassadorial/Briefing Books, HI; Gardner, *Shared Hopes, Separate Fears*, 198.

92. Ransom, "Ford Country," 96; MacDougall, "Technocrats as Modernizers," 323; Memo from McNamara to Johnson, March 1, 1967, *FRUS, 1964–1968*, v. 26, 497; McFerridge, "SESKOAD."

93. Record of Conversation with General Soekoewati, June 14, 1966, Series A1838/2, Item 3034/2/1/8/Pt. 15, Indonesia—Political Coup 30-9-65 Folder, National Archives of Australia.

94. Memo from John McNaughton to Defense Secretary McNamara, August 3, 1966, *FRUS, 1964–1968*, v. 26, 497; Telegram 6577 from Jakarta to State, May 9, 1968, RG 59, Central Files, 1967–1969, DEF 19-8, U.S.-Indonesia, NA; Paget, "The Military in Indonesian Politics," 303.

95. Telegram 1661 from Jakarta to State, October 4, 1966, RG 59, Central Files, 1964–1966, DEF 19, U.S.-Indonesia, NA.

96. Pauker, "Toward a New Order in Indonesia"; Memo from Samuel Berger to Llewellyn Thompson, October 15, 1966; and Memo from Llewellyn Thompson to McNamara, October 19, 1966, both in RG 59, Central Files, 1964–1966, DEF 19, U.S.-Indonesia, NA.

97. Telegram 1357 from Jakarta to State, December 1, 1966, RG 59, Central Files, 1964–1966, DEF 19, U.S.-Indonesia, NA.

98. Paget, "The Military in Indonesian Politics," 301.

99. Telegram 40 from Jakarta to New Delhi, December 7, 1966; and Telegram 1453 from Jakarta to State, December 12, 1966, both in RG 59, Central Files, 1964–1966, DEF 19, U.S.-Indonesia, NA.

100. Winters, *Power in Motion*, 52; "Indonesia Is Told to Limit Imports," *New York Times*, December 2, 1966; Panglaykim and Thomas, "Road to Amsterdam and Beyond."

101. CIA Intel Memo, RR IM 67-8, "Prospects for Economic Development in Indonesia," February 1967, NSF, CO Files, Indonesia, v. 7, Memos, May 1966–June 1967, LBJL.

102. Report of the President's General Advisory Committee on Foreign Assistance Programs, October 25, 1968, *FRUS, 1964–1968*, v. 9, 227–229.

103. Memo for the President from Hubert Humphrey, May 13, 1966, NSF, Name File, Box 4, Memos from Vice President, v. 2, LBJL.

104. Telegram 316 from Jakarta to State, RG 59, Central Files, 1964–1966, AID, U.S.-Indonesia, NA; Telegram 3294 from Jakarta to State, May 27, 1966, RG 59, Central Files, 1964–1966, POL, Indonesia-U.S., NA.

105. Memo, "Indonesia: The Scope of United States Relations," November 1968, RG 59, SNF, 1967–1969, POL-US, Box 2212, NA.

106. Robison, *Indonesia*, 133.

107. Airgram A-259 from Jakarta to State, December 7, 1966, RG 59, Central Files, 1964–1966, POL 15-1, Indonesia, NA.

108. MacDougall, "Technocrats as Modernizers," 272; Telegram 3019 from Jakarta to State, April 22, 1966, RG 59, Central Files, 1964–1966, INCO Mining, Indonesia, NA; Soedjatmoko and Odaka, *Proceedings of the Japan-Indonesia Seminar on Modernization and Nation-Building*.

109. Telegram 4096 from Jakarta to State, April 15, 1965, RG 59, Central Files, 1964–1966, INCO Mining, Indonesia, NA.

110. Telegram 2771 from Jakarta to State, March 29, 1966, RG 59, Central Files, 1964–1966, INCO Mining, Indonesia, NA; on Moyers see *New York Times*, September 10, 1965; Leith, *Politics of Power*, 2; Wilson, *Conquest of Copper Mountain*, 1–157.

111. Telegram 1259 from State to Jakarta, April 12, 1966; and Telegram 3019 from Jakarta to State, April 22, 1966, both in RG 59, Central Files, 1964–1966, INCO Mining, Indonesia, NA; Airgram A-62 from Jakarta to State, August 6, 1966, RG 59, Central Files, 1964–1966, PET 10, Indonesia, NA.

112. Telegram 933 from Jakarta to State, August 25, 1966, RG 59, Central Files, 1964–1966, INCO Mining, Indonesia, NA.

113. Winters, *Power in Motion*, 75; "The End for Sukarno," *The Economist*, January 28, 1967.

114. Airgram A-769, Biweekly Economic Review, June 15, 1966, RG 59, Central Files, 1964–1966, E 2-2, Indonesia, NA; Airgram A-121 from Jakarta to State, June 9, 1966; and Telegram 3400 from Jakarta to State, June 10, 1966, both in RG 59, Central Files, 1964–1966, FN 9, Indonesia-U.S., NA; Airgram A-55, Biweekly Economic Review, July 30, 1966, RG 59, Central Files, 1964–1966, E 2-2, Indonesia, NA.

115. Airgram A-769, Biweekly Economic Review, June 15, 1966, RG 59, Central Files, 1964–1966, E 2-2, Indonesia, NA.

116. Robert Keatley, "Indonesia Courts Firms It Earlier Ousted in Bids to Improve Deteriorating Economy," *Wall Street Journal*, April 18, 1967; Airgram A-62 from Jakarta to State, August 6, 1966, RG 59, Central Files, 1964–1966, PET 10, Indonesia, NA.

117. "Oil and Nationalism Mix Beautifully in Indonesia," *Fortune*, July 1973, 154; Keatley, "Indonesia Courts Firms."

118. Airgram A-96, Biweekly Economic Review, August 26, 1966, RG 59, Central Files, 1964–1966, E 2-2, Indonesia, NA; Telegram 539 from Jakarta to State,

August 30, 1966, RG 59, Central Files, 1964–1966, E-INDO, Indonesia, NA; Airgram A-164 from Jakarta to State, October 6, 1966, RG 59, Central Files, 1964–1966, PET 10, Indonesia, NA; Telegram 2105 from Jakarta to State, November 2, 1966, RG 59, Central Files, 1964–1966, PET 15-2, Indonesia, NA.

119. Telegram 3390 from Jakarta to State, June 9, 1966, RG 59, Central Files, 1964–1966, FN 9, Indonesia, NA.

120. Telegram 749 from Jakarta to State, August 13, 1966; and Telegram 509 from Jakarta to State, August 26, 1966, both in RG 59, Central Files, 1964–1966, AID (U.S.), Indonesia, NA.

121. Telegram 1444 from Jakarta to State, September 23, 1966, RG 59, Central Files, 1964–1966, FN 9, Indonesia, NA; on Van Sickle, see Airgram from Medan to State, September 21, 1966, RG 59, Central Files, 1964–1966, FN 9, Indonesia, NA.

122. Telegram 97490 from State to Jakarta, December 7, 1966, RG 59, Central Files, 1964–1966, FN 14, Indonesia, NA.

123. Telegram 2616 from Jakarta to State, December 5, 1966; Telegram 2815 from Jakarta to State, December 15, 1966; and Airgram A-269 from Medan Consulate to State, "Why Doesn't Suharto Depose Sukarno?" December 15, 1966, all in RG 59, Central Files, 1964–1966, POL 15-1, Indonesia, NA.

124. Telegram 100467 from State to Jakarta, December 9, 1966, RG 59, Central Files, 1964–1966, FN 14, Indonesia, NA; Memo from Robert Barnett to Harriman, December 13, 1966, Harriman Papers, Box 451, Library of Congress; on Brown Brothers Harriman, see Airgram A-92 from State to Jakarta, March 16, 1964, RG 59, Central Files, 1964–1966, AID (U.S.) 15-8, Indonesia, NA.

125. Telegram 9505 from Paris to State, December 21, 1966, RG 59, Central Files, 1964–1966, FN 14, Indonesia, NA.

126. Telegram 57980 from State to Jakarta, September 30, 1966; and Telegram 2545 from Jakarta to State, November 30, 1966, both in RG 59, Central Files, 1964–1966, FN 9, Indonesia, NA; for a description of the Foreign Investment Law, see Robison, *Indonesia*, 138.

127. Telegram 3087 from Jakarta to State, January 5, 1967, RG 59, Central Files, 1967–1969, FN 11, Indonesia, NA; Winters, *Power in Motion*, 57–75.

128. Among the companies he had spoken to were GM, Ford, Lockheed, Freeport, U.S. Steel, GE, Westinghouse, and International Minerals Corporation; Telegram 1570 from Geneva to State, November 14, 1966, RG 59, Central Files, 1964–1966, FN 14, Indonesia, NA.

129. Memo of Conversation, January 5, 1967, RG 59, Central Files, 1967–1969, FN 9, Indonesia-U.S., NA.

130. Sullivan, "The U.S. and the New Order in Indonesia," 542.

131. Airgram A-301, "Year End Analysis, Current and Prospective Problems," January 4, 1967, RG 59, Central Files, 1967–1969, POL 2, Indonesia, NA.

132. NIE 55-67, February 15, 1967, "Prospects for Indonesia," NSF, CO Files, Indonesia, v. 7, May 1966–June 1967, LBJL.

133. Telegram 2815 from Jakarta to State, December 15, 1966, RG 59, Central Files, 1964–1966, POL 15-1, Indonesia, NA: Telegram 2898 from Jakarta to State, December 21, 1966, RG 59, Central Files, 1964–1966, POL, Indonesia, NA.

134. Telegram 2831 from Jakarta to State, December 16, 1966, RG 59, Central Files, 1964–1966, POL 15-1, Indonesia, NA.

135. Pauker, "Indonesia: The Year of Transition," 146; "Indonesia: Dilemma in Djakarta," *Newsweek*, December 29, 1966.

136. State Department Backgrounder for the NSC, August 4, 1967, RG 59, NSC Meeting Files, 1966–1970, Box 1, NA.

137. Telegram 4287 from Jakarta to State, March 15, 1967, RG 59, Central Files, 1967–1969, POL 15, Indonesia, NA.

138. Memo from Rostow to Johnson, February 20, 1967, NSF, CO Files, Indonesia, v. 7, Memos, LBJL.

139. Memo from Rostow to Johnson, February 20, 1967, NSF, CO Files, Indonesia, v. 7, Memos, LBJL; Airgram A-301, "Year End Analysis, Current and Prospective Problems," January 4, 1967, RG 59, Central Files, 1967–1969, POL 2, Indonesia, NA.

140. Memo from Rostow to Johnson, February 21, 1967, *FRUS, 1964–1968*, v. 26, 491.

141. Memo from Rostow to Johnson, February 20, 1967, NSF, CO Files, Indonesia, v. 7, May 1966–June 1967, LBJL; Memo for the President from Nicholas Katzenbach, February 23, 1967, RG 59, SNF, 1967–1969, AID (U.S.), Indonesia, Box 477, NA.

142. The IGGI was composed of fourteen Western donor countries and four international organizations: the IMF, IBRD, UNDP, and ADB; Posthumus, "The Inter-Governmental Group on Indonesia."

143. Sullivan, "The United States and the New Order in Indonesia," 359. The BE system allowed Indonesian businessmen to purchase dollars for the import of goods from a restricted list of items prioritized to meet basic commodity and production needs.

144. Telegram from State to Jakarta, February 27, 1967; and Memo from Robert Barnett to Eugene Rostow, March 2, 1967, both in RG 59, Central Files, 1967–1969, FN 14, Indonesia, Box 478, NA; Telegram 216750 from State to Jakarta, June 27, 1967, RG 59, Central Files, 1967–1969, POL, Indonesia-U.S., NA; Telegram 127464 from State to Jakarta, January 28, 1967, RG 59, SNF, 1967–1969, Econ. Aid, Indonesia, Box 478, NA; "U.S. Agrees to Provide Aid for Indonesia's Stabilization," *International Commerce*, March 13, 1967.

145. NIE 55-67, February 15, 1967, "Prospects for Indonesia," NSF, CO Files, Indonesia, v. 7, May 1966–June 1967, LBJL.

146. Telegram 2258 from Jakarta to State, November 10, 1966, RG 59, Central Files, 1964–1966, POL 7, Indonesia, NA.

147. Telegram 2110 from State to Jakarta, July 6, 1967, RG 59, SNF, 1967–1969, AID (U.S.), Indonesia, Box 478, NA.

148. Telegram 216750 from State to Jakarta, June 27, 1967, RG 59, Central Files, 1967–1969, POL, Indonesia-U.S., NA; Telegram 114 from Jakarta to State, July 7, 1967, RG 59, Central Files, 1967–1969, POL 15-1, Indonesia, NA.

149. Telegram 114 from Jakarta to State, July 8, 1967, NSF, CO Files, Indonesia, v. 8, Box 249, LBJL; *Antara*, July 11, 1967, cited in American Indonesian Chamber of Commerce (AIOCC), Bulletin 837.

150. Telegram 10759 from State to Jakarta, July 21, 1967, RG 59, SNF, 1967–1969, POL 7, Indonesia, Box 2207, NA.

151. Memo of Conversation, May 31, 1967, RG 59, SNF, 1967–1969, E 1-1 Indonesia, NA; Telegram 6134 from Jakarta to State, June 15, 1967, RG 59, SNF, 1967–1969, AID (U.S.), Indonesia, Box 478, NA.

152. Lloyd Gardner, *Pay Any Price*, 377–378; Draft Memo from Secretary of Defense McNamara to Johnson, "Defense Department Budget for FY 69," December 1, 1967, *FRUS, 1964–1968*, v. 10 (available at http://www.state.gov/r/pa/ho/frus/johnsonlb/x/); Memo from Rostow to Johnson, July 31, 1967, *FRUS, 1964–1968*, v. 9 (available at http://www.state.gov/r/pa/ho/frus/johnsonlb/ix/).

153. Memo from Rostow to Johnson, July 22, 1967; and Memo from Humphrey to Johnson, July 14, 1967, both in NSF, CO Files, Indonesia, v. 8, June 1967–August 1968, LBJL; State Department Backgrounder for the NSC, August 4, 1967, RG 59, NSC Meeting Files, 1966–1970, Box 1, NA.

154. Memo from AID director William Gaud to Johnson, August 8, 1967, *FRUS, 1964–1968*, v. 26, 522–524.

155. Draft Airgram A-12 from Jakarta to State, July 21, 1967, Green Papers, Box 11, HI.

156. "Indonesia Seen as Dividend on Strong Policy in Vietnam," *Washington Post*, October 18, 1967; Sullivan, "The United States and the New Order in Indonesia," 202–217; Notes of the 578th NSC Meeting, November 8, 1967, NSF, NSC Meetings, v. 4, Table 60, LBJL.

157. Memo of Conversation of NSC Meeting, August 9, 1967; and Tom Johnson Meeting Notes, August 9, 1967, both in NSF, NSC, NSC Meetings, v. 4, Table 55, Indonesia, LBJL; on the MDDA, see Ekbladh, "'Mr. TVA.'"

158. Memo from Marshall Wright to Rostow, September 27, 1967, *FRUS, 1964–1968*, v. 26, 529–530.

159. Record of Cabinet Meeting, October 18, 1967, Cabinet Papers, Cabinet Meeting, October 18, 1967, LBJL.

160. Memo from Vice President Humphrey to Johnson, September 25, 1966, *FRUS, 1964–1968*, v. 26, 470–474; Document 390, Summary of Notes of the 578th Meeting of the NSC, Washington, November 8, 1967, 10:05–10:55 a.m., *FRUS, 1964–1968*, v. 5, 997–1002; "Holt Says U.S. Actions Protect All Non-Red Asia," *New York Times*, July 18, 1966, 5; Seymour Topping, "Southeast Asia Isn't Scared of the Chinese Dragon," *New York Times*, January 16, 1966, p. SM7.

161. Moyar, *Triumph Forsaken*, 380–381. Moyar inexplicably ignores the CIA memo, made public long before he published his book.

162. Intelligence Memo, OCI 0815/66, "The Vietnam Conflict and International Developments," NSF, CO Files, Indonesia, Box 248, Indonesia Memos, v. 6, November 1965–May 1966, LBJL.

163. Telegram 2614 from Jakarta to State, November 6, 1967, RG 59, SNF, 1967–1969, POL 7, Indonesia, Box 2207, NA; Notes of the 578th NSC Meeting, November 8, 1967, NSF, NSC Meetings, v. 4, Table 60, LBJL; Memo for the President from the Vice President, November 13, 1967, NSF, CO Files, Indonesia, Box 249, Indonesia Cables, v. 9, September–November 1968, LBJL.

164. Note from Johnson to Rostow, November 21, 1967, NSF, CO Files, Indonesia, v. 8, June 1967–August 1968, LBJL.

165. CIA Intel Memo, RR IM 67-8, "Prospects for Economic Development in Indonesia," February 1967, NSF, CO Files, Indonesia, v. 7, Memos, May 1966–June 1967, LBJL; McCloy, cited in Cullather, "Fuel for the 'Good Dragon,'" 254.

166. "International Envoy Stresses Nation's Needs, Chances for Private Firms to Aid Development Effort Profitably," *International Commerce*, April 17, 1967; "Indonesia Enacts More Measures to Attract New Investors, Bring Back Firms Formerly Active There," *International Commerce*, May 15, 1967; "Post-Sukarno Welcome Mat: Indonesia Courts Firms It Earlier Ousted in Bids to Improve Deteriorating Economy," *Wall Street Journal*, April 18, 1967.

167. Airgram A-37 from Jakarta to State, July 21, 1967, RG 59, SNF, 1967–1969, FN 9, Indonesia, NA; see also the embassy's biweekly economic reviews for 1967, RG 59, SNF 1967–1969, E 2-2, Indonesia, NA; Cumings, *Origins of the Korean War*, v. 2, 144; Manning, "The Timber Boom with Special Reference to East Kalimantan."

168. "Indonesia: The Timber Industry," First National City Bank, 1968, Jones Papers, Box 62, HI; "Indonesia: An Economic and Political Survey," report prepared for the International Banking Department of Continental Illinois National Bank and Trust Company, 1966, Jones Papers, Box 59, HI.

169. Sullivan, "The United States and the New Order in Indonesia," 368; H. L. Hunt, "Sukarno's Debacle," March 22, 1966, in his *HLH Columns*, 87; Telegram 7048 from Jakarta to State, May 28, 1968, RG 59, SNF, 1967–1969, PET 10-3, Indonesia, NA.

170. French, "The Emergence of U.S. Multinational Enterprise."

171. Indonesia Bi-Weekly Economic Summary, April 18–31, 1967, RG 59, SNF, 1967–1969, E 2-2, Indonesia, NA; AICOC Information Bulletin 830, April 1967.

172. Airgram 806 from The Hague to State, May 26, 1967, RG 59, Central Files, 1967–1969, T7, Indonesia-Netherlands, NA; Winters, *Power in Motion*, 57.

173. Telegram 114 from Jakarta to State, July 7, 1967, RG 59, Central Files, 1967–1969, POL 15-1, Indonesia, NA.

174. Airgram A-100 from Jakarta to State, August 23, 1967, RG 59, Central Files, 1967–1969, LAB 1, Indonesia, NA. Djamin noted that Indonesia's monthly wage, at $35–$40 per month, was among the lowest in Asia, although the embassy noted that there "are relatively few workers . . . earning either of these amounts."

175. Howard Jones Memo on Stanford Research Institute meeting, October 3, 1967, Jones Papers, Box 61, HI; "Indonesia," prepared for the Pacific-Indonesia Business Association (PIBA) Conference, August 3–5, 1967, Stanford Research Institute, Jones Papers, Box 61, HI.

176. Telegram 114 from Jakarta to State, July 7, 1967, RG 59, Central Files, 1967–1969, POL 15-1, Indonesia, NA; Letter from James A. Linen to Acting President Suharto, March 22, 1967, RG 59, Central Files, 1967–1969, FN 9, Indonesia, NA.

177. Proceedings of the Indonesian Investment Conference, November 2–4, 1967, RG 59, Central Files, 1967–1969, FN 9, Indonesia, NA; Winters, *Power in Motion*, 56–76, provides a detailed account of the weekend meeting.

178. Letter from Hubert Humphrey to Johnson, November 29, 1967; and Letter from Johnson to James Linen, December 1, 1967, both in Oversized Attachments, Box 1910, LBJL.

179. Airgram A-189 from Jakarta to State, October 14, 1967, RG 59, SNF, 1967–1969, E 2-4, Indonesia, NA.

180. "The Pacific-Asia World: Profit Opportunities and Challenges for U.S. Business," Gallatin Special Report, December 1967, Jones Papers, Box 75, Subject File, HI; Johnson and McKeen, *Business Environment in an Emerging Nation*.

181. "Doing Business in the New Indonesia," Business International, 1968, Jones Papers, Box 75, Subject File, HI; "Indonesia," Bank of America Report, 1968, Jones Papers, Box 75, Subject File, HI.

182. "Indonesia's Potholed Road Back," *Fortune*, June 1, 1968; Clark, *Indonesia, Sick Man on the Mend*.

183. Memo from Rostow to Johnson, October 18, 1968, *FRUS, 1964–1968*, v. 26, 563–565.

184. Airgram 358 from Jakarta to State, January 12, 1968, *FRUS, 1964–1968*, v. 26, 539–542.

185. Airgram A-423 from Jakarta to State, February 21, 1968, RG 59, Central Files, 1967–1969, POL 1, Indonesia, NA.

186. Airgram A-423 from Jakarta to State, February 21, 1968, RG 59, Central Files, 1967–1969, POL 1, Indonesia, NA; Malik, "Promise in Indonesia," 302–303.

187. MacDougall, "Technocrats as Modernizers," 272–276; Airgram A-423 from Jakarta to State, February 21, 1968, RG 59, Central Files, 1967–1969, POL 1, Indonesia, NA.

188. Sullivan, "The United States and the New Order in Indonesia," 246; see also Pauker, "Toward a New Order in Indonesia," RAND Memo P-3531 (1967), Guy Pauker Papers, HI; Moertopo, *Some Basic Thoughts*, 62.

189. Airgram A-423 from Jakarta to State, February 21, 1968, RG 59, Central Files, 1967–1969, POL 1, Indonesia, NA.

190. Airgram 358 from Jakarta to State, January 12, 1968, *FRUS, 1964–1968*, v. 26, 539–542.

CONCLUSION

1. Telegram 107241 from State to Jakarta, January 30, 1968, RG 59, Central Files, 1967–1969, Box 2205, NA; Memo from Rostow to Johnson, June 27, 1967, NSC, CO Files, Indonesia, v. 8, LBJL.

2. NIE 55-68, December 31, 1968, *FRUS, 1964–1968*, v. 26, 565–576; Michael Leifer, *ASEAN and the Security of Southeast Asia*.

3. Memo from Bundy to Johnson, October 22, 1965, *FRUS, 1964–1968*, v. 26, 334–335.

4. Levinson and Onis, *Alliance That Lost Its Way*; Scheman, *Alliance for Progress*; Dosal, "Accelerating Dependent Development and Revolution."

5. Memo from Bell to Peters, October 28, 1960, RG 59, Central Files, PET, Indonesia, 1960, NA.

6. William Bundy, cited in Green, *Indonesia*, xii–xiii.

7. State Department Backgrounder for the NSC, August 4, 1967, RG 59, NSC Meeting Files, 1966–1970, Box 1, NA; Airgram A-423 from Jakarta to State, February 21, 1968, RG 59, Central Files, 1967–1969, POL 1, Indonesia, NA.

8. "Part XI: Engineer's Venture," in Hanna, *Bung Karno's Indonesia*, 1–7; Latham, "Modernization, International History, and the Cold War World," in Engerman et al., *Staging Growth*, 3.

9. Airgram A-176, September 27, 1967, NSF, CO Files, Indonesia, Box 248, Indonesia Cables, v. 7, May 1966–June 1967, LBJL; see also Douglas, *Political Socialization and Student Activism in Indonesia*.

10. Moertopo, *Some Basic Thoughts*, 45–48.

11. Effendy, *Islam and the State in Indonesia*, 44–52.

12. Parmar, "Building a Modernising Knowledge Elite for Indonesia," 19; Hassan, *Muslim Intellectual Responses to "New Order" Modernization*, 4–13; Noer, "Ummat Islam dan Masalah Modernisasi."

13. Hefner, *Civil Islam*, 115–116.

14. Hassan, *Muslim Intellectual Responses to "New Order" Modernization*, 17.

15. Maluk, "Indonesian Army and Political Islam"; Hassan, *Issue of Modernization*; Federspiel, *Indonesia in Transition*; Federspiel, "The Military and Islam in Sukarno's Indonesia."

16. Santosa, "Modernization, Utopia, and the Rise of Islamic Radicalism."

17. Walker, "Mixing the Sweet with the Sour," 62.

18. Airgram A-816 from Jakarta to State, October 18, 1968, RG 59, SNF, 1967–1969, POL 2, Indonesia, Box 2206, NA.

19. For a broader discussion of these issues, see Schmitz, *Thank God They're on Our Side*; LaFeber, "Tension Between Democracy and Capitalism"; Smith, *America's Mission*; and Caldwell, *Ten Years' Military Terror in Indonesia*. For an honorable exception, see Mortimer, *Showcase State*.

20. Gilman, "Modernization Theory," 56. This is in addition to the critiques launched against modernization theory by its academic and intellectual critics. See,

for example, Frank, "The Development of Underdevelopment"; Huntington, *Political Order in Changing Societies*; and Escobar, *Encountering Development*.

21. Latham, *Modernization as Ideology*, 209–210.

22. Cullather, "'Fuel for the Good Dragon'"; Brazinsky, "Koreanizing Modernization"; Meredith Woo Cumings, *Developmental State*.

23. Airgram A-33 from Jakarta to State, February 16, 1970, RG 59, SNF, 1970–1973, POL 1, Indonesia-U.S., Box 2379, NA.

24. Aspinall, *Opposing Suharto*.

25. Winters, "Criminal Debt"; Marcus Brauchli, "Speak No Evil: Why the World Bank Failed to Anticipate Indonesia's Deep Crisis," *Wall Street Journal*, July 14, 1998; "Poverty in Indonesia: Always with Them," *The Economist*, September 16, 2006.

26. Leith, *Politics of Power*; Barber and Schweithelm, *Trial by Fire*; Glover and Jessup, *Indonesia's Fire and Haze*.

27. Robison and Hadiz, *Reorganizing Power in Indonesia*, 12.

28. Heryanto and Hadiz, "Post-Authoritarian Indonesia"; Colombijn and Lindblad, *Roots of Violence in Indonesia*.

29. Human Rights Watch, *Too High a Price*; Roger Mitton, "U.S. Seeks to Boost Strategic Relations with Indonesia," *Straits Times* (Singapore), December 24, 2005.

Works Cited

Abdulgani, Ruslan. *The Foreign Minister's Report to Parliament on President Sukarno's Second Tour, August 26–October 16, 1956.* Jakarta, Indonesia: Department of Foreign Affairs, 1956.

Abramson, Rudy. *Spanning the Century: The Life of Averell Harriman, 1891–1986.* New York: William Morrow, 1992.

Adas, Michael. *Dominance by Design: Technological Imperatives and America's Civilizing Mission.* Cambridge, MA: Harvard University Press, 2006.

Aden, Jean Bush. "Oil and Politics in Indonesia, 1945 to 1980," Ph.D. diss., Cornell University, 1988.

Aidit, D. N. "Dare, Dare, and Dare Again: Political Report Presented on February 10 to the First Plenary Session of the Seventh Central Committee of the Communist Party of Indonesia." Peking: Chinese Foreign Ministry, 1963.

———. "The Indonesian Revolution and the Immediate Tasks of the Communist Party of Indonesia." *Peking Review*, no. 37, September 13, 1963. 1964.

———. *The Selected Works of D. N. Aidit*, 2 vols. Washington, DC: U.S. Joint Publications Research Service, 1961.

Anderson, Benedict. "How Did the Generals Die?" *Indonesia* 43 (1987): 109–134.

———. *Imagined Communities: Reflections on the Origins and Spread of Nationalism.* London: Verso, 1991.

———. "Perspective and Method in American Research on Indonesia." In Ben Anderson and Audrey Kahin, eds., *Interpreting Indonesian Politics: Thirteen Contributions to the Debate.* Ithaca, NY: Cornell Modern Indonesia Project, 1982, 69–83.

———, ed. *Violence and the State in Suharto's Indonesia.* Ithaca, NY: Cornell Modern Indonesia Project, 2001.

Anderson, Benedict R. O. G., and Ruth McVey. *A Preliminary Analysis of the October 1, 1965, Coup in Indonesia.* Ithaca, NY: Cornell Modern Indonesia Project, 1971.

Anderson, Irvine. *The Standard-Vacuum Oil Company and United States East Asian Policy, 1933–1941.* Princeton, NJ: Princeton University Press, 1975.

Arndt, H. W. "PT Krakatau Steel." *Bulletin of Indonesian Economic Studies* 11(2) (July 1975): 120–126.

Aspinall, Edward. *Opposing Suharto: Compromise, Resistance, and Regime Change in Indonesia.* Palo Alto, CA: Stanford University Press, 2005.

Barber, Charles Victor, and James Schweithelm. *Trial by Fire: Forest Fires and Forestry Policy in Indonesia's Era of Crisis and Reform.* Washington, DC: World Resources Institute, 2000.

Barclay, Glen St. J. "In the Sticky Fly Paper: The United States, Australia, and Indonesia, 1959–1964." *Naval War College Review* 34 (1984): 67–80.

Bartlett, Anderson, Robert Barton, Joe Bartlett, George Fowler, and Charles Hayes. *Pertamina: Indonesian National Oil.* Jakarta, Indonesia: Amerasian, 1972.

Beers, Howard W. *An American Experience in Indonesia: The University of Kentucky in Affiliation with the Agricultural University at Bogor.* Lexington: University of Kentucky Press, 1971.

Belmonte, Laura. "Selling Capitalism: Modernization and U.S. Overseas Propaganda, 1945–1959." In David C. Engerman, Nils Gilman, Mark Haefele, and Michael E. Latham, eds., *Staging Growth.* Amherst: University of Massachusetts Press, 2003, 107–121.

Benda, Harry. "*The Decline of Constitutional Democracy in Indonesia,* by Herbert Feith" [review]. *Journal of Asian Studies* 23(3) (1964): 449–451.

Berger, Mark T. "Decolonisation, Modernisation, and Nation-Building: Political Development Theory and the Appeal of Communism in Southeast Asia, 1945–1975." *Journal of Southeast Asian Studies,* 34(3) (2003), 421–448.

Berman, Edward H. *The Influence of the Carnegie, Ford, and Rockefeller Foundations on American Foreign Policy: The Ideology of Philanthropy.* Albany: State University of New York Press, 1983.

Beschloss, Michael. *Taking Charge: The Johnson White House Tapes, 1963–1964.* New York: Simon and Schuster, 1997.

Best, Stephen. *The Politics of Historical Vision: Marx, Foucault, Habermas.* New York: Guilford Press, 1995.

Bienen, Henry, ed. *The Military and Modernization.* Chicago: Atherton, 1971.

Bird, Kai. *The Color of Truth: McGeorge Bundy and William Bundy—Brothers in Arms.* New York: Simon and Schuster, 1998.

Blair, John M. *The Control of Oil.* New York: Vintage, 1976.

Borden, William S. "Defending Hegemony: American Foreign Economic Policy." In Thomas Paterson, ed., *Kennedy's Quest for Victory: American Foreign Policy, 1961–1963.* New York: Oxford University Press, 1989, 57–85.

———. *The Pacific Alliance: The U.S. Foreign Economic Policy and Japanese Trade Recovery, 1947–1955.* Madison: Wisconsin University Press, 1984.

Brackman, Arnold. *The Communist Collapse in Indonesia.* New York: Norton, 1969.

———. *Southeast Asia's Second Front: The Power Struggle in the Malay Archipelago.* New York: Praeger, 1966.

Brands, H. W. "The Limits of Manipulation: How the United States Didn't Topple Sukarno." *Journal of American History* 76 (1989): 785–808.

————. *The Specter of Neutralism: The U.S. and the Emergence of the Third World,* *1947–1960*. New York: Columbia University Press, 1990.

————. *The Wages of Globalism: Lyndon Johnson and the Limits of American Power.* New York: Columbia University Press, 1995.

Brazinsky, Gregg. "Koreanizing Modernization: Modernization Theory and South Korean Intellectuals." In David C. Engerman, Michael E. Latham, Mark H. Haefele, and Nils Gilman, eds., *Staging Growth: Modernization, Development, and the Global Cold War.* Amherst: University of Massachusetts Press, 2003, 251–274.

Bresnan, John. *At Home Abroad: A Memoir of the Ford Foundation in Indonesia, 1953–1973.* New York: Equinox, 2006.

————. *Managing Indonesia: The Modern Political Economy.* New York: Columbia University Press, 1993.

Bunnell, Frederick. "American 'Low Posture' Policy Toward Indonesia in the Months Leading Up to the 1965 'Coup.'" *Indonesia* 50 (1990): 29–60.

————. "The CIA-DPP 1961 Secret Memorandum on Indonesia." *Indonesia* 22 (1976): 131–169.

————. "The Kennedy Initiatives in Indonesia, 1962–1963." Ph.D. diss., Cornell University, 1969.

Burch, Philip. *Elites in American History.* New York: Holmes and Meier, 1980.

Caldwell, Malcolm, ed. *Ten Years' Military Terror in Indonesia.* Nottingham, U.K.: Spokesman Books, 1985.

Carlisle, Donald S. "The Changing Soviet Perspective of the Development Process in the Afro-Asian World." *Midwest Journal of Political Science* 8(4) (1964): 385–407.

Central Intelligence Agency. *Indonesia—1965: The Coup That Backfired.* Washington, DC: CIA, 1968.

Challis, Roland. *Shadow of a Revolution: Indonesia and the Generals.* Gloucestershire, U.K.: Sutton, 2001.

Chalmers, Ian, and Vedi R. Hadiz, eds. *The Politics of Economic Development in Indonesia: Contending Perspectives.* New York: Routledge, 1997.

Chen, Jian. *Mao's China and the Cold War.* Chapel Hill: University of North Carolina Press, 2001.

Chetwynd, Eric J. "The Indonesian Stabilization Attempt of 1963: A Study in the Economics and Politics in Indonesia." Master's thesis, American University, 1965.

Clark, Joseph S. *Indonesia, Sick Man on the Mend: Report to the Committee on Foreign Relations, United States Senate, on a Study Mission to Indonesia.* Washington, DC: U.S. Government Printing Office, 1968.

Collado, Emilio G. "Economic Development Through Private Enterprise." *Foreign Affairs* 41(4) (July 1963): 708–720.

Collins, Robert. *More: The Politics of Economic Growth in Postwar America.* New York: Oxford University Press, 2000.

Colombijn, Freek, and J. Thomas Lindblad, eds. *Roots of Violence in Indonesia.* Leiden, Netherlands: KITLV Press, 2002.

Cooper, Frederick. "Modernizing Bureaucrats, Backwards Africans, and the Development Concept." In Frederick Cooper and Randall Packard, eds., *International Development and the Social Sciences: Essays on the History and Politics of Knowledge.* Berkeley: University of California Press, 1997, 64–93.

Cooper, Frederick, and Randall Packard, eds. *International Development and the Social Sciences: Essays on the History and Politics of Knowledge.* Berkeley: University of California Press, 1997.

Cordier, Andrew W., and Max Harrelson, eds. *Public Papers of the Secretaries General of the United Nations,* v. 6, U Thant. New York: United Nations, 1976.

Cornejo, Robert M. "When Sukarno Sought the Bomb: Indonesian Nuclear Aspirations in the Mid-1960s." *Nonproliferation Review* 7(1) (2000): 31–43.

Cottle, Drew, and Narim Najjarine. "The Department of External Affairs, the ABC, and Reporting of the Indonesian Crisis, 1965–1969." *Australian Journal of Politics and History* 49(1) (2003): 48–60.

Cribb, Robert, ed. *The Indonesian Killings of 1965–1966: Studies from Java and Bali.* Victoria, Australia: Monash University Center of Southeast Asian Studies, 1990.

———. "Unresolved Problems in the Indonesian Killings of 1965–1966." *Asian Survey* 42 (July-August 2002): 550–564.

Crouch, Harold. *The Army and Politics in Indonesia.* Ithaca, NY: Cornell University Press, 1978.

Cullather, Nick. "Damning Afghanistan: Modernization in a Buffer State." *Journal of American History* 89 (2002): 512–537.

———. "Development? It's History." *Diplomatic History* 24 (2000): 641–654.

———. "'Fuel for the Good Dragon': The United States and Industrial Policy in Taiwan, 1950–1965." In Peter Hahn and Mary Ann Heiss, eds., *Empire and Revolution: The United States and the Third World Since 1945.* Columbus: Ohio State University Press, 2001, 242–268.

Cumings, Bruce. "The Asian Crisis, Democracy, and the End of 'Late' Development." In T. J. Pempel, ed., *The Politics of the Asian Economic Crisis.* Ithaca, NY: Cornell University Press, 1999, 17–44.

———. "Boundary Displacement: Area Studies and International Studies During and After the Cold War." *Bulletin of Concerned Asian Scholars* 29(1) (1997): 6–26.

———. *The Origins of the Korean War,* v. 2, *The Roaring of the Cataract.* Princeton, NJ: Princeton University Press, 1990.

———. *Parallax Visions: American–East Asian Relations at the End of the Twentieth Century.* Durham, NC: Duke University Press, 1999.

Cumings, Meredith Woo, ed. *The Developmental State.* Ithaca, NY: Cornell University Press, 1999.

Dean, Robert. *Imperial Brotherhood: Gender and the Making of Cold War Foreign Policy.* Amherst: University of Massachusetts Press, 2001.

Derkach, Nadia. "Soviet Policy Towards Indonesia in the West Irian and Malaysia Disputes." *Asian Survey* 5 (1965): 566–572.

Dick, Howard. "Formation of the Nation-State, 1930s–1966." In Howard Dick, Vincent J. H. Houben, J. Thomas Lindblad, and Thie Kian Wie, *The Emergence of a National Economy: An Economic History of Indonesia, 1800–2000*. Honolulu: University of Hawaii Press, 2002, 153–193.

Dick, Howard, Vincent J. H. Houben, J. Thomas Lindblad, and Thie Kian Wie. *The Emergence of a National Economy: An Economic History of Indonesia, 1800–2000*. Honolulu: University of Hawaii Press, 2002.

Djojohadikusomo, Sumitro. *Bahan ceramah tentang perspektif perkembangan dalam 30 tahun mendatang* (published in English as *Structure, Performance, and Prospects of the Indonesian Economy*). Jakarta, Indonesia: Lembaga Pertahanan Nasional, 1980.

Dosal, Paul J. "Accelerating Dependent Development and Revolution: Nicaragua and the Alliance for Progress." *Inter-American Economic Affairs* 38 (spring 1985): 75–96.

Douglas, Stephen A. *Political Socialization and Student Activism in Indonesia*. Champaign: University of Illinois Press, 1970.

Doyle, Jeff, Jeffrey Gray, and Peter Pierce. *Australia's Vietnam War*. College Station, TX: Texas A&M University Press, 2002.

Easter, David. "British and Malaysian Covert Support for Rebel Movements in Indonesia During the 'Confrontation,' 1963–66." *Intelligence and National Security* 14(4) (1999): 195–208.

———. "British Intelligence and Propaganda During the 'Confrontation,' 1963–66." *Intelligence and National Security* 16(2) (2001): 83–102.

Effendy, Bahtiar. *Islam and the State in Indonesia*. Singapore: Institute for Southeast Asian Studies, 2003.

Efimova, Larisa M. "Stalin and the Revival of the Communist Party of Indonesia." *Cold War History* 5(1) (2005): 107–120.

———. "Who Gave Instructions to the Indonesian Communist Leader Musso in 1948?" *Indonesia and the Malay World* 31(90) (2003): 171–189.

Ekbladh, David. "'Mr. TVA': Grass-Roots Development, David Lilienthal, and the Rise of the Tennessee Valley Authority as a Symbol for U.S. Overseas Development, 1933–1973." *Diplomatic History* 26 (2002): 335–374.

Elson, R. E. *Suharto: A Political Biography*. Cambridge, U.K.: Cambridge University Press, 2001.

Engerman, David C. *Modernization from the Other Shore: American Intellectuals and the Romance of Russian Development*. Cambridge, MA: Harvard University Press, 2004.

———. "West Meets East: The Center for International Studies and Indian Development." In David Engerman, Nils Gilman, Mark H. Haefele, and Michael E. Latham, eds., *Staging Growth: Modernization, Development, and the Global Cold War*. Amherst: University of Massachusetts Press, 2003, 199–225.

Engerman, David, Nils Gilman, Mark H. Haefele, and Michael E. Latham, eds. *Staging Growth: Modernization, Development, and the Global Cold War*. Amherst: University of Massachusetts Press, 2003.

Escobar, Arturo. *Encountering Development: The Making and Unmaking of the Third World*. Princeton, NJ: Princeton University Press, 1995.

Essai, Brian. *Papua and New Guinea: A Contemporary Survey*. Oxford: Oxford University Press, 1961.

Evans, Brian. "The Influence of the U.S. Army on the Development of the Indonesian Army, 1954–64." *Indonesia* 47 (1989): 25–50.

Federspiel, Howard M. *Indonesia in Transition: Muslim Intellectuals and National Development*. Commack, NY: Nova Science, 1998.

———. "The Military and Islam in Sukarno's Indonesia." *Pacific Affairs* 46(3) (1973): 407–420.

Feith, Herbert. *The Decline of Constitutional Democracy in Indonesia*. Ithaca, NY: Cornell University Press, 1962.

———. "President Sukarno, the Army, and the Communists: The Triangle Changes Shape." *Asian Survey* 4 (1964): 969–981.

Feith, Herbert, and Lance Castles, eds. *Indonesian Political Thinking, 1945–1965*. Ithaca, NY: Cornell University Press, 1970.

Ferguson, Thomas. *Golden Rule: The Investor Theory of Politics and the Logic of Money Driven Political Systems*. Chicago: University of Chicago Press, 1995.

Fetzer, James. "Clinging to Containment: China Policy." In Thomas Paterson, ed., *Kennedy's Quest for Victory: American Foreign Policy, 1961–1963*. New York: Oxford University Press, 1989, 178–197.

Fifield, Russell. *Southeast Asia in United States Foreign Policy*. New York: Praeger, 1963.

Foo, Lee Kwang. "The U.S. and the Indonesian-Malaysia Dispute, 1963–1965: American Response to a Regional Conflict." Master's thesis, Cornell University, 1980.

Ford Foundation. *Celebrating Indonesia: Fifty Years with the Ford Foundation, 1953–2003*. New York: Ford Foundation, 2004.

Foucault, Michel. *Discipline and Punish: The Birth of the Prison*. New York: Vintage Books, 1979.

Fox, William T. R. "Civil-Military Relations Research: The Social Science Research Committee and Its Research Survey." *World Politics* 6 (January 1954): 278–288.

Frank, Andre Gunder. "The Development of Underdevelopment." *Monthly Review* 18 (1966): 17–31.

Fraser, Cary, "An American Dilemma: Race and Realpolitik in the American Response to the Bandung Conference, 1955." In Brenda Gayle Plummer, ed., *Window on Freedom: Race, Civil Rights, and Foreign Affairs, 1945–1988*. Chapel Hill: University of North Carolina Press, 2003, 115–140.

Freedman, Lawrence. *Kennedy's Wars: Berlin, Cuba, Laos, and Vietnam*. New York: Oxford University Press, 2000.

French, M. J. "The Emergence of U.S. Multinational Enterprise: The Goodyear Tire and Rubber Company, 1910–1939." *Economic History Review* 40 (1987): 64–79.

Frey, Marc. "Tools of Empire: Persuasion and the United States' Modernizing Mission in Southeast Asia." *Diplomatic History* 27(4) (2003): 543–568.

FRUS [Foreign Relations of the United States], *1955–1957*, v. 10, *Foreign Aid and Economic Defense Policy.* Washington, DC: Government Printing Office, 1989.

———, v. 22, *Southeast Asia.* Washington, DC: Government Printing Office, 1989.

FRUS, 1958–1960, v. 16, *East Asia Regional; Laos; Cambodia.* Washington, DC: Government Printing Office, 1992.

———, v. 17, *Indonesia.* Washington, DC: Government Printing Office, 1994.

FRUS, 1961–1963, v. 1, *Vietnam 1961.* Washington, DC: Government Printing Office, 1988.

———, v. 2, *Vietnam 1962.* Washington, DC: Government Printing Office, 1990.

———, v. 4, *Vietnam, August–December 1963.* Washington, DC: Government Printing Office, 1991.

———, v. 8, *National Security Policy.* Washington, DC: Government Printing Office, 1996.

———, v. 9, *Foreign Economic Policy.* Washington, DC: Government Printing Office, 1995.

———, v. 22, *Northeast Asia.* Washington, DC: Government Printing Office, 1996.

———, v. 23, *Southeast Asia.* Washington, DC: Government Printing Office, 1995.

FRUS, 1964–1968, v. 5, *Vietnam 1967.* Washington, DC: Government Printing Office, 2002.

———, v. 9, *International Development and Economic Defense Policy; Commodities.* Washington, DC: Government Printing Office, 2002.

———, v. 10, *National Security Policy.* Washington, DC: Government Printing Office, 2002.

———, v. 26, *Indonesia; Malaysia-Singapore; Philippines.* Washington, DC: Government Printing Office, 2001.

———, v. 31, *South and Central America, Mexico.* Washington, DC: Government Printing Office, 2004.

Gardner, Lloyd. *Pay Any Price: Lyndon Johnson and the wars for Vietnam.* Chicago: I.R. Dee, 1995.

Gardner, Paul F. *Shared Hopes, Separate Fears: Fifty Years of United States–Indonesian Relations.* Boulder, CO: Westview Press, 1997.

Geertz, Clifford. *Agricultural Involution: The Processes of Ecological Change in Indonesia.* Berkeley: University of California Press, 1963.

———. "The Development of the Javanese Economy: A Socio-Cultural Approach." Indonesia Project Paper E/56-1. Cambridge, MA: Center for International Studies, February 1956.

———. "Religious Belief and Economic Behavior in a Central Javanese Town: Some Preliminary Considerations." Indonesia Project Paper E/55-6. Cambridge, MA: Center for International Studies, January 1956.

Gendzier, Irene L. *Managing Political Change: Social Scientists and the Third World.* Boulder, CO: Westview Press, 1985.

Geyelin, Philip. *Lyndon B. Johnson and the World.* New York, Praeger, 1967.

Gilbert, Stephen P. "Wars of Liberation and Soviet Military Aid Policy." *Orbis* 10(2) (fall 1966): 830–846.

Gilman, Nils. "Involution and Modernization: The Case of Clifford Geertz." In Jeffrey H. Cohen and Norbert Dannhaeuser, eds., *Economic Development: An Anthropological Approach.* Walnut Creek, CA: Rowman & Littlefield, 2002.

———. *Mandarins of the Future: Modernization Theory in Cold War America.* Baltimore: Johns Hopkins University Press, 2003.

———. "Modernization Theory, the Highest Stage of American Intellectual History." In David Engerman et al., eds., *Staging Growth: Modernization, Development, and the Global Cold War.* Amherst: University of Massachusetts Press, 2003.

———. "Paving the World with Good Intentions: The Genesis of Modernization Theory." Ph.D. diss., University of California at Berkeley, 2000.

Glover, David, and Timothy Jessup. *Indonesia's Fire and Haze: The Cost of a Catastrophe.* Singapore: Institute of Southeast Asian Studies, 1999.

Gordon, Lincoln. "The Alliance at Birth: Hopes and Fears." In L. Ronald Scheman, ed., *The Alliance for Progress: A Retrospective.* New York: Columbia University Press, 1988, 73–81.

Goto, Ken'ichi. *Tensions of Empire: Japan and Southeast Asia in the Colonial and Postcolonial World.* Columbus: Ohio State University Press, 2005.

Gouda, Frances. *American Visions of the Netherlands East Indies/Indonesia: U.S. Foreign Policy and Indonesian Nationalism, 1920–1949.* Amsterdam: Amsterdam University Press, 2002.

Gould, James. *Americans in Sumatra.* The Hague, Netherlands: Martinus Nijhoff, 1961.

Grandin, Greg, *The Last Colonial Massacre: Latin America in the Cold War.* Chicago: University of Chicago Press, 2004.

Grasberg, Eugene. "Indonesia's Investment Requirements." Indonesia Project Publication E/55/20. September 1955,: Cambridge, MA: Center for International Studies, 1955.

Green, Marshall. *Indonesia: Crisis and Transformation, 1965–1968.* Washington, DC: Compass Press, 1990.

Gutteridge, William. *Armed Forces in the New States.* London: Oxford University Press, 1962.

———. *Military Institutions and Power in the New States.* New York: Praeger, 1965.

Halberstam, David. *The Best and the Brightest.* New York: Random House, 1972.

Hammar, Lawrence, "The Philosophy of Shared Poverty: Rethinking Agricultural Involution and the Culture of Geertz." *Journal of Historical Sociology* 1(3) (1988): 253–277.

Hanna, William. *Bung Karno's Indonesia*. New York: American Universities Field Staff, 1961.

Hassan, Mohammad Kamal. *The Issue of Modernization and Its Impact on Indonesian Muslim Intellectuals: Nurcholish Majid's Attempt at a Theology of Development*. Plainfield, IN: Association of Muslim Social Scientists, 1978.

———. *Muslim Intellectual Responses to "New Order" Modernization in Indonesia*. Kuala Lumpur, Malaysia: Percetakan Dewan Bahasa dan Pustaka, 1980.

Hatta, Mohammed. *Portrait of a Patriot: Selected Writings*. Jakarta: Gramedia, 1973.

Hauswedell, Peter Christian. "The Anti-Imperialist United Front in Chinese and Indonesian Foreign Policy, 1963–1965: A Study of Anti-Status Quo Politics." Ph.D. diss., Cornell University, 1976.

Heath, Jim F. *John F. Kennedy and the Business Community*. Chicago: University of Chicago Press, 1969.

Hefner, Robert W. *Civil Islam: Muslims and Democratization in Indonesia*. Princeton, NJ: Princeton University Press, 2000.

———. *The Political Economy of Mountain Java: An Interpretive History*. Berkeley: University of California Press, 1990.

Heryanto, Ariel, "The Development of 'Development.'" *Indonesia* 46 (1988): 1–24.

Heryanto, Ariel, and Vedi R. Hadiz. "Post-Authoritarian Indonesia: A Comparative Southeast Asian Perspective." *Critical Asian Studies* 37(2) (2005): 251–275.

Higgins, Benjamin. *All The Difference: A Development Economist's Quest*. Montreal, Canada: McGill-Queen's University Press, 1992.

———. Foreword to Clifford Geertz, *Agricultural Involution: The Processes of Ecological Change in Java*. Berkeley: University of California Press, 1966.

———. *Indonesia: The Crisis of the Millstones*. New York: Van Nostrand Searchlight Books, 1963.

———. *Indonesia's Economic Stabilization and Development*. New York: Institute of Pacific Relations, 1957.

Higgins, Benjamin, and Guy Pauker. "Economic Implications of the Asian-African Conference and Its Aftermath." Paper C/55-22. Ithaca, NY: Cornell University Indonesia Project, 1955.

Hilsman, Roger. *To Move a Nation: The Politics of Foreign Policy in the Kennedy Administration*. Garden City, NJ: Doubleday, 1967.

Hindley, Donald. "Foreign Aid to Indonesia and Its Political Implications." *Pacific Affairs* 36 (1963): 107–119.

———. "The Indonesian Communist Party and the Conflict in the International Communist Movement." *China Quarterly* 19 (1964): 99–119.

———. "Indonesia's Confrontation of Malaysia: A Search for Motives." *Asian Survey* 4 (1964): 404–414.

Holtzappel, H. "The 30 September Movement: A Political Movement of the Armed Forces or an Intelligence Operation?" *Journal of Contemporary Asia* 9 (1979): 216–240.

Horne, Alistair. *Harold MacMillan*, v. 2, *1957–1986*. New York: Viking, 1989.

House Committee on Foreign Affairs. *Foreign Assistance Act of 1962: Hearings Before the Committee on Foreign Affairs*. 87th Congr., 2nd sess., pt. 4, April 2–5, 9, 1962. Washington, DC: Government Printing Office, 1962.

House Committee on Foreign Affairs, *Foreign Assistance Act of 1963: Hearings Before the Committee on Foreign Affairs*, 88th Congr., 1st sess., April 23, 1963. Washington, DC: Government Printing Office, 1963.

House Foreign Affairs Committee. *Report of the Special Study Mission to Southeast Asia, October 13–19, 1963*. Washington, DC: Government Printing Office, November 7, 1963.

Hughes, John. *Indonesian Upheaval*. New York: David McKay, 1967.

Human Rights Watch. *Too High a Price: The Human Rights Cost of the Indonesian Military's Economic Activities*. New York: Human Rights Watch, 2006.

Hunt, H. L. *HLH Columns: A New Series of the Stimulating Daily Newspaper Columns of H. L. Hunt*. Dallas: HLH Products, 1967.

Hunt, Michael. *Ideology and U.S. Foreign Policy*. Chapel Hill: University of North Carolina Press, 1987.

Huntington, Samuel. *Changing Patterns of Military Politics*. New York: Free Press, 1962.

———. *Political Order in Changing Societies*. New Haven, CT: Yale University Press, 1968.

———. *The Soldier and the State: Theory and Politics of Civil-Military Relations*. New York: Vintage Books, 1957.

Indonesian Ministry of Foreign Affairs. *Africa-Asia Speaks from Bandung*. Jakarta: Indonesian Ministry of Foreign Affairs, 1955.

Iriye, Akira. *Global Community: The Role of International Organizations in the Making of the Contemporary World*. Berkeley: University of California Press, 2004.

Janowitz, Morris. *The Military in the Political Development of New Nations: An Essay in Comparative Analysis*. Chicago: Phoenix Books, 1964.

Johnson, John H. *The Role of the Military in Underdeveloped Countries*. Princeton, NJ: Princeton University Press, 1962.

Johnson, Rossall J., and Dale McKeen. *Business Environment in an Emerging Nation: Profiles of the Indonesian Economy*. Evanston, IL: Northwestern University Press, 1966.

Johnson, U. Alexis. "Internal Defense and the Foreign Service." *Foreign Service Journal* (July 1962): 20–23.

Jones, Howard P. *Indonesia: The Possible Dream*. New York: Random House, 1971.

Jones, Matthew. *Conflict and Confrontation in Southeast Asia, 1961–1965: Britain, the United States, Indonesia, and the Creation of Malaysia*. Cambridge, U.K.: Cambridge University Press, 2002.

———. "Creating Malaysia: Singapore Security, the Borneo Territories, and the Contours of British Policy, 1961–1963." *Journal of Imperial and Commonwealth History* 28 (2000): 85–109.

———. "'Maximum Disavowable Aid': Britain, the United States, and the Indonesian Rebellion, 1957–58." *English Historical Review* 459 (1999): 1179–1216.

———. "A 'Segregated' Asia? Race, the Bandung Conference, and Pan-Asianist Fears in American Thought and Policy, 1954–1955." *Diplomatic History* 29(5) (2005): 841–868.

———. "U.S. Relations with Indonesia, the Kennedy-Johnson Transition, and the Vietnam Connection." *Diplomatic History* 26 (2000): 249–281.

Joseph, Paul. *Cracks in the Empire: State Politics in the Vietnam War.* Boston: South End Press, 1981.

Kahin, George McT. "Indonesia's Strengths and Weaknesses." *Far Eastern Survey* 20(16) (1951): 157–162.

———. "Malaysia and Indonesia." *Pacific Affairs* 37 (1964): 253–270.

———. *Nationalism and Revolution in Indonesia.* Ithaca, NY: Cornell University Press, 1952.

———. *Southeast Asia: A Testament.* London and New York: Routledge Curzon, 2003.

Kahin, George McT., and Audrey Kahin. *Subversion as Foreign Policy: Eisenhower, Dulles, and the Indonesian Debacle.* Ithaca, NY: Cornell University Press, 1994.

Kaiser, David. *American Tragedy: Kennedy, Johnson, and the Origins of the Vietnam War.* Cambridge, MA: Harvard University Press, 2002.

Karabell, Zachary. *Architects of Intervention: The United States, the Third World, and the Cold War, 1946–1962.* Baton Rouge: Louisiana State University Press, 1999.

Khrushchev, Nikita S. *Khrushchev's Tour of Asia: Nikita S. Khrushchev's Report on His Trip to India, Burma, Indonesia, and Afghanistan.* New York: Crosscurrents Press, 1960.

Klare, Michael T., and Cynthia Arnson. *Supplying Repression: U.S. Support for Authoritarian Regimes Abroad.* Washington, DC: Institute for Policy Studies, 1981.

Kochavi, Noam. "Washington's View of the Sino-Soviet Split, 1961–63: From Puzzled Prudence to Bold Experimentation." *Intelligence and National Security* 15 (2000): 50–79.

Kolko, Gabriel. *Confronting the Third World.* New York: Pantheon, 1988.

LaFeber, Walter. *The Clash: U.S.-Japanese Relations Throughout History.* New York: Norton, 1997.

———. "The Tension Between Democracy and Capitalism During the American Century." *Diplomatic History* 23 (1999): 263–285.

Lashmar, Paul, and James Oliver. *Britain's Secret Propaganda War.* Phoenix Mill, U.K.: Sutton Publishing Company, 1998.

Latham, Michael. *Modernization as Ideology: American Social Science and "Nation Building" in the Kennedy Era.* Chapel Hill: University of North Carolina Press, 2000.

Legge, J. D. *Sukarno: A Political Biography*, 2nd ed. Singapore: Stamford Press, 2003.

Leifer, Michael. *ASEAN and the Security of South-East Asia*. London: Routledge, 1989.

Leith, Denise. *The Politics of Power: Freeport in Suharto's Indonesia*. Honolulu: University of Hawaii Press, 2003.

Lev, Daniel S. "Indonesia 1965: The Year of the Coup." *Asian Survey* 6 (1966): 103–111.

———. "Memory, Knowledge, and Reform." In Mary Sabina Zurbuchen, ed., *Beginning to Remember: The Past in the Indonesian Present*. Seattle: University of Washington Press, 2005, 195–209.

———. "Political Role of the Army in Indonesia." *Pacific Affairs* 36 (1963–1964): 349–364.

———. *The Transition to Guided Democracy: Indonesian Politics, 1957–1959*. Ithaca, NY: Southeast Asia Program, Department of Asian Studies, Cornell University, 1966.

Levinson, Jerome, and Juan de Onis. *The Alliance That Lost Its Way*. Chicago: University of Chicago Press, 1970.

Levy, Marion. "Armed Forces Organizations." In Henry Bienen, ed., *The Military and Modernization*. Chicago: Atherton, 1971, 41–79.

Lissak, Moshe. "The Role of the Military: Modernization and Role-Expansion of the Military in Developing Countries—A Comparative Analysis." *Comparative Studies in Society and History* 9(3) (1967): 233–255.

———. "Selected Literature of Revolutions and Coup d'Etat in the Developing Country." In Morris Janowitz, ed., *The New Military*. New York: Russell Sage Foundation, 1964, 339–362.

Little, Douglas. "The New Frontier on the Nile: JFK, Nasser, and Arab Nationalism." *Journal of American History* 75(2) (1988): 501–527.

Liu, Hong. "'The China Metaphor': Indonesian Intellectuals and the PRC, 1949–1965." Ph.D. diss., Ohio University, 1995.

Logevall, Frederick. *Choosing War: The Lost Chance for Peace and the Escalation of War in Vietnam*. Berkeley: University of California Press, 1999.

Lu, Soo Chun. "United States Relations with Indonesia, 1953–1961." Ph.D. diss., Ohio University, 1997.

Lyons, Terence. "Keeping Africa Off the Agenda." In William Cohen and Nancy Bernkopf Tucker, eds., *Lyndon Johnson Confronts the World: American Foreign Policy, 1963–1968*. New York: Columbia University Press, 1994, 245–278.

MacDougall, John. "Technocrats as Modernizers: The Economists of Indonesia's New Order." Ph.D. diss., University of Michigan, 1975.

Mackie, J. A. C., ed. *The Chinese in Indonesia: Five Essays*. Melbourne: Nelson Press, 1976.

———. "Indonesia's Government Estates and Their Masters." *Pacific Affairs* 34 (1961–1962): 337–360.

———. *Konfrontasi: The Indonesia-Malaysia Dispute, 1963–1966*. Kuala Lumpur, Malaysia: Oxford University Press, 1974.

———. *Problems of Indonesian Inflation*. Ithaca, NY: Cornell Modern Indonesia Project, 1967.

Maga, Timothy P. *John F. Kennedy and the New Pacific Community, 1961–63*. London: Cambridge University Press, 1990.

———. "The New Frontier vs. Guided Democracy: JFK, Sukarno, and Indonesia, 1961–1963." *Presidential Studies Quarterly* 20 (1990): 91–102.

Mahajani, Usha. "Kennedy and the Strategy of AID: The Clay Report and After." *Western Political Quarterly* 18(3) (1965): 656–668.

———. *Soviet and American Aid to Indonesia, 1949–1968*. Athens: Ohio University Southeast Asia Program, 1970.

Malik, Adam. "Promise in Indonesia." *Foreign Affairs* 46 (1968): 302–310.

Maluk, Safrul. "The Indonesian Army and Political Islam: A Political Encounter, 1966–1977." Master's thesis, McGill University, 2000.

Manning, Chris. "The Timber Boom with Special Reference to East Kalimantan." *Bulletin of Indonesian Economic Studies* 7 (1971): 30–60.

Markin, Terrence. "The West Irian Dispute: How the Kennedy Administration Resolved That 'Other' Southeast Asian Conflict." Ph.D. diss., Johns Hopkins University, 1996.

Marquis, Jefferson P. "The Other Warriors: American Social Science and Nation Building in Vietnam." *Diplomatic History* 24 (2000): 79–104.

Marxism's New Horizon: Collection of Documents on the Twenty-Second Congress of the Communist Party of the Soviet Union from the Communist Parties of Italy, France, Albania, Indonesia, Bulgaria, Hungary, Czechoslovakia, Poland, USA, Ceylon, and India. New Delhi, India: Bookman, 1962.

Mas'oed, Mohtar. "The Indonesian Economy and Political Structure During the Early New Order, 1966–1971." Ph.D. diss., Ohio State University, 1983.

May, Brian. *The Indonesian Tragedy*. London: Graham Brash, 1978.

McCalister, L. N. "Recent Research and Writing on the Role of the Military in Latin America." *Latin America Research Review* 2 (1966): 50–56.

McClintock, Michael. *The American Connection*, v. 1, *State Terror and Popular Resistance in El Salvador*. Toronto: Zed Books, 1986.

———. *Instruments of Statecraft: U.S. Guerrilla Warfare, Counterinsurgency, and Counterterrorism, 1940–1990*. New York: Pantheon, 1992.

McFerridge, Charles Donald. "SESKOAD: Training the Elite." *Indonesia* 36 (1983): 87–99.

McGehee, Ralph. "The Indonesian Massacres and the CIA." *Covert Action* 35 (1990): 56–58.

McLeod, Helen. *Cannibals Are Human: A District Officer's Wife in New Guinea*. Sydney, Australia: Angus & Robertson, 1961.

McMahon, Robert J. "The Cold War in Asia: Toward a New Synthesis?" *Diplomatic History* 12 (1998): 301–327.

———. *Colonialism and the Cold War: The United States and the Struggle for Indonesian Independence, 1945–1949*. Ithaca, NY: Cornell University Press, 1981.

————. *The Limits of Empire: The United States and Southeast Asia Since World War II*. New York: Columbia University Press, 1999.

McNamara, Robert. *In Retrospect: The Tragedy and Lessons of Vietnam*. New York: Times Books, 1995.

McVey, Ruth. "The Post-Revolutionary Transformation of the Indonesian Army," pt. 1 and 2. *Indonesia* 11 (1971): 131–147, and *Indonesia* 13 (1972): 147–181.

Merrill, Dennis. *Bread and the Ballot: The United States and India's Economic Development, 1947–1963*. Chapel Hill: University of North Carolina Press, 1990.

Metz, Steven. "American Attitudes Toward Decolonization in Africa." *Political Science Quarterly* 99(3) (1984): 515–533.

Moertopo, Ali. *Some Basic Thoughts on the Acceleration and Modernization of 25 Years' Development*. Jakarta, Indonesia: Yayasan Proklamasi, Center for Strategic and International Studies, 1973.

Moon, Suzanne. "Takeoff or Self-Sufficiency: Ideologies of Development in Indonesia, 1957–1961." *Technology and Culture* 39(2) (1998): 187–213.

Mortimer, Rex. *Indonesian Communism Under Sukarno: Ideology and Politics, 1959–1965*. Ithaca, NY: Cornell University Press, 1974.

————. *The Indonesian Communist Party and Land Reform, 1959–65*. Clayton, Australia: Monash University, 1972.

————, ed. *Showcase State: The Illusion of Indonesia's "Accelerated Modernisation."* London: Angus and Robertson, 1973.

Moyar, Mark. *Triumph Forsaken: The Vietnam War, 1954–1965*. New York: Cambridge University Press, 2006.

Mozingo, David. "China's Policy Towards Indonesia." In Tang Tsou, ed., *China in Crisis*. Chicago: University of Chicago Press, 1968, 135–144.

————. *Sino-Indonesian Relations: An Overview*. Santa Monica: RAND Corporation, 1965.

Mrazek, Rudolf. *The United States and the Indonesian Military, 1945–6: A Study of an Intervention*, 2 vols. Prague, Czechoslovakia: Oriental Institute in Academia, 1978.

Murphy, John. *Harvest of Fear: A History of Australia's Vietnam War*. Boulder, CO: Westview Press, 1993.

Nasution, A. H. *Fundamentals of Guerrilla Warfare*. New York: Praeger, 1965.

————. *Kekaryaan ABRI* [The Military's Functionality]. Jakarta, Indonesia: Seruling Masa, 1971.

Natal, Jonathan. "The Road to Vietnam: Modernization Theory in Fact and Fiction." In Christian Appy, ed., *Cold War Constructions: The Political Culture of U.S. Imperialism, 1944–1966*. Amherst: University of Massachusetts Press, 2000, 132–154.

Nishihara, Masashi. *The Japanese and Sukarno's Indonesia: Tokyo-Jakarta Relations, 1951–1966*. Honolulu: University of Hawaii Press, 1976.

Noer, Deliar. "Ummat Islam dan Masalah Modernisasi" [The Muslim Community and the Problem of Modernization]. *Api* 3 (October 1966): 7–10.

Noer, Thomas J. "The New Frontier and African Neutralism: Kennedy, Nkrumah, and the Volta River Project." *Diplomatic History* 8(1) (1984): 61–80.

Paauw, Douglas. "Financing Economic Development in Indonesia: Public and Private Mobilization of Voluntary Savings." Indonesia Project Publication A/55-12. Published in *Ekonomie dan Keuangan Indonesia* (April 1955): 171–185.

Packenham, Robert. *Liberal America and the Third World: Political Development Ideas in Foreign Aid and Social Science.* Princeton, NJ: Princeton University Press, 1973.

Paget, Roger K. "The Military in Indonesian Politics: The Burden of Power." *Pacific Affairs* 40 (1967–1968): 294–314.

Painter, David. *Oil and the American Century: The Political Economy of U.S. Foreign Oil Policy, 1941–1954.* Baltimore: Johns Hopkins University Press, 1986.

Panglaykim, J., and K. D. Thomas. "The New Order and the Economy." *Indonesia* 3 (1967): 73–119.

———. "The Road to Amsterdam and Beyond: Aspects of Indonesia's Stabilization Program." *Asian Survey* 7 (1967): 689–703.

Parker, Jason. "Cold War II: The Eisenhower Administration, the Bandung Conference, and the Reperiodization of the Postwar Era." *Diplomatic History* 30(5) (2006): 867–892.

Parmar, Inderjeet. "Building a Modernizing Knowledge Elite for Indonesia: The Ford Foundation's Role in Promoting U.S. Hegemony During the Cold War." Unpublished manuscript, 2005.

Passman, Otto. "The Report of the Clay Committee on Foreign Aid: A Symposium." *Political Science Quarterly* 78(3) (September 1963): 321–361.

Paterson, Thomas G. *Contesting Castro: The United States and the Cuban Revolution.* Oxford, U.K.: Oxford University Press, 1995.

———, ed. *Kennedy's Quest for Victory: American Foreign Policy, 1961–1963.* New York: Oxford University Press, 1989.

Pauker, Guy. "Indonesia: The Year of Transition." *Asian Survey* 7 (1967): 138–150.

———. "Indonesia in 1964: Toward a 'People's Democracy?'" *Asian Survey* 5 (1965): 88–98.

———. "The Indonesian Doctrine of Territorial Warfare and Territorial Management." RAND Memorandum RM-3312-PR. Santa Monica, CA: RAND Corporation, November 1963.

———. "Indonesia's Eight-Year Development Plan." *Pacific Affairs* 34 (1961): 115–130.

———. "The Role of the Military in Indonesia." In John H. Johnson, ed., *The Role of the Military in Underdeveloped Countries.* Princeton, NJ: Princeton University Press, 1962, 185–231.

———. "Southeast Asia as a Problem Area in the New Decade." *World Politics* 11 (1959): 339–359.

———. "The Soviet Challenge in Indonesia." *Foreign Affairs* 40 (1962): 613–626.

———. "The Strategic Implications of Soviet Military Aid to Indonesia." RAND Memorandum 3481-1-PR. Santa Monica, CA: RAND Corporation, January 1963.

————. "Toward a New Order in Indonesia." RAND Memorandum P-3531. Santa Monica, CA: RAND Corporation, 1967.

Pauker, Guy, and Benjamin Higgins. "Economic Implications of the Asian-African Conference and Its Aftermath." Indonesia Project Publication C/55-22. Cambridge, MA: Center for International Studies, May-June 1955.

Penders, C. L. M. *The West New Guinea Debacle: Dutch Colonization and Indonesia, 1945-1962*. Honolulu: University of Hawaii Press, 2002.

Perlmutter, Amos. "The Praetorian State and the Praetorian Army: Toward a Taxonomy of Civil-Military Relations in Developing Polities." *Comparative Politics* 1(3) (1969): 382-404.

Pollard, Vincent. "ASA and ASEAN, 1961-1967: Southeast Asian Regionalism." *Asian Survey* 10:3 (1970): 244-255.

Posthumus, G. A. "The Inter-Governmental Group on Indonesia." *Bulletin of Indonesian Economic Studies* (July 1972): 55-77.

Prasad, Dekvi Nandan. *Food for Peace: The Story of U.S. Food Assistance to India*. New York: Asia, 1980.

Pye, Lucian "Armies in the Process of Political Modernization." In John H. Johnson, *The Role of the Military in Underdeveloped Countries*. Princeton, NJ: Princeton University Press, 1962, 68-89.

Rabe, Stephen G. "Controlling Revolutions: Latin America, the Alliance for Progress, and Cold War Anti-Communism." In Thomas Paterson, ed., *Kennedy's Quest for Victory: American Foreign Policy, 1961-1963*. New York: Oxford University Press, 1989, 105-122.

————. *The Most Dangerous Area in the World: John F. Kennedy Confronts Communist Revolution in Latin America*. Chapel Hill: University of North Carolina Press, 1999.

Rabel, Roberto. *New Zealand and the Vietnam War: Politics and Diplomacy*. Auckland, New Zealand: Auckland University Press, 2005.

Ransome, David. "The Berkeley Mafia and the Indonesian Massacre." *Ramparts* 9 (1970): 26-49.

————. "Ford Country: Building an Elite for Indonesia." In Steve Weissman, ed., *The Trojan Horse: A Radical Look at Foreign Aid*. Palo Alto, CA: Ramparts, 1975, 93-116.

Reid, Anthony, ed. *Verandah of Violence: The Background to the Aceh Problem*. Singapore: Singapore University Press, 2006.

Report of the Citizens Committee to Strengthen the Security of the Free World, March 26, 1963 [Clay Report]. Washington, DC: Government Printing Office, 1963.

Report of the President's Committee to Study the United States Military Assistance Program. Washington, DC: Government Printing Office, 1959.

Roberts, Stanley. *Food for Peace: Hope and Reality of U.S. Food Aid*. New York: Praeger, 1973.

Robin, Ron. *The Making of the Cold War Enemy: Culture and Politics in the Military-Intellectual Complex*. Princeton, NJ: Princeton University Press, 2001.

Robinson, Geoffrey. *The Dark Side of Paradise*. Ithaca, NY: Cornell University Press, 1995.

———. "*Rawan* Is as *Rawan* Does: The Origins of Disorder in New Order Aceh." In Benedict Anderson, ed., *Violence and the State in Suharto's Indonesia*. Ithaca, NY: Cornell Modern Indonesia Project, 2001, 213–242.

Robison, Richard. *Indonesia: The Rise of Capital*. Sydney, Australia: Allen & Unwin, 1986.

Robison, Richard, with Vedi R. Hadiz. *Reorganizing Power in Indonesia: The Politics of Oligarchy in the Age of Markets*. London: Routledge, 2004.

Romulo, Carlos. *The Meaning of Bandung*. Chapel Hill: University of North Carolina Press, 1956.

Roosa, John. *Pretext for Mass Murder: The September 30th Movement and Suharto's Coup d'Etat in Indonesia*. Madison: University of Wisconsin Press, 2006.

Rosenberg, Emily S. *Financial Missionaries to World: The Politics and Culture of Dollar Diplomacy, 1900–1930*. Cambridge, U.K.: Cambridge University Press, 1999.

———. "'Foreign Affairs' After WWII: Connecting Sexual and International Politics." *Diplomatic History* 18 (1994): 59–70.

Rostow, Walt W. *The Diffusion of Power: An Essay in Recent History*. New York: MacMillan, 1972.

Rotter, Andrew. *The Path to Vietnam: The Origins of the American Commitment to Southeast Asia*. Ithaca, NY: Cornell University Press, 1987.

Ryan, Peter. *Fear Drive My Feet*. Melbourne: Melbourne University Press, 1959.

Sadli, Mohammed. "Inflation, the Drifting Kite." In Herbert Feith and Lance Castles, eds., *Indonesian Political Thinking*. Ithaca, NY: Cornell University Press, 1970, 387–389.

———. "Recollections of My Career." *Bulletin of Indonesian Economic Studies* 29(1) (1993): 35–51.

Salant, Walter S. *The United States Balance of Payments in 1968*. Washington, DC: Brookings Institution, 1963.

Salim, Emilm. "Recollections of My Career." *Bulletin of Indonesian Economic Studies* 33(1) (1997): 45–74.

Saltford, John. "United Nations Involvement with the Act of Self-Determination in West Irian (West New Guinea), 1968 to 1969." *Indonesia* 69 (April 2000): 71–92.

Sampson, Anthony. *The Seven Sisters: The Great Oil Companies and the World They Shaped*. New York: Bantam Books, 1975.

Santosa, June Chandra. "Modernization, Utopia, and the Rise of Islamic Radicalism in Indonesia." Ph.D. diss., Boston University, 1996.

Saulnier, Tony. *Headhunters of Papua*. New York: Crown, 1961.

Saunders, Frances Stonor. *The Cultural Cold War: The CIA and the World of Arts and Letters*. New York: New Press, 1999.

Schafer, Michael. *Deadly Paradigms: The Failure of U.S. Counterinsurgency Policy*. Princeton, NJ: Princeton University Press, 1988.

Schaller, Michael. *Altered States: The United States and Japan Since the Occupation.* New York: Oxford University Press, 1997.

———. *The American Occupation of Japan: The Origins of the Cold War in Asia.* New York: Oxford University Press, 1985.

Scheman, Ronald, ed. *The Alliance for Progress: A Retrospective.* New York: Praeger, 1988.

Schlesinger, Arthur M. *Robert F. Kennedy and His Times.* Boston: Houghton Mifflin, 1978.

———. *A Thousand Days: John F. Kennedy in the White House.* Boston: Houghton Mifflin, 1965.

Schmitz, David. *Thank God They're on Our Side: The United States and Right Wing Dictatorships, 1921–1965.* Chapel Hill: University of North Carolina Press, 1999.

Schurmann, Franz. *The Logic of World Power: An Inquiry into the Origins, Currents, and Contradictions of World Politics.* New York: Pantheon, 1974.

Scott, James. *Seeing Like a State: How Certain Schemes to Improve the Human Condition Have Failed.* New Haven, CT: Yale University Press, 1998.

Scott, Peter Dale. "The United States and the Overthrow of Sukarno, 1965–1967." *Pacific Affairs* 58 (1985): 239–264.

Senate Committee on Foreign Relations. *Economic, Social, and Political Change in the Underdeveloped Countries and Its Implications for United States Policy.* Washington, DC: Government Press Office, 1960.

Senate Committee on Foreign Relations. *Foreign Assistance Act of 1962: Hearings Before the Committee on Foreign Relations.* 87th Congr., 2nd sess., April 5, 9–13, 16, 18, 1962. Washington, DC: Government Printing Office, 1962.

Senate Committee on Foreign Relations. *The Vietnam Hearings.* New York: Vintage Books, 1966.

Shee, Poon-Kim. "A Decade of ASEAN, 1967–1977." *Asian Survey* 17(8) (August 1977): 753–770.

Shils, Edward. "The Military in the Political Development of the New States." In John H. Johnson, ed., *The Role of the Military in Underdeveloped Countries.* Princeton, NJ: Princeton University Press, 1962, 7–67.

Shinn, William T. "The 'National Democratic State': A Communist Program for Less-Developed Areas." *World Politics* 15(3) (April 1963): 377–389.

Sikkink, Kathryn. *Ideas and Institutions: Developmentalism in Brazil and Argentina.* Ithaca, NY: Cornell University Press, 1991.

Simpson, Christopher, ed. *Universities and Empire: Money and Politics in the Social Sciences During the Cold War.* New York: New Press, 1998.

Smith, Geoffrey "National Security and Personal Isolation: Sex, Gender, and Disease in the Cold War U.S." *International History Review* 14 (1992): 307–337.

Smith, Joseph Burkholder. *Portrait of a Cold Warrior.* New York: G. P. Putnam's Sons, 1981.

Smith, Robert. *Tiger in the Senate: The Biography of Wayne Morse.* Garden City, NY: Doubleday, 1962.

Smith, Tony. *America's Mission: The U.S. and the Worldwide Struggle for Democracy in the Twentieth Century*. Princeton, NJ: Princeton University Press, 1994.

Sodhy, Pamela. "Malaysian-American Relations During Indonesia's Confrontation Against Malaysia, 1963–1966." *Journal of Southeast Asian Studies* 19 (1988): 111–136.

Soedjatmoko and Kunio Odaka. *Proceedings of the Japan-Indonesia Seminar on Modernization and Nation-Building*. Jakarta, Indonesia: Foreign Ministry of Indonesia, March 26–28, 1973.

Stockwell, A. J., ed. *British Documents on the End of Empire*, ser. B, v. 8, *Malaysia*. London: Stationary Office, 2004.

Stoler, Ann Laura. *Capitalism and Confrontation in Sumatra's Plantation Belt, 1870–1979*. Ann Arbor: University of Michigan Press, 1991.

Streeter, Stephen. *Managing the Counterrevolution: The United States and Guatemala, 1954–1961*. Athens, OH: Ohio University Press, 2000.

Subritzky, John. *Confronting Sukarno: British, American, Australian, and New Zealand Diplomacy in the Malaysian-Indonesian Confrontation, 1961–1965*. New York: St. Martins, 2000.

Subroto. "Recollections of My Career." *Bulletin of Indonesian Economic Studies* 34(2) (1998): 67–92.

Sudjatmiko, Iwan Gardono. "The Destruction of the Indonesian Communist Party: A Comparative Analysis of East Java and Bali." Ph.D. diss., Harvard University, 1992.

Sukarno. *The People's Command for the Liberation of West Irian.*, Special Issue, no. 82. Department of Information, Republic of Indonesia, December 19, 1961.

Sulistyo, Hermanawan. "The Forgotten Years: The Missing History of Indonesia's Mass Slaughter (Jombang-Kediri 1965–1966)." Ph.D. diss., Arizona State University, 1997.

Sullivan, John H. "The United States and the 'New Order' in Indonesia." Ph.D. diss., American University, 1969.

Sundhaussen, Ulf, with C. L. M. Penders. *Abdul Haris Nasution: A Political Biography*. London: University of Queensland Press, 1985.

Suraputra, D. S. *The Role of America and Soviet Aid to Indonesia*. The Hague, Netherlands: Institute of Social Studies, 1967.

Swift, Ann. *The Road to Madiun: The Indonesian Communist Uprising of 1948*. Ithaca, NY: Cornell University Press, 1989.

Tarpley, Webster G., and Anton Chaitkin. *George Bush: The Unauthorized Biography*. New York: Executive Intelligence Review, 2004.

Taylor, Carl. "Indonesian Views of China." *Asian Survey* 3 (1963): 165–172.

Tipps, Dean C. "Modernization Theory and the Comparative Study of Societies: A Critical Perspective." *Contemporary Studies in Society and History* 15(2) (March 1973): 199–226.

Tovar, B. Hugh. "The Indonesian Crisis of 1965–1966: A Retrospective." *International Journal of Intelligence and Counterintelligence* 7(3) (1994), 313–338.

Tovar, B. Hugh, and J. Foster Collins, "Sukarno's Apologists Write Again." *International Journal of Intelligence and Counterintelligence* 9 (fall 1996), 337–357.

United Nations. *Verbatim Record of the 1144th Meeting of the Security Council, September 9, 1964.* New York: United Nations, 1964.

———. *Verbatim Record of the 1145th Meeting of the Security Council, September 10, 1964.* New York: United Nations, 1964.

———. *Verbatim Record of the 1152th Meeting of the Security Council, September 17, 1964.* New York: United Nations, 1964.

Utrecht, E. "Land Reform in Indonesia." *Bulletin of Indonesian Economic Studies* 5(3) (June 1968): 71–80.

van der Kroef, Justus M. "Indonesian Communism's 'Revolutionary Gymnastics.'" *Asian Survey* 5 (1965): 217–231.

———. "Interpretations of the 1965 Indonesian Coup: A Review of the Literature." *Pacific Affairs* 43 (1970–1971): 557–577.

———. "Peasant and Land Reform in Indonesian Communism." *Journal of Southeast Asian History* 1(1) (1963): 27–52.

———. "Political Awakening in West New Guinea." *Pacific Affairs* 36(1) (1963): 34–53.

———. "Recent Developments in West New Guinea." *Pacific Affairs* 34 (1961–1962): 279–290.

Vitalis, Robert. *America's Kingdom: Mythmaking on the Saudi Oil Frontier.* Palo Alto, CA: Stanford University Press, 2006.

Walker, William O. "Mixing the Sweet with the Sour: Kennedy, Johnson, and Latin America." In Diane Kunz, ed., *The Diplomacy of the Crucial Decade: American Foreign Relations During the 1960s.* New York: Columbia University Press, 1994.

Wallerstein, Immanuel. "The Rise and Future Demise of the World Capitalist System: Concepts for Comparative Analysis." In Immanuel Wallerstein, *The Essential Wallerstein.* New York: The New Press, 2000, 71–106.

Weinstein, Franklin B. *Indonesian Foreign Policy and the Dilemma of Dependence: From Sukarno to Suharto.* Ithaca, NY: Cornell University Press, 1976.

Weis, W. Michael. "The Twilight of Pan-Americanism: The Alliance for Progress, Neo-Colonialism, and Non-Alignment in Brazil, 1961–1964." *International History Review* 23(2) (2001): 322–344.

Welfield, John. *An Empire in Eclipse: Japan in the Postwar American Alliance System.* London: Athlone Press, 1993.

———. "Whose Plot? New Light on the 1965 Events." *Journal of Contemporary Asia* 9(2) (1979): 197–215.

West, F. J. "The New Guinea Question: An Australian View." *Foreign Affairs* 39 (1961): 504–511.

Westad, Odd Arne. *The Global Cold War: Third World Interventions and the Making of Our Time.* New York: Cambridge University Press, 2005.

White, Ben. "Rice Harvesting and Social Change in Java: An Unfinished Debate." *Asia Pacific Journal of Anthropology* 1(1) (2000): 79–102.

White, Theodore. *The Making of the President, 1964*. New York: Signet, 1965.

Wick, Robert S. *God's Invasion: The Story of Fifty Years of Christian and Missionary Alliance Missionary Work in Irian Jaya*. Camp Hill, PA: Buena, 1990.

Wieringa, Saskia. "The Birth of the New Order State in Indonesia: Sexual Politics and Nationalism." *Journal of Women's History* 15(1) (2003): 70–91.

Wilson, Forbes. *Conquest of Copper Mountain*. New York: Atheneum, 1981.

Winters, Jeffrey. "Criminal Debt." In Jeffrey A. Winters and Jonathan R. Pincus, *Reinventing the World Bank*. Ithaca, NY: Cornell University Press, 2002, 101–131.

———. *Power in Motion: Capital Mobility and the Indonesian State*. Ithaca, NY: Cornell University Press, 1996.

Woo, Jung-En. *Race to the Swift: State and Finance in Korean Industrialization*. New York: Columbia University Press, 1991.

Wright, Richard. *The Color Curtain: A Report on the Bandung Conference*. New York: World, 1956.

Young, Kenneth. "Local and National Influences in the Violence of 1965." In Robert Cribb, ed., *The Indonesian Killings of 1965–1966: Studies from Java and Bali*. Victoria, Australia: Monash University Center of Southeast Asian Studies, 1990, 63–101.

Young, Marilyn. "The Age of Global Power." In Thomas Bender, ed., *Rethinking American History in a Global Age*. Berkeley: University of California Press, 2002, 274–295.

Zegwaard, Gerard. "Headhunting Practices of the Asmat of Netherlands New Guinea." *American Anthropologist* 61 (1959): 1020–1041.

Zurbuchen, Mary Sabina, ed. *Beginning To Remember: The Past in the Indonesian Present*. Seattle: University of Washington Press, 2005.

Index

Abdulgani, Ruslan, 109–110, 199–200
Adbullah, Hadji Abdul Malik Karim, 254
Accommodationists, 39, 42–43
Acheson, Dean, 10, 16, 46
Achmad, Tirtosudiro, 190, 196
Adjie, Ibrahim, 78
AFL-CIO, 25, 30, 222
Aidit, D. N., 56, 91, 147, 163, 174–175
American Indonesian Chamber of Commerce, 216, 243
Amory, Richard, 42, 81
Anderson, Benedict, 31
ANZUS (Australia, New Zealand, United States Security Treaty), 118, 124, 137, 195
Army Staff and Command College. *See* SESKOAD
Association of South East Asian Nations (ASEAN), 215–216, 247, 250
Authoritarianism, 35
Australia: and Malaysia, 113, 118, 124, 129, 132–133, 137, 160; and petroleum, 199; and resumption of aid to Indonesia, 196; September 30th Movement, 178–179, 184, 190; and views of Indonesia, 242; West New Guinea, 46, 56–57
Australia, New Zealand, United States Security Treaty. See ANZUS

Ball, George, 154, 169, 176–178, 195, 199
Bandung Conference, 17–18
BAPPENAS. *See* National Development Planning Agency

Barnett, Robert, 120, 235
Barwick, Garfield, 132
Bayh, Birch, 134–135, 249
Bell, Bernard, 90, 92
Bell, David, 80
Bell, James, 151, 165
Benson, George, 159
Bissell, Richard, 40, 42–43
Body for the Protection of Sukarnoism, 147
Bogor, Agricultural University at, 23
Borneo, 180
Bowles, Chester, 10–11, 54
Bratanata, Slamet, 232–234
Brazil, 142–143
Broomfield, William, 58, 61, 95–97, 118, 121
Brown and Root, 232–233
Brunei, 114–116
Budjiardjo, Ali, 232
Bundy, McGeorge, 127, 129, 132, 154, 162, 195, 202,250
Bundy, William, 4, 137, 141, 156, 167, 208, 251
Bunker, Ellsworth, 58, 155–156, 158
Burnham, James, 94
Bush, George H. W., 132

Caltex, 4, 100–109, 153–154, 197–199
Catholic Party, 110
Central Intelligence Agency: 50, 138, 165, 167; and covert operations, 140–144, 156–157, 185–190; and involvement in massacres, 186–192; and relationship between Indonesia and Vietnam, 242;